MORE
THAN
A
METHOD

CONTEMPORARY APPROACHES TO FILM AND TELEVISION SERIES

A complete listing of the books in this series can be found on our Web site at http://wsupress.wayne.edu.

General Editor
BARRY KEITH GRANT
Brock University

Advisory Editors
PATRICIA B. ERENS
Dominican University

LUCY FISCHER
University of Pittsburgh

PETER LEHMAN
Arizona State University

CAREN J. DEMING
University of Arizona

ROBERT J. BURGOYNE
Wayne State University

TOM GUNNING
University of Chicago

ANNA McCARTHY
New York University

PETER X. FENG
University of Delaware

Trends and Traditions in Contemporary Film Performance

MORE
THAN
A
METHOD

Edited by
Cynthia Baron
Diane Carson
and **Frank P. Tomasulo**

WAYNE STATE UNIVERSITY PRESS   DETROIT

Library of Congress Cataloging-in-Publication Data

More than a method : trends and traditions in contemporary film performance / edited by Cynthia Baron, Diane Carson, and Frank P. Tomasulo.
p. cm. — (Contemporary approaches to film and television series)
Includes bibliographical references and index.
ISBN 0-8143-3078-9 — ISBN 0-8143-3079-7 (pbk.)
1. Motion picture acting. I. Baron, Cynthia A. II. Carson, Diane.
III. Tomasulo, Frank P. IV. Series.
PN1995.9.A26M67 2004
791.4302'8—dc22
2004000534

Chapter 3, "Performance in the Films of Robert Bresson: The Aesthetics of
Denial," by the late Doug Tomlinson, appeared originally in *Making Visible
the Invisible: An Anthology of Original Essays on Film Acting*, ed. Carole
Zucker (Metuchen: Scarecrow, 1990) 365–90. Copyright © Carole Zucker.
Reprinted by permission.

Chapter 11, "Thinking through Jim Carrey," by Vivian Sobchack, appeared
originally in a slightly different form in *Closely Watched Brains*, ed. Murray
Pomerance and John Sakeris (Toronto: Pearson Educational, 2001) 199–213.
Copyright © 2001 Vivian Sobchack. Reprinted by permission.

CONTENTS

ILLUSTRATIONS

ACKNOWLEDGMENTS

Grateful acknowledgment is made to the University Research Council and the good offices of Dr. U. Narayan Bhat, Dean of Research and Graduate Studies, at Southern Methodist University for their generous support of the publication of this volume.

The chapters in this book are the result of individual research and extensive conversations in person and across cyberspace. Several chapters reflect the influence of the various panels and workshops on film acting that the editors and contributors have organized over the course of the last several years at academic conferences. We would like to thank the Society for Cinema and Media Studies and the University Film and Video Association for allowing us to present our ideas in a public forum, test different methods of analysis, and exchange ideas with interested colleagues.

We also want to thank the people who assisted us at Wayne State University Press, in particular Barry Keith Grant, Adela Garcia, Robin DuBlanc, and Jane Hoehner.

Introduction

More Than *the* Method, More Than One Method

Cynthia Baron, Diane Carson, and Frank P. Tomasulo

Despite the diversity of method and material, the studies in this collection all begin from the perception that film acting is best understood as a form of *mediated performance* that lies at the intersection of art, technology, and culture. Contributors' observations also reflect a shared understanding that technological developments, such as cinema, have transformed our ideas about performance, the body, and the self. Given their focus on work from the 1950s forward, the essays feature analyses of film performances that give expression or respond in some way to contemporary notions about fragmented subjectivity and illusory identity.

Interestingly, these studies also reveal the contributors' shared awareness that in spite of the apparent disappearance and promised transcendence of the body, twentieth-century film and media technology actually confirmed the centrality of corporeal bodies—for bodies became the only "authentic" ground for mediated and typically hcightcncd displays of beauty and grace, physical pain and emotional torment, quotidian naturalness and arch inhumanity. While each chapter addresses distinct questions about working relationships between actors and directors, the interplay between performance and filmic elements (for example, framing, sound design, editing patterns), and the affective qualities of actors' expressions, gestures, and voices, a thread that unites all twelve chapters is the view that contemporary film performances and contemporary understandings of film performance are themselves informed at least in part by a century of acting in the cinema.

1

While several patterns emerge in the performances analyzed, the diversity in film acting is the most salient point established in this collection. The surprising range in the performances studied can be linked to differences between and changes in the cultural and cinematic conventions that shape quotidian performances of gender, class, age, ethnicity, and locality. It can also be attributed to the more subliminal shifts in ideology that subtend filmmakers' and audiences' changing and sometimes disparate assumptions about the "correct" way to conceive dramatic and fictional character. Contributors to this volume consistently find that a variety of extracinematic factors influence filmmakers' choices about and audiences' responses to *actors'* expressivity (the degree to which performers do or do not "project" their characters' subjective experiences). Contributors also find that extracinematic factors influence choices and responses to *cinematic* expressivity (the ways in which filmic elements enhance, truncate, or somehow mediate and modify access to actors' performances).

The collection's tacit but fundamental polemic is that there is more to film performance than Method acting. The authors' consistent emphasis on *performance as presented on screen* challenges the idea that reference to training or working method is the best or only way to categorize performances.[1] These case studies of acting in films range from Robert Bresson's *A Man Escaped* (1956) to Stanley Kubrick's *Eyes Wide Shut* (1999), and they provide counterevidence to the notion that the Method style (presumably found in performances by actors such as Marlon Brando and Robert De Niro) is the norm in film acting and the standard by which all film performances should be evaluated.[2] Designed to balance the numerous publications about Lee Strasberg and Method acting, such as David Garfield's *The Actors Studio: A Player's Place* (1980), Foster Hirsch's *A Method to Their Madness* (1984), and Steve Vineberg's *Method Actors: Three Generations of an American Acting Style* (1991), this collection's circumscribed survey of contemporary film performance calls into question the belief that Strasberg's formulation of Method acting is the only "scientific" method used in film performance.[3]

Paul McDonald's and Sharon Marie Carnicke's chapters (1 and 2) articulate considerations pertinent to all the essays by directly addressing some of the misconceptions that have circumscribed the analysis of film performance. McDonald's introductory essay shows how analysis of screen acting can contribute to work on the processes of interpretation and identification. It also challenges Lev

Kuleshov's (in)famous dictum that editing choices create film performances. Closing with a description of the minute details in Ingrid Bergman's expressions and gestures in a moment from *Notorious* (1946), McDonald argues for the importance of analyzing the *material elements of actors' performances* in film: vocal intonation, gesture, facial expression, posture, and so on.

Carnicke's essay begins the work of distinguishing Stanislavsky's System from traditions of naturalism, by noting that labels such as "Stanislavskian" and "Brechtian" simply do not describe the complexity of actors' working methods.[4] It also establishes that film directors do in fact work with actors in a variety of different ways: put in the simplest terms, sometimes directors see actors as collaborators, other times they treat them like puppets.

The comprehensive studies by McDonald and Carnicke also indicate ways to update John O. Thompson's proposal that "commutation test" methodology be used to analyze screen performances. With the text serving as the constant, Paul McDonald uses a comparative study of *Psycho* (Hitchcock, 1960, and Van Sant, 1998) to illustrate how subtle differences in gesture and expression shape audiences' perception of the characters and interpretations of the meaning of the films as a whole. Using directors as the variable, Sharon Marie Carnicke illuminates the specific features of actors' performance by setting up three case studies: Jack Nicholson in *The Passenger* (Antonioni, 1975) and *The Shining* (Kubrick, 1980); Shelley Duvall in *Nashville* (Altman, 1975) and *The Shining*; and Tom Cruise in *Interview with the Vampire* (Jordan, 1994) and *Eyes Wide Shut* (Kubrick, 1999).

Building on McDonald's and Carnicke's essays, the chapters in the main body of the collection are primarily case studies in film performance (rather than auteur or star studies). The dialectic between a director and an actor is a complicated issue to analyze. The studies in our collection do not offer essentializing statements about the respective roles and functions of directors and actors. They also reject the idea that any style of acting is or should be seen as the norm or evaluative standard for screen performance. Recognizing the integral relationship between acting and aesthetic/ideological context, the case study chapters consistently demonstrate that "*acting has a history . . . with identifiable styles and trends and influences*" (Hornby 56; emphasis added). Working with this premise, our contributors use (sometimes disparate) views of modernism, neonaturalism, and postmodernism as conceptual lenses through which to historicize and interrogate acting

3

styles. These sometimes overlapping categories provide a starting point for inquiries into some of the aesthetic, cultural, and ideological developments that shaped film performances in the latter part of the twentieth century.

The studies in part 2, on films by Robert Bresson, Michelangelo Antonioni, and Robert Altman, isolate modernist elements in selected film performances. Individually and collectively, the studies by Doug Tomlinson, Frank P. Tomasulo, and Robert T. Self challenge the view that film acting should be discussed primarily or exclusively in "such terms as 'believable,' 'truthful,' and 'realistic'" (McDonald 30). The three modernism studies also effectively articulate the ways in which certain film performances give expression to the notion that "all forms of human interaction are in one sense stagy and that notions of 'character,' 'personality,' and 'self' are merely outgrowths of the various roles we play in life" (Naremore 3).

We open with studies of modernist performances that set aside conventions of realism in part to begin the process of dislodging the long-standing focus on Method acting and "realistic" screen performance. Beginning with work on modernist aspects of film performance also signals our belief that studies of screen acting can and should be integrated into the process of "analyzing and contesting how film reproduces ideological beliefs and 'truths'" (McDonald 30). We hope to make an intervention in this regard, for as Carole Zucker points out, while cinema's "natural" disposition to record reality "has been, if not repudiated, then certainly contested, [this paradigm shift] has not yet resulted in a serious, concomitant reexamination of performance aesthetics" (56).

The chapters in part 3, on performances in films by John Cassavetes, John Sayles, and Neil Jordan, focus on what we have termed neonaturalistic elements in selected films from the 1970s forward. Each essay reckons with the impact of modernism and/or the important distinctions between late-twentieth-century naturalism and various incarnations of Hollywood "realism." In many respects, trends in neonaturalism prove to be the most difficult to describe in distinct and persuasive ways. First, in contrast to modernist and postmodern traditions that differentiate themselves in unique ways from the "realist" norm, neonaturalist performances often share more "family resemblances" to each other than do modernist or postmodern acting styles. Second, it is more difficult to demonstrate significant differences between neonaturalist performances and acting that conforms to Hollywood "realism." In contrast to modernist or postmodern films, neonaturalist and "realist" films often present performances in comparable ways. It can be difficult to describe the slightly "unconventional" way that neonaturalist films use compositional and editing strategies to present performances.

By comparison, in part 2, Tomlinson, Tomasulo, and Self isolate several distinct strategies in modernist films that are diametrically opposed to framing and editing choices in Hollywood "realist" films. These authors clarify ways that frame compositions in modernist films often exclude facial close-ups and character-related camera movements. Their studies find that actors are frequently decentered and diminished in the frame while props, costumes, setting, and locale become more significant. The analyses of modernist film performances show how compositional departures from the "realist" norm are often compounded by editing strategies that fail to provide traditional figurations for projection and identification. For example, Tomlinson points out that Bresson's elliptical editing style eliminates "onscreen representation of cathartic or paroxysmal acts" and instead features "juxtaposition that is used to effect the communication of ideas and information." The sharp contrasts in the way modernist and Hollywood "realist" films present performances are not found in the subtle distinctions between neonaturalist (or even postmodern) films, in which the compositional and editing strategies used to present performances sometimes differ from the realist norm more in degree than in kind.

In spite of this challenge, the studies by Maria Viera, Diane Carson, and Carole Zucker effectively make the case for examining certain performances under the rubric of neonaturalism, often by locating the influence of modernism on naturalistic conceptions of character. Analyzing acting that is as carefully crafted as performances in the other traditions, chapters 6, 7, and 8 on performances in films directed by Cassavetes, Sayles, and Jordan use *neonaturalism* as a term to designate certain aesthetic/ideological performance elements. Describing performances that are grounded in a twentieth-century conception of character as social type, these three chapters examine work in film performance that owes as much to the fiction of Emile Zola and the theater of André Antoine as it does to the modernist interventions of novelists such as Marguerite Duras and Alain Robbe-Grillet.

The chapters in part 4 explore, among other things, the legacy of modernism in postmodern screen performances. Focusing on performances by Jorge Perugorria, Nicole Kidman, Tom Cruise, Jim

Carrey, and Chow Yun-Fat, these essays examine films that do not treat "performance as an outgrowth of an essential self" but instead imply "that the self is an outgrowth of performance" (Naremore 19). The studies by Ronald E. Shields, Dennis Bingham, Vivian Sobchack, and Cynthia Baron locate a discrete collection of characteristics in postmodern film acting. Despite the range of material considered, they all describe ways that intertextual quotation figures in postmodern performance. They also locate instances of extreme minimalism and/or exaggeration in postmodern screen acting. In addition, they all explore ways in which media-saturated culture comes to play a pivotal role in the creation and apprehension of postmodern film performances.

The organization of the essays into modernist, neonaturalist, and postmodern trends has been established to reflect historical development to some degree. For example, the minimalist performances found in Bresson's films from the 1950s are in some sense antecedents of Tom Cruise's truncated performance in Kubrick's *Eyes Wide Shut* (1999). The three rubrics should not, however, be seen as mutually exclusive historical categories: studies in the modernist section look at work from the 1950s to the 1970s; the neonaturalist studies discuss films from the 1970s to the 1990s; chapters in the postmodern section explore performances from the late 1980s to the 1990s. Moreover, individual essays sometimes analyze performance elements that belong in more than one of the three aesthetic traditions considered in the volume. That conceptual pluralism does not signify a confusion in scholarship but instead should be seen as a reflection of the eclectic deployment of performance styles in the films themselves. Therefore, this collection of studies offers no overriding argument that there is a single continuum that separates "artificial, codified, self-reflexive" acting from "natural, realistic, lifelike" performance. Instead, the volume's nuanced studies locate lifelike elements in the most self-reflexive performances and discuss the formalistic, codified features of the most verisimilar acting.

The collection's three principal divisions are essentially ways to open discussion, prompt descriptive rather than evaluative analyses of film acting, and begin analysis of the ways in which "acting is the form of performance specifically involved with the construction of dramatic character" (McDonald 30)—however character is defined. We have found that this last element, about conceptions of character, is highly significant to the study of acting, for there is simply no getting around the fact that performances are grounded in various conceptions of character, person, and identity. The human figures seen in modernist film narratives are often minimalist traces stripped down to their essential qualities. Characters in neonaturalistic films generally belong to clearly delineated social environments and their actions are often a consequence of personal history and environmental determinants. Performers in postmodern films often assume or quote a collection of identities drawn (or "sampled") from a media-saturated society.

Working with rubrics such as modernist, neonaturalist, and postmodern performance elements is intended as an alternative to traditional film criticism that distinguishes between impersonation that is supposed to be a mark of "great" acting and personification that is thought to be the purview of certain stars and inexperienced actors. Discussing performance elements in relation to the aesthetic or ideological orientation of individual films signals our disinterest in teleological studies that find film performances developing greater degrees of "realism" over time. Our circumscribed focus on film performance also means that the volume is not designed to provide an exhaustive study of modernism, neonaturalism, or postmodernism. We hope and expect that readers' understanding of these traditions will facilitate their apprehension of the "new" application of those categories to film performance. Anticipating that existing knowledge will facilitate the process of visualizing the case studies considered, some contributors have chosen to examine films by directors whose signature styles are already identified with aesthetic traditions, as Antonioni is with modernism, Sayles is with neonaturalism, and Woo is with postmodernism.[5]

The case study chapters are also organized to show that *films incorporate performance in a variety of ways*. The collection's opening essays on acting in modernist films reveal that actors are sometimes presented as mere plastic elements in the mise-en-scène. In Robert Bresson's *A Man Escaped* (1956), François Leterrier is required *not* to project emotion, and filmic elements are orchestrated to confound easy identification. Analyzing Michelangelo Antonioni's *Blow-Up* (1967), Tomasulo demonstrates that the phenomenological (rather than psychological) significance of the scenes through which Thomas/David Hemmings passes is often conveyed largely through frame composition and mise-en-scène rather than dialogue or the actor's voice, gesture, and expression.

The next three chapters demonstrate that actors are also presented as members of ensembles. In Robert Altman's *Nashville*

(1975), a collage of fragments from the ostensibly naturalistic but ultimately expressionistic performances by Henry Gibson, Lily Tomlin, Michael Murphy, Shelley Duvall, Karen Black, Keith Carradine, and others intersect to create a view of modern subjectivity as "splintered, unstable, and insecure," as Self explains in chapter 5. In John Cassavetes's *Opening Night* (1977), the actions and reactions of Gena Rowlands, John Cassavetes, Ben Gazzara, Zohra Lambert, and others play off each other to reveal the workings of characters soaked in their specific environment(s). Because the performers limn characters defined by explicit situations, the composite and fundamentally naturalistic picture that emerges in Cassavetes's film does not conform to Hollywood "realism," which includes ostensibly "realistic" touches in what are primarily formulaic and/or mythic narratives. In John Sayles's *Matewan* (1987), the interlocking performances of Chris Cooper, James Earl Jones, David Strathairn, John Sayles, and others depict characters so clearly bound to a specific period and place that the social significance of their encounters generates interest and sometimes empathy without triggering the forms of primary and secondary identification produced by classical Hollywood "realism."

Chapters 8 and 9 explore divergent ways in which films feature performances by actors whose characters come into sharp focus through interaction with other players. For example, in Neil Jordan's *The Crying Game* (1992), the layers and complexity of the character Fergus build as Stephen Rea inhabits the circumstances that force Fergus/Rea into close contact first with Jody/Forest Whitaker and later with Dil/Jaye Davidson. In Jordan's *The End of the Affair* (1999), the world as seen through the eyes of Henry (Rea) finally comes into clear view through the complex interplay between Henry/Rea, his wife/Julianne Moore, and her lover/Ralph Fiennes. In *Strawberry and Chocolate* (1994), directed by Tomás Gutiérrez Alea and Juan Carlos Tabio, the film's deft social commentary and the dense psychosexual identity of the gay Cuban artist emerges from Jorge Perugorria's cleverly orchestrated performance both for the audience within the text, the young Marxist David (Vladimir Cruz), and for the film's spectator.

The two chapters that follow, 10 and 11, provide studies of Nicole Kidman, Tom Cruise, and Jim Carrey as rather different instances of "stars-as-performers" (see Geraghty 191–96). As Dennis Bingham points out, in Stanley Kubrick's *Eyes Wide Shut*, Kidman and Cruise are required to present audiences with performances in which "acting is a showing of the character, not an

8

embodiment of it," while Kubrick creates additional layers of social commentary by folding Cruise's star image into his portrayal of Dr. Bill Harford, and the Cruise-Kidman marriage into the encounters between Dr. Harford and his wife, Alice. In her study of Jim Carrey's films, such as *Ace Ventura: Pet Detective* (1994), Vivian Sobchack shows how Carrey's over-the-top and metacritical performances "focus on and heighten our attention to the thoroughly acculturated and performative nature of human behavior in mass-mediated culture." Reminding us that actors as well as directors can provide the authorial signature in a film, Sobchack uses Carrey-the-actor (not Carrey-the-star) as the frame for her analysis.

Returning in some respects to the presentation of performance in the first studies, the final case study chapter looks at a performance by Chow Yun-Fat in a John Woo film as an instance of a star-model serving as an evocative element in a glossy media-saturated mise-en-scène. Informed as it is by Peking Opera aesthetics and a cosmopolitan worldview perhaps specific to Hong Kong before it became a Special Administrative Region of China, *The Killer* (1989) mobilizes hyperbolic filmic elements in ways that establish (and sometimes confound) audience identification. At the same time, its predominately (although not exclusively) truncated performances are simultaneously engaging and distancing insofar as and precisely because they are constituted by gestures and poses that "quote" images from international consumer culture.

While the studies in this volume are designed to illustrate the important distance between the presentation of performance in a film such as Bresson's *A Man Escaped* and Woo's *The Killer*, opening and closing with studies of these texts underscores the idea that selected (and sometimes surprising) elements traverse a spectrum of contemporary screen performances. There is, for example, a curious bond that links the aesthetic choices of filmmakers like Bresson and Woo, whose work emerges from different eras and different parts of the globe. Their connection is due, at least in part, to a casting process that goes beyond the more familiar strategies of typecasting and typage by considering what Doug Tomlinson terms actors' "moral resemblance" to their characters.[6] While associations of this sort frustrate efforts to delineate mutually exclusive categories of film acting, they do prompt scholars to remain open to the complexities of analyzing screen performance.

In addition to emphasizing the idea that there is more than one method to film performance, the individual chapters also illustrate that there is more than one way to analyze film performance. Within the collection, therefore, there is a diversity (and even a dissonance) in methodology and terminology. While textual analysis of screen-performance-as-presented is central to every chapter, several essays draw on interview material and/or references to cultural knowledge about stars to flesh out their arguments. Even though contributors most often analyze performance in relation to parameters set by directors, selected essays focus on actors as the isolated variable. Some of the most interesting inconsistencies in the collection emerge from contributors' conflicting understandings of Stanislavsky, Kuleshov, and Brecht. We have elected to retain rather than suppress these divergent perspectives to ensure that the collection fosters diverse studies of screen acting.

Despite their differences, all of the essays analyze performances as filmic elements that create meaning and emotional effects. In doing so, they implicitly address certain fundamental questions. Does analysis of performance contribute to our interpretations of films, and if so, how? Can we study the relationships among film acting, directors' artistic visions, and/or their respective working methods; if so, what material should we consider? Can we analyze performance in relation to film narrative, national cinemas, aesthetic movements, and socioeconomic developments in local and global cultures; if so, what methods of analysis are appropriate or effective?

Examining the selection and orchestration of performance choices in a range of films, these studies explicitly consider a constellation of related questions. Are performance choices related to other cinematic elements in a scene; if so, how? Does the choreography of performances within a scene relate to other features of a film's style, mood, and mise-en-scène? How are gestures, facial expressions, and line readings integrated into frame composition and editing patterns to convey dramatic units of action, shifting relations of power, or characters' goals, desires, and objectives? Considered in isolation and as elements of an orchestrated ensemble, how do actors' voices and physical appearances contribute to style and meaning in a given scene or an entire film? What do comparisons of thematically similar scenes in markedly different films reveal about performance choices?

The essays in the collection all go against what Jonas Barish has described as an "antitheatrical prejudice" that has persisted through "many transformations of culture" (4). Outlining Barish's findings, Richard Hornby explains that this prejudice has been "directed primarily against actors [who have been] attacked on the usual grounds of being libidinous, thievish, vulgar"—charges that cover an intolerance of actors because they "pretend to be persons who they are not" (13). Matthew H. Wikander makes a similar point by noting that "the distinction between real life—spontaneous, sincere, authentic—and the hypocritical falsehoods of the actor is a constant thread in the antitheatrical polemic" (xxi). The deep-seated mistrust of actors warrants circumspect analysis, Barish argues, because "it has infiltrated the spirits not only of insignificant criticasters and village explainers but of giants like Plato, Saint Augustine, Rousseau and Nietzsche" (2). Building on Barish's work, Wikander's analysis of views expressed by playwrights, pamphleteers, and major writers shows that more than anything else, antitheatricalism "provides the evidence of a continuous privileging of the inner life," the authentic self (xviii).

It may be that the way academic film studies has gotten around the problem of actors' legitimacy has been to focus on the complex interplay between movie star images and their cultural context. Detour or not, such star studies have provided an exceptional springboard for the analysis of film performance. The substantial work on movie stars and stardom has effectively shown that star images exist within a specific social context and that subjective responses to them help to create a milieu that in turn contributes to shaping those images. That conceptual model is a useful one for exploring the reciprocal relationship among performances, cultural environments, and technological developments.[7]

The studies in this collection also go against the long-standing perception that film technology and cinematic technique produce screen performances. Our authors have carefully analyzed screen performance in spite of the largely accurate perception that the final form results from filmmakers' manipulation of technology. Acknowledging the veracity of that perception, the volume's contributors still challenge the lingering belief that the collaborative nature of cinema means that film acting need not be studied. That challenge is based on two interlocking premises. The first supposition is that while film audiences encounter performances that have been modified by the work of directors, editors, cinematographers, makeup artists, music composers, and others, *films nonetheless create meaning and emotional effects at least in part by the way they present performances*. The collection issues from the insight that a film's presentation of performance warrants interrogation. An editor's decision to cut away from an actor's face at a moment of emotional intensity is a choice about how the character should be presented. A sound editor's choice to highlight a musical motif already associated with a protagonist in a sequence that features an opponent is a choice that contributes to a film's orchestration of performance elements. Such manipulations of cinematic technique shape spectator positioning and the process of identification. They affect the way audiences encounter characters. They influence how viewers experience and interpret basic acting elements like gesture and intonation.

The second shared premise is that while film audiences encounter performances that are created in part by decisions of directors and other members of the production and postproduction staffs, the "material elements of the actor's voice and body" (McDonald 31) contribute to the final visualization of character. As a consequence, those material elements warrant close consideration. Regardless of who originates or selects a particular performance choice, and in spite of performance elements having a basis in intention and (sometimes serendipitous) chance, it is *actors' voices* that carry the paralinguistic features that create nuances of meaning in their intonations, inflections, rhythms, tone, and volume. Similarly, it is the *bodies of actors* that provide (at least the basis for) the facial expressions, gestures, postures, and various gaits film audiences encounter.

In short, contributors to this volume recognize and assume that actors are elements of a film's mise-en-scène and as such are integrated into the set design, lighting scheme, costume and makeup design, and choreography of performance and camera movement. Yet they do not dismiss a film's visualization of character and presentation of performance because an actor working in film is, as Rudolf Arnheim once suggested, "a stage prop chosen for its characteristics and . . . inserted at the proper place" (Benjamin 232).

Stephen Heath's 1977 essay entitled "Film Performance" can perhaps be seen as marking a point of departure for more recent studies of acting in the cinema. A cogent analysis that reflects the concerns of its era, Heath's study of performance does not consider actors or acting but instead the "performance of the subject in language" (118). Heath uses this linguistic model of performance to discuss ways in which film representation, like all representation, "is performance" (115). In the years since Heath's essay was first published, studies of performance in film have explored many of the points Heath articulates.

They have also considered substantially different terrain than Heath in focusing inquiry on actors and acting. The work on stars and the star system includes texts such as Charles Affron's *Star Acting* (1977), Richard Dyer's *Stars* (1979) and *Heavenly Bodies* (1986), Barry King's "The Hollywood Star System" (Ph.D. dissertation, 1984), Richard de Cordova's *Picture Personalities* (1990), and the contributor volumes *Stardom: Industry of Desire* (1991), edited by Christine Gledhill, and *Contemporary Hollywood Stardom* (2003), edited by Martin Barker and Thomas Austin.

The special issue of *Cinema Journal* devoted to film acting (fall 1980), edited by Virginia Wright Wexman, along with John O. Thompson's essays in *Screen* (1978 and 1985), sketched out the possibilities for scholarship focused directly on screen performance. Studies such as Jane Feuer's *The Hollywood Musical* (1982) and Rick Altman's *The American Film Musical* (1987) examined the thin line that "separates normal from choreographed movement" (Feuer 9) and the "combination of rhythmic movement and realism" in acting in musicals (Altman 110). The pivotal study in film performance, James Naremore's *Acting in the Cinema*, was published in 1988. Distinguished by its comprehensive scope, clarity of argument, and lucid, nuanced analysis of the multidimensional character of film performance, Naremore's volume marked out areas of study that still await consideration. It also led to publications such as Roberta Pearson's *Eloquent Gestures* (1992), Virginia Wright Wexman's *Creating the Couple* (1993), Danae Clark's *Negotiating Hollywood* (1995), and collections such as *Making Visible the Invisible* (1990), edited by Carole Zucker, *Star Texts* (1991), edited by Jeremy Butler, and *Screen Acting* (1999), edited by Alan Lovell and Peter Krämer.

Doug Tomlinson's massive volume, *Actors on Acting for the Screen: Roles and Collaborations* (1994), represents an often overlooked landmark in contemporary studies of film performance. Other useful collections of interviews with actors working in film include *Actors on Acting* (1981), edited by Joanmarie Kalter, *The Player* (1984), edited by Lillian and Helen Ross, *Figures of Light* (1995), edited by Carole Zucker, and *Playing to the Camera* (1998), edited by Bert Cardullo, Harry Geduld, Ronald Gottesman, and Leigh Woods. A better understanding of film performance can be derived from analysis of manuals such as Tony Barr's *Acting for the Camera* (1982), Robert Barton's *Acting On Stage and Off*, 3rd ed. (2003), Michael Caine's *Acting in Film* (1989), Robert Benedetti's *Action! Acting for Film and Television* (2001), and Judith Weston's comprehensive guidebooks: *Directing Actors: Creating Memorable Performances for Film and Television* (1996) and *The Film Director's Intuition: Script Analysis and Rehearsal Techniques* (2003). Sheridan Morley's *Tales from the Hollywood Raj* (1983) and Foster Hirsch's *Hollywood Film Acting* (1991) offer interesting observations on acting in American films. Work by film scholars can be enriched by the information and analysis in Joseph Roach's *The Player's Passion* (1985), *Acting (Re)considered* (1995; 2nd edition 2002), edited by Phillip B. Zarrilli, Colin Counsell's *Signs of Performance: An Introduction to Twentieth-Century Theatre* (1996), Carnicke's *Stanislavsky in Focus* (1998), and *Twentieth Century Actor Training* (2000), edited by Alison Hodge. Raymond Williams's insights in *Drama and Performance* (1954; revised 1968; reprinted 1991), *Modern Drama* (1966), *Drama from Ibsen to Brecht* (1968), the collection titled *English Drama: Forms and Development* (1977), and "Drama in a Dramatised Society," a public lecture delivered in 1974, warrant reconsideration by scholars analyzing performance in the age of mechanical reproduction, electronic transmission, and virtual experience.

The range of film performances that can be considered in future studies has no discernible limit. A more nuanced analysis of "realism" in Hollywood films from the 1960s forward would be valuable, as would studies that rethink the place of Method acting in millennial stardom and film performance. Studies of performances in American independent film would be welcome; films like *Daughters of the Dust* (Julie Dash, 1991) and *Flirt* (Hal Hartley, 1995) belong to the legion of independent films that invite audiences to rethink ingrained habits of consuming film performance. Work on acting in films by transnational women directors like Chantal Akerman, Jane Campion, and Mira Nair would also enrich our understanding of screen acting; monolithic notions about film performance become impossible when one has to account for performances as disparate as those in Akerman's *Night and Day* (1991), Campion's *Sweetie* (1989), and Nair's *Monsoon Wedding* (2002).

As our use of modernism, neonaturalism, and postmodernism as conceptual lenses suggests, we see analysis of screen performance as part of an inquiry that can and should be integrated into existing trajectories in film and media studies. We believe, for example, that understanding ways in which texts mediate performances is crucial in studies of text-spectator relationships as well as cultural studies of star images. We find that analyzing a film's orchestration of performance can clarify how specific cinematic moments generate identification. We think that examining the material elements of screen acting can facilitate studies of audience responses to representations of gender, ethnicity, class, age, region, and other categories of cultural identity. We hope that the collection fosters further investigation into these possibilities, as well as into trends and traditions in screen performance not yet defined.

NOTES

1. Stephen Prince's *Movies and Meaning* (1997) and William H. Phillips's *Film: An Introduction* 2nd ed. (2002) are indicative perhaps of prevailing views on film acting within cinema studies. In both textbooks, the authors place Method actors in a separate category. Phillips contrasts Method actors with character actors and nonprofessionals (23). Prince opposes Method acting to antiquated acting, describing the period before 1950 as a primitive one in which "most Hollywood acting tended to be technical and without much psychologizing about a character's motivations and personality" (93). Method acting's privileged position in the accounts by Phillips and Prince is consistent with views of Method acting that still circulate in popular culture. It is, however, inconsistent with current views on Method acting in theater practice and performance studies.

David Krasner notes that while "Method acting has been the most popular . . . form of actor training in America," in contemporary academic programs, "Method acting has fallen into disfavor" (6). Refining that point, Marc Gordon observes that "outside of the Actors Studio, not even a handful of universities or conservatories teach Strasberg's Method [with the consequence that] Method actors have, for quite some time, been the 'exceptions,' not the rule, in very diversified American university training programs" (49). Rhonda Blair balances the views of Krasner and Gordon by recognizing that "the various 'Methods,' as taught by Stella Adler, Sanford Meisner, Lee Strasberg, and others, remain the foundation for much of the actor training in the United States [even though] their ideas have been weakened by misunderstanding on the parts of actors, acting teachers, theorists, and even the master teachers themselves" ("The Method and the Computational Theory of the Mind" 201). Outlining a range of developments, Blair explains that the different formulations of the Method have also been called into doubt "by the rise of postmodern theories; mistrust of Freudian views of psychology and humanist-modernist views of identity; critiques of realism, representation, and mimesis; and the impact of performance modes resistant to psychological realism" (201).

Even a cursory review of contemporary actor training practices and theoretical perspectives on performance suggests that film scholars need to revise the way they have considered Method acting. At the same time, even an outline of perspectives in theater and performance studies also indicates starting points for research that will provide the basis for more sophisticated analyses of film performance, analyses that recognize the distinctions between Stanislavsky's System and Strasberg's Method, the possible connections between the orientations of Stella Adler and Bertolt Brecht, and the remarkable points of contact between postmodern notions of identity and Sanford Meisner's vision of performance (see Gordon 43–60, Krasner 23–25, Stinespring 97–109).

2. In her essay "Re-examining Stardom," Christine Geraghty's lucid analysis of stars as celebrities, professionals, and performers serves as a compendium of studies by scholars such as Richard Dyer, Barry King, Colin Counsell, and Christine Gledhill that presented Method acting as "strongly associated with certain modes of film stardom" and with "realistic" film performance (192). Geraghty explains that since the 1950s, Method acting style that combined "naturalism" with "heightened emotionalism" (and was believed to be grounded in a "vision of the individual as divided between an 'authentic' inner and a potentially repressed/repressive outer self") has seemed to resonate with certain views of cinema (192). Geraghty explains that Method acting's "emphasis on emotion expressed through gesture and sound (rather than words) fitted the dethroning of the script and the word by cinema's visual possibilities; the emphasis on the expressiveness of the body could be accommodated in cinema's use of the body as spectacle; the emphasis on inner character was consonant with cinema's promotion of stars as unique and authentic individuals" (192).

3. Sharon Marie Carnicke's essay "Lee Strasberg's Paradox of the Actor" provides valuable information about the "unscientific" working methods of Elia Kazan and his application of Method acting principles. Carnicke's *Stanislavsky in Focus* also clarifies the distinctions between Stanislavsky's System and Strasberg's Method, which "privileged the psychological techniques of Stanislavsky's System over those of the physical" (1). For a look at how the Method became seen as a new, "scientific" approach to film performance, see Baron, "The Method Moment: Situating the Rise of Method Acting"; for information about "scientific" methods practiced in the 1930s and 1940s, see Baron, "Crafting Film Performances: Acting in the Hollywood Studio Era."

4. Carnicke's remarks on Stanislavsky in this volume provide only a glimpse of the research presented in her book, *Stanislavsky in Focus*, which now serves as the foundation for discussions of the Stanislavsky System (see Beck 261–82; Blair, "Reconsidering Stanislavsky" 179). Today, many scholars in theater and performance studies find that the apparent opposition between Stanislavskian and Brechtian acting styles and acting methods has depended largely on the perception that Strasberg's Method was equivalent to Stanislavsky's System (see Gainor 165; see Herrington 159–60). In the 1960s and 1970s, practitioners seeking alternatives to

Strasberg's Method and to performances designed, for example, to fit "realist texts that continued to privilege the male point of view," turned to what they saw as Brechtian acting, which seemed to allow "the actor to critique character and circumstances" (Stroppel 112). More recently, however, actors and directors have come to believe that identifying Stanislavsky with acting styles and acting methods designed to create the impression of psychological realism "ignores the immense range and variety of his work" (Blair, "Reconsidering Stanislavsky" 179). Practitioners have discovered that the basic elements of Stanislavsky's System "can be used in a range of theatrical environments" (Gainor 165). In addition, scholars now see connections between "Stanislavsky's core concept of the performer's dual consciousness [and] poststructuralist approaches beholden to Bertolt Brecht" insofar as the concept provides "a framework within which identities and their formative influences can be questioned and critiqued" (Beck 261–62).

    5. One of the additional benefits to using directors' work as an organizing element is that studies such as Robert Self's on Altman as a modernist, rather than postmodern director, and Ronald Shield's on Alea as a postmodernist, rather than neonaturalist director, effectively demonstrate how the analysis of film performance can enrich and amend prevailing views of directors' oeuvres.

    6. John Woo explained that Chow Yun-Fat and Danny Lee were cast in *The Killer* because he sees them as modern knights (61).

    7. Analyses of film performance can benefit from more direct contact with work on performance in television and new media: working methods in television challenge assumptions about actor-director relationships; the kinesthetic nature of new media's alternative narrative structure requires us to sharpen analyses of the affective aspects of fragmentary performance.

WORKS CITED

Altman, Rick. *The American Film Musical*. Bloomington: Indiana UP, 1987.

Barish, Jonas. *The Antitheatrical Prejudice*. Berkeley: U of California P, 1981.

Baron, Cynthia. "Crafting Film Performances: Acting in the Hollywood Studio Era." *Screen Acting*. Ed. Alan Lovell and Peter Krämer. London: Routledge, 1999. 31–45.

———. "The Method Moment: Situating the Rise of Method Acting." *Popular Culture Review* 9.2 (1998): 89–106.

Beck, Dennis C. "The Paradox of the Method Actor: Rethinking the Stanislavsky Legacy." *Method Acting Reconsidered*. Ed. David Krasner. New York: St. Martin's, 2000. 261–82.

Benjamin, Walter. "The Work of Art in the Age of Mechanical Reproduction." *Illuminations*. New York: Harcourt, Brace and World, 1968. 219–53.

Blair, Rhonda. "The Method and the Computational Theory of the Mind." *Method Acting Reconsidered*. Ed. David Krasner. New York: St. Martin's, 2000. 201–18.

———. "Reconsidering Stanislavsky: Feeling, Feminism, and the Actor." *Theatre Topics* 12.2 (2002): 177–90.

Carnicke, Sharon M. "Lee Strasberg's Paradox of the Actor." *Screen Acting*. Ed. Alan Lovell and Peter Krämer. London: Routledge, 1999. 75–87.

———. *Stanislavsky in Focus*. Amsterdam: Harwood, 1998.

Feuer, Jane. *The Hollywood Musical*. 2nd ed. Bloomington: Indiana UP, 1993.

Gainor, Ellen. "Rethinking Feminism, Stanislavsky, and Performance." *Theatre Topics* 12.2 (2002): 163–75.

Geraghty, Christine. "Re-examining Stardom: Questions of Text, Bodies, and Performance." *Reinventing Film Studies*. Ed. Christine Gledhill and Linda Williams. London: Arnold, 2000. 183–201.

Gordon, Marc. "Salvaging Strasberg at the Fin de Siècle." *Method Acting Reconsidered*. Ed. David Krasner. New York: St. Martin's, 2000. 43–60.

Heath, Stephen. "Film Performance." *Ciné-tracts* 2 (1977): 7–17.

Herrington, Joan. "Directing with the Viewpoints." *Theatre Topics* 10.2 (2000): 155–68.

Hornby, Richard. *The End of Acting*. New York: Applause, 1992.

Krasner, David. "I Hate Strasberg: Method Bashing in the Academy." *Method Acting Reconsidered*. Ed. David Krasner. New York: St. Martin's, 2000. 3–39.

McDonald, Paul. "Film Acting." *The Oxford Guide to Film Studies*. Ed. John Hill and Pamela Church Gibson. New York: Oxford UP, 1998. 30–35.

Naremore, James. *Acting in the Cinema*. Berkeley: U of California P, 1988.

Phillips, William H. *Film: An Introduction*, 2nd ed. New York: Bedford/St. Martin's, 2002.

Prince, Stephen. *Movies and Meaning*. Boston: Allyn and Bacon, 1997.

Stinespring, Louise M. "Just Be Yourself: Derrida, Difference, and the Meisner Technique." *Method Acting Reconsidered*. Ed. David Krasner. New York: St. Martin's, 2000. 97–109.

Stroppel, Elizabeth C. "Reconciling the Past and the Present: Feminist Perspectives on the Method in the Classroom and on the Stage." *Method Acting Reconsidered*. Ed. David Krasner. New York: St. Martin's, 2000. 111–23.

Thompson, John O. "Beyond Commutation: A Reconsideration of Screen Acting." *Screen* 26.5 (1985): 64–76.

———. "Screen Acting and the Commutation Test." *Screen* 19.2 (1978): 55–69.

Wikander, Matthew H. *Fangs of Malice: Hypocrisy, Sincerity, and Acting.* Iowa City: U of Iowa P, 2002.

Woo, John. "Chinese Poetry in Motion." *Sight and Sound* 4.7 (1997): 61.

Zucker, Carole. "The Concept of 'Excess' in Film Acting: Notes toward an Understanding of Non-naturalistic Performance." *Post Script* 12.2 (1993): 54–62.

1

ANALYZING
FILM
PERFORMANCE:
LOGIC AND
METHODS

1

Why Study Film Acting?
Some Opening Reflections

Paul McDonald

Since the early days of cinema, film has displayed a continuing fascination with capturing the human body in action. In narrative cinema, this preoccupation is witnessed in the circuit of meaning between actor and character. Given the continuing presence of the actor throughout film history, it is therefore surprising that film scholarship has not undertaken a more sustained engagement with the contribution of acting to film aesthetics or representation. So central is the signification of the actor to the workings of narrative cinema that it is debatable if film scholarship can offer a satisfactory understanding of the meanings and affects of film without attention to screen performance.

The absence of acting analysis from the existing body of film scholarship cannot be explained as merely a matter of accident or neglect. Rather, this situation has emerged as film studies has developed an intellectual agenda with lines of inquiry that have firmly encouraged a disregard for acting. In their examination of film form, the pioneering film theorists were concerned with what Victor Perkins describes as the "twin mystiques" of image and montage (17). With the image, "the decorative and expressive use of pictorial space was given precedence over the dramatic use of real space" (19). Montage was valued for how meaning was found in the uniquely filmic materiality of shot transitions. In his famous exercise, Lev Kuleshov shot two scenes, one in which a prisoner stared at an open cell door and a second where the protagonist was a starving man facing a bowl of soup. Kuleshov claimed that when close-ups of the actor responding to these circumstances were reversed and inserted into the opposing scene, in both cases the meanings derived from the actor's face could fit comfortably into the new contexts (Kuleshov 192). Supposedly, the changes had no effect on what the actor was believed to be thinking or feeling. For Kuleshov, this confirmed the power of montage over performance, so that he concluded: "Apart from montage, nothing exists in cinema. . . . the work of the actor is absolutely irrelevant . . . with good montage it is immaterial how he works" (192). Kuleshov went on to concede that acting did have a limited effect on creating meaning within the shot, but he could only understand that effect in terms of creating "intra-shot montage" (193). Kuleshov remained rather unclear about what he meant by this but seemed to suggest that the actor's action contributed to the plays of rhythms internal to any shot. Potentially, this insight may have provided a point for opening out onto a wider consideration of the specific work of the actor on film, yet Kuleshov continued to regard the significance of the actor as subservient to the general rhythm of montage segments. For the pioneering formalists, it was film that produced meaning, not the actor.

Auteurist analysis also submerged the signification of the actor under the authority of the director. While the auteur-structuralist variation on the debate raised some questions about reading films as the statements of solitary expressive individualists, still the director remained at the center of analysis. For Peter Wollen, the auteur theory would find certain films "indecipherable because of 'noise' from the producer, the cameraman or even the actors" (104). It was therefore understandable that when Wollen struck the analogy between film authorship and musical performance, the performance of the director would be of primary concern.

Following the post-structuralist challenge to authorship, acting and the actor were unlikely to emerge as a key area of analysis as film studies sought to dismiss focus on the individual in the making of film meaning. The structuralist turn in film theory called into doubt claims for the individual creation of meaning. While such claims could reasonably be questioned, individuals in films still remained meaningful. Developing in this context, spectatorship studies saw the actor as a figure, an object to be looked at, for a body of theory concerned with conceptualizing the abstract category of the subject.

After the original 1979 publication of Richard Dyer's *Stars*, studies of actors would appear regularly in film scholarship. Although Dyer offered suggestions for the analysis of performance, star studies developed in such ways that analysis became concerned with the meaning of the performer but not, paradoxically, the meaning of performance (that is, acting). Possibly as a result of this new focus on the individual on screen, a scattering of notable writings on film acting did appear around the 1980s (for example, Thompson, "Screen Acting," "Beyond Commutation"; King; Naremore). Since that time, work has appeared that attempts to bring acting into focus (for example, Zucker; Lovell and Krämer), yet the serious study of film performance can be described as intermittent at best.

Since the decline of structuralist analysis and the emergence of star studies, film scholarship has diversified in its concerns. It may be wondered therefore why film acting should still continue to be an undeveloped area of scholarly analysis. One explanation for this would seem to be the very complexity that acting presents to any serious work of film analysis. Although film scholarship has changed its conceptual frameworks and priorities, the concern to understand the workings of the film text has remained constant over time. Examination of acting has a vital role to play in that task, through considering how the signification of the actor's voice and body contribute to a film's meaning. However, it is in this fundamental task that acting is found to present considerable problems for the work of analysis.

In what stands as one of the important contributions to the study of film acting, Roberta Pearson's analysis of D. W. Griffith's Biograph films identifies not only a major historical transformation in performance style but also raises some general questions about the problems and issues involved in analyzing film acting. As Pearson points out, with the gestures of the performer's body lacking the limited lexicon, digital distinctions, and clear system of oppositions found in language, it is impossible for the analysis of acting to work at the level of individually discrete sign units. This would suggest there is an inevitable futility in attempting to embark on a semiotics of film acting in the pursuit of comprehensive and exact analytic rigor. By recognizing these difficulties, Pearson's approach, instead of studying signs, identifies a combination of elements working together at the higher order of what she calls the "super sign," or the code. This change of emphasis provides an important analytic foundation for future work. It must be acknowledged, however, that a code remains a rather imprecise construct, and this very imprecision is likely to forever greet the study of film acting and frustrate confident analysis.

It is one thing to recognize the neglect of film acting by cinema scholarship, but it is still another to think of why that neglect should need to be corrected. Acting is not alone in being neglected: sound and lighting design have suffered a similar fate. So merely to note that film acting has not received sustained attention does not offer a compelling reason for why it should do so now. If film acting is to become an established aspect of film analysis, it must be because reading the uses of the voice and body can inform a larger understanding of any film and of films in general. Analyzing film acting will only become a worthwhile and necessary exercise if the signification of the actor can be seen to influence the meaning of film in some way. In other words, acting must be seen to count for something. A fundamental concern is therefore to uncover what is significant about film acting. This raises a range of basic questions. What will count as significance in performance? How will we know that significance when we see it? In taking the work of the actor to be significant, on what terms are we judging that significance?

Diacritical Analysis of the Actor's Voice and Body

One way of progressing on the issue of significance is suggested by John O. Thompson's application of the commutation test to film acting. Thompson's method is to suggest that by hypothetically substituting performers in roles, significant differences in the meaning of the actor are made visible. Although this simple diacritical exercise is undoubtedly useful, I have argued that Thompson's application of the exercise is limited because his substitutions operate only at the level of the whole actor (McDonald). What Thompson does not consider is how the meaning of gestures and vocal inflections may also result from a play of differences—and therefore he studies the actor but not acting. In a self-critical turn, Thompson ("Beyond Commutation") acknowledges problems in seeing meaning only through the effect of oppositions, for actors work by creating "positivities"—what *is* rather than what *is not*—in performance. While this criticism would seem correct with regard to the creative work of acting, the diacritical technique remains a most useful tool and, if applied to a reading of the actor's voice and body, it can be used as a starting point from which to assess significance in a performance.

The commutation test can work through a variety of imaginative substitutions; however, remakes of films provide tangible examples with which to work on a diacritical analysis of differences produced entirely at the level of the actor's voice and body. With remakes, differences are often produced by changes in mise-en-scène and editing, all of which influence and transform performances. Gus Van Sant's 1998 version of *Psycho* reduces this additional "noise," claiming to be a shot-for-shot remake of the original Alfred Hitchcock thriller (1960).

Van Sant aimed to be as close to the original production process as possible, producing the film through the same studio (Universal), on parts of the original backlot, keeping to Hitchcock's six-week production schedule, shooting scenes in the same sequence, and similarly refusing press previews (A. Smith). However, from the opening panoramic sweep over Phoenix, the claim of shot-for-shot fidelity is discredited, for differences immediately appear in settings, editing patterns, and camera movements. While these differences exist, however, use of shot scale, editing patterns, camera movement, and script all appear to *roughly* approximate the original. Where Van Sant's remake really struggles to create an exact imitation is with its performers and their performances. Janet Leigh is replaced by Anne Heche as Marion Crane. Vince Vaughn takes over from Anthony Perkins as Norman Bates. Marion's sister Lila, originally played by Vera Miles, is now Julianne Moore, and in the role of the detective, Milton Arbogast, Martin Balsam is replaced by William H. Macy.

On its release, Van Sant's remake was greeted with uniform dismissal by reviewers, who judged the film inferior to the original. It is difficult to disagree with this evaluation, but my purpose here is not to measure the remake against the original but rather to compare the two versions for how, most other things being more or less equal, differences in acting performance come to the fore and how these divergences affect the meaning of the respective films.

For William Rothman, Vaughn does not work as Bates because "his obvious weirdness makes it inconceivable that any woman worth caring about would willingly accept his invitation to dine with him" (30). In contrast, I find Vaughn does not work in the role for precisely opposite reasons. Vaughn's bulky frame and healthy appearance contrast with Perkins's lean and hungry look in the original. Against Perkins, Vaughn looks too "normal" to be Norman. Of course, it is entirely possible that real-life killers can conform to conventions of regular appearance, but this is a movie, and Perkins's physicality fits plausibly with playing what could be described as, to borrow a term from Thompson, a "category-meaning"—in this case, the weird killer type.

While Vaughn's body suggests imposing physical strength, Perkins's frail frame becomes a metaphorical somatotype for the character's mental weakness. In terms of acting, Vaughn can be found throughout the remake imitating the nervous laugh Perkins adopted in the original, an idiosyncrasy that is the foundation for Rothman's evaluation of the actor's weirdness. Even without comparison to the original, Vaughn's laugh appears obtrusive. Vaughn makes the laugh appear very self-conscious, whereas with Perkins the laugh emerged purely from what could be described in Stanislavskian terms as the given circumstances of the scene.

Thus, while I share Rothman's discomfort with Vaughn in the Bates role, for me this uneasiness does not arise from seeing a character who acts weird but from being presented with an actor performing weirdly. Vaughn laughs because Perkins laughed, whereas Perkins laughed because someone like Norman probably would in such a situation. This sense of derivation therefore supports Rothman's contention that "Van Sant's actors seem to be going through the motions, to be following a bad script, to be reading lines that do not even seem to have been written for them" (29). However, evaluations aside, the overall impact of the change in actors may be to create a significant change in meaning regarding the relationship of the killer to social normality. As Gavin Smith comments, "Where Hitchcock's Norman is conclusively Other, Van Sant's is one of us" (37).

Further significant differences emerge in the characterization of Marion. When she arrives at the Bates Motel, Marion is shown to cabin 1 by Norman. While the set is almost identical in the two films, small differences in script and editing become apparent, as do contrasts in how the actors use their voices and bodies. After Norman leaves Marion's cabin, she is alone and begins to unpack her bags before hiding the stolen money in a rolled-up newspaper. When Heche rolls the money in the paper and places it on the bedside table, her actions exactly follow Leigh's—it is rumored that Van Sant used a portable DVD player on the set so the performers and crew could copy the original.

Other acts of imitation appear throughout the remake of the scene, but there are also just as many differences in the performance decisions made by the two actresses. After placing the suitcase on the bed, both Marions pull out a dress, which they handle in different ways. Nothing appears significant about this difference. However, before she hangs the dress, in both versions Marion returns to her handbag to take out the money, and it is at this point that the differences introduced suddenly appear significant.

1.1. Handling the money: Leigh/ Crane's dilemma

1.2. Handling the money: Heche/ Crane's liberty.

Leigh/Crane stands on the spot, slowly taking the envelope containing the money from the bag, holding it in her left hand while the right appears to hover away from the money (figure 1.1). Heche/Crane is more hurried in her retrieval of the envelope and, once it is in her left hand, she opens out her arms, swinging from side to side to look around for a place to stash the money (figure 1.2). During this moment, something noticeably present in the Heche/Crane performance but absent from Leigh/Crane's is a rather wicked smile. In contrast, Leigh/Crane evinces only concerned seriousness.

Differences in how the respective performers held the dress did not appear important, but in their handling of the envelope, the two actresses significantly change the attitude of Marion toward the purloined money. With Leigh/Crane, the combination of her gestures suggests a moral struggle about wanting and not wanting the money: one hand holds it while the other seems reluctant even to touch it. While the money may enable Marion to "buy off unhappiness," she is facing a trap of her own making. In contrast, Heche/Crane's quicker pace suggests a livelier wish to get on with the business of hiding the money. Her loose swinging body indicates a sense of liberty involved with having the money, supplemented by a smile that, in these circumstances, appears rather mischievous. Together the combination of Heche/Crane's actions would all seem to suggest an attitude of "Aha, I have the money, so where shall I hide it?"

These small differences are significant for they contribute to a larger understanding of how Marion is characterized and to the respective overall meanings of the two films. A similar difference in acting occurs earlier, during the sequence in which Marion is driving to Fairvale and imagines the voice of Tom Cassidy criticizing her for planning to steal the money while, he claims, flirting with him. Here again, Heche/Crane produces her mischievous smile, making clear her sense of satisfaction in having duped the lascivious male (figure 1.3). At the equivalent moment in the original, Leigh/Crane offers only the faintest hint of a smile, so faint that it could easily be missed, and it is questionable whether it ever even fully registers as a smile at all (figure 1.4).

Watching this same moment in Scottish artist Douglas Gordon's *24 Hour Psycho* (1993) (a gallery installation in which the duration of Hitchcock's original 104-minute feature is stretched over an entire 24-hour period), Leigh's smile becomes much more obvious. Yet although slowing the temporal passage of the film clarifies this detail, the smile seems transformed. What in the original is at best the briefest hint of a sly smile—a smile that Marion hardly seems able to reveal to herself or the outside world—becomes a long, lingering, beaming expression of joy. This would suggest that film duration introduces a paradox into acting analysis: while slowing or halting the film frame may be necessary to precisely determine performance details, thereby resolving denotative issues (smile or no smile?), by modifying time, the connotations of any given performance moment may become radically

1.3. Triumphant amusement: Heche/ Crane escapes unhappiness.

1.4. Anxious amusement: Leigh/ Crane enters the night.

altered. This would suggest that acting analysis must remain mindful of the effects that different temporalities may have on the analytic process.

Comparing details in Leigh and Heche's acting reveals the differences Gavin Smith finds between the two versions of Marion: "[Heche's] Marion lacks Leigh's guilt, melancholy and mounting sense of entrapment. Where Leigh's Marion maintained a careful diplomatic distance from her boss' flirtatious client, Heche's Marion responds with ironic/sarcastic indulgence. Where Leigh is solemn, even grim, Heche is light, untroubled, and almost breezy. Van Sant has reconceived her as someone lacking moral ballast and emotional complexity" (37). Smith ascribes responsibility for these differences to the director, thereby detracting from the contribution of the performers. In addition, by judging the remake as simply lacking the moral weight of the original, Smith does not consider how the details of Heche's performance transform the place of the woman in the narrative. Leigh/Crane is the transgressive woman who questions her actions in a patriarchal society, while Heche/-Crane appears to embrace and take pleasure in her wrongdoing. With the former, the woman appears conscious of her fate at the hands of male authority, while the latter is either unaware of that authority or excited by disrupting its power.

In this case, significance is judged in terms of how the minute actions of the actor reveal a larger understanding of the character's involvement with the circumstances of the narrative. If this principle forms a basic criterion for judging significance in film acting, then it would suggest that the work of analyzing performance need not require reading a performance for the totality of its actions but only in key selected parts. Those parts are unlikely to involve the analysis of even a whole scene, for it is frequently only in brief and fleeting moments that the actor's voice or body may present something of significance. Although only transitory, those moments are nevertheless disproportionate in their impact. They are instances that can only be detected in the minutest details of the actor's vocal and physical actions. At these moments, the voice and body produce micromeanings, the significance of which affects a film as a whole.

Acting, Authenticity, and the Fracturing of Narrative Containment

The study of film acting can gain from the authorship debate the idea that analysis does not need to be caught up with questions of intentionality—whether the actor did or did not consciously produce those details. For the work of analysis, it does not matter how the details got there, only that they are there and seem significant. Whether those details can claim the status of a sign seems unlikely. They can, however, be viewed as the product of an acting code. A starting point for the study of film acting is therefore to analyze the signification of the body and voice in those fragmentary moments when the actions and gestures of the performer impart significant meanings about the relationship of the character to the narrative circumstances.

It would be easy to mistake this principle to mean that acting is only significant when it can be seen to integrate the body and voice of the actor into advancing the progression of the narrative. But acting may also become significant when it can be seen to work *against* the preferred line of the narrative. Although not intended as a performance analysis, Andy Medhurst's study of the sexual politics in *Victim* (Basil Dearden, 1961) finds a tension between the film's tolerant but contained treatment of homosexuality and those moments when desire is unequivocally expressed.

At the center of this tension is Dirk Bogarde's performance as the lawyer Melville Farr. Bogarde brought to the role the quality of gentlemanly poise found so frequently in his performances. That poise breaks down, however, in the key "confessional scene," during which Farr's wife, Laura (Sylvia Syms), questions him about his lover. When pressed by Syms/Laura, Bogarde/Farr forcefully tells her, "I stopped seeing him because I wanted him. Do you understand, because I wanted him." For Medhurst: "Simply writing those words cannot convey the strength of Dirk Bogarde's delivery" (31). It is easy to see Medhurst's point. At this moment, the strength of Bogarde's voice conveys a passion that is not found anywhere else in the film. He speaks with such force that the muscles across the left side of his face and neck can be seen to tense and flex. Although his eyes widen the first time he says, "because I wanted him," the second time they narrow to convey a quite palpable sense of passionate anger. In danger of sounding flippant (although on-screen Bogarde's performance makes the moment anything but frivolous), one of the subtle things that seems to really indicate the degree of the actor/character's conviction is how Bogarde/Farr's neatly coiffured hair shakes as he speaks. Quite simply, at this point, the combination of effects gives the performance the impression that Bogarde/Farr really means it (figure 1.5).

Such an overloading of meaning into the smallest of physical and vocal actions defines what Dyer describes as the "rhetoric of authenticity" in performance: "Authenticity is established or constructed in media texts by the use of markers that indicate lack of control, lack of premeditation and privacy. These return us to notions of the truth being behind or beneath the surface" (*"A Star Is Born"* 137). In terms of the narrative development, the scene places Farr in the privacy of the home, away from the public world of his professional responsibilities, in a situation in which he is forced to admit his hidden desires. But it is not just these circumstances that make the scene a moment of real revelation. In the

1.5. Explosive emotionality: Bogarde delivers Farr's confession.

context of a film concerned with repression, Bogarde's performance in this scene creates a moment of compelling emotional intensity. As Medhurst suggests, the significance of the moment comes in how "this exchange . . . shatters *Victim*'s carefully tolerant project. It is the moment when irresistible sexual desire finds, literally, its voice" (31–32). The moment is given added significance because not only does no other performer/character in the film display an equal level of passion but also, apart from another brief lapse when Bogarde/Farr hits Peter Copley/Paul Mandrake, he retains the air of decorum demanded by the respectability of his profession. The tension Medhurst sees between the film's control and its expression of desire is therefore played out in Bogarde's performance as the momentary loss of his dignified restraint. In short, the actor's voice and body become not only indices of emotionality but also disrupt the social containment of illicit desire.

Acting, Identification, and Emotion

A further way of considering the significance of performance is in the construction of identification. Many theories of spectatorship have regarded identification as formed under the determining power of the gaze. For Christian Metz, identification with actors/characters was secondary to primary identification with the spectator's own look. Despite this dual emphasis, as spectatorship theory developed, it became preoccupied with the look and not the looked-

at. Robin Wood questions the absolute power of the look in determining identification, arguing that "the construction of identification within a film is a delicate and complex matter, that can never
be reduced simply to the mechanics of the 'look,'" but involves
dealing with "the whole spectrum of spectator response from feelings of sympathy through empathy to total involvement" (305).
Although Wood does not consider acting in this context, his sugges-
tion for investigating how identification is formed beyond the look
opens a space in which to consider the place of acting in forming
sympathy and involvement.

Working with the example of *Notorious* (Alfred Hitchcock,
1946), Wood proposes a range of ways in which identification is
achieved in the film. Although Wood first suggests the formation of
identification through a relationship to a male gaze, his analysis
allows one to consider how the work of acting can become significant in constructing empathetic identification in ways that respond
to and challenge the power of such a look.

To use Wood's example, in the very first scene of *Notorious*,
Ingrid Bergman/Alicia Huberman emerges from the courthouse,
where she is greeted by a barrage of looks. This opening sets the
foundation for the film's larger investigation of her character at the
hands of the men—Cary Grant/Devlin, Claude Rains/Alexander
Sebastian, and Louis Calhern/Paul Prescott. From the very beginning, she is placed under the intrusive scrutiny of a male look. As
she emerges from the courtroom, however, Bergman subtly conveys
something of Alicia's response to the look. Confronted by the
reporters, Bergman/Huberman walks upright with her eyes lowered, until flashbulbs illuminate her and make her conscious of the
reporters. She raises her eyes and glances briefly to her right in the
direction from which the flashes came, lowers her eyes, opens her
mouth for a moment but does not speak, looks ahead, closes her lips
tightly, glances at the first reporter who asks her questions, ignores
the second reporter, glances at the third, and then leaves. Here she
is on the end of the look but Bergman's performance conveys clearly
the character's discomfort with that position (figure 1.6).

The significance of these details can be found in the second
form of identification Wood proposes: identification with the threatened or victimized. Alicia may be placed under an investigating look,
but Bergman's performance immediately demonstrates her response
as the victim of the gaze, producing a tension that will remain
throughout the entire film's examination of the notorious woman.
Wood is correct to see the "natural" tendency to identify with the

1.6. Identification with the victimized: Bergman/ Huberman reacts to the look.

victim as culturally determined, but it is Bergman's performance that has the deepest effect on making that connection at this moment. Also at work here is the form of affinity Wood describes as "identification with the star," where the qualities of "healthiness," "naturalness," and "niceness" define Bergman's image (311–14).

The performance also begins to work at establishing how the film develops what Wood describes as "degrees of sympathy": "Irrespective of the mechanics of point of view, we identify with characters to the degree to which we are able (are encouraged) to sympathize, or, better still, empathize with them" (306). Bergman/ Huberman is at the center of what Wood describes as the "female system" of the film: "It is not a film that reinforces patterns of male aggression, but a film that identifies us . . . with the woman's experience of that aggression, the mechanics and motivation of which are uncompromisingly exposed" (326).

This effect can be witnessed in the scene in which Alicia comes to understand that she is being poisoned by Rains/Sebastian and his mother, Leopoldine Konstantin/Madame Sebastian. Wood discusses this scene in great detail as an example of the construction of identification through cinematic devices. Indeed, the scene involves devices like the traveling close-up of the poisoned coffee cup carried by Madame Sebastian and the use of subjective viewpoint shots to place the moviegoer in the position of Alicia. Then there is the swift track in as Alicia attempts to stand after realizing what is happening and the distorted viewpoint shot as she loses consciousness.

All these devices make the scene develop from an objective witnessing of events in the room to inscribing a close identification with Alicia's subjective perception and feelings. This transition changes the distribution of knowledge between the audience and Alicia. The moviegoer already knows the poisoning is taking place so, as Wood suggests, the "first part of the scene . . . recounts the process whereby she catches us up," whereas later "the second part involves us more and more intimately in her experience" (309). Alicia comes to share the moviegoer's secret knowledge before we come to identify with her response to the situation. The scene can therefore be seen to progress through the forms of identification Wood describes as "the sharing of a consciousness"—the "intellectual identification" produced when the knowledge of the character and moviegoer are equivalent—to the emotional identification resulting from empathy with the victim.

Wood reads this process as developing entirely through how the scene is shot and edited. Although his point is perceptive, one can also consider the contribution made by acting. At the moment of crossover from the objective to the subjective, intellectual and emotional identification collide as Alicia realizes the plotting of her fate. Shot scale, music, and editing all work toward creating the impact of the moment. A medium shot of Bergman is followed by a medium shot of Konstantin, accompanied by a zoom in, then back to Bergman before a similar cut and change of framing looks toward Rains. The Kuleshov effect could be credited with constructing meaning at this point: we see Alicia and then what she looks at, and so we infer what she is thinking. But this would only explain the cognitive effect of intellectual identification as we see Alicia realizing what is happening. It is Bergman's acting that makes the cognitive collide with the emotional. Across the exchange of shots, Bergman's breathing appears to intensify, and after the look at Rains/Sebastian, she throws her head back in her chair, closes her eyes, rolls her head from side to side, and her mouth slightly trembles or quivers (figure 1.7). The moment may last only a second or two but it is exactly at this point that the full combination of the scene's intellectual and emotional identifications are achieved. The character knows what we know and now the audience, thanks to Bergman's acting, can witness the distress and depth of suffering Alicia is feeling.

1.7. Knowledge and emotion: Bergman/ Huberman feels the danger.

Bergman's body completes the combining of knowledge with feeling at this moment. If the Kuleshov effect were as effective as the account of his legendary exercise would suggest, then there would be no need for Bergman to offer anything at this point. She could have sat blank faced and the camera and editing would have said it all. However, if this could be imagined, the scene would have an entirely different meaning and different emotional effect. It is necessary for the audience to see that Alicia is arriving at knowledge about what is going on, and then to witness her horror at that realization. These effects depend on performance.

Something interesting arises from this example about acting and the construction of point of view. Frequently, point of view is understood simply as how the flow of narrative information is delivered or withheld through the arrangement of shots and editing. Knowledge is thereby equated with looking, a connection encouraged by the term point of *view*. However, Richard Maltby draws an important distinction between viewpoint, "the camera's position in space: its angle, level, height, and distance from its subject," and point of view, the "position of knowledge in relation to the fiction" (212). Clearly, the positioning of the camera in cinema will become linked to the position of knowledge offered the moviegoer, and so viewpoint and point of view will frequently be intertwined. But Maltby's definition of point of view is open enough to suggest that the construction of knowledge is not just an effect of the camera's position. Lighting, sound, music, and script will all influence what the moviegoer comes to know at any given time—as will acting. The intonations and inflections of an actor's line readings, and the details of his or her facial expressions, gestures, and postures, all influence what we can know about a character's situation at any particular time. We see Bergman/Huberman reaching a point where she realizes what we already know, but it is her acting that gives back to the moviegoer an understanding of what the character is experiencing at that moment.

Some Conclusions

What is significant about seeing the role of acting in the organization of point of view is how identification is achieved not only through the cognitive effect of imparting knowledge but also through the affective realm of creating emotional meaning. Through Bergman/Huberman, the moviegoer identifies with a moment of knowledge but also with her emotional response to that realization. Analyses of point of view have often concentrated on the cognitive to the exclusion of the affective. However, in films, identification is achieved not only through the construction of a cognitive point of view but also through the forming of an emotional point of view. Acting has a vital role to play in constructing both categories. By reading performance, we can learn both what a character knows and what a character feels. If the study of film acting develops further, it may illuminate not only our understanding of how performances construct meaning but it may also have a deeper conceptual influence on the intellectual agenda of film studies by encouraging attention to the significance of emotion when assessing the impact of the movies.

Discussing the effect of Bogarde's performance in the confession scene of *Victim*, Medhurst reflects on what he sees as his own "helpless subjectivism," saying it is impossible to pin down precisely how or why Bogarde's delivery is significant "until we have some adequate account of film acting beyond the loose and impressionistic" (31). As suggested earlier, the analysis of acting will never become a precise semiotic science. Yet that imprecision should not be mistaken for lack of detail, nor should impressionism be regarded as preventing insightful analysis and criticism. Instead, what is at issue is how to integrate those impressions into an understanding of the contributions that acting makes to the construction of meaning in cinema. It is only in the details of the actor's voice and body that the meaning and significance of acting's contribution to film can be found. Impressions will cease to appear vague if the readings they provide inform a larger and substantial understanding of a film's meaning.

This chapter has aimed to highlight just a few examples of how useful insights may be arrived at through close attention to the significance of acting in film. The analyses undertaken here have looked at the role of acting in determining the situations of characters within the larger dramatic dynamics or ideological conditions of film narrative. There has also been the attempt to draw the reading of acting into the mounting of a more complex understanding of how identification works in narrative cinema. Central here is the importance of acting's emotional impact. As suggested earlier, the study of performance will make a valuable intervention in film scholarship if it can encourage a greater and more intensive engagement with the affective impact of movies. Acting analysis will become integral to the study of film if, through attention to the micromeanings of the voice and body, it becomes possible to find in the very smallest of details the most significant of moments.

NOTE

My thanks to Tamar Jeffers for offering valuable insights that helped develop this chapter.

WORKS CITED

Dyer, Richard. "*A Star Is Born* and the Construction of Authenticity." *Stardom: Industry of Desire*. Ed. Christine Gledhill. London: Routledge, 1991. 132–40.

———. *Stars*. Rev. ed. London: British Film Institute, 1998.

King, Barry. "Articulating Stardom." *Screen* 19 (1985): 27–50.

Kuleshov, Lev. "The Principles of Montage" (1935). *Kuleshov on Film*. Ed. Ron Levaco. Berkeley: U of California P, 1974. 183–95.

Lovell, Alan, and Peter Krämer, eds. *Screen Acting*. London: Routledge, 1999. 59–74.

Maltby, Richard, *Hollywood Cinema*. Oxford: Blackwell, 1995.

McDonald, Paul. "Film Acting." *The Oxford Guide to Film Studies*. Ed. John Hill and Pamela Church Gibson. Oxford: Oxford UP, 1998. 30–35.

Medhurst, Andy. "*Victim*: Text as Context." *Screen* 25 (1984): 22–35.

Metz, Christian. *Psychoanalysis and Cinema*. Basingstoke: MacMillan, 1982.

Naremore, James. *Acting in the Cinema*. Berkeley: U of California P, 1988.

Pearson, Roberta E. *Eloquent Gestures: The Transformation of Performance Style in the Griffith Biograph Films*. Berkeley: U of California P, 1992.

Perkins, Victor. *Film as Film*. Harmondsworth: Penguin, 1972.

Rothman, William. "Some Thoughts on Hitchcock's Authorship." *Alfred Hitchcock: Centenary Essays*. Ed. Richard Allen and S. Ishii Gonzalès. London: British Film Institute, 1999. 29–42.

Smith, Adam. "So Good They Made It Twice!" *Empire* 116 (1999): 83.

Smith, Gavin. "Playing with Horrific Farce." *Sight and Sound* 9 (1999): 36–37.

Thompson, John O. "Beyond Commutation—A Reconsideration of Screen Acting." *Screen* 26 (1985): 64–76.

———. "Screen Acting and the Commutation Test." *Screen* 19 (1978): 55–69.

Wollen, Peter. *Signs and Meanings in the Cinema*. London: Secker and Warburg/British Film Institute, 1987.

Wood, Robin. *Hitchcock's Films Revisited*. London: Faber and Faber, 1989.

Zucker, Carole, ed. *Making Visible the Invisible*. Metuchen: Scarecrow, 1990.

2

Screen Performance and Directors' Visions

Sharon Marie Carnicke

As the generally acknowledged heads of collaborative teams who make films, directors often set the tone for the production process, define the parameters of collaboration, and largely determine the ways in which each individual's efforts are used. As such, directors can be considered, in most cases, authors of the final film product. No more or less than other individuals working in cinema, actors too rely on directors to make their contributions count. Screen performances, after all, are shaped in part by directorial decisions made in editing rooms, where actors' images and voices are manipulated in their absence. Given this reality, I invite you to turn your attention instead to actors' working relationships with directors on sets and locations where the actors physically perform. Selected case studies show not only the range and complexity of such relationships but also, more pointedly, that screen actors accommodate different directorial visions by adjusting their performances to suit the aesthetic and narrative styles of the films in which they appear.

Actors working in movies consistently explain that directors become their primary source of feedback, replacing the responses of a traditional theatrical audience.[1] This professional and creative relationship is so essential in film that most screen actors tend to measure their satisfaction against it. Sidney Poitier, for example, unequivocally states that "to get pleasure out of being in a movie, I have to work with a director who is able to inspire me" (Ross and Ross 109). When directors' feedback proves unreliable or when trust is betrayed, film actors are left unsatisfied and sometimes profoundly shaken. Discussing his work during the Hollywood studio era, Melvyn Douglas recalls "ghastly frustrations, especially when I had the kind of directors I couldn't hold an intelligible conversation with, and I had a lot of that" (Ross and Ross 33). Shelley Duvall has described stress-related health problems that developed during the production of *The Shining* (1980), when Stanley Kubrick subjected her to a record number of takes (127 for a single scene), kept her in tears for twelve hours a day, and blamed her inexperience for delays in filming (Lo Brutto 442). No wonder actors with professional leverage, such as Liv Ullman and Jack Nicholson, prefer to choose directors rather than roles (Cardullo et al. 162, 308). As Robert De Niro explains, even after having had "leads in movies . . . a director would come along and I'd want to work with him. It would be a small part, but I'd do it because I wanted to work with him" (Cardullo et al. 285).

Actors understand that film directors affect performances by contributing to decisions about what will be seen in the completed film. As early as 1916, E. H. Southern remarked, "You may express the most abounding beauty, the profoundest emotion, the richest gesture, but if the camera is not making a note of it, you have not accomplished the task the director has set for you" (Cardullo et al. 31). Still, in the final cut, performance represents "a combination of actor and director," to quote Richard Widmark. "There's no way of distinguishing what the director does and what the actor does. You can't tell by the screen how it came about" (Ross and Ross 308). Echoing that point in his reflections on working with Alberto Cavalcanti in *Dead of Night* (1945), Michael Redgrave remembers that "we both felt that it was impossible to tell where direction or acting ended or began. This is, I must stress, ideal not only from the actor's point of view, but from every point of view" (Cardullo et al. 104).

While the ways in which directors and actors work together vary greatly, Jean Renoir suggests a useful axis for comparison when he divides film directors into two types: those who start work with the camera and those "who start with the actors" (Sherman 162–63). Of the first group, Renoir writes, "You put your camera in a certain spot which is carefully chosen . . . and then you take actors and you put them in front of the lens, and you go on. That means the role of director is based on the service of the camera" (162). Actors see most film directors as belonging to this group.[2] Renoir describes the second group of directors, in which he places himself, as "midwives" who nurture actors' contributions to performance. Renoir explains that for these directors, attention to the acting process is central: "You rehearse, you rehearse, and when you decide that you can give the run to the cameraman, you ask the cameraman to come with you, . . . and you decide what will be the angle" (163).[3] Directors who seek to assist actors often change tactics as need dictates. Diane Carson (in chapter 7) points out that John Sayles adjusted to the different ways in which Mary McDonnell and Alfre Woodard worked during the filming of *Passion Fish* (1992). Jeff Daniels calls those who "know how to direct different actors in different ways" the "best" directors (Cardullo et al. 258).

Renoir's axis bears expansion, however. First, one might add consideration of other directorial approaches. For example, as suggested by Carole Zucker in chapter 8, directors like Neil Jordan employ the imagination of a short story writer and novelist. Second, Renoir suggests no clear correspondence between directorial approach and the encouragement of creative input from actors. This second point especially bears a closer look.

On the one hand, directors who start with the camera and emphasize visual design may place high priority on collaborating with actors, while directors who attend to actors' objectives and their vocal and physical choices do not necessarily work collaboratively with them. Those directors who start with the camera but leave actors alone to do their creative work often view them as experts who contribute specialized knowledge and talents to the enterprise. Because "most cinema directors are cinema," as Henry Fonda puts it, "they hire the best actors they can find and expect a performance from them" (Cardullo et al. 212). Robert Altman perhaps represents the extreme of this laissez-faire approach. He wants the actor to surprise him, to "bring something to me that I've never seen before, but that I know is right" (Sherman 161). In developing character, he urges actors to use their personal creative impulses and to write their own dialogue (Breskin 271). In Altman's view, collaboration produces a richer film. He explains, "If the vision were just mine, just a single vision, it wouldn't be any good" (Sterritt 129). Echoing Richard Widmark's observations about the joint effort behind the performances we see on screen, Altman describes screen performances as "the combination of what I have in mind, with who the actor is and then how he adjusts to the character, along with how I adjust" (Sterritt 129).

On the other hand, directors who start with the camera sometimes become master puppeteers who limit actors' creative input.

These can view actors primarily as objects for the camera. Describing his experience with Fritz Lang, Fonda explains that Lang "would actually manipulate you with his hands" (Cardullo et al. 216) to get the physical position he desired. Michelangelo Antonioni tends to follow this "master puppeteer" approach insofar as he asserts that "it is the director . . . who should decide the pose, gestures, and movements of the actor" (48). Rejecting collaboration with actors as "not possible" and pointing out that "sometimes the actor and director necessarily become enemies," Antonioni has argued that the film actor should be "a kind of Trojan horse in the citadel of the director" (48–49).

Even these brief observations by Altman and Antonioni, both of whom can be said to start with the camera, suggest the difficulty of mapping collaboration to directorial approach. From such observations, however, an axis of comparison other than Renoir's emerges that charts the amount of control a director exerts over actors' choices. This axis cuts across all modes of directorial inspiration, whether visual, performative, or narrative, and maps instead the dynamic working relationship between director and actor. Along this axis, a director like Neil Jordan, whose films spring from his deep engagement with screenwriting, can be compared with Robert Altman. Both welcome actors' contributions within the stylistic boundaries set by the narrative. As Stephen Rea says of Jordan, "Neil doesn't direct me as an actor; he doesn't try and orchestrate my performance, he just reminds you what the story is, and where he wants the story to go" (Zucker 110). Given their view of actors as collaborators, directors like Jordan and Altman stand at the opposite pole from directors like Lang, Antonioni, and, as we shall see, Stanley Kubrick, who see actors primarily as props to manipulate within the mise-en-scène.

Whatever the working relationship between actor and director during filming might have been, the performance seen in the final cut is assembled by selecting those performed moments in which actors' physical and vocal expressions best embody the film's underlying themes and aesthetic style. Screen actors take this as given. When Robert De Niro says that "the director should let the actors know what he's trying to do in the style" (Cardullo et al. 282), he suggests that actors can assist in creating such moments. Like other film professionals, actors recognize that narrative and aesthetic demands differ from film to film. Furthermore, they expect to adjust and attune the details of their performances to suit a director's vision.

Academic inquiries into performance, however, have often aligned styles we see in film with specific acting techniques. Realistic and naturalistic narratives that feature recognizable characters with coherent personalities and familiar desires usually line up with "Stanislavskian" modes. Moreover, the "Stanislavskian" actor presumably works to create character authentically by merging self with role.[4] Performances in modernist or postmodern narratives that stress ambiguity of character and question the nature of identity are often viewed as featuring "Brechtian" elements such as estrangement and episodic structures that lack causal or motivational relationships. Thus, actors in these films presumably use "Brechtian" techniques to stand outside their characters and to maintain an objective opinion of the role's behavior.[5]

Reference to Stanislavskian and Brechtian techniques do not, however, capture the full complexity of actors' work. Recall that the division between directors who start with the camera and directors who start with the actor is complicated by differences even within a group: among directors who start with the camera, some collaborate with actors while others use actors as props. Dividing actors into those who create "realistic" performances and nonrealistic ones is similarly complicated. The final performance on screen tells us virtually nothing about the acting technique used during filming. What reads as realistic might arise from any variety of acting techniques, including those of Stanislavsky, Brecht, Delsarte, Suzuki, and so on.

Reference to Stanislavskian and Brechtian techniques also fails to capture the complexity of the theoretical systems ostensibly identified by the terms. Take, for example, the work of Konstantin Stanislavsky. The nearly exclusive identification of Stanislavsky with realism ignores much of his career. His famous Chekhov productions represent only one phase in his directing and, indeed, one that precedes his most concentrated efforts to develop an acting system. Over time, he not only directed realist plays but also operas, symbolist plays, and verse dramas by Pushkin, Shakespeare, and Molière.

Even early in his career, Stanislavsky adapted his approach when directing actors in roles that resisted coherent development. For the 1909 production of Turgenev's *A Month in the Country*, Stanislavsky advised Olga Knipper-Chekhova to play each scene independently of the others in order to embody the changeable nature of her character, an idea that director David Kaplan sees as the anticipation of Brecht's episodic structure (61–62). Moreover, throughout his career as a teacher, Stanislavsky insisted that "one must give actors various paths" for their work (565) and so designed many more techniques than the ones that feature identification of self with character. His system articulates methods for utilizing emotional memory, physical and mental exercises from Yoga, the Method of Physical Actions, and his last, most innovative approach, Active Analysis, through which the text is viewed as a dynamic structure of actions and counteractions that produce chains of events.

Viewing the actor's body and voice as productive of performance offers the cinema scholar a methodology that transcends the limitations of identifying styles with specific acting techniques. Examining the physical and vocal choices that appear on screen as both interpretive and constitutive of style offers a more useful means by which to analyze performance than those based primarily on actor training. This approach charts an actor's ability to adapt his or her choices and training to suit the demands of different narrative, cinematic, and shooting styles. By setting aside presumed connections between acting techniques and performance styles, one is able to analyze the work of actors as more or less flexible, more or less supple, rather than as primarily "Stanislavskian" or "Brechtian." Many actors see their ability to adapt to narrative and directorial demands as the special expertise for which they are hired. Jack Nicholson argues that "your job [as an actor] is to give the director what he wants ultimately, no matter what it is" (Sherman 191). He notes that his truncated performance in *The Passenger* (1975) "is exactly what [Antonioni] wanted" and that his exaggerated performance in *The Shining* was just what Kubrick wanted (Thompson 133, 166).

An analogy between acting and playing the piano clarifies the distinction between acting technique and performance. Musician Charles Rosen makes two interesting observations about ways that pianists interact with musical style. He explains that players adjust their level of physical exertion to the demands of the music; louder music necessitates more exertion, softer music, less. Second, Rosen points out that players develop individualized techniques for fingering based on the anatomy of their hands (the length of the fingers, the width of the palm), not on theory (22, 15–16).

Applying Rosen's observations to the actor proves illuminating. Like the pianist, who uses different levels of exertion and yet the same fingers to play ballads or jazz, an actor like Jack Nicholson uses different kinds of energy but the same physiognomy to embody Antonioni's subdued protagonist in *The Passenger* and Kubrick's manic monster in *The Shining*. Recall two similar moments in these films: the Antonioni scene set in a baroque church, in which David Locke meets two guerrillas wishing to buy arms from the person whose identity Locke has stolen, and the Kubrick scene in which Jack Torrance interviews for the caretaking job at the Overlook Hotel. The screenplays present Nicholson with similar narrative demands. Both are interviews; in both the protagonist meets his interlocutors for the first time; in both he is unsure of how to handle the situation. Yet within these narrative similarities, Antonioni and Kubrick employ different aesthetic styles. *The Passenger* depends on modernist minimalism while *The Shining* breaks through naturalistic assumptions, anticipating postmodernism disruptions in identity, chronological time, and spatial orientation.

In the first case, in sympathy with Antonioni's minimalist vision, Nicholson uses facial gesture sparingly, barely moving his lips and eyes to embody a man profoundly empty of purpose. While he speaks to the guerrillas, Nicholson's body remains poised in attentive stillness. Critic Julian Hoxter calls this work Nicholson's "most natural, his least affected, and, I would submit, in many ways his most accomplished to date" (87). By comparison, to suit the hyperbolic style of the Kubrick film, Nicholson exaggerates the tension in his lips and jaw while he stares wide-eyed. During this job interview scene, Nicholson telegraphs the character's effort to sit still and listen by shifting his position in the chair and looking rapidly from one interviewer to the other. As Mario Falsetto observes, Nicholson's work in *The Shining* "is notable for its physicality and expressiveness." Especially in comparison to his minimalist performance for Antonioni, Nicholson gives a "wildly inventive and emotionally charged performance" for Kubrick (164). Using his training well, Nicholson adjusts his physical vocabulary to the needs of the film, transforming himself and his performance style in the process.

At the same time, like the pianist who always works within the gifts and limitations of his or her own anatomy, Nicholson renders the portrayal of the two characters using the specific features of his own body and physiognomy. Despite differences in physical exertion from slack expression to tense exaggeration, Nicholson's facial anatomy individualizes his work: however small or large his gestures, his eyebrows always raise themselves into perfect Vs. In *The Passenger*, his eyebrows contribute to the image of a man for whom identity is a performance. In *The Shining*, they become yet another sign of the character's out-of-control insanity.

Actors like Jack Nicholson draw upon a wide range of traditions and techniques. Contemporary actor training programs commonly teach Stanislavsky and Brecht alongside training derived from the American Method and Japanese director Tadashi Suzuki. Thus, like pianists, film actors can pick and choose as they create performances that suit narrative and directorial demands. Moreover, like pianists, who cannot change the anatomy of their hands, actors always access character through their bodies, using not theory but the physical and vocal attributes that mark their individualities. In this regard, training and technique provide the means by which they use their bodies as "instruments" to respond to various aesthetic styles and professional demands. As the following case studies suggest, actors working in film create the performances required by the director's vision of the narrative by drawing on their own, often eclectic, training. Moreover, in moving from film to film, character to character, and director to director, the same actor can employ technique quite differently by adjusting physical means, if not anatomy, to the needs of narrative and aesthetic style. This adjustment lies at the heart of the performer's art.

Jack Nicholson: Working with Antonioni and Kubrick

Nicholson's performances in the interview scenes from *The Passenger* and *The Shining* suggest how widely actors can adjust their performances. Nicholson's gestural and vocal choices in each film allow him to present two distinct characters. Under Antonioni's direction in *The Passenger*, Nicholson "is enervated as the world-weary reporter" (Vineberg 316). He "seems to have been selected precisely because his blandness and inexpressive deadness of feature suggest so convincingly the look of a man in desperate need of an identity" (Arrowsmith 129). The interview scene shows "that this quintessentially rootless, identity-less modern man is just as out of place there, in the church, as he was in the desert" (Brunette 135). Overall, he gives an "imploded performance" by directing his energy inward (McGilligan 247).

By comparison, under Kubrick's direction in *The Shining*, Nicholson creates a writer down on his luck, whose "phony" behavior at the interview is "evident in the way he tries so hard to be affable and accommodating" (Falsetto 165). Depending upon the critic's personal taste, Nicholson's performance may be considered either "desperately mannered" (Vineberg 319) or "invigorating" (Falsetto 164). However interpreted, critics agree that Nicholson's energy explodes outward, often directed toward Shelley Duvall as his wife.

Critics have often identified Nicholson with heightened performances that feature the broad facial and physical gestures exemplified by his work in *The Shining*. As a consequence, his minimalist use of gesture in a film like *The Passenger* seems to go "against type" (Hoxter 87). In reality, Nicholson reveals great flexibility. Dennis Bingham, for example, charts Nicholson's stylistic range from the exaggerated work in *Batman* (1989), in which his face registers as "a Delsarte chart," to his "mostly naturalistic and understated" acting in *Five Easy Pieces* (1970), in which he embodies a character who "seems cut from the antihero mold at which Method actors so excelled" (103, 115, 111).

Interviews with Nicholson indicate that he consciously adjusts to the material. When asked about his work in *The Border* (1982), he explained: "I was able to give a naturalistic performance . . . that wasn't possible in the films that preceded it. *Going South* was a farce; *The Shining* was a *Grand Guignol*; *Postman* was a *film noir*; *Reds* was biographical. All had their own stylistic demands. [*The Border*] didn't and in many ways it was easier to do" (Shepherd 146–47).[6] Nicholson's training has given him many different ways to negotiate the disparate styles of the films in which he has appeared. He learned techniques drawn from the traditions of François Delsarte, Bertolt Brecht, Konstantin Stanislavsky via the Method, and Jerzy Grotowski via British director Peter Brook (Bingham 116).

Moreover, throughout his career, Nicholson has sought to exercise the full range of his skills by seeking roles that challenge him, as his wanting to "do an Antonioni movie" (Hoxter 85) suggests. Despite Antonioni's known antipathy toward collaboration with actors, Nicholson saw the modernist director as "one of the greatest influences on filmmaking in the past three decades" (Thompson 133). Antonioni responded by casting Nicholson as David Locke but commented that "if the actor is different from the part, if the feeling doesn't work, even Jack Nicholson won't get the part" (336).

How did the working relationships between Nicholson and these two directors result in the actor's successful transformation into two such distinct characters? The answer lies somewhere in the articulation between each director's working method and

Nicholson's collaborative and technical abilities to embody different physical and vocal attributes as encouraged by directorial visions, narratives, and shooting styles.

In working together, Antonioni and Nicholson both found that they had to compromise. As noted earlier, Antonioni belongs to the group of directors who serve the camera, expecting control over every element in the frame, whether it be landscape, architecture, or human being. In prompting actors, Antonioni used what he called a "hidden method" (McGilligan 246). He would tell actors to "just say the lines and make the movements" and then "trick an actor by demanding one thing and obtaining another." As he explains, "What I do is try to provoke [actors]. . . . And then I watch through the camera and at that moment tell them to do this or that. But not before. I have to have my shot" (Antonioni 49, 136). Antonioni cites the opening scene from *The Passenger* in which David Locke tries to dig his Land Rover out of the Algerian sand as an example of his "method." Antonioni felt that the scene succeeded because he fought with Nicholson in order for the actor to "enter into a state of crisis. . . . When we filmed, the crisis came naturally. The weeping was natural. It was real" (175–76). Antonioni asserts that Nicholson "did not even realize" the ruse (175), while Nicholson called the experience a case of "No communication. No give and take" (McGilligan 247).

Antonioni expected to dictate Nicholson's performance, explaining, "I tried to control him in such a way as to produce this type [of character]" (175). The willful director considered Nicholson a "great actor" in large part because of the star's willingness to cooperate: "He's intense, yet he doesn't create any problems—you can cut his hair (I didn't), he's not concerned about his 'good' side or whether the camera is too high or too low; you can do whatever you want" (336). In turn, Nicholson said, "They told me I was the first actor who got along with him in twenty-five years, probably because I gave him the performance he wanted" (Thompson 133).

Working with a star pressured and in part surprised the auteur. On a practical level, Antonioni bristled because he had to work much faster than he wanted to accommodate Nicholson's other engagements (Brunette 135). On the artistic level, Nicholson left a personal mark on the film especially identifiable in the humorous undercurrents in his performance. Peter Brunette speculates that "an interesting exploration could be made of the influence of an American star . . . on Antonioni's working methods and even on his script." Brunette points to moments such as the one in which

David Locke, left alone after his meeting with the guerrilla fighters, catches himself swearing under his breath. Brunette identifies Locke's humorous apology to God for swearing in church as one of Nicholson's interventions in the film (177 n. 16).

Turning to the working relationship on *The Shining*, interview material suggests that Kubrick cast Nicholson precisely because of his reputation for exaggerated acting. Kubrick explains that he had admired Nicholson's ability to go beyond realism, pointing out that Nicholson's "work is always interesting, clearly conceived and has the x-factor, magic" (Ciment 188). Nicholson, in turn, was interested in the director's non-naturalistic impulses. Discussing his work with Kubrick on *The Shining*, Nicholson noted: "You can go on for years saying 'I'm going to get this thing real, because they really haven't seen it real' . . . and then you come up against someone like Stanley who says, 'Yeah, it's real, but it's not interesting'" (Lo Brutto 443). Nicholson agreed with Kubrick's stylistic approach to the screenplay, explaining that "when the material is as unusual as *The Shining*, dealing with ghosts and spirits, the actor has to be larger than life" (McGilligan 312). Yet Nicholson also knew that such stylistic experiments entailed risks. He has observed that "the affectation of style within cinematic acting is something the audience heavily penalizes you for, because they're stuck at the turn of the century; they're interested in naturalism" (Bingham 101).

A link exists between Nicholson's experiences on *The Passenger* and *The Shining* insofar as both directors begin with the camera. Kubrick's attention to visual detail has consistently astonished and delighted audiences. Note, for example, the extraordinary use of mirrors in *The Shining* to reflect the schizophrenic duality in the protagonist's character.[7] But in contrast to Antonioni, Kubrick sees himself as a director who focuses intensively on acting. He has said that he learned how to work with actors by reading Nikolai Gorchakov's *Stanislavsky Directs* (Walker, Taylor, and Ruchti 21). Considering Kubrick's working methods, his avowal makes sense in light of the book's history. Published in the Soviet Union in 1954 when censors had banned information about Stanislavsky's most innovative acting experiments, Gorchakov suggests something of Stanislavsky's last directorial approach without actually naming or describing it. Active Analysis becomes Gorchakov's subtext. A Russian reader, used to such literary ploys, would unpack the author's hidden associations. Kubrick's idiosyncratic work with actors suggests that as a Western reader, he picked up only some aspects of Active Analysis.

Broadly speaking, Active Analysis makes the actor aware of the play's narrative structure through repeated improvisations that function as drafts of the final performance. Emulating late Stanislavskian technique, Kubrick developed a clear focus on the link between actor and narrative. Describing Kubrick's view that performance style should reflect the demands of the narrative, Mario Falsetto notes that "performance and how to communicate meaning through character have consistently been crucial components in Kubrick's aesthetics" (151).

Moreover, as in Active Analysis, Kubrick expected actors to explore the parameters of their scenes through repetition. He became famous for his exhaustive number of takes, many of which he considered to be rehearsals (much as Active Analysis views repeated improvisations as multiple drafts of a scene). He has noted, "I'm not sure that the early takes aren't just glorified rehearsals with the added adrenaline of film running through the camera" (Ciment 188).[8] Examples of Kubrick's method abound. Barry Nelson repeated "Hi ya, Jack" thirty-five times to start the interview scene in *The Shining* (Lo Brutto 429). Scatman Crothers, who played Halloran at the age of seventy, witnessed Kubrick's terrible perfectionism when he had to get out of a snowcat and walk silently across a snowy expanse forty times. The work was so physically extreme that Nicholson intervened on behalf of the elderly actor, asking Kubrick to "pay attention to the actor's exhaustion" (Kazan 208).

While Kubrick emphasizes narrative and repetition, he leaves out one aspect of great significance to Stanislavsky: the actors' discussion that occurs before each repetition. Active Analysis establishes a shared understanding of the play and promotes agreements on the goals for each repetition in order to move the cast as a whole toward successful embodiment of the play as well as their characters. Kubrick does not encourage such collaboration, expecting actors to work on their own. "Teaching actors how to act," he explains, "is something that should be done by somebody else" (Walker, Taylor, and Ruchti 21). This attitude has led to incommunicative silence. As Tony Burton reports, "When he's on the set working he doesn't talk to anyone. He doesn't explain anything. He just says 'Let's go again. Let's go again.' . . . Why did he stop me? . . . You'll never know" (Lo Brutto 444). Anne Jackson, playing a doctor in one scene, bitterly complained that he subjected her to multiple takes without telling her what he wanted her to change or improve in her work. Although Shelley Duvall consoled her, assuring her that "he's done this with everyone," Jackson was particularly irked when she realized that her first take was used in the final film (Lo Brutto 428–29).

Kubrick does, however, share Stanislavsky's directorial eye. As accurately reflected by Gorchakov, the older Russian master did not impose a priori patterns of movement on his actors, but rather watched them move freely as narrative logic suggested. When he noticed a pattern expressive of the production's concept, he would set it as "blocking." Similarly, Kubrick explains that he has to "work out clearly what the objectives of a scene are from the point of view of narrative and character, but once this is done [he finds] it much more profitable to avoid locking up any idea about staging or camera or even dialogue prior to rehearsals." Kubrick believes that throughout his career as a director he has sought to "arrive in some way as an observer looking at something that has a degree of freshness to me" (Walker, Taylor, and Ruchti 22). When he saw what he wanted, he selected it for inclusion in the final cut.

While Kubrick makes the acting process difficult, Jack Nicholson successfully adapted to Kubrick's approach and attuned his performance to the aesthetic demands of the film. His broadly based training not only gave him many tools with which to access his character but also many ways to work, and thereby to adjust his means to Kubrick's method. As a result, there is a close fit between Nicholson's acting and Kubrick's vision for *The Shining*. Dennis Bingham sees the performance as a "brilliant example" of why both "formalists [who] see the actor as an expressive figure in the mise-en-scène" and critics who "argue that actors' presences are so strong that they themselves can be auteurs" deserve equal attention (143). In short, Nicholson's differing use of his body and voice in *The Passenger* and *The Shining* demonstrate how a single actor can move from one character to another and adjust to two directorial approaches. Nicholson emerges from the study as a highly flexible and collaborative actor.

Shelley Duvall: Working with Altman and Kubrick

In contrast to Nicholson's work, Shelley Duvall's with Robert Altman and Kubrick suggests the difficulties actors sometimes encounter as they move from one director to another. Her "Modigliani" face and "kooky, funny looking" appeal (Eisenberg 3) attracted the attention of both directors. Altman cast her as L. A. Joan in his 1975 *Nashville*, using her unusual looks and skimpy costumes to challenge conventional expectations about sexuality (Jahr). For *The Shining*, Duvall was Kubrick's "first and only choice" for Wendy, whom he saw as "mousy and vulnerable" (Lo Brutto 415). Her "eccentric quality—the way she talks, the way she moves, the way her nervous system is put together" (Ciment 189) seemed to Kubrick already stylized and hence interesting. Dressed in eccentric clothes that cover her body completely (red long johns under a pinafore dress and big furry boots that make her shuffle), she is made to seem an oversized child.

Discovered by Altman at a party in Texas, she lived the American myth of a star, suddenly born from obscurity (Segrave and Martin 135). As an actor, Duvall relied on her innate ability to observe people. She explains, "I was always a good observer. A lot of what my characters do is taken from people I've watched: friends, family, strangers" (Sherman 188). Her canny observations of women obsessed with consumerism and magazines for Altman's *Three Women* led to her receiving the award for Best Actress at the 1977 Cannes Film Festival.

During the filming of *Nashville*, Altman encouraged actors to contribute liberally to the project, even by mining as much of their personal lives as they wished. As screenwriter Joan Tewkesbury reports, Altman wanted them "to embroider with as much detail from their own lives as was required to make them at home with their assignments" (Stuart 18). In some cases, he provoked near parodies of the Method actor's dredging up of personal experience. For example, he cast Keith Carradine as one-third of a sexual triangle, playing opposite his real-life friend and actual lover. Carradine suggests that such parallels with real life were not always comfortable. "You could get stroked, or you could get shafted. There was an invitation to bring everything you could to the party. But it was at your own peril" (Stuart 156).

Duvall contributed to the development of L. A. Joan in a number of ways. To establish the look of her character, she shopped in thrift stores for platform shoes, sequined tube tops, short shorts, wildly patterned socks, and large bags to hold seemingly innumerable wigs (Stuart 122). On-screen Altman draws attention to Duvall's talent for costume metamorphosis in the scene that features L. A. Joan in a bar, just after she has changed her wig and thus her look. The scene shows Duvall walk past her latest conquest, who registers no recognition, as she seeks out the next flirtatious encounter.

She also used her powers of observation to humanize her eccentric-looking character. Tewkesbury describes L. A. Joan as "among those girls . . . who were disgruntled at home because they couldn't get close enough to fame" (Stuart 63). Duvall researched such women. "I hung around with groupies at rock clubs in Los Angeles. That kind of investigation is useful, just watching everyday people is what works best for me" (Sherman 188). She decided that her character's "insecurity" was "expressed by an obvious bid for attention" (Lane). As Duvall explains, L. A. Joan "craves affection but doesn't have a high regard for herself. She hasn't learned the big lesson, that before you can have a happy life, you have to be a happy person" (Lane, n.p.). Duvall's vision of L. A. Joan dovetails nicely with Altman's use of her within the frame. He often makes her the visual focus, while simultaneously marginalizing her character's involvement in the scene's main action. For example, in her uncle's rooming house, she parades around in her underwear, distracting the new boarder from his telephone call to his mother. Duvall stands in the center of the shot but remains uninvolved in the primary conversation. Altman underlines her bid for attention by showing the boarder turn his back to the camera as he looks at her.

Duvall weaves the fabric of her role from a series of small, simple, everyday gestures that Altman presents in short takes, as his shooting style for the film dictates. Consider the scene in the hospital where her aunt lies dying. L. A. Joan asks a man to light her cigarette, then rebukes her uncle for interrupting the conversation, and finally walks down the hall toward the exit with her new beau. These three moments are not continuous in the film, but rather function as briefly glimpsed images. Altman also uses short takes in the barroom scene that features the character Tom Frank (Carradine). All the women who have slept with him, including L. A. Joan, are there when he dedicates his song to a new lover. Duvall uses simple gestures to express her reactions. She smokes her cigarette; her eyes dart from side to side; she smiles knowingly as Tom takes the stage. She cocks her head in confusion at his dedication, and finally, when she understands, she turns her head with an ironic smile toward her rival (Keyssar 160–62).

Duvall found Altman's approach "so easy, I couldn't believe I was getting paid to do this" (Segrave and Martin 135). Critic Pauline Kael pointed to Duvall's success in this working environment, noting that Duvall seemed "able to be herself on the screen in a way that nobody has ever been before" (Stuart 96).

Yet Altman's approach could not prepare Duvall for working with Kubrick. While Altman had included her in the collaborative team, Kubrick controlled her work by psychologically beating her into a frenzied emotional performance. According to Duvall, Kubrick's "way of working is to do take after take until your spontaneity goes quite dead. Then, when you think you've got no resistance left, you come back again, full force" (Mann). Kubrick complained that she had "great difficulty" with the level of emotion necessary for her role. In discussing the scene on the hotel staircase in which her husband threatens her, Kubrick admits that she ultimately found an "authentic sense of hysteria," but, he comments, "It took her a long time to achieve this" (Ciment 188). Working with Kubrick, she suffered and blamed herself. "My biggest problem was my own insecurity," Duvall said (Lo Brutto 441). Making matters worse, Kubrick either paid her little attention or reprimanded her for causing unnecessary delays, while he dealt directly and easily with Nicholson. Duvall could not entirely tell whether Kubrick did not respect her or whether he merely played a psychological "game" to get the performance he wanted from her (Lo Brutto 443).

In *The Shining*, Duvall's emotional portrayal of Wendy, again woven from familiar gestures, differs starkly from Nicholson's broad, exaggerated work. As Mario Falsetto writes, "Jack mugs and limps his way through many scenes, in contrast to the genuine terror and piercing screams emanating from Wendy" (171). Also in stark contrast to Altman's fleeting glimpses of her, Kubrick presents Wendy primarily through long scenes of extended reactions to her husband. This directorial decision required Duvall to sustain Wendy's emotional reactions for long periods of time and over the course of many takes. Moreover, Kubrick often wanted her to express a single unmodulated emotion, usually fear. Take, for example, the scene in which Torrance angrily pursues his wife up the stairs (figures 2.1 and 2.2). As Nicholson gesticulates wildly, his hands flailing, his arms extended outward, Duvall barely moves. She pulls her elbows in close, clutching a baseball bat in her tense hands. As Nicholson advances with eyes wide, his voice loudly reprimanding and mocking her, she backs up the stairs cautiously, her eyes narrowed in fear, her voice hoarse and her words blurred. Her head wavers on her shoulders in exhaustion. Given Nicholson's active, changeable performance, Duvall's seems long-suffering and homogenous in comparison. She functions as the measure of his abuse rather than as an independent force in the scene. Writing

2.1. Shelley Duvall exhausted, her head drooping, her body drained of all energy.

2.2. Jack Nicholson on the attack, the tension in his body turning his face into a mask.

about this scene and others, Falsetto envisions the spectator as "torn between the enjoyment of Nicholson's performance and revulsion at the cruelty of his displays" in ways that make the scenes between husband and wife fascinating but "unsettling" (170).

In examining how actors attune their performances to suit specific roles, the comparison of Duvall's performances for Altman and Kubrick again brings to light how technical and stylistic demands, in this case the length of the shot and Wendy's prolonged reactions, make necessary the actor's adjustments in body and voice. When both films wrapped, Duvall had successfully transformed herself into the two different characters. As L. A. Joan, Duvall creates a nuanced performance that works simultaneously on different levels. She accesses the character through small, telling, everyday gestures. As Wendy, she gives a sustained performance that works through emotionally telling gestures. Given Kubrick's desire that Duvall portray Wendy in monochromatic terms, he made Duvall appear, however, less supple and expressive an actor than her costar, a choice he would make again with Tom Cruise.

Tom Cruise: Working with Kubrick and Jordan

Tom Cruise's work with Kubrick and Neil Jordan suggests the limitations of viewing acting in terms of star image. Having taken acting classes "like a junky" in New York (Sanello 33), Cruise first came to public attention in *Risky Business* (1983). With his boyish good looks and clean-cut charm he became a "top box-office star, whose fame has been built portraying heroic, decent men" (*Interview with the Vampire*). As Dennis Bingham explains in chapter 10, Kubrick would trade on Cruise's star image in *Eyes Wide Shut* (1999), typecasting him as the handsome, successful doctor who has everything. In contrast, when Neil Jordan chose Cruise for *Interview with the Vampire* (1994), he cast against type. "Sometimes when you go the opposite way from what people expect, you get the best results," Jordan said (Salamon 74).

The casting of Cruise in both films intensified publicity. Before the release of *Eyes Wide Shut*, Cruise and Nicole Kidman fielded scandalous rumors that the sexually explicit scenes on screen allegedly paralleled their married life. For *Interview with the Vampire*, the novel's author Anne Rice reportedly criticized Cruise as "no more my Vampire Lestat than Edward G. Robinson is Rhett Butler" (Rowe).[9] As controversies surrounding casting suggest, Cruise's star image initially overshadowed considerations of his work as an actor.

In *Eyes Wide Shut*, Tom Cruise's Dr. William Harwood proves to be as empty and vacuous as Jack Nicholson's modernist wanderer David Locke in *The Passenger*. With Cruise's stardom providing its own field of allusions, Kubrick uses the actor ironically to explore and expose the emptiness of success. Cruise physicalizes Dr. Bill's vacuity by means of a blank, noninteractive performance that suggests Brechtian techniques of estrangement (see Bingham's chapter 10). By making the familiar appear strange, the actor draws attention to the artifice of performance. For Cruise, the expression of estrangement consists primarily of turning his face into an immobile mask, however provocative the situations he encounters. For long reactive shots, his face remains slack, moving little and expressing less, even when confronted with his wife's sexual confessions. When Bill later dons a literal mask, viewers are prompted to recall his earlier masklike stares and see them as an aesthetic choice.

At first glance, Nicole Kidman also appears to use estrangement when her speech becomes unnaturally slow and when, during her first lovemaking scene, she glances directly into the camera as if to acknowledge the spectator. However, in contrast to his presentation of Dr. Bill, Kubrick always provides logical explanations for Alice's (Kidman's) odd behavior. In the one instance, her speech is slowed by alcohol and marijuana. In the other, she glances, not into the camera, but into a mirror strategically placed. In short, Kubrick uses narrative elements in a way that make Cruise's choices seem stylized while Kidman's appear, albeit at second glance, believable.

The stylistic distinction between Cruise's and Kidman's performances is further marked by their different levels of interaction with each other. For example, when Alice confesses her desire for another man, Cruise maintains an unchanging look and pose. His face has already become the inexpressive mask he will later wear. Cruise accomplishes this feat by doing literally nothing. In contrast, Kidman's face changes rapidly with the story she tells and in reaction to her husband. Her high level of interactivity is naturalistically embedded in the emotional situations and relationships through which her character moves.

By distinguishing Cruise's performance from Kidman's, Kubrick sets a stylized male performance against a more familiarly framed female one, just as he had done in *The Shining*.[10] However, while Nicholson's broad performance with its endless invention seems more innovative that Duvall's, Cruise's blank performance seems to pale in comparison to Kidman's expressive work. Has Kubrick set Cruise up to look like a "bad" actor? Had he done the same with Duvall by insisting on a monochromatic performance? Certainly, Cruise and Duvall lack the interactive details of their costars. As one critic notes, Bill's facial masks make him look "dead or at best false," especially in contrast to Alice, who becomes Kubrick's "most psychologically complete character"

(Nelson 284, 296). While the performances by Cruise and Duvall are comparable in being less interesting than those created by their costars, they do not share stylistic traits: Cruise's performance is distinctly nonrealistic while Duvall's performance is largely "authentic," to borrow Kubrick's adjective for it. The axis of comparison, therefore, shifts from aesthetic style to levels of interactivity in physical and vocal work.

Such observations lay a foundation for evaluating performance in ways that help illuminate the total film and the director's propensities. The counterpoint of acting choices made by Nicholson and Cruise, when juxtaposed to those of Duvall and Kidman, suggest that Kubrick is using nonrealistic acting to define male characters against the women's emotional authenticity. By comparison, Nicholson's and Kidman's constant and varied adjustments to their partners make their performances seem more nuanced. While the interactive performances by Nicholson and Kidman might conform more closely to conventional ideas of good film acting, this fact does not mean that they create better performances than the actors who provide their counterpoint. To understand the work of Cruise and Duvall, it is useful to recall that when actors are denied interactive opportunities, their contributions become less legible. On the one hand, Antonioni ensures the ambiguity of character in *The Passenger* by limiting the occurrences of sustained interaction. He spends more screen time on brief emotionally neutral transactions (renting a car or hotel room) and on views of the surrounding landscapes (sand, streets, towns) than on scenes between characters. On the other hand, in both *Eyes Wide Shut* and *The Shining*, Kubrick uses long interactive sequences but demands differential levels of involvement from the actors playing opposite each other. Under his direction, Cruise and Duvall seem relatively uninvolved because they modulate their expressions so very little, while Kidman and Nicholson, who react with rapidly changing, varied expressions, seem utterly present.

Unlike Kubrick, Neil Jordan allows Cruise to exercise his interactive abilities more fully. By comparing Cruise's work in *Interview with the Vampire* with his performance in *Eyes Wide Shut*, the spectator glimpses the star's acting expertise. Consider the scene in which Lestat gives a doll to Claudia, the child vampire. When she asks whether the gift betokens her birthday, Cruise's face plays an emotional scale for the camera. In the next moments, when she presses him to explain how she became a vampire, Cruise uses a multitude of expressions and gestures ranging from silent denial to an angry, impulsive attempt to strangle her. As one reviewer observed, "Tom Cruise, who has walked through most of his films with a sneer or a clench-jawed scowl, is a kinetic marvel here" (Barra). Physically transformed from his usual star image by a loss of weight and by period costumes, wigs, and makeup, in Jordan's film Cruise also transforms his usual on screen persona. The critics, on balance, praised him as "willing to loosen that noble jaw, to be openly erotic toward another man" (Salamon 72), seeing his casting against type as an ironic strength. "Here is the most clean-cut of American movie stars, decked out in ruffles and long blond wig, gliding insinuatingly through a tale in which he spiritually seduces another foppish, pretty young man. And here is the surprise. Mr. Cruise is flabbergastingly right for this role" (Maslin).

As noted briefly at the beginning of this chapter, Jordan's approach to directing does not fall into the two categories outlined by Renoir; he does not start with visual design or performance but instead with narrative, preferring to take, as he says, "the most outrageous chances with narration" (Barra 39). Against Anne Rice's wishes, Jordan's screenplay emphasizes moments of sardonic humor (*Interview with a Vampire*). As Jordan put it, "They're eating rats? It's hilarious. Well, then, let's have 'em eat a poodle" (Anderson). He grounded his vision of the film in an even greater irony, namely, that there was "something funny in Louis's dilemma—a vampire who won't kill" (Anderson). Jordan entrusted Cruise's portrayal of Lestat to carry this ironic point of view. The plan seemed to work; as one reviewer observed, "Mr. Cruise's smart performance is, intentionally, campier and funnier than anything else in the film" (Janes).

Like Altman, Jordan welcomes actors' contributions within the stylistic boundaries set by the narrative. He reports that he especially enjoys actors like Cruise, who "want to invent their parts themselves" (Zucker 110). Cruise said that he brought to Lestat an "emotional reality" and "rooted" his performance in "a strong foundation of who this guy is" (Cruise). Cruise explains that he sympathized with "Lestat's loneliness." Invoking a classic Stanislavsky trick (to play an evil person, look for the good), Cruise observed that "people don't do things because they think they're evil, they do things because they think they're right. . . . [Lestat] really does love Louis, he really does love Claudia, and he really does feel what he's giving them is this wonderful gift of eternal life" (Cruise).

Comparing Cruise's work in *Eyes Wide Shut* and *Interview with the Vampire* demonstrates that his abilities as an actor exceed the limits of his star persona. The two very different performances show that he can adjust to different aesthetic frameworks and adapt to different working relationships with directors. At the same time, his casting in both movies takes advantage of his stardom. In the same way that Kubrick uses Cruise's star status to create layers of meaning in the film, Jordan's deliberate miscasting of Cruise establishes ironic connections between the film's characters and contemporary stardom. As Jordan explains, "The world of a vampire is not that different from the world of a massive Hollywood star. . . . You're kept from the harsh daylight, you live in a strange kind of seclusion, every time you emerge a kind of ripple runs through people" (Jordan).

Concluding Remarks

Film performances emerge from complex artistic and technical collaborations that center in the working relationships between actors and directors; the three case studies above begin to suggest that complexity. As the one who sets the tone for collaboration, the director can either embrace or limit the actors' contributions. Altman, Jordan, and even Kubrick in his way encourage actors to determine the physical and vocal gestures expressive of their characters. In contrast, Antonioni strives to be the sole auteur, determining every detail in his films including those of the actor's performance. Yet the force of cinematic collaboration is so great that even Antonioni's vision can be modified by certain actors; however compliant Nicholson may have been, he left his mark on *The Passenger*.

Moreover, when examining specific screen performances and their contributions to the film as a whole, attention paid to the actors' use of body and voice offers a more productive avenue for discussion than do alignments of specific acting approaches with performance styles. As all the case studies demonstrate, single actors adjust their techniques as they move from film to film within the limits of their skills and anatomies. While performances in individual films emerge from the complex connections among directorial vision, narrative demands, camera work, mise-en-scène, sound and design, the actors still embody characters by means of physical and vocal gestures. The three case studies begin to suggest how complicated the intersections among these elements are. True, no single element is sufficient to account for actors' representation of characters or the performances we see on screen. And it is true

63

that cinema's complex integration of artistic and technical elements makes actors' work seem elusive. Yet the contributions they make bear consideration, as they not only adjust but contribute to directors' different working methods and attune their performances to suit directors' visions.

NOTES

1. Mai Zetterling calls the director "the only witness of the acting during the shooting of the film." Anthony Quinn notes that "the director is your audience, and if he's pleased, you feel you've done your job" (Cardullo et al. 151). Lee Remick points out that "you need to be able to rely on your director, because there is no other audience" (Ross and Ross 378). As Michael Redgrave recognizes, the partnership between actor and director can become quite "intimate" (Cardullo et al. 102). Robert De Niro says of Martin Scorsese, "I used to talk to him in private, in front of no one. . . . I like sometimes to be very personal with the director" (Cardullo et al. 290). Of Elia Kazan, Remick observes, "Actors confide in him. They tell him things they'd never tell another living soul" (Ross and Ross 254).

2. Jason Robards, Sr. reminds fellow actors that "in movies . . . the important things are the lights, the dollies, the cold camera eye" (Ross and Ross 385). Henry Fonda reports, "There are fewer directors in cinema who have real communication with an actor, who can help an actor build a performance" (Cardullo et al. 212). Robert De Niro agrees. "Newer directors," he says, tend to "know less about acting *per se*. Their tradition is not the theater" (Cardullo et al. 282). Implicitly supporting these views, Michelangelo Antonioni and Robert Altman stand as examples of this type of director. Antonioni sees actors as "an element of the image—and not always the most important element" (175), while Altman concedes that acting "is the one job on the set that I can't do as well or better than anyone else" (Stuart 109). He admits that "I'm embarrassed in a rehearsal because I don't know what to do" (Sherman 86).

3. Many directors who approach film from an acting perspective began their careers as actors. Richard Boleslavsky, John Cassavetes, and Sidney Lumet, all "great communicators" (Fonda in Cardullo et al. 212), did so. Actors praise Elia Kazan precisely because he brought his acting experience to the set. Marlon Brando said, "Kazan is the best actor's director you could ever want, because he was an actor himself" (Cardullo et al. 277). Some directors function as acting teachers and coaches. According to Lillian Gish, D. W. Griffith taught his casts to act by insisting that they "live" their roles and "train their bodies" (Cardullo et al. 258). Andy Griffith said of his work on Kazan's *A Face in the Crowd* (1957), "I learned all I know about acting . . . with Kazan" (Ross and Ross 222).

4. See, for example, Cima 7–8; Aston 65–66; and Love 276.

5. See, for example, Cima 7–8; Diamond 83–86; and Aston 66.

6. In view of the prevalence of "realism" in American cinema, Nicholson considers it an absence of style.

7. See Falsetto's analysis of the scene between Torrance and his son, in which the real Jack and his mirrored image appear together in the frame, "indicating that perhaps Jack's two personas are merging, [that] Jack and his alter ego, the public and the private, are becoming less and less distinguishable" (167).

8. Kubrick wanted actors to find what was necessary to play the scene through physical repetition rather than through discussion. As his cameraman put it, "If he requires several takes, it's in order to get the most out of the actors" (Ciment 213). Kubrick himself, however, tended to blame actors. "When I have to shoot a very large number of takes, it's invariably because the actors don't know their lines. . . . [When an actor] has learned his lines only well enough to say them while he is thinking about them, he will always have trouble as soon as he has to work on the emotions in the scene or find camera marks" (Ciment 188). As a result of his tactics, actors often appear drained on screen, as if Kubrick were "trying to get performances that come out of extremity, exhaustion," to quote John Boorman (Lo Brutto 431).

9. Following the film's release, Rice resolved the controversy she had created when she praised Cruise "as a great actor" in a two-page advertisement in the *New York Times* and an eight-page "open letter" in *Daily Variety* ("Interview with a Vampire").

10. Thomas Allen Nelson points out that Cruise's character shares more than just a stylistic impulse with Nicholson's. Dr. Bill, like Jack Torrance, represents "a Kubrickian male character discovering his own paradoxical duality." Moreover, the search involves a similar behavioral pattern. "Like Jack Torrance in *The Shining*, [Dr. Bill] expresses a latent male urge to blame his wife for all his inadequacies as a husband and father" (265, 268, 267).

WORKS CITED

Anderson, John. "Some Ill Winds Swirled over Directing of *Vampire*." *Los Angeles Times* 25 Nov. 1994.

Antonioni, Michelangelo. *The Architecture of Vision: Writings and Interviews on Cinema*. Ed. Carlo di Carlo and Giorgio Tinazzi, Marga Cottino-Jones, American ed. New York: Marsillo, 1976.

Arrowsmith, William. *Antonioni: The Poet of Images*. New York: Oxford UP, 1995.

Aston, Elaine. *An Introduction to Feminism and Theater*. New York: Routledge, 1995.

Barra, Allen. "Here Comes Mr. Jordan." *American Film* (Jan. 1990). Clippings on Neil Jordan. Margaret Herrick Library, Academy of

Motion Pictures, Los Angeles.

Bingham, Dennis. *Acting Male*. New Brunswick: Rutgers UP, 1994.

Breskin, David. *Inner Views: Filmmakers in Conversation*. Boston: Faber and Faber, 1992.

Brunette, Peter. *The Films of Michelangelo Antonioni*. New York: Cambridge UP, 1998.

Cardullo, Bert, Harry Geduld, Ronald Gottesman, and Leigh Woods, eds. *Playing to the Camera: Film Actors Discuss Their Craft*. New Haven: Yale UP, 1998.

Carnicke, Sharon Marie. *Stanislavsky in Focus*. New York: Harwood/Routledge, 1998.

———. "Stanislavsky's System: Pathways for the Actor." *Twentieth Century Actor Training*. Ed. Alison Hodge. New York: Routledge, 2000. 11–36.

Cima, Gay Gibson. *Performing Women: Female Characters, Male Playwrights, and the Modern Stage*. Ithaca: Cornell UP, 1993.

Ciment, Michel. *Kubrick*. Trans. Gilbert Adair. New York: Holt, Rinehart, and Winston, 1980.

Cruise, Tom. *In the Shadow of the Vampire*. Videocassette. Warner Bros., 1994.

Diamond, Elin. "Brechtian Theory/Feminist Theory: Toward a Gestic Feminist Criticism." *Drama Review* (spring 1988): 83–86.

Eisenberg, Laurence. "Shelley Duvall: Filmdom's Most Unlikely Star." *Cosmopolitan* Aug. 1983: 3.

Falsetto, Mario. *Stanley Kubrick: A Narrative and Stylistic Analysis*. Westport: Praeger, 1994.

Gorchakov, Nikolai M. *Stanislavsky Directs*. Trans. Miriam Goldina. New York: Grosset and Dunlap, 1954.

Hoxter, Julian. "The Passenger." *Jack Nicholson: Movie Top Ten*. Ed. Mikita Brottman. London: Creation Books International, 2000. 83–91.

Interview with the Vampire. Press kit and clippings. Margaret Herrick Library, Academy of Motion Pictures, Los Angeles.

Jahr, Cliff. "Shelley Duvall Delivers It." *Village Voice* 11 May 1977.

Janes, Caryn. "In Search of the Man within the Monster." *New York Times* 13 Nov. 1994.

Jordan, Neil. *In the Shadow of the Vampire*. Videocassette. Warner Bros., 1994.

Kaplan, David. *Five Approaches to Acting*. New York: West Broadway, 2001.

Kazan, Norman. *The Cinema of Stanley Kubrick*. New York: Frederick Ungar, 1989.

Keyssar, Helen. *Robert Altman's America*. New York: Oxford UP, 1991.

Lane, Lydia. "Love Thyself to Love Others." *Los Angeles Times* 15 Aug. 1975.

Lo Brutto, Vincent. *Stanley Kubrick: A Biography*. New York: Donald I. Fine, 1997.

Love, Lauren. "Rejecting the Organic: A Feminist Actor's Approach."

Acting (Re)Considered: Theories and Practices. Ed. Phillip Zarilli. New York: Routledge, 1995.

Mann, Roderick. "Shelley Duvall Gets the Call—for Olive Oyl." *Los Angeles Times* 6 May 1979.

Maslin, Janet. "Interview with the Vampire." *New York Times* 11 Nov. 1994.

McGilligan, Patrick. *Jack's Life: A Biography of Jack Nicholson.* New York: W. W. Norton, 1994.

Nelson, Thomas Allen. *Kubrick: Inside a Film Artist's Maze.* Bloomington: Indiana UP, 2000.

Rosen, Charles. "On Playing the Piano." *Doing It: Five Performing Arts.* Ed. Robert B. Silvers. New York: New York Review of Books, 2001. 15–44.

Ross, Lillian, and Helen Ross, eds. *The Player: A Profile of an Art.* New York: Limelight, 1984.

Rowe, Douglas J. "Interview with the Director." *Entertainment Today* 18 Nov. 1994.

Salamon, Julie. "Interview with the Vampire." *Wall Street Journal* 17 Nov. 1994.

Sanello, Frank. *Cruise.* Dallas: Taylor, 1995.

Segrave, Kerry, and Linda Martin. *The Post-Feminist Hollywood Actress.* Jefferson: MacFarland, 1990.

Shepherd, Donald. *Jack Nicholson: An Unauthorized Biography.* New York: St. Martin's, 1991.

Sherman, Eric, ed. *Directing the Film: Film Directors on Their Art.* Los Angeles: Acrobat, 1976.

Stanislavskii, K. S. *Stanislavskii repetiruet.* Ed. I. Vinogradskaia. Moscow: STD, 1987.

Sterritt, David, ed. *Robert Altman: Interviews.* Jackson: U of Mississippi P, 2000.

Strasberg, Lee. "Acting." *Encyclopedia Britannica,* 14th ed. 1957.

———. "The Actors Studio." Sound recording no. 339A. 1956–69. Wisconsin Center for Film and Theater Research, University of Wisconsin, Madison; Tape A1. 26 Nov. 1963. State Historical Society of Wisconsin, Madison.

Stuart, Jan. *The "Nashville" Chronicles: The Making of Robert Altman's Masterpiece.* New York: Simon and Schuster, 2000.

Thompson, Peter. *Jack Nicholson: The Life and Times of an Actor on the Edge.* Secaucus: Birch Lane, 1997.

Vineberg, Steve. *Method Actors: Three Generations of an American Acting Style.* New York: Schirmer, 1991.

Walker, Alexander, Sybil Taylor, and Ulrich Ruchti. *Stanley Kubrick, Director: A Visual Analysis.* New York: W. W. Norton, 1999.

Zucker, Carole. *In the Company of Actors: Reflections on the Craft of Acting.* New York: Routledge, 1999.

2

....

MODERNISM

AND

FILM

PERFORMANCE

3

Performance in the Films of Robert Bresson

The Aesthetics of Denial

Doug Tomlinson

•••

If Renoir's aesthetic is that of complexity and Hitchcock's is of complicity, Bresson's is that of denial. Where Renoir's characters are complex within an ambivalent moral system and Hitchcock's are guilty within a Manichean schema, Bresson's are near reclusive within asceticism.

In Bresson's cinema, this ascetic philosophy is in evidence from his invention through visualization of character.[1] Not only are his characters denied the pleasure of existence, his performers (whom he refers to as models) are denied purposeful expression, his collaborators denied artistic input, his spectators denied access to character psychology traditionally communicated through systems of projection and identification. In his *Notes on Cinematography*, he quotes Pascal: "They want to find the solution where all is enigma only" (Bresson 40).[2]

Bresson's conviction that cinema must be unique unto itself and unlike any other form of artistic communication means that performance, traditionally the main element of narrative cinema, is presented in a radically altered form. In order to understand his radical use and presentation of performance, one must understand his conception of character as well as his theory of performance, his editing strategies as well as his placement of the performer within individual compositions.

The Bressonian Character

Each of Bresson's characters is imprisoned in this life. For some, this involves physical incarceration; for most, spiritual. *The Diary of a Country Priest* (1950), *A Man Escaped* (1956), and *Pickpocket* (1959) form a trilogy examining male alienation: religious, political, sexual. The three protagonists—the country priest, Fontaine (*A Man Escaped*), and Michel (*Pickpocket*)—share certain characteristics: they are all outsiders, all somewhat wary of the society that surrounds them. This creates a sense of restraint, a guarded or shy appearance as if avoiding direct confrontation. All three are amateurs: at profession (priest), project (Fontaine), and craft (Michel). All three have a ritualistic obsession that effaces their physical personality: the priest's devotion to an ascetic existence, Fontaine's to his project of escape, Michel's to perfecting his prestidigital technique. All three are alienated: the priest from his community by his asceticism; Fontaine from his nuclear family, his political family (the Resistance), and prison mates by his incarceration in a jail cell; Michel by his homosexuality and its emergence in criminal behavior. Each of these male protagonists takes refuge in a hermetic posture; all seem prone to despondency. And yet in privation there is release.

Many adjectives have been used to describe these examples of the typical Bressonian character: alienated, despondent, stubborn, hermetic, effaced. While such adjectives are indeed apt, they need to be augmented by a series with a more positive connotation: modest, shy, introspective, focused, guarded, even noble. In retrospect, Bresson's characters are more complex than they appear at first. The perceived stubbornness is often merely hiding the more sensitive and intelligent aspects of a character who has been, to use Bresson's term, "flattened" by the experience of life and thus forced to seek refuge in seemingly antisocial behavior (Godard and Delahaye 17).[3]

The hermetic posture in these males is, however, temporarily ameliorated by a catalyst, the protagonist's release into communication facilitated by a cathartic encounter. The country priest's acceptance of his imminent death is facilitated by his encounter with the countess, her acceptance of his counsel giving him a fulfilled sense of purpose; Fontaine's acceptance of Jost is a positive force in his escape plan; Michel's acceptance of himself is facilitated by Jeanne's acceptance of him. Communication aids resolution and release.

3.1.

There is, however, in Bresson's films, an inconclusive nature to that release, no sense that the new situation will be any less alienating. That Bresson's characters remain imprisoned even after their narrative release is indicated by his denial of any sense of release through psychological projection. At the end of *Pickpocket*, Michel and Jeanne communicate through a screen, Michel's face unendowed with a purposeful expression. In *A Man Escaped*, Fontaine and Jost walk away from the prison into a dark void; we are not allowed access to their faces in this moment of release, for freedom is but a temporary reality (figure 3.1).

Bresson denies access to easy solutions, thus reiterating Pascal. He denies his models any expression of resolution, insisting that a level of ambiguity be maintained beyond the final image; he denies the spectator psychological closure, positing that ultimately the question of character is unresolvable.

Performance Theory

No actors.
(No directing of actors.)
No parts.
(No learning of parts.)
No staging.
(But the use of working models, taken from life.)

Being (models) instead of Seeming (actors) (Bresson 1).
Choose your models well, so they lead you where you want to go (41).

Bresson has discussed at length and in detail the inaptness of traditional modes of performance for the film medium. Accordingly, he developed a visual strategy for the presentation of performance that involved the denial of both the actor's and spectator's habitual access to emotional and psychological properties of a character.

His basic mistrust of traditional performance involves the psychological obviousness of "pretending," his belief being that "the actor's obligation to his art is to be somebody else." This notion is anathema to Bresson; his desire is to reveal character rather than construct it. His process involves a reduction rather than an increment in strategies; his desired result being an increase in the spiritual value obtained by his "models." He feels that human beings are complex and that what actors are trained to do is to simplify that complexity.

Bresson believes that the training actors receive also causes them to develop the habit of projecting and thus making visible the thoughts and feelings of their characters. Their habitual way of portraying character, according to Bresson, is not suitable for presenting his characters, who never really show what they are thinking and feeling. Based on his observation of actors who attempt to portray character that do not reveal their inner experiences through conventional external signs, Bresson finds that actors simply are not equipped to portray non-actor characters (See Hayman 16–23). He explains:

> For there are actors who try, yes. But when the actor simplifies himself, he is even more false than when he is the actor, when he plays. For we are not simple. We are extremely complex. And it is this complexity that you find with the non-actor.
> We are complex. And what the actor projects is not complex. (Qtd. in Godard and Delahaye 16)

While Bresson does not disavow its validity for the stage, he finds this theatrical approach inappropriate for the cinema, particularly his own. Bresson's desire is not to document the art of performance and thus pay tribute to the double nature of character and performer, but to present uniquely conceived models of human character. The public, he claims, has been wrongly "schooled to cherish the alternate presence of 'him and the other'" (Bresson 53),[4] his most damning statement in this regard being from *Notes on Cinematography*: "Failure of *Cinema*. Ludicrous disproportion between immense possibilities and the result: the Star-system" (47).

An avoidance of that duplicity has informed his casting strategy since 1950, his refusal to hire those with acting experience extending to his own models.[5] Bresson claimed that knowledge of his process and its results on the screen would ultimately jeopardize his control.[6]

Initially, this approach involved casting for moral resemblance, a process wherein he attempted to find someone whose moral outlook approximated that of the character.[7] Bresson believed that from such a person he would get an unconscious honesty and thus erase the line between character and performer. The camera—which he regularly referred to as "that extraordinary instrument"—would then reveal that honesty.[8]

Having secured a level of authenticity through this approach to casting, Bresson then moved to ensure its continued effect through a very rigorous style of rehearsal.

Bresson's antitheatrical approach to performance includes a disavowal of the process of character building and the exploration of psychological motivation. His preference has been to have his models execute simple actions removed from narrative or emotional context, in an unknowing void. As he has said: "I may have my character walk to a desk and place a book on it for as many as 10, 20, 30, 40 times. When I see what I want, when he gives me what I want—this tiny glimpse of him—I take it" (qtd. in interview with Green, n.p.). The desired effect is a level of automatism, of moving in a fashion in which there is no exteriorizing of emotion or psychology, no form of purposeful expression. The repetition of movement in rehearsal is meant to suppress intentionality and thus free authenticity.

"Model. Reduce to the minimum the share his consciousness has. Tighten the meshing within which he cannot any longer not be him and where he can now do nothing that is not *useful*" (Bresson 26). Bresson either adopted this theory from Montaigne or found confirmation of it in that writer's work. As he said to Charles Thomas Samuels:

> Anyway, mechanics are essential. Our gestures, nine times out of ten, are automatic. The way you are crossing your legs and holding

your head are not voluntary gestures. Montaigne has a marvelous chapter on hands in which he says that hands go where their owner does not send them. I don't want my non-actors to think of what they do. Years ago, without realizing any program, I told my non-actors, "Don't think of what you are saying or doing," and that moment was the beginning of my style. (Samuels 60)

What Bresson attempted to do was recover the automatism of everyday life, those unconscious moments which he felt were the true indicators of personality. What he sought was the revelation of instinct.[9]

Bresson's approach to achieving this unconscious automatism involved the flattening of both external elements of performance: the physical and the vocal. By denying the intentionality of these exterior aspects, Bresson believed he was moving his models closer to being in a state to reveal authentic character.

It has been suggested that the key to Bresson's physical presentation exemplifies the *tabula rasa*, Locke's theory that all ideas and rational experience are empirically built up from sense impressions (as opposed to the doctrine of innate ideas). It has also been suggested that Bresson renders the face expressionless so as to impute expression through the principles Kuleshov derived from his Mozhukhin experiment. I would argue that neither assumption is correct, the two being somewhat interconnected by the implication of construction. While it is true that Bresson denies his models overt expression, it is not for the purpose of construction but rather for the possibility of revelation. For Bresson, the expression is not on the face, it is *in* the face, his aim being a presentation of physiognomy rather than a *re*presentation of psychology.

Bresson strives for the same ironed-out quality for the vocal track. Here Bresson insists again that overt expression be removed, that the words simply be read with proper attention to their rhythmic structure. Inflection and projection are not necessary, as individual timbre is what embodies authentic character. Bresson instructs his models to speak all their lines as if in monologue, thus removing any level of expression that might be engendered in the attempt to communicate ideas to another person. As he has stressed, monotone is not synonymous with monotonous, and authentic meaning will erupt only when intentionality has been eradicated.

The purpose of these strategies is to serve Bresson's overall conception of a cinema free of artificiality. Because Bresson perceives the performance code as the most prone to artificiality, he works to delimit its traditionally communicative powers.

Narrative Style and Structure

An understanding of the third level of Bresson's utilization of the performance code involves examining his narrative style and structure so as to determine the place accorded performance in his compositional strategies and editing patterns. In his compositions, Bresson systematically downplays the importance of the human figure, generally rendering it the equal of environment; in his editing, he avoids traditional narrative systems that are used to clarify and focalize. He removes the emphasis from performance values, as would be consistent with his approach to the casting and rehearsal of his models.

His compositional strategies include: a reduction in purposeful facial close-ups; attention to nonfacial gestural synecdoche; a use of setting and lighting to maintain the balance in compositional effect of figure and environment; a reduction of character-related camera movements.

As Bresson has noted: "Shooting is not making something definite, it is making preparations" (Bresson 53). While he takes enormous care to ensure that his mise-en-scène has a very specific hieratic quality, ultimately he is more concerned with his montage.

His editing strategies as they relate to performance include: an avoidance of traditional figurations for projection and identification; an elliptical style by which he avoids the on-screen representation of cathartic or paroxysmal acts, including moments of heightened emotion; a style of juxtaposition that is used to effect the communication of ideas and information rather than Kuleshovian-derived emotions; a reliance on repetitive rhythmic editing structures.

Beyond the compositional and editing strategies, one must also take note of Bresson's unique use in this trilogy of first-person voice-over narration. Where most first-person narrators are generally talkative and informative, Bresson's are shy and guarded. Where most speak of emotional trauma and mystery and embroider their *récit* with editorial comments, Bresson's impart factual information. Where most speak with first-person egocentricity, Bresson's present themselves as both subject and object. Where most examine a situation in a series of flashbacks to lend a sense of psychological investigation, Bresson's narrate a straight or near-linear chronology.

Most important, Bresson's use of voice-over divorces the two performance aspects of face and voice, thereby downplaying the effect of their simultaneity. Delivered in monotone and generally without an accompanying facial close-up, Bresson's voice-overs give primacy to the word over the speaker. The voice, thus removed, reinforces the overall environment of isolation and alienation.

Communicative powers in the cinema are largely embodied by systems of projection and identification. As outlined, Bresson rehearses his models so as to avoid the former; in his style and structure, he works to avoid the latter.[10] Where Hitchcock essentially encourages both projection and identification, and Renoir generally encourages projection but avoids identification, Bresson denies both. In the case study of *A Man Escaped*, I will examine some of the methods by which he denies these systems.

A Man Escaped

A Man Escaped, like other Bresson films, is the story of a struggle, in this case against both the self and the physical confines of a prison. Fontaine will be free physically only when he is free spiritually; he will be free only when he gives himself up to grace.

The film is set in Lyon in 1943 during the Nazi occupation. Based on the actual account of French Resistance member André Devigny, the film details the planning and execution of an escape. In an attempt to indicate both the factual nature of the story and his devotion to an ascetic style, Bresson prefaces the film with the title: "This story actually happened. I set it down without any embellishment."

In the course of the narrative, Fontaine (who is in every scene) encounters both encouragement and discouragement from his fellow inmates, some anxious for him to succeed, others fearful of repercussions for all if he fails. Throughout, Fontaine remains committed to the idea of escape, but—being human—allows himself to procrastinate. Even after his sentencing (he is to be shot), he hesitates. It is not until he overcomes his fear and allows fate to intervene (hence the film's alternate title, "The Spirit Breathes Where It Will," from St. John's Gospel) that Fontaine is released from both his physical and mental imprisonment.

Bresson cast the film using his moral resemblance principle, choosing François Leterrier, a twenty-seven-year-old philosophy graduate who had recently completed his military service, for the role of Fontaine. (Leterrier was also the same age and rank as Devigny.) The role of the skeptical prisoner Blanchet was played by an elderly Belgian man of letters. German students played Gestapo officers.

Roland Monod, a former theology student, was cast as Pastor de Leiris. In the November 1956 issue of *Cahiers du cinéma*, Monod published an article entitled "Working with Bresson." In that article he confirmed Bresson's theoretical approach to characterization:

> Bresson told me that since the pastor's strength lay in the intensity of his inner life, the more I turned in upon myself, the less I seemed outwardly to give, the more this depth of being would impose its strength and authority on the screen. . . .
>
> "Forget about tone and meaning," Bresson told me. "Don't think about what you're saying; just speak the words automatically. . . . The film actor should content himself with *saying* his lines. He should not allow himself to show that he already understands them. Play nothing, explain nothing. A text should be spoken as Dinu Lipatti plays Bach. His wonderful technique simply *releases* the notes; understanding and emotion come later. . . ."
>
> The dialogue directly recorded at the studio . . . [Bresson found] *still too human*, too anecdotal. We had to go back and re-record our lines in a sound studio. There, phrase by phrase, word by word almost, we spoke our lines after their author—ten, twenty, thirty times over, trying to match as exactly as possible the intonations, *the rhythm*, that in the end Bresson played every part. (n.p.; emphases two, three, and four mine)

In *A Man Escaped*, Bresson involves us exclusively with the activities of Fontaine. We meet other characters only as their activities intersect with his, notably in the communal washroom. Fontaine's contact with others outside this communal space is limited by his solitary incarceration. He does manage to communicate with others, but under conditions in which they are physically separated, their communication illegal. Mostly we witness Fontaine alone in his cell, fashioning the tools of his escape.

Of the four characters he speaks to surreptitiously outside the washroom, only Terry, an inmate who is inexplicably allowed to walk the courtyard, is visible to him. The others are in their cells. He speaks with Orsini through the peephole in his door, to Blanchet while both are at their exterior windows. His communication with a fourth prisoner is limited to tapping messages through their shared wall. Late in the film, after his imminent execution has been announced, Fontaine receives a roommate. While the boy, Jost, is at first perceived as an obstacle, his true function is soon revealed. Forced to include or kill him, Fontaine opts for the former and finally discusses his plan. It is under such dire circumstances that Bresson generally structures and examines the difficulties of communication.

Fontaine's central preoccupation during the first part of the film is with releasing the panels of his cell door. It is in the structure of these scenes that we most clearly witness Bresson's avoidance of systems of projection and identification.

An analysis of a typical sequence is instructive:

Shot 1: close-up of two hands holding a spoon wedged in the door panel (figure 3.2). This shot is taken from an oblique angle without an establishing shot; the vertically panning camera traces the push of the spoon down, up, then back down.

Shot 2: close-up of Fontaine, in profile, the face somewhat obscured in shadow (figure 3.3). VOICE-OVER: "I made slow progress because I was afraid to make noise."

Shot 3: close-up of hands (figure 3.4). The camera is positioned as in shot 1. Hands move downward with the spoon wedged in the door panel; the camera pans vertically with the hands as they put the spoon on the floor. VOICE-OVER: "I had to sweep up my shavings with a straw plucked from my broom."

Shot 4: long shot of the hallway, with Fontaine's door in the midground (figure 3.5). A straw sweeps up shavings, pulling them under the door

Shot 5: close-up of hands sweeping the shavings into the cell, then picking them up (figure 3.6). The camera is positioned as in shots 1 and 3.

One hand then picks up the spoon, puts it in the door panel, withdraws it to a pocket, pulls it out again and gets it partway back to the door panel before withdrawing it completely. Fontaine then retreats to a seated position on the bed, eyes pulled to the extreme screen left. He then looks down and off right for a few seconds until he hears: "Is that you, Fontaine?" (figure 3.7)

In this five-shot sequence we see four key aspects of Bresson's style of projection and identification avoidance: (1) the absence of a clear traditional close-up of the protagonist for means of gaining reaction to the visualized proceedings; (2) the camera placed at an angle oblique to the action so that literal point of view is clearly not

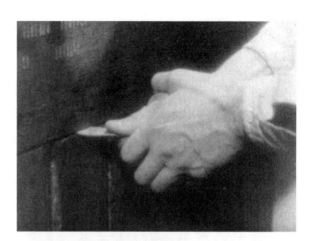

3.2.

3.3.

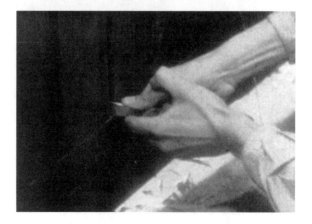

3.4.

3.5.

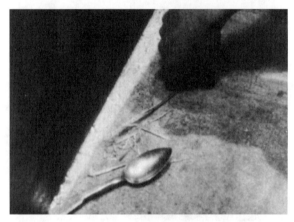

3.6.

3.7.

3.8.

intended, and moving the camera in a panning motion to reinforce the presence of the camera as the agent of narrative; (3) the use of gestural synecdoche to communicate Fontaine's caution; and (4) most radically, cutting to the other side of the door, a space Fontaine is unable to see.

The scenes of Fontaine working on his door are not completely devoid of facial close-ups, but it is generally at moments of achievement or frustration that Bresson tends to remove them completely, deny clear access, or locate the reaction in a nonfacial gesture. Projection in a close-up would generally be anticipated in such intense scenes; a director like Hitchcock would heighten the suspense by employing figurations that would induce or enforce identification with the character's cognitive processes.

> Shot 1: close-up of hands working on the door with spoon blade. The camera, positioned at an oblique angle to the action, pans upward with hands and spoon. VOICE-OVER: "After three weeks, trying to be noiseless, I managed to loosen three boards."
>
> Shot 2: brief close-up of Fontaine, eyelids down, no access to pupils (figure 3.8).
>
> Shot 3: close-up of hands pushing down on the spoon wedged horizontally in the door frame (figure 3.9). VOICE-OVER: "But their ends were held by tenons too strong for my spoon."
>
> Shot 4: close-up of Fontaine, as in shot 2. Sound of snapping. No facial reaction, very minimal body jerk.

3.9.

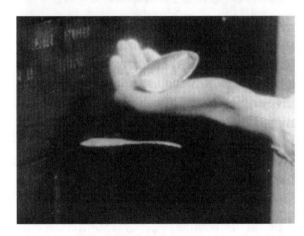

3.10.

3.11.

Shot 5: close-up of hand, palm up, holding the bowl of the broken spoon (figure 3.10). The hand then exits screen right, leaving as the image just the spoon handle still wedged horizontally in the door. A sound of excruciating pain is heard as he attempts to free the panel. Fontaine withdraws his hands, cut on movement to shot 6.

Shot 6: continued movement of hand withdrawing. Fontaine backs up until his body is seen from the ribs down (figure 3.11). VOICE-OVER: "To split the frame (*as he sits*), I needed another spoon to use as a lever." Sitting on the edge of the bed, Fontaine is seen in profile hunched over with his left elbow on his left knee, eyes downcast at the end of the shot as he begins to raise his head toward the door (and away from the camera). Fade to black.

In this six-shot sequence, Bresson uses two close-ups of Fontaine's face, neither having a particular function vis-à-vis the action, neither functioning as a purposeful reaction component or to anchor a voice-over or figuration for visual identification.

In shot 4, the main catharsis occurs when the spoon handle breaks. Curiously, there is neither a facial nor overt body movement to correspond to the breaking action. Bresson uses only the sound of the spoon snapping to convey their occurrence. Importantly, the next shot is to a close-up of Fontaine's hand with the severed spoon and then the spoon blade alone, their reactions to the disaster being far more significant in the Bressonian system than any facial gesture.

Shot 5 covers a significant period of time, Bresson never cutting or panning to Fontaine's face. It is not until he has completed the activity and moves to sit on his bed that Bresson deigns to give us a shot of Fontaine that includes the face. That shot, however, like the previous one, involves a nonfacial reaction to the disaster, Bresson detailing Fontaine's frustration through posture rather than facial gesture. A facial close-up at this point would have been within the standard cinematic presentation, affording the performer an opportunity to project frustration and providing the spectator the occasion to strongly identify with this moment of crisis. Bresson purposely eschews the obviousness of such easy resolution.

Another sequence where traditional close-up reaction-shot editing is elliptically denied is when Fontaine successfully removes the panels of his door, walks around the corridor, and speaks briefly with Orsini. In this extended (sixty-two-foot) two-shot scene, Bresson not only denies us visual access to Orsini but also refuses a clear facial close-up of Fontaine, downplaying completely any sense of traditional projection or identification as structured though facial indicators.[11] Hence Bresson counteracts what we might intuit as Fontaine's joy and sense of freedom by keeping him obscured, for the most part, in darkness and/or long shot, reducing his body to a vague element in a severely darkened composition. A close-up would not only have removed the possible ambiguity of dual emotion (free, but not free) but foregrounded psychology over ambiance. Bresson avoids such standard formulation here, preferring to convey emotion only at the end of the scene, and then by voice-over, as Fontaine walks away from the camera and into darkness. Continuing to deny tradition, he situates the content of Fontaine's monotone voice-over as his perception of Orsini's reaction: "His surprise pleased me."

In this scene, Bresson does not attempt to build emotional impact through a shot/reaction shot structure of alternating close-ups or to impute cognition through specific psychologically endowed figurations. He simply inserts it. As such, we are encouraged to respond to words communicated *through* the model, not verbal or visual expression communicated *by* the model.

Fontaine effects this release from a cell, on the upper level of the prison, having been moved there after his first meeting with the prison official and after his series of conversations with Terry.

When Fontaine is moved to this new cell, he encounters, as one of his neighbors, an old man named Blanchet. Resistant at first to communicating or even acknowledging his presence, Blanchet is eventually moved by Fontaine's dedication to escape and sacrifices his blanket to help make the necessary ropes.

On ten separate occasions Fontaine and Blanchet converse, each man situated at his exterior window. In visualizing these conversations, Bresson used only two camera setups, repeating them in each scene: a two-shot in which Blanchet is deeper in the frame and a close-up of Fontaine. Throughout, the physical setup forbids them eye contact; the bars impede our access to their faces.

Repetition of the same camera setup is one aspect of Bresson's style of rhythmic editing (the first two scenes analyzed in this case study were marked by this structure: the inexorability of returning to the same spot). A second involves the structure of dialogue. For example, the rhythmic structure of the first three conversations is that of question and answer. In all, Blanchet asks six questions—two in the two-shot configuration, the other four offscreen while Fontaine is shown in close-up. The two most penetrating questions are those posed in two-shot, the first being the opening question of the second conversation: "Why do you do it?" (referring to Fontaine's plan to escape), the second being the last of the third conversation: "How will you escape?" The response to Blanchet's first question: "To fight . . . to fight against myself," is rendered in two-shot. Similarly, Bresson chose this setup for Blanchet's two most poignant statements: "Then stop scraping, we'll all be punished," at the end of the first conversation, and "I need courage to kill myself. I tried a shoelace. It broke," during the second. These question-and-answer dialogues, rendered in isolated close-ups, would have increased the potential for systems of projection and identification to intensify the drama. Bresson, however, is particularly careful to avoid the psychological and emotional ramifications of a close-up of either man during these key moments, preferring to place the accent on the inexorability of fate through rhythm and setting, rather than the projection of character through performance.

All close-ups of Fontaine during these conversations involve seemingly less significant moments, save one; appropriately, it is his most ambiguous response. When Blanchet asks, "How will you escape?" Fontaine answers, "I haven't the slightest idea." Bresson, who generally refuses the close-up for pointed responses, here renders visually significant his protagonist's most confused statement. Not surprisingly, Bresson saves this moment for the end of the scene, then has Fontaine climb down from his window, leaving us to contemplate those words while looking at the barred window. Bresson does not keep Fontaine on screen long enough to have him relay the importance of that statement through facial gesture. Rather, we come to understand the ramifications of his words through a sustained visual reiteration of the environment of the prison.

The communal washroom is the main location for visual as well as verbal contact. Bresson never once gives us a sense of how large the space is, how many inmates are there at any given time, how many guards are present, where they are located, or how they oversee the space. He does, however, establish an environment of necessary caution: in the first washroom scene in which Fontaine meets other inmates, conversation has barely begun when from off-screen comes the command of "Silence!" Not only does this effectively establish an atmosphere that pervades further scenes in this location, but it activates a seminal figure of Bresson's choreographic style: eyes darting in and out of eyeline matches with extreme precision. These scenes are emblematic of conversation in

Bresson's work: the frustration of communication signaled by a precise choreography that inhibits projection by and identification with character.

Of these washroom scenes, twelve focus on the encounters of Fontaine and Pastor de Leiris, while three focus on Fontaine and Orsini, the will of God and the mistakes of Orsini being the two factors that enable Fontaine to escape successfully at the film's end. The scenes with the pastor are rife with hesitation on the part of Fontaine, his choreographed eye movements connoting uneasiness and/or embarrassment, as well as the necessary caution. Typical is the following section of the washroom scene immediately following the night when Fontaine climbs through his door and walks around the corridor.

> Shot 1: group shot of Fontaine, the pastor, and three other inmates.
> PASTOR: (*handing a note to Fontaine*) Read and pray. God will help you.
> *Fontaine moves to put the note in his pocket, the camera moving with him to the coat rack.*
> Shot 2: FONTAINE: (*as he passes behind the pastor*) We must help ourselves, too (figure 3.12).
> PASTOR: Do you pray?
> Shot 3: FONTAINE: (*in a close-up at the trough*) Sometimes (figure 3.13).
> PASTOR (*offscreen*): When things look bad?
> FONTAINE (*looking offscreen in the opposite direction to where the pastor is*): Yes.
> Shot 4: PASTOR: (*in a close-up*) That's easy (figure 3.14).
> Shot 5: FONTAINE: (*in close-up*) Too easy (figure 3.15).
> Shot 6: PASTOR in close-up as he turns to look at Fontaine without speaking.
> Shot 7: FONTAINE: (*in a close-up*) God can't do everything for you (figure 3.16).
> *Fontaine looks left to the pastor, quickly disengaging his glance by returning his eyes to the downward position, then up to look offscreen right.*

Bresson reinforces the religious/philosophical differences between these two men by filming this discussion about prayer as a series of close-ups rather than the two-shots they had previously cohabited. This strategy not only emphasizes the fragmentation of this particular conversation, but more effectively communicates the awkwardness this level of personal interaction obtains for Fontaine. Note particularly shot 3, when Fontaine turns away from

3.12.

3.13.

3.14.

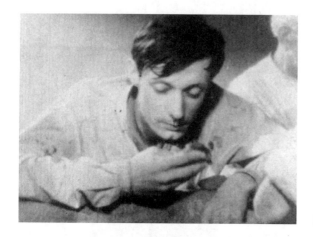

3.15.

3.16.

the pastor, and shot 7, when he quickly disengages his glance. The choreography of turning away is ultimately more effective than the verbal admission of guilt.

Conclusion

In traditional narrative cinema, as in most theater, characters are developed and performance created for the most part through the visualization of conversation. In such situations, a director can extend the projection of character through performance to effect a system of spectatorial identification, encouraging it through any number of configurations involving characters in purposeful or sustained action or reaction, or enforcing it through sustained point-of-view editing. These strategies form a dominant aesthetic but are not the only approach to the presentation of character.

In Bresson's cinema, conversation is severely limited and generally cryptic, reflecting the director's belief that communication between humans is fraught with difficulty. Extended conversations are rare, the uneasy quality of the exchanges typified by the avoidance of eye contact between the speakers. Bresson's characters are denied the explication of actions and reactions on any psychological or emotional level, as such explication is an affront, marked by disingenuousness and a lack of authenticity.

Performance in Bresson's films is a product of the aesthetics of denial, notably a denial of all traditional rhetorical approaches. In his films, he attempts to defocalize performance by removing the immediacy of its effect. His central approach involves a denial of systems of projection and identification.

If asceticism is the pathway to a greater spiritual awareness, then Bresson's cinema is an exemplification of that doctrine. Therein lies his unique contribution: he forces us to reassess our cinematic aesthetic, specifically our spectatorial needs; he forces us to forestall our habitual reliance on performance.

NOTES

1. Bresson has written all his scripts since his third feature, *The Diary of a Country Priest*, in 1950. (He collaborated on the first two.) Having complete control meant writing his scripts by himself.

2. Typically ambiguous, this note could refer to his characters, models, and/or audience.

3. Bresson has consistently used a 50mm lens to flatten the image and thus further visualize this concept.

4. The actual wording is, "The actor is double. The alternate presence of him and of *the other* is what the public has been schooled to cherish."

5. The genesis of this dictum apparently began when problems arose on the set of his second feature, *Les dames du Bois de Boulogne* (1944), due to his inability to suppress performance virtuosity to suit his aims. The case of Bresson vs. Maria Casarès is well documented, his difficulty stemming from her inability to satisfy his needs, hers from a feeling of being reduced to a prop. See particularly Casarès.

6. Bresson did break this rule once, when he cast Jean-Claude

Guilbert as both Arnold in *Au hasard, Balthazar* and Mathieu in *Mouchette*, filmed in the same year. Bresson was able to keep Guilbert from having access to his screen image until both films were shot.

7. Later he would redefine that strategy, claiming that vocal quality was the more important aspect and admitting to a procedure of casting his nonprofessionals by telephone. By the 1970s, he had further refined that strategy to a point where casting was a matter of what he called "luck and intuition." See particularly Carlos Clarens's interview with Bresson and Michael Ciment's for Bresson's comments on these changes in strategy.

8. Whether schematized or not, there is also a physiognomic dimension to his casting. The facial and physical similarities of Claude Laydu (the priest), François Leterrier (Fontaine), and Martin Lassalle (Michel), for example, can be seen easily.

9. The key passage from Montaigne is the following from his *Essays*:

We cannot command our haire to stand on end;
nor our skinne to startle for desire or feare.
Our hands are often carried where we direct
them not.

10. While projection is a function of performance, the method of its presentation is controlled by the director; while identification can by *enforced* (through sustained point-of-view editing), it can also be suggested by the director (through sustained use or repetition of purposeful image) or suggested through the projection of character psychology or actor persona. (Hitchcock, for example, cast many of his leads for the benefits of habitual identification with the star persona.)

11. If eye contact had been desired, Orsini could have opened his peephole; if Bresson had wanted to visualize him, he could have cut to the inside of his cell, having committed a similar act when he visualized the hallway and door shavings outside Fontaine's cell. Bresson denies our visual access to Orsini, preferring to have us imagine him through the sound of his voice. A two-shot does not negate systems of projection and identification. It can, however, deemphasize them.

WORKS CITED

Bresson, Robert. *Notes sur le Cinématographe.* Paris: Editions Gallimard, 1975. Reprinted in *Notes on Cinematography: 1950–1958.* Trans. Jonathan Griffin. New York: Urizen (distributed by E. P. Dutton), 1977.

Casarès, Maria. "The Actress Faces the Camera." *World Theatre* 8.1 (1959): 43–52. Reprinted in *Voices in Film Experience: 1894 to the Present.* Ed. Jay Leyda. New York: Macmillan, 1977.

Ciment, Michel. "The Poetry of Precision." *American Film* 9.1 (1983): 70–73.

Clarens, Carlos. "Four Nights of a Dreamer." *Sight and Sound* 41.1 (1971/72): 2–4.

Godard, Jean-Luc, and Michel Delahaye. "La Question, entretien avec Robert Bresson." *Cahiers du cinéma* 178 (1966): 26–35. Trans. in "The Question: Interview with Robert Bresson." *Cahiers in English* 8 (1967).

Greene, Marjorie. "Robert Bresson." *Film Quarterly* 13.3 (1960): 4–10.

Hayman, Ronald. "Robert Bresson in Conversation with Ronald Hayman." *Transatlantic Review* 46/47 (1973): 16–23.

Monod, Richard. "Un Condamné à mort s'est échappé." *Cahiers du cinéma* (1956). Trans. in "Working with Bresson: A Man Condemned to Death Has Escaped." *Sight and Sound* 27.1 (1957): 30–33, 53.

Samuels, Charles Thomas. *Encountering Directors*. New York: G. P. Putnam's Sons, 1972. 57–76.

4

"The Sounds of Silence"

Modernist Acting in Michelangelo Antonioni's *Blow-Up*

Frank P. Tomasulo

> On or about December 1910, human character changed. . . . And when
> human relations change, there is at the same time a change in religion,
> conduct, politics, and literature.
> *Virginia Woolf*

· ·

Whether or not human character changed in a particular month in
1910, the *depiction* of human subjectivity certainly changed radically from earlier epochs. Investigations of human behavior and
motivation by modern thinkers such as Darwin, Marx, Freud, and
Husserl repositioned the role of the self in an increasingly complex
universe. As a result, twentieth-century fiction, painting, sculp-
ture, and later cinema redefined *la condition humaine*. As the
nature of the individual self became problematized in the modern
world, creative artists began to "ambiguate" the human beings represented in their works, thereby rendering more accurately that
diachronically changing psyche. In this "art-imitates-life" sense,
then, modernism can be seen as a new realism, the realism of our
times, so to speak—at least in regard to the representation of
human subjectivity.

The Modernist Character/The Modernist Actor

Whereas the epic hero of the classical age represented and stood in
for a collectivity, a nation or a people, and formed part of a meaningful and cohesive (albeit closed) world, the modern, "open" pro-

tagonist (or even antihero) is a more solitary subjectivity, who often stands in opposition to the natural or social universe of the fiction. Such "open" characters—what Lucien Goldmann (following Georg Lukács) called "problematical heroes"—became the staples of twentieth-century literature and film. Divorced or alienated from both their social situations and themselves, their inner lives and personal identities could no longer be assumed from their Serlean "speech acts" or outward behavioral tropes. Indeed, the unidimensional, easily knowable character (*ethos*) in the traditional Aristotelian model, whose external actions (*pratton*) were assumed to be congruent with his or her internal being—in that the inner life "motivated" outer action and, conversely, outer behavior was "explained" by inmost psychological motives—gave way to more indeterminate, less unified ciphers whose emotional lives and thought processes were ambiguous, if not polysemic.

While Virginia Woolf, James Joyce, William Faulkner, and other modern novelists attempted to apprehend the new subjectivity through a stream-of-consciousness style, modern cinematic auteurs had to develop neoteric ways to depict the internal lives of characters, since the medium they were working in was characterized by such a strong objective surface. As Thomas Elsaesser put it, "If the cinema is a projection of vision, then it cannot also be one of consciousness" (7). Because of its indexical and iconic nature, most filmmakers forswore internal monologue in favor of a phenomenological presentation and observation of the outer world. This latter approach—what I would dub *monologue extérieur*—is most evident in the *nouveau roman* school of French literature and in the *école du regard* cinemas of Robert Bresson, Alain Resnais, and Alain Robbe-Grillet (Tomasulo, "Intentionality of Consciousness" 58–62).

In this discursive mode of character representation, the great characterological events (the *peripateia*) of the Greek drama give way to the modernist minutiae of quotidian existence, the sheer facticity of human *being*. Although this branch of the modernist school often eschews traditional depth psychology (the basis of much Method acting), the melodramatic "mugging" and stentorian performance style of the stage, the declamatory, "hammy" pantomimes of the silent cinema, and the "psychological realism" inherent in the verisimilar and naturalistic performance codes of the classical Hollywood cinema, it *is* attentive to "geography" and to the cinematic means by which character can be articulated. In modernist cinema, then, ontology and cinematography become psychology. In this sense, the objects of perception (by the character and the filmmaker) define consciousness through an assumed existential intentionality; in short (and in French), *chosisme* (thingness) implies *choisisme* (choice).

Although Michelangelo Antonioni is not the most extreme film director to use the Brechtian *Verfremdungseffekt*, or "Alienation effect" (Godard, Fassbinder, Resnais, and Straub clearly use the "A-effect" more than Antonioni), his films tend to play down psychological convention and call self-conscious attention to the fiction, by "baring the device" and thereby exposing the means of production of meaning-production. Nonetheless, in Antonioni's oeuvre, even a moderate use of Brechtian or Pirandellian formalist devices is enough to renegotiate and/or problematize the habitual "identification-effect" that spectators have come to expect from mainstream cinematic fiction.

Certainly, *all* film directors shape the performances of their actors by utilizing wardrobe, hairstyle, and props. What sets Antonioni apart is that he relies equally on mise-en-scène, découpage, camera angles, color, lighting, set design, sound track articulations, music, *and* pared-down performances to construct his singular cinematic language of characterization. As he once put it, "Only one person fuses in his mind the various elements involved in a film . . . the director. The actor is one of those elements, *and sometimes not even the most important*" (qtd. in Billard 8). More naturalistic film directors exploit the theatrical codes of their actors' facial expressions, gestures, and dialogue to effectuate audience understanding and empathy. In contrast, Antonioni uses a cinematic syntax that problematizes such clarity. The viewer is thus presented with a paradoxical modernist morphology, one that ultimately underplays his characters' individuality and "personality." Indeed, the Antonioni character is often just a small part of a larger visual and social field, a "figure in a landscape" as Ted Perry called it (3).

By foregrounding the background, Antonioni redefines the nature of film dramaturgy—and the nature of cinematic performance. Just as Tomlinson observes about Bresson in chapter 3, Antonioni "systematically downplays the importance of the human figure, generally rendering it the equal of environment." Whereas the Aristotelian drama was defined as "character is destiny," Antonioni's teleology of character might be called "environment is destiny," in that an empty mise-en-scène often defines the hollow plight and circumstances of his protagonists. As such,

Antonioni seems to follow Jean Renoir's realist prescription: "One starts with the environment to arrive at the self" (171).

Of course, although Antonioni transcends many of the tenets of the Italian neorealist school from which he emerged and its reliance on physiognomy, he retains an interest in human beings, their social roles, and their interactions. As he once put it, "Film has always been for me, conflict. A man, a woman: drama" (Tomasulo, "Life Is Inconclusive" 62). Thus, both the auteur and the spectator are involved in an ambiguous push-pull, "approach-avoidance" relationship with the people in an Antonioni film. His protagonists often stand condemned *sub specie aeternitatis*, yet their pathetic plights elicit sympathy; their situations and their sufferings are presented from an aloof and distanced perspective, but their confused feelings and perceptions are evident. As such, the filmmaker provides a context that, in effect, denies viewers the luxury of a single-faceted response but that does not negate the moral reality of their individual choices and predicaments. On the one hand, his characters may be viewed as abstractions—Contemporary Woman or Bourgeois Man—without individual identities; on the other hand, they can be judged, albeit without the mitigating emotional baggage of empathy and identification. In this sort of cinematic universe, Antonioni's actors tend to be embodied themes rather than flesh-and-blood people.

In such a universe, in which screen acting is only one part of a directorial language system, characters can be both external *and* internal, real *and* symbolic, *actantes et personnages* (to use Roland Barthes's distinction). This "mixed use" is especially relevant to a discussion of film performance, given both the resolute indexicality of the motion picture apparatus and the filmmaker's and performers' assumed need to express the private emotional lives of the characters.

Although emotions are usually thought of as highly personal and individual matters, Antonioni's signature modernist-formalist manner of externalizing and representing inner feelings gives them a wider scope and meaning. The director essentially depicts the dissolute and decadent emotions of an entire class—the bourgeoisie—with all its human failures and foibles. Antonioni's ideological thematic has portrayed the dialectics of decay of the aristocratic class since the beginning of his career.[1]

It is intriguing that Antonioni has described his principle for depicting inner feelings as follows, "Our acts, our gestures, our words are nothing more than the consequences of our own personal situation in relation to the world around us" ("A Talk with Antonioni" 26). These words are remarkably similar to the words of Karl Marx in *Critique of Political Economy*: "It is not the consciousness of men that determines their existence but, conversely, their social existence that determines their consciousness" (425).

Being the Part

A basic tenet of Stanislavskian/Method acting is that the actor is the auteur (Carnicke 80) or, as Tony Barr has said in discussing screen acting, "The actor's primary function is to communicate ideas and emotion to an audience" (3). However, in the work of Antonioni, as well as some other film directors, the communication of ideas and emotion has become the job of the filmmaker, not the performer. In fact, Michelangelo Antonioni has stated this directly: "Actors feel somewhat uncomfortable with me; they have the feeling that they've been excluded from my work. And, as a matter of fact, they have been" (qtd. in Billard 8). This may be because the director also believes that his actors are only one part of a larger composition: "I regard [the performer] as I regard a tree, a wall, or a cloud, that is, as just one element in the overall scene" ("A Talk with Antonioni" 36). This may be why Antonioni has explained his work methods on the set as follows: "The film actor ought not to understand, he ought to *be*. . . . The director owes the actor no explanations except general ones about the character and the film. It is dangerous to go into details" (Leprohon 101–3).

This essay will focus on the anti-"Methodist," modernist means by which Antonioni uses actors and performance to convey meaning and character in *Blow-Up* (1967).[2] This zero-degree acting style is defined as modernist in part because it fits the pattern in modern art that was so succinctly characterized by Ludwig Mies van der Rohe as "less is more." In fact, in Antonioni's cinema, *all* the conventional techniques of the performer's "instrument" are pared down and minimized: facial expression, gesture, body language and movement, costume, and especially dialogue.[3] Nonetheless, Geoffrey Nowell-Smith is correct to say that "Antonioni's films can be described as texts written on the body of the actor" (43). This "silent treatment" will be explored below, with particular emphasis on the depictions of sexuality in *Blow-Up* and the final scene in Maryon Park in London.

Silence Is Golden, but Talk Is Cheap: *Blow-Up* as Polysemic Performance Text

The very first sequence in *Blow-Up* establishes a conflict between sound and silence, as Antonioni crosscuts between a group of youthful, energetic, modishly dressed, and noisy Rag Week students who look like "mimes" and a group of older, exhausted, shabbily clad, and quiet derelicts exiting a doss-house. The contrast in colors and pace of the movements of the two juxtaposed groups of performers is stark, and that performance difference is reinforced by the respective editing rhythms. In addition, the students are wearing heavy white pancake makeup on their faces, thereby allying them with some of the film's fashion models and adding a Brechtian masklike dimension to their appearance. (Although the photographer-protagonist is not made up, his facial expressions are often masklike in their vacuity.) The mimes seem to epitomize the performative—life itself as a performance—in this scene and in the final scene of the film, but the "documentary" aspects of the doss-house scene are undercut because, like the mimes but unbeknownst to the derelicts, Thomas (David Hemmings) is also playing a part. After bidding farewell to his compatriots in poverty, he walks furtively down the street and gets into a Rolls-Royce convertible.[4] Throughout the film, Thomas acts a part—that of the hip, world-weary artist—just as actor David Hemmings limns the role of the brash, sexist studio photographer.[5]

The Rag Week students are not, technically speaking, mimes since their performances are, especially in the opening scene, rather boisterous—kinetically and aurally. They run through the streets and shout exuberantly in the first scene of the film. Their shouts, however, do not communicate much more than their excitement and passion within staid, stiff-upper-lip British society (epitomized by the Royal Guard, African nuns, and other solemn people they pass on the streets). In the opening of the film, the mummers "converse" with Thomas exclusively through gestural synecdoche and other unspoken means. Nonetheless, their shared gazes—their imploring requests for a donation and Thomas's lackadaisical facial response—establish an ambiguous link between them that causes the photographer to give them some cash at the beginning of the film and to retrieve their invisible tennis ball at the end. Like Antonioni, who uses atypical "wires" to communicate meaning and character, the mimes use atypical performance channels to convey information about themselves.

At his studio, Thomas whistles (another nonverbal device) to get the attention of his models, his "birds." When the photographer does speak, he barks out demanding orders ("Have that stuff developed, eh? Right away," "Get the birds down here, will ya?") to his assistant, Reg, and is vocally and physically abrupt with everyone he encounters. He keeps Veruschka von Lehndorff (playing herself), one of the world's leading fashion models, waiting for almost an hour. At the start of that photo session, the photographer gestures with a shrug of his head for Reg to open the blinds and let in some light, not even deigning to speak to the hired help.

Later, at a haute-couture modeling session, Thomas shouts rudely at the anorexic women ("Terrible!" "Put the head *up!*"), roughly positioning their limbs into static poses, and struts smugly around the set like a military martinet.[6] These interactions establish the photographer as a Marcusean one-dimensional man, a phallic narcissist, an egotistical "control freak." Hemmings gets to act a bit in this scene, but his performance is just that: a performance— as "prima don" photographer for the benefit of his minions.

Acting Sexy

In a famous passage from *Das Kapital,* Karl Marx linked the changing relations of production in his epoch to the libidinal impulse. He diagnosed the capitalist era as follows: "There followed on the birth of mechanization and modern industry . . . a violent encroachment like that of an avalanche in its intensity and its extent. All bounds of morality and nature, of age and sex, of day and night, were broken down. *Capital celebrated its orgies"* (21; emphasis added). In 1962, Erik Erikson, whose psychoanalytic books were largely responsible for the 1960s (and 1990s) vogue of "identity," noted that "the patient of early psychoanalysis suffered most under sexual inhibitions which prevented him from [attaining his identity]" (279). By contrast, the contemporary patient is constrained not by sexual repression but, according to Christopher Lasch, by narcissism. Overtly charming and successful, the modern-day narcissist is socially and sexually promiscuous as a way of avoiding close involvements (Lasch 71–103). As a result, compulsive copulation becomes perfunctory and sterile: no longer a blissful pleasure shared by two (or more) people, but a self-indulgence for solitary monads.

Herbert Marcuse offered a similar diagnosis. He pointed out that images of sexual gratification that had such explosive negative force in Victorian society have been harnessed—in a postindustrial *societé de consommation* that no longer needs the cement of sexual taboo—to the service of the status quo and consumerism ("Sex sells"). He called this contemporary phenomenon "repressive desublimation" (72–79).

These same issues are part and parcel of the cinematic world of Michelangelo Antonioni, particularly his portrayal of the "sexual crisis" of the modern libidinal apparatus (Leprohon 168). In an interview following the release of *Zabriskie Point* (1969), he made his view explicit: "In my other films, I looked upon sex as a *malattia dei sentimenti, a disease of love*" ("A Talk with Antonioni" 40; emphasis added). In addition to his depiction of characters and situations that reflect the "Sick Eros" of our time, Antonioni uses cinematic signifiers to convey the despair of contemporary desire. Although his films are often considered "sexy"—part of an international marketing strategy by European filmmakers who gave the world auteurs and sex in contradistinction to Hollywood's stars and sexual repression—Antonioni frequently provides a "cold shower" for his viewers and characters by focusing on the sociopolitical determinants of the failures of latter-day lust and love. In particular, his dispassionate, almost clinical, mise-en-scène, découpage, and sound track articulations during actual love scenes and during symbolic sex sequences create the exact opposite effect of Hollywood cinema's lyrical romantic imagery and music. These Brechtian distanciation devices make it difficult for audiences to identify emotionally with Antonioni's characters; instead, the spectator views them from the outside. Put another way, Antonioni is interested less in the personal *psychology* of love and sexuality than in the social *phenomenology* of contemporary erotic behavior.

The classical Hollywood cinema's sexual regime generally involves a narrative trajectory toward marriage as a closural device, a suppression of the erotic impulse, except for the inscription of fetishization of the female body through the agency of the male gaze, and a privatization of emotions, a withdrawal of the couple from the social milieu. This "us-against-them" retreat from the public sphere reflects the more individualistic ethos of American capitalism and American cinema. For Antonioni, even when his damaged subjects find a moment alone, they bring their social baggage with them. Indeed, the dynamic is more "me against you" than "us against them." And he often uses the sexiopolitics of narrative space to convey that idea, as in Thomas's one-on-one session with the model Veruschka—a scene that was selected as "the sexiest scene in film history" by the British journal *Premiere* in 2003.

When we first see Veruschka, she seems to be seated on the floor in Thomas's studio, but when he snaps his finger on a sheet of Plexiglas, we realize that it is only her reflection. This complex mise-en-scène suggests the artificial nature of the model's presence as well as the photographer's view of her as insubstantial. The shot also introduces the "to see or not to see" theme that vision is ambiguous (Antonioni, *Blow Up* 14). With jazz music by Herbie Hancock playing in the background, Thomas—still wearing his torn and grubby clothes from the flophouse—starts the photo shoot with a series of standard locked-down camera positions with Veruschka posed in somewhat stiff, albeit alluring, positions against a backdrop of feathers, but he eventually shifts to using a handheld camera and interacting directly with the model. The photographer's movements create a decidedly erotic tone, and he even straddles his subject on the floor of his loft. "Work! Work!" he shouts at her strenuously, although his behavior is closer to a sexual conquest than to professional rapport. In the context of a film that minimizes dialogue, his repeated verbal entreaties—"On your back!" "Go! Go!" "Give it to me!" "Lovely, yeah!" "Make it come!" "For me, love, for me!"—display a paroxysmal outburst of ersatz passion that belies the otherwise "cool" exterior of David Hemmings's performance.

Antonioni uses the quickened pace of the action and editing, as well as a sexually charged saxophone recording on the sound track, to emphasize the sexual simulacrum, but the scene is also photographed in an unemotional way and clearly shows that the woman is estranged and unsatisfied by the experience. Indeed, the camera zoom into her face as she writhes on the floor as if in the grip of orgasm is an authorial (and male spectatorial) intrusion and penetration of the woman's "sexual space."

At the crescendo of the scene, Thomas screams out *his* pleasure ("Yes! Yes!"), then nonchalantly dismounts and walks away from the model. The cut is to a view of Veruschka sprawled out on the floor as the photographer lies collapsed on the sofa in the background. A phallic wooden beam appears to emerge from the woman's crotch, suggesting the impersonal, "wooden," and unconsummated nature of their make-believe "intercourse" (figure 4.1). Here, Antonioni replaces dialogue and performance with precise articulations of the mise-en-scène to reveal Thomas's career-driven,

4.1. A phallic wooden beam in the background appears to emerge from Veruschka's crotch.

locked-up ego. As the director once said, "Often, an actor viewed against a wall or a landscape, seen through a window, is much more eloquent than the line you've given him" (qtd. in "Apropos of Eroticism" 162). Indeed, for Antonioni, this use of aesthetic language is the true protagonist of his films, not the traditional hero figure of the classical cinema, who is sublimated and/or derealized beyond recognition in Antonioni's oeuvre. In a similar way, Antonioni rarely seeks an authentic collaboration with his performers or encourages them to improvise on the set.[7]

Later, in the loft, Thomas has an encounter with Jane (Vanessa Redgrave), the mystery woman from the park.[8] Once again, Antonioni relies on cinematic signifiers rather than performance tropes to convey their ambiguous emotions and motives (figure 4.2). For instance, the "passion" of their meeting is evoked not so much by their actions (she removes her blouse without a word; he casually tosses aside the roll of film) but by the mauve color of the seamless backdrop behind them as they kiss. Before they kissed, the photographer had treated Jane in the only way he knew how to relate to a female—as a model. He wants to see "how she sits," poses her against a backdrop, and directs her to "keep still" and to move "slowly, slowly, against the beat" of the mood-enhancing music playing on his stereo. In this sense, Thomas orchestrates the scene like a cinema director; indeed, he orchestrates the scene like Michelangelo Antonioni, who in many respects treats his performers like models (if not mannequins).[9]

4.2. Thomas (David Hemmings) and Jane (Vanessa Redgrave) hardly look at each other, and Jane's alienating posture is an impediment to intimacy.

Of course, Thomas's fashion milieu could explain *some* of the wordlessness in the film, since haute-couture models are not usually expected to speak while posing, but his occupation does not account for *all* the displaced emotional affect. While he is with Jane, Thomas even smokes a cigarette in a sexually suggestive manner (his fingers form a V at his nose as he inhales), but there is no mutual self-surrender here, only cold, egoistic calculation: she wants the incriminating roll of film, and he wants another notch on his belt. And, although their sex takes place offscreen and is interrupted by the delivery of Thomas's propeller, the similarity between this scene and the modeling session with

4.3. The teenyboppers return to Thomas's studio.

Veruschka points out Thomas's "repetition compulsion" without the need for direct references to it.

Thomas's repetition compulsion is also evident in another scene, in which he engages in an "orgy" with two adolescent would-be models (Jane Birkin and Gillian Hills). In an earlier scene, Thomas shows the girls a little trick of manual dexterity by deftly rolling a coin back and forth between the fingers of his right hand, suggesting his bodily control and smooth sensuality, but, significantly, the prop he uses is a coin—money—an indication of the cash nexus that intrudes on all of Thomas's relationships. In a sly bit of acting "business," Hemmings buttons up one button on his blue shirt, an understated gesture that signals his professional and sexual rejection of the young women.

Later that day, the teenyboppers return to Thomas's studio (figure 4.3). They would like him to photograph them, but instead he removes their clothes and cavorts with them on his seamless backdrop paper. Although at least one critic sees this scene as a sign of the "cool" cameraman's "humanization" in that he treats the girls as human beings rather than in the manner of a detached professional (Meeker 11), Thomas once again dismisses the teenagers ("Later!") after having his orgiastic way with them. Hemmings provides insight into the character's interior life here by cracking an occasional smile during his romp with the teenyboppers, but for the most part, his cool demeanor and rude behavior predominate: he has the girls make coffee for him, thus putting them to work; looks up their skirts as they mount the staircase (a handheld low-angle point-of-view shot leaving no doubt about Thomas's male gaze and "sexual politics"); has them remove his shoes like servants; and chases them out after they have serviced him sexually.

Subtle facial expressions and gestural codes also convey volumes in two scenes in which Thomas visits his painter friend Bill (John Castle), who lives next door. When Thomas first visits his neighbor, Bill invites him in with a subtle gesture of his head; once in, Thomas asks Bill if he can purchase one of the artist's abstract canvases. The painter shakes his head, indicating "no." Thomas then asks if the artist will give him the painting; again, Bill just shakes his head. This sort of nonverbal communication recurs throughout *Blow-Up*. Later, Thomas wanders into a "primal scene" (Restivo 113) between Bill and his girlfriend, Patricia (Sarah Miles), who are making love on the floor. The photographer does not look away or leave discreetly; instead, true to his "cool" persona, he observes the scene impassively. The woman looks up at Thomas and reaches her hand toward him in an imploring, albeit ephemeral, manner. She then smiles in an equally fleeting and indecipherable manner. She appears to be neither shocked nor embarrassed by Thomas's presence or gaze. There is even a hint that she is involved with him, since she goes up to his loft shortly afterward. Indeed, her silent monologue with "peeping" Tom suggests that she is more interested in communicating with him than with the man who is penetrating her.

Given the limited range of emotion evinced, it is difficult to imagine why Antonioni needed to shoot twenty-one takes of this one interaction between Hemmings and Miles (Antonioni, *Blow-Up* 14). Maybe, like Stanley Kubrick, Antonioni needed to decondition his performers from reacting with their usual gesticulatory and vocal exaggerations (see Dennis Bingham's chapter 10 in this volume), or perhaps, like Bresson, Antonioni used the repeated takes "to suppress intentionality and thus free authenticity" (Tomlinson 370).

One possible explanation for Thomas's lack of affect in these and other scenes in *Blow-Up* is that he appears to be a substance abuser; he always seems to be drinking or smoking pot. At a pot party held at the home of his agent, he indulges so indiscriminately that he has to sack out overnight at his agent Ron's (Peter Bowles) pad.[10] The next morning he has to shake out the cobwebs before proceeding to try to solve the murder mystery, which by now has become the raison d'être of his existence.

"His Master's Voice"

In classic Hollywood movies, characters often emerge not only from their physical actions but also from their bodies in the form of speech acts. Often, these speech acts can be interpreted through the Barthesian "grain of the voice," those individual and recognizable characteristics of a performer's persona manifested in his or her speech patterns (Greta Garbo's accent, Marlon Brando's "mumbling," Marilyn Monroe's breathiness, Wallace Beery's raspy drawl). In *Blow-Up*, Antonioni's eschewal of these defining attributes is most evident in David Hemmings's generally flat and deadpan line readings, creating a character who is not the traditional "strong, silent type" but a more modernist figure: a man without qualities.[11] Indeed, in the parlance of the acting profession, he is a character without subtext. Antonioni's methods of working with actors are such that "they appear to recite their lines with the monotonous detachment of non-performers who have no involvement with what they are saying" (Scott 88).

There are exceptions to this monotonal vocal pattern, especially at the beginning of *Blow-Up* when the character's macho identity is being established. For instance, he is decidedly harsh and loud when he scolds one model for chewing gum ("No chewing gum! Get rid of it! . . . Not on my floor!"), two others for standing in an awkward position ("How about the leg a little further *forward*!" "You, arm down!"), and them all for not being suitably perky (after a piercing whistle: "Wake up!" "I asked you to smile, *eh*!"—a remark that visibly startles the model nearest him). Just before leaving the teenyboppers for the first time, he tells one to "get rid of that bag; it's *diabolical*," his voice dripping with professional sarcasm. As these

4.4. Thomas's entrapment is presented in a graphic visual manner rather than through David Hemmings's performance.

examples show, Thomas may possess *some* of the traits attributed to Bresson's heroes—alienation, stubbornness, automatism, effacement of emotion, and ambiguity—but he clearly does not have the positive aspects of temperament—modesty, shyness, introspection, and nobility—that coexist in the Bressonian "flattened" yet complex protagonist (Tomlinson 366–69).

Hemmings's face throughout much of the film remains as expressionless and deadpan as his voice. As just one example, when Thomas goes back to the park at night to search for the corpse, he slowly and deliberately approaches the tree where he saw the corpse. The camera tilts down to reveal the dead body. When Thomas kneels down and gently touches the cadaver (like the original "doubting" St. Thomas, who physically had to touch the resurrected Christ before he would believe), the photographer is mute and his face is impassive—as impassive as the dead man's.[12] Rather than overt movement or dialogue, Antonioni uses faint sound effects—an offscreen dog barking in the distance, the click of a camera shutter (?)—to disclose the fear that the once overconfident Thomas feels. Thomas is equally poker-faced when he stares at the enlargements hung about his loft like the Stations of the Cross. Although Hemmings's face at this point expresses at most slight curiosity, conveyed by his knitted brow, the shot composition communicates the character's situation more directly (figure 4.4). Thomas's face is trapped between two of the blow-ups, which impinge on his "personal space" and occupy most of the frame. As such, his entrapment by the mystery in the park is presented in a graphic visual manner, rather than through any overt techniques in David Hemmings's performance.

Although his characters' faces are often expressionless and they communicate little though dialogue, Antonioni nonetheless puts the viewer in their minds and thoughts. This is often achieved by using an *école du regard* editing strategy. In the above scene, for example, the director shows us what Thomas is successively looking at: consecutive shots of Jane and her older male companion, the man alone near an Edenic tree, a wooden fence, Jane approaching the camera, a telltale shot of what appears to be a man with a pistol in the bushes behind the fence, and then the tree, where, underneath, there appears to be the corpse of the older gentleman. As the frame fills with these shots, Thomas's general ideation is revealed without the usual trappings of acting. The only hints of a performance in this solo scene are the beads of perspiration that cover Hemmings's face as he contemplates the pictures, his rubbing gesture across his lips (reminiscent of both Humphrey Bogart's recurring "tic" and Jean-Paul Belmondo's homage to Bogie in Jean-Luc Godard's *Breathless* [1959]), and Hemmings's hands-on-hips pose, which convey his anxiety and puzzlement. At one point, Hemmings points his finger, suggesting he has had an epiphany, and he rushes into the darkroom to develop more negatives.[13]

In the next scene, one of the most significant "silent" scenes in the film, we watch for more than fifteen minutes as Thomas silently stares at, rephotographs, develops, and enlarges his original shots from the park, until the grain patterns of the crucial images (is it a corpse under the tree? a gun?) become indistinguishable from the abstract-expressionist paintings of Thomas's neighbor Bill.[14] Although his movements from the studio to the darkroom are determined and brisk, Hemmings's acting in this extended scene consists mainly of running his fingers nervously through his hair several times and projecting "intense moments of quiet concentration" (Zucker, "Making Friends" 153) as he ponders the images and attempts to organize the shots to tell a coherent story. In doing so, Thomas again plays the role of a film director or editor. As Antonioni cuts from one still to the next, we begin to understand Thomas's ineffable thought process and the narrative connections he makes between the disparate angles as he follows the eyeline glances of the woman to a wooded area near the fence (figure 4.5).

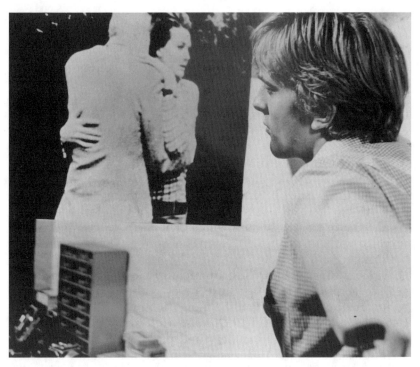

4.5. Hemming's projects "intense moments of quiet concentration" as he follows the eyeline glances of the woman.

Hemmings's performance does not convey the photographer's exact interpretation of the "montage" until he reveals to his neighbor's lover, Patricia, that he believes he prevented a murder, a judgment he reconsiders later. As in much of the film, the characters "converse" in this scene but hardly listen to each other and end up talking past each other in a string of non sequiturs:

> **Patricia**: Who was he?
> **Thomas**: Someone.
> **Patricia**: Shouldn't you call the police?
> **Thomas**: (*nods toward the photo of the dead man*) That's the body.
> **Patricia**: It looks like one of Bill's paintings. . . . Will you help me? I don't know what to do.
> **Thomas**: What is it? Huh?

Patricia: I wonder why they shot him. . . .
Thomas: I didn't ask.

At this, Patricia starts to exit, running her fingers along a string that had held up the pictures. She seems about to say something but instead smiles enigmatically once again at Thomas. Miles's soft voice, gentle stroking of Thomas's hair, quiet demeanor, red see-through crochet dress, and expressionless face are all that Antonioni needs to suggest her character's unrequited passion for the photographer.

The Sounds of Silence

As Ludwig Wittgenstein once said, "Words are also deeds." This idea has important implications for the cinema. Especially in classical Hollywood cinema, words *are* often deeds, in that wall-to-wall scripted dialogue is often the predominant device by which dramatic action, narrative significance, and characters' emotions are conveyed. The transparency of spoken language, at least in "realist" cinema, makes an obvious and overt source of information for least-common-denominator audiences. Most moviegoers would have no difficulty accepting Wittgenstein's notion.

However, Wittgenstein's dictum has a corollary: silence is also a deed. In contrast to, say, talkathon Hollywood movies or the films of Eric Rohmer, Antonioni's cinema is replete with silence, which often becomes the principal agency of communication in a scene. Indeed, the lack of verbal articulation in his films subverts the traditional codes of theatrical and cinematic melodrama, in which characters' feelings and ideas are expressed ad nauseam through speech (think of *My Dinner with André*), facial expression (think of almost any Jack Nicholson movie except Antonioni's *The Passenger* [1975]), and overt action (think of most genre films that involve a chase, fistfight, dance, combat, pratfalls, and so on). Antonioni's films exhibit a counterpropensity to those conventional codes of characterization: "My aim is to achieve the suppression of outward physical action . . . and, where possible, eliminate dialogue" (qtd. in Gessner 396).

The near muteness of Antonioni's characters "speaks" to a "failure t' communicate" between alienated monads. In blocking his two-shots so that characters are positioned on opposite sides of the screen and not facing each other, the director enables the audience to see *all* the performers' facial expressions while also suggesting that there is a physical and emotional gulf between them, that they fail to "see eye to eye." As the filmmaker has said, "A speech which the actor makes in profile gives a different weight from one spoken full-face" ("A Talk with Antonioni" 28). It could also be said that the characters' silence bespeaks a vacuity, an inner emptiness, in his "hollow men" (and semihollow women). In the case of many Antonioni characters, like Gertrude Stein's Oakland, "there's no there there." To put this another way, many of the people in Antonioni's films are characters without *character*.

On another level, this "silent treatment" suggests that any belief in a shared language system that enables human beings to interact is an illusion. As Wittgenstein also said, "Whereof one cannot speak, thereof one must be silent" (6.54). Serlean speech acts may be fine, Antonioni may be trying to tell us, but nonspeech is also an act in a world of ambiguous language relations and debased public discourse. Furthermore, as a film artist, the director appears to give greater emphasis to the mise-en-scène, sound effects, understated gestural codes (what Brecht would call *gestes*), and music—leaving the gaps to be filled in by the spectator.

Thus, in Antonioni's universe, the voicelessness of the characters signals that words spoken from the screen are no longer the only way to tell a story or to create a character. Spectators used to the conventions of the Hollywood cinema therefore go through a process of defamiliarization as they attempt to understand characters who hardly communicate in verbal language. The director's nearly wordless people become *tabula rasa* whose quietude requires a viewer who is highly attentive and projective, one who is willing to read the visual and sonic fields for clues to characterization. In addition, the paucity of synch sound detracts the spectator from another erogenous pleasure of the text: the oral and aural gratification of taking in the overheard or eavesdropped conversations of others.

Having labeled the director's minimalist audio field as modernist and equated it with a "less-is-more" aesthetic, there may be a counterfactual, equally valid argument: Antonioni's "sounds of silence" can be construed as a *realistic* technique. After all, real-life human beings do not generally converse as much as fictional characters in the movies. The characters' muteness could therefore be explained as an essentially realist project of verbal representation. In this sense, Antonioni's use of mime is mimetic.

Antonioni's silences are not dramaturgical pregnant pauses, those emotionally coded (and emotionally loaded) moments that interrupt the free flow of chatter so common to Western theatrical traditions; indeed, *speech* in Antonioni acts as the interruption of the free flow of quiet. If his people are not completely silent, they nonetheless exist in a state psychoanalysis characterizes as *parole vide*, or empty speech, which has no basic function other than to express the relation that its lack of significance elides—that is, to contribute to an aural vacuum, a void that must be filled by gesture, music, sound effects, or the spectator's own perusal of the image.

The tendency in Antonioni's films to break with the traditional aural codes of the classical cinema frustrates the spectator's desire to hear—what Jacques Lacan calls *un pulsion invocante*, an invocatory drive, which is dependent on a lack—and breaks the implied unity of the senses for the viewer accustomed to the mind-body conflation of the dominant cinema. The abundance of lip-synchronized dialogue (and broad, ostentatious gestures) in the classical cinema creates an illusion of wholeness and supports the overall strategy of audience identification with a coherent fictional character. As Mary Ann Doane put it, "The sonorous envelope . . . sustains the narcissistic pleasure derived from the image of a certain unity, cohesion, and, hence, an identity grounded by the spectator's fantasmatic relation to his/her own body" (45).

When Thomas does talk, much of his communication is remote, mediated, and artificial. He uses a car phone repeatedly to convey messages to his agent, his studio, and others, using a code name—Blue 4-3-9—to establish his anonymous identity for the call service. He often gives orders to his models through intermediaries—his Asian woman assistant, for example, or his aide-de-camp, Reg, whom Thomas tells to "get the birds down here, will ya," and gives a telephone to take down an address of a "bloody junk shop." He matter-of-factly calls his female subordinate and most women he encounters "love" in the oily British style of the period, but such plastic endearments merely debase the language. He calls one model "Stripes" because of the black-and-white pattern on her costume; no attempt is made to know her as a human being.[15]

Beyond the individual *style* of a film actor's voice, though, the specific *words* he or she utters are as important to the spectator, who seeks identification with and understanding of the character. The words and expressions of classical cinema ("Frankly, my dear, I don't give a damn," "Go ahead, make my day," "I made him an offer he couldn't refuse," "May the Force be with you") enable viewers to misrecognize their own selves through a process of aural interpellation. The secondary status of dialogue in Antonioni's oeuvre is thus equivalent to the removal of the Father, as Language and Law, for the spectator-auditor. The resulting Lacanian "lack" impels the viewer to fill in the gaps with his or her own "inner speech."

What does pass for conversation in Antonioni's work cannot be properly called dialogue; the latter is too strong a term for such banal pseudo-exchanges, especially since the characters rarely face each other directly while speaking. In addition, the frequency of repetitive phrases and non sequiturs evokes the mood of a Harold Pinter drama, without the obvious wordplay. Thus the solitude of Antonioni's characters, rather than their interactions, is foregrounded. A case in point is Thomas's interchange with Jane after the telephone rings in his loft. At first he ignores the persistent sound, but then he suddenly scrambles all over the floor looking for its source. After he locates the telephone and picks up the receiver, he hands it to Jane without a word. The following incoherent exchange ensues:

> **Jane**: Is it for me?
> **Thomas**: It's my wife.
> **Jane**: Why should I speak to her?
> **Thomas**: *Into phone* Sorry, love, the bird I'm with won't talk to you. *He hangs up. To Jane* She isn't my wife really. We just have some kids. . . . No, no kids. . . . Sometimes, though, it feels as if we had kids. She isn't beautiful; she's . . . easy to live with. *Pause* No, she isn't. That's why I don't live with her.

This monologue is emblematic of Antonioni's redirection of traditional acting paradigms. As described in both classical writing manuals and "Methodist" performance primers, actors need to establish a "backstory," a life history, of their characters that they can use in developing the delivery of their lines. Thus, in the example above, although Thomas seemingly reveals important information about his personal situation, what he says is so self-contradictory that Jane and the viewers do not know what to believe, thereby undercutting the expository purpose of the conversation. Hemmings's disinterested performance style contributes to this effect: he follows Jane around the loft as she ducks under ceiling beams and taps her knuckles impatiently on the wood. As he talks, he runs his finger over an Op Art painting, building the tension between him and

Jane but not advancing the backstory one iota. It is as if Thomas's voiceless gestures and movements override the character "revelations" in his speech, leaving the viewer "in the moment" rather than in the past.

Prop It Up

In Antonioni's cinema, props can take on huge symbolic importance, while at the same time remaining real objects in a phenomenological world of things. Whereas in most films (and plays), actors use props to convey meaning and character and to *enhance* their performances, in *Blow-Up*, props actually *take the place of* performance and communicate directly with the spectator. One instance of a "prop" substituting for performance is the literal prop, or propeller blade, that figures prominently in the antique shop scene and as the coitus interruptus mechanism during Thomas's sexy scene with Jane in his studio. (It is of some Freudian interest that Thomas drops the propeller while trying to place it in his car.) Similarly, another prop—the broken-off neck of a guitar—serves as a modern castrated phallus when it is prized at a rock concert, where it is thrown out to a frantic crowd, and devalued when Thomas and, a few seconds later, another man, throws the propeller to the street.[16]

Props also substitute for performance (or lack thereof) during the scene following the Veruschka photo shoot. Thomas is shaving in his bathroom, presumably having showered and changed into the clothing he wears throughout the rest of the film (straight-legged white jeans, wide black belt, black half-boots, and a light blue shirt—usually seen with the top three buttons left open). As Thomas shaves and confronts his identity in the bathroom mirror, a shelf filled with cologne bottles is visible on screen right. The sheer number of glass props sums up this character, who would rather perfume himself than examine his inmost self, who would rather cover up his sordid soul with fragrant emoluments than confront the emptiness within.

Even more significant, the gallery of phallic icons in *Blow-Up*—from Thomas's camera lens to the propeller ("I *must* [have it today]! I can't live without it!") to the guitar neck to the marijuana joints he smokes with Jane at the beginning of the film and at his agent Ron's home at the end—symbolize objects that enable the protagonist to escape temporarily from his epistemological ennui and experience a modicum of ersatz pleasure. Ultimately, however, all of the props provide a cold shower of disturbing disillusionment and detumescence.[17] These phallic objects also provide a phenomenological substitute for Thomas's lack of emotional affect and true masculinity, and Hemmings's correspondingly low-key performance.

Hemmings's flat facial expression throughout *Blow-Up* also needs to be understood in the context of the era in which it was produced. Thus, Hemmings's flat affect is surely meant to express the sangfroid and *impassibilité* of the 1960s "Mod" lifestyle. In contrast to the "Rockers" of the period, who reveled in passionate displays and working-class violence, the Mods were more concerned with their Carnaby Street fashions and detached decadence. The rock concert scene in the Rikki-Tikk Club epitomizes the use of contradictory sonic articulations to record the tensions both within Thomas and within the British subculture.

The anticipatory sound of a driving rock beat is heard as Thomas approaches the club in search of Jane, whom he spotted on the street; however, when he enters the discotheque, the young patrons are inappropriately silent. They are also rigidly immobile, except for one interracial couple who dances listlessly to the pounding beat and the photographer's slow movement through the club. Although the youngsters' clothes are "loud," we cannot hear their voices. The music and lyrics of the Yardbirds seem to speak for the youngsters, and Jeff Beck's song even conveys apposite thematic messages from those of the director—"You're tellin' me you didn't see"—helping to fill in the characterological void. But even the song is not communicated properly. A technological failure causes the rock group's performance to go sour: one of the musicians' electric guitars malfunctions, producing annoying static on the sound track. This failure of technology to create or improve meaningful rapport between people mirrors the protagonist's own overreliance on his ineffective camera apparatus.

It is only when the rock performer smashes his obstreperous instrument to bits and hurls the guitar neck out into the statue-like crowd that they react. This direct frontal assault on their zombie-like performances provokes them to shout and scream loudly and to chase after the prop, which ends up in Thomas's besieged hands. However, the pandemonium and all the impassioned movements of the crowd do not communicate anything more than the mimes' histrionic excess. They are still dead-in-life characters, like Thomas, who are stirred by ersatz phallic symbols (the propeller, the guitar neck) to move or shout inarticulately but do not share authentic intimacies or joy with their fellow human beings.

The Tennis (End) Game

In a personal interview with me, Antonioni quoted Anton Chekhov: "Give me new endings, and I can reinvent literature!" The director also invoked a realist (as opposed to a formalist) justification for his problematic closures: "Life is inconclusive" (Tomasulo 64). Nonetheless, the antiteleological structures of his narratives call into question the syllogistic progression of the Aristotelian dramatic mythos of narrative continuity and causality, the ancient basis for contemporary master narratives. The open texture of these modernist "stoppings" deny closure within the diegesis and thus throw back to the viewer any Aristotelian raveling and unraveling.

This renegotiation of the narrative contract relates to the general problematics of artistic language in the modern world. The endings of Antonioni's films are independent entities, texts apart from the body of the narrative. Rather than being structured around a single cathartic event (for example, the blinding of Oedipus), Antonioni's films are cyclical in structure, with little noticeable rise and fall—that is, they are what Paul Schrader has called "a continuous continuation" (33). Despite their modernist configurations, though, many of Antonioni's endings evince a silence of signification that leaves the spectator with an unfulfilled mania for explanation.

In *Blow-Up*, the protagonist's repeated state of silence contributes to the film's narrative and thematic ambiguity. As a still photographer, Thomas is used to silent work: when he is not shouting at his vapid models or bossing around his staff, he is in the darkroom or working silently in the doss-house. His silence conveys his incivility: he never thanks anyone who helps him. Nonetheless, at the beginning and especially at the end of the film, Thomas and the mimes *do* communicate with each other, through subtle facial and gestural codes, emphasizing again Antonioni's refutation of dialogue as the chief mode of characterological portrayal.

At the end of *Blow-Up*, in the tennis court scene, Antonioni and actor David Hemmings finally communicate something to the viewer. The photographer puts down his ever-present camera (and what a meaningful gesture *that* is, because Thomas had, up until this point, mainly communicated with others through his camera lens) and moves into close-up as he tosses back an imaginary ball to the mimes. Antonioni holds on Hemmings's blasé facade while the character experiences a slow series of internal emotions and thoughts that appear to overwhelm him (figure 4.6). This is silent

4.6. Antonioni holds on Thomas's blasé facade while the character experiences a slow series of internal emotions and thoughts.

acting at its most sophisticated best, exemplifying what Béla Belázs called "the silent soliloquy" (63) or, as Angela Dalle Vacche has noted, the "visual ventriloquism" in the cinema of Antonioni, whereby the director "speaks through the actor's body" (48).

Even before this final moment, Thomas had begun to communicate with the mimes, albeit nonverbally. The students' overt and mannered gesticulations (the way they play tennis, for instance) and the photographer's more delicate and lackadaisical responses establish an ambiguous link between them that causes him to cooperate and retrieve the invisible tennis ball. Of course, Antonioni's autonomous camera also cooperates by following the path of the "ball" as it bounces and finally settles in the grass near Thomas. Here, Antonioni's camera takes on a performative role in the discourse and actually upstages Hemmings's material enactment of Thomas's character.[18]

Since a film's ending is such a privileged site, spectators try to extract some ultimate significance (and signification) from Hemmings's enigmatic and uncertain expressions and the subtle changes in his countenance. This subdued performance contains the whole psychological and semiotic resolution of the entire film. The offscreen sound of a tennis ball pinging and bouncing (especially since it is gradually podded up on the sound track over the length of the entire shot) may skew the spectator's interpretation somewhat, but each viewer still comes away with a different meaning from Hemmings's polysemic articulation. If, as actor Alan Bates suggests, "Thought does register on camera" (qtd. in Barr 42), then we should be able to discern what Thomas is thinking—sans dialogue or overt facial expression.

Much of the critical literature on *Blow-Up* offers conflicting interpretations of the photographer's final gesture, his retrieval of the mimes' imaginary tennis ball. Despite many nuances and subtleties, these arguments often boil down to whether the ending is "happy" (the hero has a positive experience with other people and puts down his camera) or "sad" (Thomas surrenders his hold on reality).[19] These value judgments aside, Thomas's act is indisputably a thoughtful and imaginative leap in the direction of another reality, calling into question much of what came before in the narrative. More judgmental readings presuppose that Thomas (and the spectator) should experience catharsis.

The change in narrative voice is apparent as the character disappears (after first being minimalized by a cut to an overhead long shot) to leave the grass behind for our inspection. Thomas, who had been the center of that final image (and of the whole film), vanishes through a cinematic trick and thus deprives us of a vanishing point; we are left with a flat image with no sense of depth. As such, Antonioni's art is based on absence, including the absence of overt acting. In *Blow-Up*, there are numerous diegetic absences: the photographer's disappearance, the corpse's Fort/Da presence/absence, the stolen blowups, and so on. Indeed, the theft of the incriminating photos denies Thomas the "happy ending" to his book; sounding a bit like a Hollywood producer, in the pub scene Ron had said that a happy ending "rings truer." The status of the narrative's closure is thus openly discussed within the narrative.

Thus the erotic and emotional involvement usually associated with plot and characters is, in Antonioni, replaced by an aesthetic appreciation. To momentarily revive the language of semiotics, it is precisely *this* conflict—the coterminous distinction between the polyvalent language of the images (oriented toward the signifier) and the univocal language of the ideological (oriented toward the signified)—which produces the oft-discussed "ambiguity" of the director's films. The work of closure, then, in an open-ended film would seem to involve an ideologically inspired passage between two modes of discourse: the poetic and illusive order of film style, which keeps meaning and desire in a state of suspense, versus the cognitive and definite domain of the dialogue, which seeks to fix meaning and to lodge desire in a safe haven. Ultimately, one must distinguish between the emotional/dramaturgical climax of classical cinema and the other sorts of endings—thematic, chromatic, cinematic, and the like—associated with modernist, formalist films.

Unlike classical cinema, which depends on the device of the memorable tag line of dialogue ("Tomorrow is another day," "Nobody's perfect," "This could be the beginning of a beautiful friendship"), Antonioni most frequently ends his films in silence or with music. His characters' voices are generally still for several shots, if not several minutes, before the end. Related to this characterological silence is an authorial stance similar to indirect discourse. Like Flaubert, Antonioni affirms a perspective superior to his characters, while simultaneously challenging his viewers to assume that same place.

The director eschews the use of dialogue at the end of *Blow-Up* as he often does in the final scenes of his films. He often relies on elements of the mise-en-scène: in this case, a chimerical "prop"—an invisible ball—is used to convey character and meaning. Certainly this ball is a Metzian "imaginary signifier" if ever there was one (Metz 18–34). The imaginary ball also plays a role in the performance of meaning—in this case, the Fort/Da appearance/disappearance of the ball mirrors the appearance/disappearance of the mimes (who appear at both the beginning and the end of the film) and, more important, the appearance/disappearance of the corpse Thomas found in the park. Furthermore, Antonioni uses the camera to accentuate that theme: in the final shot, Thomas himself "disappears" from the screen through the use of a self-reflexive cinematic special effect, a dissolve-out.

Conclusion

Antonioni's predilection for "No Words," the slogan painted on the stolen airplane in *Zabriskie Point*, is part of his postlinguistic cinematic language and nonverbal aesthetic. Performance figures into this equation through the de-emphasis on speech and theatrical gesture throughout *Blow-Up*, as well as other Antonioni films. In contrast to, say, Federico Fellini, whose histrionic characters use broad, stereotypical Italianate gestures and wear their hearts on their sleeves (and in their dialogue), Antonioni's actors use a much more limited "palette." They are part of an overall visual and color design, not just a talking tongue. The last word is Antonioni's: "Films are always in prose. Why? One could tell a story by images alone, without words, as pure as poetry" (qtd. in Wyndham 13).

NOTES

1. Antonioni expressed his political passion most directly in an interview with the author: "I was so against the bourgeoisie and wanted to say something against it. The aristocrats are sliding into nothingness. They're disappearing slowly" (Tomasulo, "Life Is Inconclusive" 62).

2. Actor-director John Cassavetes once told me that he was "a Methodist," meaning that he subscribed to many of the tenets espoused by Lee Strasberg and the Actors Studio.

3. Many seasoned film actors advise beginners to tone down their performances before the camera. In an educational film about screen acting produced by Carnegie-Mellon University, Academy Award–winning director Ron Howard proffered the following guidance: "In a long shot, act as if you're on the stage; in a medium shot, take it down a notch; and in a close-up, take it down *two* notches." (Needless to say, Opie's recommendation did not come with a working definition of a "notch.") Alec Guinness affirmed that it had taken him twenty-five years to learn "to do nothing" when in front of the camera lens (Barr 7), and Michael Caine opined: "If you catch someone 'acting' in a movie, that actor is doing something wrong" (Caine 4). Despite this minimalist discourse from mainstream neonaturalist actors, Antonioni's modernism takes this sort of restraint to an extreme.

4. Angelo Restivo compares the doss-house scene in *Blow-Up* to the Lumière brothers' *Workers Leaving a Factory* (1895), one of the first motion pictures ever screened for an audience (109). That "*actualité*," however, should not be held up as an unvarnished exemplar of "the realist impulse" (Restivo 18) because the factory workers were wearing their Sunday-best clothing, were aware of the camera (operated by their employers!), and were exiting a factory (owned by the Lumières) in the middle of the workday—all indications that the film had been set up. Furthermore, the *Blow-Up* scene involves a British flophouse, not a factory, so the men who emerge represent the *lumpenproletariat* class rather than proletarian factory workers.

5. Antonioni "discovered" Hemmings in a small London stage production ("Apropos of Eroticism" 162).

6. This was, of course, the era of the rail-thin British fashion model, with Twiggy and Jean Shrimpton being the most renowned exemplars of the Mod look. The Hemmings character was apparently based on a real-life British fashion photographer, David Bailey, who was notorious for his demanding persona.

7. At least one modernist director, Robert Altman, allows his performers to improvise and even write their own dialogue (see Robert Self's chapter 5 on *Nashville* in this volume). In an interview with me, Antonioni responded to my question about Jack Nicholson's alleged use of improvisational gestures in *The Passenger*: "They weren't so spontaneous. I told Nicholson to do that. As for dialogue, it can be completely changed by the lighting scheme of the shot, by the colors, by camera movement" (Tomasulo, "Life Is Inconclusive" 64).

8. One of the most common ways to convey character semes—the proper name—is absent in *Blow-Up*. The two main characters are never identified by name within the diegesis, although their first names—Thomas and Jane—are noted in the film's published screenplay and in most of the scholarly literature. The very absence of a cognomen provides symbolic inferences, just as it does in the modernist novels of Kafka (K. in *The Trial*) or the plays of Samuel Beckett. Since one's name is often associated with one's identity (Who are you? John Doe), the failure to provide an appellation suggests a characterological anonymity or veritable nonexistence. It can also be seen as part of Antonioni's Brechtian strategy to undermine facile audience identification. Finally, this namelessness (also found in *The Passenger* [The Girl], *Il mistero di Oberwald* [The Queen], and *all* the family names in *L'avventura*, *L'eclisse*, *Il deserto rosso*, and *Zabriskie Point*) bespeaks a lack of or loss of personal identity that Antonioni thematizes throughout his work.

By providing extratextual information about the characters' names through the *Blow-Up* script and interviews, however, the director encourages individual associations that attach to those designations: "doubting" Thomas, "peeping" Tom, or "plain" Jane, all of which have some resonance with the people in *Blow-Up*. In combination, however, Thomas and Jane are sexually charged names to readers of D. H. Lawrence's *Lady Chatterley's Lover*, in which Mellors, the groundskeeper, uses "John *Thomas*" and "Lady *Jane*" to designate, respectively, the male and female sex organs. Neither the script nor the film, however, offers a surname for either character (or for any other character in the entire film), thus setting them apart from any roots, traditions, or family ties, and makes them modern tabulae rasae.

9. Another modernist filmmaker who minimizes acting flourishes is Robert Bresson (see Tomlinson's chapter 3), who espouses the use of amateur actors and "automatism" in his book *Notes sur le ciné-matographe*. Bresson referred to his players as "models" (Tomlinson 365).

10. Ron (Peter Bowles) appears to be even more of a pothead than Thomas is. At one point, he is seen with *two* joints in his mouth.

11. The reference here is to Robert Musil's novel, *The Man without Qualities*.

12. This scene is strongly reminiscent of a doppelgänger sequence in Antonioni's *The Passenger* in which Locke (Jack Nicholson) discovers a corpse in an adjacent hotel room and stares blankly at the dead man's face for quite some time. The facial resemblance is uncanny, not only because the other actor's (Chuck Mulvehill) features are similar to Nicholson's but also because Nicholson is figuratively "playing dead," that is, his characterization is of a spiritually dead man. In addition, Antonioni's framing of the shot—a two-shot close-up—emphasizes the Lacanian "mirror stage" aspects of the scene (Scott 135).

13. Another wordless finger gesture occurs in the pub scene, when Thomas meets with his agent, Ron. He stops a passing waiter by grabbing his arm, points to a dish on a plate, and says, "And a pint." He is thus able

to order his entire lunch by uttering only three words.

14. The connections to the conspiracy theories about the assassination of John F. Kennedy are clear: a gunman possibly hiding behind a fence on a grassy knoll, the failure of a camera (Abraham Zapruder's 8mm movie apparatus) to answer all the troubling questions, and so on.

15. Even if Thomas were interested in getting to know any of these models, Antonioni's mise-en-scène and costumes would be prohibitive. The models are first seen behind a black, smoked-Plexiglas screen, thus alienating them from the photographer. In addition, behind-the-scenes images show an assistant using clothespins to make the fashions fit properly on the models' bodies and hiding the price tags that dangle from the necklines. Like Thomas, these "birds" are revealed to be all surface.

16. This scene takes place at night outside a fashionable dress shop, whose windows are filled with mannequins that resemble both Thomas's posed fashion models and the stiff, immobile concertgoers.

17. Fredric Jameson has pointed out that after the sex romp with the two teenyboppers, Thomas is drawn to images of death: "Before that episode, [he] thinks he has prevented a murder; after satiety, the well-known link between sex and death causes him to look more closely, and to discover the traces of the corpse" (195).

18. This idea was called to my attention by Cynthia Baron.

19. These two positions are most clearly exemplified in the contradictory interpretations of Arthur Knight and Ian Cameron and Robin Wood. Knight claims: "When the hero joins the game, one has the feeling of a final affirmation, that he is aligning himself with people who are joyfully alive" (5); Cameron and Wood insist that Thomas's "grasp of objective reality [is] fatally undermined" and that Hemmings's face "is that of a man near the verge of insanity" (138).

Works Consulted

Affron, Mirella Jona. "Bresson and Pascal: Rhetorical Affinities." *Quarterly Review of Film Studies* 10.2 (1985): 118–34.

Antonioni, Michelangelo. "Apropos of Eroticism." *The Architecture of Vision: Writings and Interviews on Cinema*. Ed. Carlo di Carlo and Giorgio Tinazzi. New York: Marsilio, 1996. 148–67.

———. *Blow-Up*. New York: Lorrimer, 1971.

———. "A Talk with Michelangelo Antonioni on His Work." *The Architecture of Vision: Writings and Interviews on Cinema*. Ed. Carlo di Carlo and Giorgio Tinazzi. New York: Marsilio, 1996. 21–47.

Arrowsmith, William. *Antonioni: The Poet of Images*. New York: Oxford UP, 1995.

Austin, J. L. "Performative Utterances." *Philosophical Papers*. Oxford: Oxford UP, 1970. 233–52.

Barr, Tony. *Acting for the Camera*. New York: Harper and Row, 1986.

Belázs, Béla. *Theory of the Film: Character and Growth of a New Art.* Trans. Edith Bone. New York: Dover, 1970.

Billard, Pierre. "An Interview with Michelangelo Antonioni." *Blow-Up.* New York: Lorrimer, 1971. 5–10.

Bislinghoff, Gretchen. "On Acting: A Working Bibliography." *Cinema Journal* 20.1 (1980): 79–85.

Brecht, Bertolt. *Brecht on Theatre.* Trans. John Willett. London: Methuen, 1964.

Bresson, Robert. *Notes sur le cinématographe.* Paris: Editions Gallimard, 1975.

Brunette, Peter. *The Films of Michelangelo Antonioni.* Cambridge: Cambridge UP, 1998.

Butler, Judith. *Bodies That Matter: On the Discursive Limits of "Sex."* New York: Routledge, 1993.

Caine, Michael. *Acting in Film.* New York: Applause Theater Books, 1993.

Cameron, Ian, and Robin Wood. *Antonioni.* New York: Praeger, 1969.

Cardullo, Bert, et al., eds. *Playing to the Camera: Film Actors Discuss Their Craft.* New Haven: Yale UP, 1998.

Carnicke, Sharon Marie. "Lee Strasberg's Paradox of the Actor." *Screen Acting.* Ed. Alan Lovell and Peter Krämer. London: Routledge, 1999. 75–87.

Della Vacche, Angela. *Cinema and Painting: How Art Is Used in Film.* Austin: U of Texas P, 1996.

Doane, Mary Ann. "The Voice in the Cinema: The Articulation of Body and Space." *Yale French Review* 60 (1980): 33–50.

Dyer, Richard. *Stars.* 2nd ed. London: British Film Institute, 1997.

Elsaesser, Thomas. "Reflection and Reality: Narrative Cinema in the Concave Mirror." *Monogram* 2 (summer 1972): 2–9.

Erikson, Erik H. *Childhood and Society.* 2nd ed. New York: Norton, 1963.

Esslin, Martin. *Brecht: The Man and His Work.* Rev. ed. New York: Norton, 1974.

Gessner, Robert. *The Moving Image: A Guide to Cinematic Literacy.* New York: Dutton, 1971.

Jameson, Fredric. *Signatures of the Visible.* London: Routledge, 1992.

Knight, Arthur. "Three Encounters with *Blow-Up.*" *Film Heritage* 2 (spring 1967): 3–6.

Kuleshov, Lev. *Kuleshov on Film.* Ed. Ron Levaco. Berkeley: U of California P, 1974.

Lasch, Christopher. *The Culture of Narcissism.* New York: Norton, 1979.

Leprohon, Pierre. *The Italian Cinema.* Trans. Roger Greaves and Oliver Stallybrass. New York: Praeger, 1972.

Lovell, Alan, and Peter Krämer, eds. *Screen Acting.* London: Routledge, 1999.

Marcorelles, Louis. "Albert Finney and Mary Ure Talking about Acting." *Sight and Sound* 30.2 (1961): 56– 61, 102.

Marcuse, Herbert. *One-Dimensional Man: Studies in the Ideology of Advanced Industrial Society.* Boston: Beacon, 1964.

Marx, Karl. *Capital*. Vol. 1. New York: Modern Library, 1936.

———. *The Communist Manifesto*. In *Essential Works of Marxism*. Ed. Arthur P. Mendel. New York: Bantam, 1965. 13–44.

———. Preface. *A Contribution to a Critique of Political Economy*. In *Early Writings*. Trans. Rodney Livingstone and Gregor Benton. New York: Vintage, 1975. 424–28.

Meeker, Hubert. *"Blow-Up." Film Heritage* 2 (1967): 7–15.

Metz, Christian. *The Imaginary Signifier: Psychoanalysis and the Cinema*. Trans. Ben Brewster. Bloomington: U of Indiana P, 1982.

Naremore, James. *Acting in the Cinema*. Berkeley: U of California P, 1988.

Nowell-Smith, Geoffrey. *L'avventura*. London: British Film Institute, 1997.

Perry, Ted. "Men and Landscapes: Antonioni's *The Passenger*." *Film Comment* 11 (July–Aug. 1975): 2–6.

Pudovkin, V. I. *Film Technique and Film Acting*. New York: Grove, 1970.

Renoir, Jean. *My Life and My Films*. Trans. Norman Denny. New York: Atheneum, 1974.

Restivo, Angelo. *The Cinema of Economic Miracles*. Durham: Duke UP, 2003.

Schrader, Paul. *Transcendental Style in Film: Ozu, Bresson, Dreyer*. Berkeley: U of California P, 1972.

Scott, Michael Alan. "Michelangelo Antonioni's *The Passenger*: A Film Analysis." Diss. Columbia U Teachers College, 1979.

Searle, John R. *Speech Acts: An Essay in the Philosophy of Language*. Cambridge: Cambridge UP, 1969.

Smith, Barbara Herrnstein. *Poetic Closure: A Study of How Poems End*. Chicago: U of Chicago P, 1968.

Tomasulo, Frank P. "The Intentionality of Consciousness: Subjectivity in *Last Year at Marienbad*." *Post Script* 7 (winter 1988): 58–71.

———. "Life Is Inconclusive: A Conversation with Michelangelo Antonioni." *On Film* 13 (fall 1984): 61–64.

Tomlinson, Doug. "Performance in the Films of Robert Bresson: The Aesthetics of Denial." *Making Visible the Invisible: An Anthology of Original Essays on Film Acting*. Ed. Carole Zucker. Metuchen: Scarecrow, 1990. 365–90.

Wittgenstein, Ludwig. *Tractatus Logico-Philosophicus*. Trans. D. F. Pears and B. F. McGuinness. London: Routledge, 1961.

Wyndham, Frances. "Antonioni's London." *London Sunday Times* 12 Mar. 1967: 13–15.

Zucker, Carole, ed. *Figures of Light: Actors and Directors Illuminate the Art of Film Acting*. New York: Plenum, 1995.

———. "Making Friends with the Camera: An Interview with Ian Richardson." *Screen Acting*. Ed. Alan Lovell and Peter Krämer. London: Routledge, 1999. 152–64.

———. *Making Visible the Invisible: An Anthology of Original Essays on Film Acting*. Metuchen: Scarecrow, 1990.

5

Resisting Reality
Acting by Design in Robert Altman's *Nashville*

Robert T. Self

. . . .

"I want to hear a little more Haven this time," says country-western singer Haven Hamilton (Henry Gibson) in a recording session at the beginning of *Nashville* (1975). This request for more volume in his recorded voice reflects an intersection of personality, public persona, and mediated presence shaped by the controlling authority of electronic playback. Haven's assertion establishes a paradigm for the representation of character in Robert Altman's modernist film as a site where the force of acting, the demands of script, and the design of direction compete and cohere. The film further develops a sense of personality as a construct of public performance, private subjectivity, and cultural politics. Personality, art, and acting all emerge, like those fragments the poet "has shored against my ruin" in T. S. Eliot's *The Waste Land* (1922), as artifices of resistance against the all-too-debilitating nature of reality. In *Nashville*, naturalistic acting constitutes the antinaturalistic design of art. The actor performs personification as impersonation.

Acting in the cinema is always the site of a complex interaction among three forces—the script, which delineates some drama with particular character functions developed through certain behavior; the actors, whose performances themselves comprise a complex interaction of craft, physiognomy, and professional, career, and personal autobiography; and the director, who shapes performance and selects camera setups in production and who (in postproduction) emerges as the intentionality behind the editing of specific shots and sounds in the final cut of the film.

126

In modernist cinema, that complexity is compounded by the dissolution of the concept of character. Classical narrative cinema assumes the possibility of communication and persuasion and asserts a unified social identity grounded in the secular humanism that optimistically posits "man" as the position of intelligibility, meaningful action, and ethicality. Acting in these texts performs a scripted concept of whole, intentional, efficacious individuals held in place by the "zero degree" style of classical cinema. In contrast, modernist cinema presupposes the world as splintered and centerless, meaning as imprecise and indeterminate, and morality as divisive and illusory. It asserts that the human being is neither an autonomous individual nor a meaningful unity, but a process of divergent and conflicting constraints, both internal and external. Performance, then, is developed not to ultimately convey some sense of an "individual" "identity" but to portray personality as a subjectivity proscribed by contradictory forces. Thus, acting in modernist discourse works inevitably in the service of the depiction of splintered, unstable, and insecure identity.

The discontents of modernist narration in the twentieth century bequeath a particular vision about the nature and possibility of aesthetic form, social identity, and cultural value. Modernism is formalist in structure, reflexive in subject, experimental in expression, ironic in worldview, and generally conservative and pessimistic in philosophical stance, as it surveys an early-twentieth-century "waste land" in Western culture, economy, politics, and morality. It calls attention to its artifice as an interrogation of realism. It asserts the value of aesthetic as opposed to moral absolutes. It seeks a dispassionate and detached voice to speak about passionate and traumatic matters. It experiments with the limits of artistic form to discover new and fragmentary forms of expression. It takes an existential stance toward the disruption, alienation, and despair that it takes to characterize contemporary life. Malcolm Bradbury and James McFarlane assert that modernism

> is the one art that responds to the scenario of our chaos. It is the art consequent on Heisenberg's "Uncertainty principle," of the destruction of civilization and reason in the First World War, of the world changed and reinterpreted by Marx, Freud and Darwin, of capitalism and constant industrial acceleration, of existential exposure to meaninglessness or absurdity . . . the art consequent on the dis-establishing of communal reality and conventional notions of causality, on the destruction of traditional notions of the wholeness of individual character, on the linguistic chaos that ensues when public notions of

127

language have been discredited and when all realities have become subjective fictions. (27)

From *M*A*S*H* (1969) to *The Company* (2003), Robert Altman's films generally—and *Nashville* in particular—reflect these modernist qualities everywhere. They conceive social identity as multiple and unstable. They reflect on the role of the entertainment business in the debasements of contemporary values. Their narratives are fractured and fragmentary and ask to be read not as logically and causally inflected conflicts and resolutions but as formal, abstract designs. Acting involves amateur performers, improvisation, fragmentary performances, and unusual physiognomies. *Short Cuts* (1993), for instance, conveys the multiple lines of characters inexorably and unintelligibly woven together around death from accidents, murder, and suicide—the whole structured through the complex musical interactions of classical, jazz, and new age music. Actors perform naturalistic roles in truncated moments that are subsumed to subliminal structural relationships. Rick Altman explicitly describes the bleakness of Robert Altman's vision of America's capitals of entertainment: "*Nashville* provides a terrifyingly effective critique of the mythology which serves as a foundation for the entire enterprise of American life" (*The American Film Musical* 327).

The novelistic tradition embraces the certainties of social realism, but modernist discourse puts the intelligibility of these conventional orders at risk. Says Altman of the logic of assassination in *Nashville*: "The reason we look for plots and collusions is that we are looking for a reason that computes. . . . We demand logic, but it doesn't necessarily have to be there" (Bryne 25). Such work questions social, temporal, and especially characterological stability. A central quality of modernist cinema is its claim to represent a truer reality. Its human figures are "people," not "characters." Their physiognomy is ordinary rather than idealized. The behavior of these people frequently seems motivated by unseen events and unknown causes and therefore necessitates active audience participation in the closing of narrative gaps or in rationalizing incoherent behavior. Actions prompt reactions but not in any logical or sequential way. Narrative order disappears. Narrative lines multiply. People assume major roles in some stories and minor ones in others. These textual qualities engage a conventional reading strategy that discovers meaning through a correlation with everyday reality that films like *Nashville* and *Short Cuts* describe as the shallow and chance encounters of human interaction.

This debilitating quality of the contemporary frequently emerges in Altman's depiction of entertainment as complicit in the fragmentation of social identity. In *Buffalo Bill and the Indians* (1976), *The Player* (1993), *Prêt-à-Porter* (1996), and *Nashville*, actors emerge, like audiences, as the victims of an industry that makes human need the basis for commodities sold by stars, by glamour, and by false illusions. In particular, acting in *Nashville* becomes a metaphor for this negative effect because it centrally explores the relationship between public performance and the personal persona behind that performance. Performance constantly emerges out of a complex mix of public persona, personal "reality," and the politics of individual moments. As usual in the musical, this tension reflects the onstage/backstage dichotomy involved in the generic structure of putting on a show. But, as Jane Feuer has argued, "the musical could incorporate the myth of entertainment into its aesthetic discourse" (172) and thus works to break down the barriers between performance and real life, between acting and personality.

As a documentary in style, however, *Nashville* is less concerned to blur than to examine and expose the fissures between motive and behavior, between acting and individuality, between seeming and being. The film thus reflexively models in its content the modernist issues of acting explored in this essay. Jerome Delamater describes this process in the musical: "Performance in its ritualized form often functions as *discours*; the characters are no longer just characters whose existence is restricted to the text, but they are performers as characters who frequently invite the audience to participate in the ritual with them" (45).

In *Nashville*, acting is a complex, painful, and occasionally tragic business. Putting on a show involves a process of debasement symbolized graphically in the scene in which Sueleen Gay (Gwen Welles) performs a striptease at a "smoker" arranged to raise money from wealthy male contributors to presidential politics. Performance built on aspiration, self-deception, and humiliation finally represents the politics of selling the body. Altman's films frequently invite a reading of character and identity as textual devices communicating values implicit in the discourses and ideologies that intersect to produce them; personal identity is constructed and constrained by divergent external forces—linguistic, economic, biological. In *Nashville*, the ability to perform, the struggle for success, and the need for human relationship are, as the roving sound truck campaigning for Hal Phillip Walker reminds us throughout the film, all politics.

An irony in Altman's narratives is the energy devoted to creating a verisimilitude in acting that ultimately must be read not as naturalistic but as expressionistic. This contradiction in modernist cinema maintains a rigorous commitment to a real world of human behavior, both internal and external, less stylized, less idealized, less narrativized than in classical discourse; at the same time it valorizes the aesthetic demands of form engaged by the filmmaker in the personal creation of an impersonal art. This confluence of the drive toward a greater realism on the one hand and artistic craft on the other produces a cinematic modernism in which acting works as part of aesthetic form. Fletcher and Bradbury summarize the historical context of this work as the modernist "obsession with formal matters, aesthetic wholeness, and the use of language and design, rather than contingency and imitation" (394). They assert: "Modernist works frequently tend to be ordered, then, not on the sequence of historical time or the evolving sequence of character, from history or story, as in realism and naturalism; they tend to work spatially or through layers of consciousness, working toward a logic of metaphor or form" (50).

Thus, Joyce builds the structure of *Ulysses* on the metaphoric association, among many others, of Dublin and the *Odyssey*. Faulkner employs the Easter narrative to order *The Sound and the Fury*. Eliot shapes *The Waste Land* on the "seeing blindness" of Tiresias. The green light at the end of Daisy's dock and the snowing glass knickknack structure the metaphoric design of *The Great Gatsby* and *Citizen Kane* respectively. Masks and unmasking motivate story, style, and performance in *Persona* (1966). The anima makes the pictures move in *8 1/2* (1963).

Rick Altman specifically discovers motivation in *Nashville* as formal: "the process of mixing sound serves as Altman's guiding metaphor for the process of creation itself. Reality is a twenty-four track affair" ("24-Track" 4). More particularly, the film eschews the contiguity of characterological behavior for a five-day structure that asks to be read as a meditation wheel. Early in the conceptualization of the Nashville project, scriptwriter Joan Tewkesbury established this metaphoric design. At a country music nightclub during her visit to research the film, "She realized all at once that she had found her movie. Here, so it seemed, was the nucleus of the circular city that was Nashville. Anyone you saw at breakfast you'd inevitably see, later in the day, as if they had all been thrown back together by the centrifugal force of the city's ever-turning wheel. Somewhere in all of this was an overlapping circle of characters, butting up against one another through a linear series of events" (Stuart 57).

Altman's major reconstruction of this concept was to require that the film end with a death. The final scene of the film and the inexplicable shooting of Barbara Jean constitute an ironic tableau of cultural understanding that exceeds classical narrative order. This last scene depicts the initial vision of *Nashville* as the modernist Image described by Ezra Pound, "that which presents an intellectual and emotional complex in an instant of time" (Frank 9).

In his seminal essay "Spatial Form in Modern Literature," Joseph Frank provides a framework for comprehending this phenomenon. Modernism's loss of faith in temporal order occurs directly as a result of modern man's loss of "a relationship of confidence and intimacy with a world in which he feels at home" (53). Frank goes on to note: "Now time is the very condition of that flux and change from which . . . Man wishes to escape when he is in a relation of disequilibrium with the cosmos; hence non-naturalistic styles shun the dimension of depth and prefer the plane" (56). *Nashville* develops no sustained story through time with a teleology of human efficacy; rather it represents "the spatial interweaving of images and phrases independently of any time-sequence of narrative action" (49). The separate personalities caught in the film's last scene at the Parthenon are just one of the images patterned into the plane of this sequence, because all the personalities in the film, abstracted from their patterned circulation through the text, are simultaneously here as well. "For the duration of the scene, at least, the time-flow of the narrative is halted; attention is fixed on the interplay of relationships within the immobilized time-area. These relationships are juxtaposed independently of the progress of the narrative, and the full significance of the scene is given only by the reflexive relations among the units of meaning" (15).

The figures of the twenty-four characters at the Parthenon compose a line of performance drawn between a false facade of classical antiquity and the naïveté of an audience manipulated by political cynicism. Rather than being a narrative analysis of the causal logic of cultural reality that explains the tragedy of public assassination, *Nashville* develops a formal meditation on the complex contemporary symbiosis of identity, performance, entertainment, and politics. Its final sequence is an irrational drama whose actors

5.1. Constructing the final performance in *Nashville*.

represent neither characters nor individuals but images simultaneous with their imagistic interaction with others throughout the film. The Parthenon sequence is but a point on this wheel. For the only time in the film, the entire cast of twenty-four actors assembles, all standing facing each other in various degrees of waiting and observing as straight lines of performers and audience, a group portrait of the personas that whirl through the three-hour experience of the film. The cast describes a 180-degree line—appropriately, before the classical Greek facade, recalling the origins of Western drama—positioning the audience before the denouement of a modern tragedy. Time past and time present commingle here. This tableau is the point at which everything else in the film becomes clear, or rather it is that point that precedes and shapes an understanding of the past images that now follow (figure 5.1).

The paradox of realistic performance in expressionistic form is replicated in the complex and unique dynamics of acting and production in an Altman film. From *M*A*S*H* to *The Company*, observers, participants, and Altman himself similarly describe the director's construction of a community among the actors and the production company. Actors usually stay with the production from start to finish. The entire crew assembles nightly to watch dailies in a party atmosphere. Actors enjoy great freedom to develop their own concept of the character posited by the script, which is generally an operational outline of the different scenes in the film. All he does, says Altman, is create an arena in which his assembled actors interact (*Nashville*). Generally, his practice in shooting is to put microphones on all the actors and put them in motion, shooting them unobtrusively with long lens in a manner that "typifies a documentary approach to a real event." Rick Altman describes this process: "In order to create a space permitting multiple, overlapping dialogues, Altman early adopted the use of a broad-range zoom lens, permitting continuous focus from extreme long shot to large close-up" ("24-Track" 6). Thus, as actors perform, Altman's camera roams in and across and around the dramatic space, all the while recording the dialogue and ambient sound coming from twenty-four different sources. Subsequent aural and visual editing among shots develops the dramatic space as a rich overlay of sounds, what Henry Gibson called "Altmanscope." In the meantime, nobody on the set knows who or what the camera actually shoots. As Karen Black describes it, "Altman radio mikes you and you're not aware of where the camera is, and then you invent things" (qtd. in Tomlinson 50).

This complex interaction in *Nashville* begins with a script by Tewkesbury that diagrams the five-day structure of the action, identifies the various locales for that action, and generally sketches out the range of roles in the film. Part of the popular and professional perception of Altman is the freedom he is famous for allowing his actors in the development of their roles. At the same time, Altman has tended to work with a repertory company of actors whose repeated casting reflects the director's appreciation for them both as actors and as types who fill important spaces in the canvases he paints. Many of the actors and actresses in *Nashville* had worked with Altman before and would again: Henry Gibson, Lily Tomlin, Michael Murphy, Shelley Duvall, Karen Black, Geraldine Chaplin, Keith Carradine, Bert Remsen, and Robert Doqui. Some of these actors appear in Altman films across the thirty-year span of his Hollywood career. Gibson and Tomlin brought popular television images to the film from several years as regular performers on *Rowan and Martin's Laugh-In* (1968–73), and Black had featured roles in *Easy Rider* (1969), *Five Easy Pieces* (1970), and *The Great Gatsby* (1974), but few of the actors in *Nashville* has ever enjoyed major status as a movie star. And all comment on the creative flexibility that the director accords them as actors. Keith Carradine, for instance, observes: "Altman lets you create for yourself. You have so much freedom. He doesn't manipulate you . . . much" (qtd. in Tomlinson 187). Geraldine Chaplin, however, also asserts: "People say that Bob allows you the most enormous freedom and that they're creating their own part, which is an enormous lie. . . . He gives you the *impression* you're creating and that marvelous ego trip, but you're the same marionette you are with other directors" (qtd. in Tomlinson 93). Altman asserts that he chooses his actors "for who they are" and then asks them "to play themselves" (*The Player*).

The complicated nexus among writer, director, and cast that Altman authorizes is captured by Jan Stuart in his study of the making of *Nashville, The "Nashville" Chronicles*: "While many of the characters would find their origins in Tewkesbury's travels and travails, they would eventually be transformed by a free-flowing exchange between the director's sensibility and the actor's own personality and history" (63). Part of this directorial intentionality occurs in the selection of these actors in the first place. Altman says of his construction of the acting community for his films, "I'm looking for behaviors rather than actors" (qtd. in Yacowar 24). This tension reflects another of the traditional distinctions in acting: between the actor's craft in impersonating a character on the one hand and the physiognomy of the actor on the other, which personifies the character. As Barry King observes:

> The predominant tendency is for the norm of impersonation to be abandoned at the level of casting in favor of a strategy of selection based on personification—let the actor be selected by physical type anyway and let these physical attributes mean in and of themselves. In other words, the actor becomes the most rudimentary form of the sign, the ostensive sign in which the substance of the signifier is the substance of the signified: the actor is the person, has the personality, his or her appearance suggests s/he is, notwithstanding the fact that this construction relies on a first order conventionality in the culture which the actor re-presents and, sometime, redefines. (143)

In addition to this mode of casting in *Nashville*, however, the complexity of acting derives from the paradoxical conceptualization of the naturalistic as the antinaturalistic—from a representation of the actor as a sign in which impersonation is personification. The freedom of the actor on the Altman set engages the actor beyond the requirements of Method acting—where the actor reaches into personal experience in order to understand and represent particular emotional dimensions of a role—to craft the character as the personification of him- or herself. Says Stuart of the actors in *Nashville*: "Altman encouraged them to embroider with as much detail from their own lives as was required to make them at home with their assignments" (18). Little bits and pieces of detail from actors' lives offscreen appear throughout the film: Ronee Blakley's visit to see her parents in Idaho, Geraldine Chaplin's work in Israel before the film, the accident of a personal friend of Lily Tomlin. Maurice Yacowar asserts that "Altman's process is to individuate, to move from the general type to the personal character" (20). In fact, the acting depicts the general type *as* the personal character.

Yacowar's analysis of the "private vocabulary of actors" in the first decade of Altman's Hollywood career explicitly marks out the relationships that shape our understanding of acting in *Nashville*: "Altman invites his cast into a community that will create his film. The invitation may be prompted by the director's personal response to the performer's image or nature, or by his awareness of the performer's associations from other films or from real life" (15, 27). He indicates too how these actors signify particular personalities: "Bert Remsen as a cantankerous, usually crippled, nasty old man"; Michael Murphy "a glib, sophisticated hustler" (16); Shelley Duvall the "dippy hippie" (23); Henry Gibson "the self-aggrandizing magnate with the false image of avuncular warmth" (22). These personally revealed/revealing types constitute part of the design *Nashville* represents, and the cultural resonance resides in part in the actors themselves—their voices, body language, and bodies. Stuart notes that "their origin is a typically Altmanesque chicken-egg conundrum of which came first, the actor or the character" (73). Assistant director Alan Rudolph describes Michael Murphy's presence in the film: "Bob cast him so well that as soon as you see him on the screen a lot of the work has been done" (qtd. in Stuart 75). Sue Barton, the unit publicist (who plays herself in the film), generalizes even further about the significance of Altman's actors: "He has a knack for knowing who you are and putting you in situations where that is very apparent. He does see people in a way that no one else does, and he can use that to tremendous advantage to himself" (qtd. in Stuart 89).

With twenty-four characters, the film hardly devotes sufficient space for any one of them to "grow" into a classical well-rounded character. Impressions of them as "real" characters, however, emerge not simply from physiognomy or casting but from the performance work of the actors. Despite their presence almost as figures or just pigments in a painting, these actors contribute to the impression of personality by naturalist performance. The modernist interest in portraying a heightened realism, like the documentary cinematography, creates an impression of a personality as in life rather than a character as in fiction. The acting thus creates real if minimal surfaces that may only be types but that also suggest depths of both personal and imagined reality.

For example, Karen Black plays Connie White alternately as stiff, bored, and unfriendly and as a silly blond in a scarlet red prom gown when she is not performing. Onstage, she moves awkwardly and sounds very artificial in her address to members of the audience standing at the stage, suggesting that her attempt at the personal is as counterfeit as the smile she suddenly turns off and on at one point when being photographed by a fan. When she begins to sing, however, her strong, off-key voice and her energetic body movements, in synchronization with the music, convey heartfelt emotion that reinforces her lyrics. In particular, her song—about wanting to go to Memphis but not knowing the way and wanting to go to heaven but forgetting how to pray—combines with Black's discordant mix of cold detachment and shallow engagement. Together, they develop a complex image of haughty stardom and depleted personality.

Barbara Baxley as Lady Pearl plays the role of a nightclub owner and Haven Hamilton's mistress as an assertive, brash player in the business of country music but brings to the political surface of the film's social fabric the bitter voice of a Catholic outsider who mourns the assassination of the "Kennedy boys." In her nightclub, she is loud and brassy, like her curly red hair; she wears two cowboy pistols on her belt and aggressively dares her customers to misbehave. In contrast, the most striking aspect of her performance is her nuanced reminiscence of her work in Bobby Kennedy's election campaign, of the attitudes of southern conservatives, of the numbers of Tennesseans who voted for "the asshole" Nixon, of the details of Jackie's bloody clothing in the aftermath of the shooting of the president. This center of her performance was actually shot in one long monologue that Altman subsequently cut apart and distributed across the film. Drinking bourbon and seated for an interview with Opal, Baxley plays mournful, angry, and tipsy; shaking her head, compressing her lips, slurring her words, spitting them out, she alternately speaks with a tortured sadness, with scorn, with regret. Her voice rises in hostility, croons in happy memory, falls in confusion, and breaks in despair. The audience knows little else about these two "minor" roles, Connie White and Lady Pearl, played by actresses whom Stuart's *Chronicles* describes as playing themselves. But these personalities contribute important images of discordant subjects to the *Nashville* canvas.

So too does the performance of Robert Doqui as Wade. He plays a working-class black man as the clear-eyed truth sayer about the crass Nashville scene. Provocatively and loudly, he thrusts himself across a nightclub floor to call African American singer Tommy Brown "the whitest nigger in town." He looks at the star Barbara Jean at the Nashville airport and says dismissively, "She ain't gonna sing 'less she gets paid for it." His voice is plaintive and pleading when he tells Sueleen Gaye that she "can't sing a lick" and that "they're gonna kill you in this town." Counter to any image of African American subservience in the South, Dogui plays Wade as self-assured; his voice and body language are brash and rude, secure and aggressive, self-confident and assertive. Doqui raises the black voice in the film almost like a chorus whose alternative gaze throws light on the dark places of Altman's canvas, not just here but in other films as well. White behavior is also marked as variously curious, corrupt, and callous by marginal black figures in *Buffalo Bill and the Indians* (1976), *Health* (1979), *Kansas City* (1996), and *Cookie's Fortune* (1999). At the end, Wade shouts to anyone who can hear: "All y'all goin' the wrong way!"

Geraldine Chaplin plays the ironic counterpoint to Wade as Opal, the phony BBC reporter who barges in everywhere with her tape recorder, trying to make sense of the country music scene. Ironically, the personality she attempts to limn is Altman's. He told her during production: "In this movie, you're me. I just want you to follow me around, watch me, and imitate me" (qtd. in Stuart 153). He wanted her to communicate the "very false and very fake" (152). Chaplin plays the role in outlandish flowing dresses and vests of garish and clashing colors that are wholly appropriate to the mix of inane, obsequious, chatty, and oblivious gestures that characterize her performance. She creates Opal as a thoroughly obnoxious, opinionated, intrusive, and inattentive person. That the role is meant to add a self-conscious dimension to the film's design is clear from Altman's explicit description. Her role "was supposed to represent us . . . outsiders, full of bullshit. I don't know anything more about Nashville than she did" (qtd. in Viertel and Walker). The circularity here is telling. Altman chooses Chaplin to perform her own personality, and the personality he wants her to realize is his own. Her European-accented English marks her as an outsider, and Chaplin's performance of flighty heedlessness characterizes the arrogant and intrusive mass media.

Among the "major" roles in the film, measured by their filling greater space in the canvas, that of Barnett, like Opal, is least sympathetic. Heavyset, wearing a brown leather jacket and undone tie and unshaven, Allen Garfield raises both hands, tilts his head to the side, and shouts, "I got no time." This repeated figure denotes a man of authority full of tension and anxiety. Stuart's *Chronicles* indicates that Garfield's combative, angry, and confrontational performance of Barnett replicated the actor's relationship with others in the production community. Garfield plays Barbara Jean's husband-manager as the controlling, domineering business partner of the big star. He carries his large body with a forward thrust, gestures threateningly with both hands toward friends, associates, and agents who would greet his wife and client. His routine shouting and brusque manner indicate a man who wants to manage it all, but public relations demands, Barbara Jean's illness, and political pressures are forces beyond his command. He wants to manage Barbara Jean's image and keep it free from entangling political associations, but his arrogant and harried demeanor reflects his lack of control. Garfield performs this aggressive anxiety in a remarkable scene in her hospital bedroom.

The scene begins with Garfield sitting feet up on the bed, listening intently to Connie White on the radio as she performs in Barbara Jean's place at the Opry. He matter-of-factly asserts to Barbara Jean, sitting in the middle of the hospital bed, that he needs to know what White is singing if he is to thank her later at the club. When Barbara Jean insists that all he really wants to do is "hobnob" later, he angrily leaps from the chair to stand over her and aggressively asserts that since he never interferes with her singing, she should not complain about "how I run your life." As her reactions become hysterical, he bends down to her and menacingly asks if she is going "nutsy on me again," forcefully telling her that he "won't stand for it." Her tearful acquiescence to his berating leads to his moving around the end of the bed in preparation to leave; having verbally beaten her into submission, he speaks to her now as a child, forcing her to repeat to him what he's about to do and why. He moves from an exasperated but practical realization that he must go and thank Connie White for taking Barbara Jean's place on the Opry stage, to combative insistence about the onerousness of the chore, to browbeating his wife for questioning him, to baby talking her into submission. Officious, hostile, and loud, Garfield's Barnett contains and displays the coercive pressures of entertainment, publicity, and stardom.

As a political front man for presidential candidate Hal Phillip Walker, John Triplette is a different sort of manager. Michael

Murphy plays the suit from politics, a smooth and straight-talking, intense but low-key organizer. Murphy's slight build, youthful face, and relaxed posture imply an open, easy-going friendliness offset by an intense gaze that implies an alert, probing purposiveness. Stuart describes the image: Triplette was "Watergate oiliness tempered by Murphy's hands-in-pocket finesse" (74). Tewkesbury further conceptualizes the role: "He'll do anything to get his candidate taken care of. Lying brilliantly and lying to the point where it was the truth. The most polished out-of-towner in Nashville. He knows the drill, he knows how long to be nice to people, he knows who to juice, he knows when to get out. He is ruthless. Ambition taken up to the level of sophistication" (75).

Murphy's performance and persona actualize a more charming personality than the screenwriter describes. He smiles readily and easily, gestures in self-deprecating ways, and analyzes and persuades calmly as he stands intimately close to the personal space of his interlocutors. His voice, body language, and face communicate an articulate magnetism, sincerity, and sympathy that fifteen years later would perfectly suit him to play the candidate for president in Altman's *Tanner '88* (1988). Murphy's performance is chameleonlike. At times, his voice and eye carry a steely edge; at other times, he sets his face blankly and his eye intently on attractive young women; at still other times, he stands quietly, observantly, and unobtrusively at the edge of a medium shot. Then, in a close-up, he leans in to joke intimately and confidentially, and elsewhere he persuades glibly. Always standing in close proximity to his listener, he soothes with a quiet voice, cajoles with a frank, flat directness in his voice, fraternizes through the easy familiarity of his movements and laughter, or else, standing flat-footed and squarely in front of his listener, he intimidates with a strong voice and short, emphatic hand gestures. He plays lechery, cynicism, and duplicity with the same boyish charm that fully reinforces the character's iconic name, tellingly mispronounced at one point by Barnett as "Triple." Yacowar asserts that here, as in his other roles for Altman, "a sinister, corrupt force lurks behind Murphy's handsome mien, . . . another instance of ethically compromised handsomeness" (16).

Lily Tomlin received an Academy Award nomination for her performance as Linnea, the wife of a music-business lawyer, mother of two deaf children, and object of the amorous attentions of itinerant womanizer and rock star Tom (Keith Carradine). In this complex role, Tomlin focuses a sincerity and devotion exactly opposite that of Triplette and her slick and folksy "good ol' boy" husband, Delbert (Ned Beattie). Liberal politics apparently motivate her to sing gospel, off-key but exuberantly, in the black choir from Fiske University and to attend a black church on Sundays. Her long, plain face makes this middle-aged mom the unlikely object of womanizer Tom's seductive singing, but during the scene in which they are in bed together in his motel room, Tomlin plays Linnea as serene and comfortable in quite unexpected circumstances. After sex, she rests on one arm looking at him; she quietly criticizes his smoking, then reaches over to take an experimental drag from his cigarette, and leans back to blow smoke awkwardly into the air as he laughs gently at her. It is an intimate moment that parallels the same shot and space of Tom's sexual escapes with three other women in the film. In Altman's medium close shot, Tomlin's relaxed posture and movements signal composure as she uses her hands to show Tom how to say "I love you" in sign. Finally, just as steadily and complacently, she looks at her watch, says she must leave, and begins dressing to exit this scene of adultery.

Tomlin has two other remarkable moments in the film. Standing in their dining room, Linnea listens intently to her deaf son speak and sign his success in swimming class. Delbert shifts his body impatiently and stares at his son with a look of resignation and blankness that indicates he cannot understand his son's signing. In contrast, Tomlin stands with her arms around her daughter's shoulders as she watches and listens to the boy. As she waves a hand at Delbert to silence him, her body is still, her lips half smiling, and her eyes, crinkled in attentiveness, never swerve from her son's face. Tomlin's performance here luminously signals attention, pride, and joy in his accomplishments. Altman's medium close-up looks at her in profile with the same intensity she devotes to her child. Then, in the scene of seduction in which the Keith Carradine character sings the Academy Award–winning song "I'm Easy," Altman's camera slowly pans across a nightclub full of Tom's other conquests—Opal, Mary, and L. A. Joan. Each thinks he sings to her, but the camera moves past them finally to begin a slow zoom in to a close shot of Lily Tomlin. Oblivious of her surroundings, hand at her throat, mouth half open, she stares intently in the direction of the musician, whose lyrics hypocritically declare:

It's not my way to love ya when no one's lookin'

It's not my way to take your hand if I'm not sure,
It's not my way to let ya see what's goin' on inside of me.
When it's love you won't be needing, you're not free.

Tomlin performs a surprising mix of parental and sexual intensity: she conveys a complex nexus of devotion, commitment, desire, and relaxed ease that makes her performance a space of grace in the *Nashville* canvas.

The figures created by two other roles also stand out in the film, both by virtue of their space in the film's overall design and in their position as stars in the fictive world. Based ostensibly on Nashville superstars Hank Snow and Loretta Lynn, Haven Hamilton and Barbara Jean constitute sites of success and power, adoration and insecurity. The film opens with Henry Gibson performing Haven in the recording studio. As he sings a song of patriotism ("we must be doing something right to last two hundred years!"), he exudes confidence, authority, and force. He glares around the studio as if expecting challenges to his words; he emphasizes certain lines with energy and bites off words as though directing the song at imagined enemies of the country. He interrupts the recording twice to assert his authority over the intruding Opal and a musician who cannot play the piano to his satisfaction. When he asks the recording engineer for "a little more Haven this time," he explicitly asserts his organizing ego in the opening space of the movie. In the next sequence, when he arrives at the Nashville airport to welcome the recovering Barbara Jean, Hamilton quarrels assertively and nastily with his mistress. Seconds later, he greets the airport crowd and introduces his fellow star, but now Gibson plays Hamilton as congenial, smiling, and friendly. These two personae, the private self-aggrandizing Haven and the onstage obsequious Haven, occur as major images throughout the film. On the one hand, he is the popular and unctuously formal country music star whose hits represent national fervor, ethical correctness, and personal fortitude. Immaculately dressed in white embroidered western clothes, Gibson plays this Hamilton as a smiling, waving, cheerleading personality who nevertheless always stands ramrod straight and stiff in public. On the other hand, in private, Hamilton is arrogant, reserved, cautious, and assertive, and Gibson plays his dialogue and body language in a way that bespeaks a hard, knowing, and defensive ruthlessness. Yacowar describes his role here and in other Altman films as "always discovering a treachery and cunning beneath Gibson's persona of innocence" (21).

In contrast, the epitome of innocence and tragedy is Barbara Jean. Actress Ronee Blakley develops a personality of sincerity, sweetness, and vulnerability. Blakley's performance, also nominated for an Academy Award, strikingly reflects the merger of script, direction, and actor, especially because Altman promotes that interaction among his actors. As he explains: "When an actor is looking for something to talk about and they have something in their own lives, I say talk about that. It pushes them into using themselves as research rather than trying to make up a character. It comes out with the smell of truth about it. It's a shortcut device for me, rather than having some writer just writing a history and then making the actor fit into it. And I still find that very valid" (qtd. in Stuart 160).

As apparently the biggest country music star in the fictional world of the film, Barbara Jean is played by one of the few professional musicians in the cast. Like that of others in the cast—in particular Henry Gibson and Lily Tomlin, who come to Altman's films from television comedy—Ronee Blakley's acting has the ring of the amateur, which, coupled with the random camera setups and live sound recording, enhances the documentary quality of the film. Blakley's singing is one of the central energies of the film, and the lyrics of her songs establish the kind of disability that emerges in her acting as well. In Barbara Jean's first public appearance, during the Opryland sequence, Blakley performs two songs that she wrote. She sings the first, about a cowboy lover, with body-swaying energy and smiling enthusiasm, but the second, "Dues," details a broken marriage. In the latter performance, her slightly bent-over posture, her closed eyes, and the contraction of her facial muscles connote painful emotional distress as she sings about "this careless disrespect I can't stand no more." Similarly, in her last performance at the Parthenon, she reveals this tension between joy and suffering. One song expresses the importance of music as a defense—"When I feel my life perishing like waves upon the sand"—and the other longs nostalgically for "Momma and Daddy in my Idaho home." Blakely's face, as she sings in Altman's close-up frames, is a luminous mix of joy and pain. Indeed, the way she raises and lowers her eyebrows, and the way she contracts and relaxes her facial muscles, signal both happiness and sorrow, in keeping with the stark black and white contrasts in the mise-en-scène—notably Blakely's black hair and white dress and the overcast sky.

Frequently looking drawn and haggard, the actress reflects the stress and illness of her personal life during the shooting. And one of the most remarkable scenes in the film—Barbara Jean's breakdown at Opryland—was written by Blakley from incidents in her own life, "stitched together from the real-life detritus of Blakely's own Idaho family album" (qtd. in Stuart 223). As she concludes singing about wanting "to walk away from this battleground," she begins to reminisce about her grandparents, about the fifty cents she won as a little girl from an appliance store for singing the lyrics on a promotional record, and about her feeling that "I've been working ever since." Blakely steps out of a performance mode; her voice becomes childishly chatty, and she stands with hand on hip, her eyes either closed or avoiding the audience. Then her voice becomes somber and starts to falter and she brings her hand to her bowed head; she clearly communicates emotional distress as Barnett finally escorts her away from the stage and the booing crowd.

This is her second collapse in the film, the earlier one occasioning her first song, the old Protestant hymn "In the Garden"—a plaintive song of need and reassurance that Jesus "walks with me / and He talks with me / and He tells me I am His own." Blakley, in her characteristic white gown, sings the hymn with a moving, delicate elegance from a wheelchair in the hospital chapel, her hands clasped in front of her, her eyes closed, while her head moves slowly in time with the gentle rhythms of the hymn. Here, in the middle of the film, is a central metaphoric representation of Nashville's thematic exploration of need and nurture as backdrops to the country music scene. Barbara Jean's popularity ostensibly resides in the tension between her palpable vulnerability and the music that resists it, as she sings in the film's final sequence, "Writing it down kinda makes me feel better / Keeps me away from them blues." There is an effervescent and childlike energy in her public demeanor—her broad smiles, thrown-back head, sparkling eyes, and eager directness—that contrasts strikingly with the petulant acquiescence in her private response to Barnett's bullying. Her omnipresent white gowns, her black hair, and her scarlet red lips significantly mark the contrasts she represents and constantly foreshadow the shooting upon which the film ends, with Barbara Jean as literally a victim of her tragic success.

In every one of these roles, the acting naturalistically evokes a range of cultural knowledge that makes the performances recognizable, but in none is there any sustained, developed portrayal of character. The acting in *Nashville* does not participate in the classical realist project of creating fully developed identities. Among the shaping forces of scripted role, acting skill, and characterological physiognomy, acting in *Nashville* is intermittently displayed by its twenty-four performers. This analysis of these performances represents the distillation of bits and pieces of acting dispersed across the text. Moreover, this summation of performance ignores how the moments of acting are juxtaposed with other performances in the scattered discourse of the film. Indeed, these summaries imply a coherence far from palpable in the viewing of *Nashville*, and far from the modernist conception of character, identity, or subjectivity that underlies the film. Naturalistic performance works for expressionistic effects shaped by the aesthetic form of the whole work. Acting efforts to impersonate the roles named in Joan Tewkesbury's script approach personification, as twenty-four characters achieve the representations they were cast to produce.

Altman observes that they cast the cars very carefully in the airport parking lot scene—the Cadillac, the Nash, the Volkswagen, and the remodeled pickup—to match their owners, and of the actors he says similarly, "I chose them because they had the characteristics and could portray the characteristics of these various characters" (*Nashville*). The individualized performance of actors tends toward the paradigmatic function of stereotype, which Barry King describes as the person of acting: "an understanding that the physical presence of the actor is already coded in the general sense of having the socially recognized attributes of an individual in the host culture" (142). These energies must be understood not in the function of classical character formation but in the function of modernist spatial form.

The major units of meaning in *Nashville* are the actors and their scattered performances. Each of these twenty-four roles is an image, a pigment, a shape in the revolving wheel that constitutes the figure this modernist poem makes. Part of the modernist reflexivity of the film resides in its self-conscious participation in the very debilitation of the mass media it critiques. But there is another aspect to its reflexivity. Despite its heightened sense of documentary realism, the film works ultimately as expressionistic, nonnaturalistic discourse. Reflexivity is not so much the self-conscious reference to the discursive process itself but the intra-textual reference in any point of the text to other aspects of the same referent elsewhere in the text. Here the signs of the text are not so much signifiers of the external world of American society but of their internal relationships to themselves and to each other within the text. Barbara Jean's closed eyes as she sings "In the Garden," her descending arm as she concludes "Dues" at Opryland, her little girl's voice saying bye-bye to Barnett in the hospital, her enthusiastic thank you to her fans at the airport—these acting touches are fragments of the poetic image, not the narrative character. His blank face as he hears Triplette offer national support for a gubernatorial campaign, his stiff back as he sings "Keep a-Goin'," the glare he fixes on Opal in the recording studio, and the timbre of his voice as he welcomes Elliot Gould to "my lovely home"—these performance details are constituent elements in the overall image of Haven Hamilton.

The separate moments of twenty-four performances in the film represent less the development of character than the fleshing out of a discrete image. As Barry King argues about non-naturalistic performance, "The regime of signification creates its own signified(s) as it were sub-consciously by the deployment of highly conventionalized systems and subcodes of reference—the audience not expecting verisimilitude (in the naturalistic sense) but an internal consistency in the relationship between signifiers and signified" (137). "Barbara Jean," then, is a unit of meaning (a formation deriving from script, actor, and director) whose whole significance in part appears as an accumulation, an accrual of references across the text, and in part derives from its juxtaposition with particular aspects of other "units of meaning"—Barnett, Haven, audiences ("characters" in naturalistic discourse)—all of which taken together constitute Pound's "intellectual and emotional complex in an instant of time." Thus the viewer of *Nashville* reads the same way as the reader of modernist cinema, "by continually fitting fragments together and keeping allusions in mind until, by reflexive reference, he can link them to their complements" (Frank 18). Part of the complexity of modernist cinema is its requisite reading strategies that recognize the simultaneity of time. Meaning emerges from the simultaneous perception of connections among images and phrases in space that have no consecutive relationship to each other in time. The Parthenon sequence works just this way in *Nashville*. Its almost classical delineation of time and space simultaneously contains the intricate pattern of the whole film: desire, politics, musical performance, and violence.

The revolving wheel of these patterns is announced in the complex opening images of the film that look and sound like an advertisement for the sound track album of the film, one of those loud television pitches that promotes the songs and the singers available "for one low price if you act now." The sequence exactly delineates the way in which naturalistic acting in the film is contained within a larger expressive design. The actors play musicians who are bit players in an ensemble album that packages and sells them as stars. This pre-credit sequence is remarkable for the nature of its movement. Six different image tracks provide information to the viewer simultaneously. In the center of the screen is the album cover for the sound track songs of the film; one by one, images of the faces of the characters in the film fill the cover as its borders remain stable. At the same time, the titles of the songs scroll up one side of the screen as the names of the performers scroll down the other side. On the sound track, audio clips from each song play as the singer's face appears in the album. The titles of the songs are simultaneously splashed in large letters across the whole screen. Throughout this scene, the strident voice-over of an announcer touts the singers and the songs, and constantly repeats with emphasis "IN NASHVILLE!" Most important for the metaphor of the film's circular design is the dominant movement that revolves the painted, not photographed, faces of each of the performers in the film around the central image of the album. The actors are already, as the film begins, formalized, abstracted into a series of signs—painted visage, a name, a character, a song. All this cacophony of motion, words, images, and music concludes with a spinning and shrinking collapse of the entire image into a black hole as the announcer's voice concludes, "All without commercial interruption." That was the ad, now here's the entertainment. But the entertainment is also an ad in a world where everyone is selling. Even as the actors impersonate the roles signified by characters' names, they personify complex figures in a tapestry depicting the relationships of public entertainment and social identity in mass culture.

The film's sequence of five days runs from Friday to Tuesday in a way that offers no explanation of how we get from everyone arriving at the Nashville airport to the assassination of Barbara Jean. Rather, each of the major sequences in the film repeats the constellation of images that informs the film's vision of the new entertainment capital of America. Each of the characters slowly comes into focus with their repeated revolution through its different venues. Says Altman, "Everybody was supposed to be representative of the music and the culture and what went on in Nashville in the seventies" (*Nashville*). Each of the actors and the roles they simultaneously impersonate and personify represents parallel or

5.2. Gwen Welles
performing pain in
Nashville.

divergent patterns: Gibson's sincere and sinister Haven, Garfield's controlling and organizing Barnett, Murphy's ingenuous and manipulative Triplette, Beattie's glad-handing toady Delbert, and Carradine's genuine and unscrupulous Tom are all sellers. The Vietnam vet, the would-be singer, the housewife, and the groupie are consumers. Mary, Connie, Sueleen, Barbara Jean, and Mr. Green are victims (figure 5.2). Opal, Wade, and the Tricycle Man are observers. Kenny, the assassin, is the innocent sojourner through Nashville who is caught up in and bewildered by its swirl of need, nurture, and violence.

Each venue in these five days also comes slowly into focus as a major aspect of the visual design constructed by the film. The airport connotes mobility. The freeway accident signifies chaos and violence. The hospital represents illness and death. Haven's party presents politics. The "picking parlors" contain seduction and humiliation, and the Opry provides entertainment. The Parthenon sequence sums up all these patterns but, no end, is just another point on this circulation of people and images. At the center of the revolving wheel is Sunday morning with its dramatic montage of worship, hymns, and a baptism. Critics at the time of the film's release argued about the problematic conclusion that failed to close the narrative, explain the three hours just experienced, or rationalize the multiple energies of the film. But the spinning ad at the beginning, the cycle of worship in the center, and the camera's final tilt up and long-held gaze into blue sky define the film as a modernist meditation.

According to Stuart, *Nashville* was born in the music, which won an Academy Award and which concludes the film on the sound track long after the credits have rolled. Keith Carradine had written "I'm Easy" and "It Don't Worry Me" earlier and sang them at a weekend party during Altman's production of *Thieves Like Us* (1974). Altman was "dazzled": "When I heard them I knew I wanted to build a whole movie around them, a movie that would simply give me an excuse to put them in" (37). The first of these songs is sung with a tender persuasion by the gentle Keith Carradine. He sings words of caring with a quiet earnestness that strikingly belies his other performance of Tom as a callous womanizer; his guileless and sincere singing signals both a compelling confession and a cynical seduction:

> Don't lead me on if there's nowhere for you to take me,
> If lovin' you would have to be a sometime thing.
> I can't put bars on my insides—my love is somethin' I
>   can't hide.
> It still hurts when I recall the times I've tried. . . .
> Give the word, I'll play your game
> As though that's how it ought to be
> Because I'm easy.

The song, its singer, its performance, and its results are full of irony, contradiction, and hypocrisy, as is the song that courses throughout the film as the hit on everybody's mind, on everybody's lips:

> Economy's depressed, not me.
> My spirit's high as it can be.
> And you might say that I ain't free
> But it don't worry me.

The last two lines are sung over and over again as the movie ends. They form the mantra of emotions that crack and strain across the text. They inform the acting, which is both naturalistic and expressive. They contain the patterned dichotomies of nurture and need, entertainment and death. They shape the film's design, which, in the words of Emily Dickinson, "revolves with a revolving wheel."

WORKS CONSULTED

Altman, Rick. *The American Film Musical*. Bloomington: Indiana UP, 1989.

———. "24-Track Narrative? Robert Altman's *Nashville*." *CiNéMAS: Journal of Film Studies* 1.3 (2000) <http://www.revue-cinemas.umon-treal.ca>.

Bradbury, Malcolm, and James McFarlane, eds. *Modernism, 1890–1930*. New York: Penguin, 1976.

Braudy, Leo. *The World in a Frame: What We See in Film*. Garden City: Anchor, 1976.

Bryne, Connie, and William Lopez. "*Nashville* (an Interview 'Documen-tary')." *Film Quarterly* 29 (winter 1975–76): 13–25.

Butler, Jeremy G., ed. *Star Texts: Image and Performance in Film and Television*. Detroit: Wayne State UP, 1991.

Caramello, Charles. *Silverless Mirrors: Book, Self, and Postmodern American Fiction*. Tallahassee: UP of Florida, 1973.

Delamater, Jerome. "Ritual, Realism, and Abstraction: Performance in the Musical." *Making Visible the Invisible: An Anthology of Original Essays in Film Acting*. Ed. Carole Zucker. Metchuen: Scarecrow, 1990. 44–63.

Dyer, Richard. *Stars*. Rev. ed. London: British Film Institute, 1998.

Ellman, Richard, and Charles Feidelson, Jr., eds. *The Modern Tradition: Backgrounds of Modern Literature*. New York: Oxford UP, 1965.

Faulkner, Peter. *Modernism*. London: Methuen, 1977.

Feuer, Jane. "The Self-Reflexive Musical and the Myth of Entertainment." *Genre: The Musical—A Reader*. Ed. Rick Altman. London: Routledge and Kegan Paul, 1981. 159–74.

Fletcher, James, and Malcolm Bradbury. "The Introverted Novel." *Modernism, 1890–1930*. New York: Penguin, 1976.

Frank, Joseph. "Spatial Form in Modern Literature." *The Widening Gyre: Crisis and Mastery in Modern Literature*. New Brunswick: Rutgers UP, 1963. 3–62.

Gaggi, Silvio. *Modern/Postmodern: A Study in Twentieth-Century Arts and Ideas*. Philadelphia: U of Pennsylvania P, 1989.

Higson, Andrew. "Film Acting and Independent Cinema." *Star Texts: Image and Performance in Film and Television*. Ed. Jeremy Butler. Detroit: Wayne State UP, 1991. 155–82.

Huyssen, Andreas. *After the Great Divide: Modernism, Mass Culture, Postmodernism*. Bloomington: Indiana UP, 1986.

Kiely, Robert, ed. *Modernism Reconsidered*. Cambridge: Harvard UP, 1983.

King, Barry. "Articulating Stardom." *Star Texts: Image and Performance in Film and Television*. Ed. Jeremy Butler. Detroit: Wayne State UP, 1991. 125–44.

Lovell, Alan, and Peter Krämer, eds. *Screen Acting*. London: Routledge, 1999.

McDonald, Paul. "Film Acting." *Film Studies: Critical Approaches*. Ed. John Hill and Pamela Church Gibson. New York: Oxford UP, 2000. 28–33.

Naremore, James. *Acting in the Cinema*. Berkeley: U of California P, 1988.

Self, Robert T. *Robert Altman's Subliminal Reality*. Minneapolis: U of Minnesota P, 2002.

Stuart, Jan. *The "Nashville" Chronicles: The Making of Robert Altman's Masterpiece*. New York: Simon and Schuster, 2000.

Tomlinson, Doug, ed. *Actors on Acting for the Screen: Roles and Collaborations*. New York: Garland, 1994.

Viertal, Jack, and David Walker. "The Long Road to Nashville." *New York Times* 13 June 1975: 56.

Wexman, Virginia Wright. "The Rhetoric of Cinematic Improvisation." *Cinema Journal* 20.1 (1980): 29–41.

Wicker, Tom. "*Nashville*: Dark Perceptions in a Country Music Comedy." *New York Times* 15 June 1975: 1+.

Yacowar, Maurice. "Actors as Conventions in the Films of Robert Altman." *Cinema Journal* 20.1 (1980): 14–28.

Zucker, Carole. *Making Visible the Invisible: An Anthology of Original Essays in Film Acting*. Metuchen: Scarecrow, 1990.

3

....

DEVELOPMENTS IN NEONATURALIST FILM PERFORMANCE

6

Playing with Performance
Directorial and Acting Style in John Cassavetes's *Opening Night*

Maria Viera

· ·

Two elements are always in play when dealing with John Cassavetes's work: (1) the impression of improvisation, although we know his films are not improvised; and (2) his "antifilmic" technical elements, which do not "construct" a performance on the screen but allow for one to take place before the camera. Cassavetes prefers that the filmic tools used to construct a performance in a given scene, such as camera angles, lighting, and camera movement, be used sparingly, only when necessary, with the performance always given top priority. It is not just a question of a long-take style that "records" a performance—Cassavetes does edit, although he rejects conventions such as the shot/reverse shot regime—but that he views film technique as something to keep out of the way of the performance. Thus the distinguishable performance style in his films emerges in the dynamic between his script, his shooting and editing style, and his work with his actors.

Cassavetes preferred to remain an independent director working outside the Hollywood system. Although he directed several films with traditional studio funding, the money he made as an actor allowed him to make eight films that were solely under his control.[1] Cassavetes was more interested in making art that expressed his personal worldview than in producing traditional Hollywood "product." The films that evince his rejection of Hollywood and the "realism" it offered therefore fit into the more modernist trajectory of Italian neorealism—with which he was familiar and with which he was impressed—and the European art film. Cassavetes's films also share certain characteristics with modernist works by the French New Wave directors—self-reflexivity, for example. However, unlike Jean-Luc Godard's ideologically motivated intervention, Cassavetes developed working methods distinct from Hollywood production processes in order to get to the characters, their situations, and the kind of performance style that personally interested him. Throughout his career, Cassavetes always emphasized that his films were not made to be easily understood. Like other artists working in the modernist tradition, he created a body of work that requires an active spectator working through such innovative, complex, and original material. To use Bertolt Brecht's neologism, Cassavetes was not interested in "culinary" theater that served up "its fare to be savored, tasted, gobbled up, and consumed [by] an audience that would have its palate tickled, titillated and satisfied" (qtd. in Ewen 201).[2] Cassavetes thus anticipated Robert Altman's statement: "I don't know how to make a film for fourteen-year-olds" (qtd. in Gritten).

At the same time, Cassavetes's work, with its radical departure from more pictorially oriented styles, comes out of a strong artistic sensibility that aligns itself with naturalism. Although his characters are quirky and often on the edge, if not "under the influence," they come from everyday life. They live in specific social environments and their actions are a consequence of their personal histories and environmental forces. As with other tendencies associated with naturalism, Cassavetes's characters, as performed by his actors, often cannot express or even understand the situation in which they find themselves. Like real people making their way through concrete but continually changing social situations, they improvise as they go along.[3]

Often shooting in his own house over a long period of time, Cassavetes created a working environment that is similar to that developed by Konstantin Stanislavsky early in his career. In selected productions he directed for the Moscow Art Theater, Stanislavsky insisted that the set and lighting should be used for their effects on the actors rather than for impressing audiences. Likewise, Cassavetes was not distracted by concerns about how the film looked pictorially or with elaborate set or lighting design. His focus, in the tradition of naturalism, was on the characters and how they might behave in the situations in which he placed them (figure 6.1).

At first glance, Opening Night (1977) may seem a strange choice to illustrate Cassavetes's naturalistic tendencies and to use

6.1. John Cassavetes supervises a scene in *Opening Night.* (Courtesy of Ray Carney and www.Cassavetes.com)

as an example of how he is part of a reemerging naturalism in mid-twentieth-century cinema. The reason is that *Opening Night* includes two "nonrealistic" elements that are deviations from the usual Cassavetes style. The first appears after the prologue of the play in its tryout in New Haven. The sequence shows the main character, Myrtle Gordon (or is it the actress Gena Rowlands, who plays the role?) from behind, in a flowing evening gown with large sleeves of pleated nylon producing a winglike effect, superimposed over an applauding audience. This image is a visual metaphor for Myrtle's (and by implication, all actors') most basic desire: to be loved. The film's second "nonrealistic" element is the "vision" of Nancy Stein (the ghost, the other woman, the younger Myrtle—played by Laura Johnson), which we actually see in shots with Myrtle, although none of the other characters see her. Needless to say, a ghost is not a standard element in naturalism. However, Cassavetes did not intend the "ghost" to be taken as a possible apparition. As the director explained: "This is a figment of [Myrtle's] imagination, it's not a fantasy, it's something that's controllable by her" (Carney, *Cassavetes on Cassavetes* 410).

In spite of these nonrealistic elements, *Opening Night* is the film par excellence to use to discuss Cassavetes's naturalistic tendencies precisely because its characters are so completely defined by their theatrical world. *Opening Night* is thus a naturalistic film about theatricality, about acting, about "putting on a performance," both literally and figuratively. As Raymond Williams explains, "In high naturalism, the lives of the characters have soaked into their environment [and] moreover, the environment has soaked into their lives" (qtd. in Innes 5). *Opening Night* is a film about a play with players who are playing with their performances in life as well as on the stage.

Scripting

Ray Carney's excavational work in *Cassavetes on Cassavetes* outlines the determinants at play in the genesis of the *Opening Night* script.[4] These include Cassavetes's interest in doing a "backstage drama" because of his admiration of *All about Eve* and his discussions with Barbra Streisand about the possibility of directing *A Star Is Born*. Cassavetes was also interested in exploring material from his and Rowlands's lives, especially what their lives would have been like if they had never met. Rowlands might have ended up becoming like Myrtle, devoting her life to the theater without marriage or family. Cassavetes might have become the cynical but charming user, Maurice Adams, he played in *Opening Night*. In addition, both Cassavetes and Rowlands were now in their late forties and although Cassavetes had explored the theme of women and aging in earlier films, this theme had become more immediate and more personal. Cassavetes said the script for *Opening Night* began with the idea of exploring "people's reactions when they start getting old; how to win when you're not as desirable as you were, when you don't have as much confidence in yourself, in your capacities" (Carney, *Cassavetes on Cassavetes* 409).

In developing the script, Cassavetes followed a naturalistic stratagem—the "scientific observation" of external physical existence—looking at people in their environments. According to Carney, Cassavetes did his "research" by speaking with Sam Shaw's wife on the phone almost every night for a year. He spent time with Rowlands, her mother, and his own mother—absorbing their conversations. In an interview with Bo Harwood, who composed the music for *Opening Night*, Carney reveals that Cassavetes acted out his characters while working on his scripts. He would "come into the office 'as Myrtle'—trying out her lines for the script, doing her tones, experimenting with gestures to see what they felt like" (*Cassavetes on Cassavetes* 408). Cassavetes explains that "you can't do this kind of exploration through film techniques. You have to write and write and write."

Another part of the process Cassavetes used to develop *Opening Night* involved looking back at the experiences of his friends and colleagues. He worked this material into the film "to show the life of an artist, of a creator" (Carney, *Cassavetes on Cassavetes* 409). In *Opening Night*, Cassavetes's characters are "theater people" in their specialized environment—a theater company putting on a play. The characters are all defined by their relationship to the production. Myrtle Gordon (Gena Rowlands) is an actress. Maurice Adams (Cassavetes) is an actor. Manny Victor (Ben Gazzara) is the director. Dorothy Victor (Zohra Lambert) is the director's wife. Sarah Goode (Joan Blondell) is the playwright. David Samuels (Paul Stewart) is the producer. Nancy Stein (Laura Johnson) is a fan. Yet Cassavetes extends the idea of theatricality beyond those who work in the theater. He explains that "*Opening Night* was about the sense of theatricality in all of us and how it can take us over, how we can appear to be totally wrong on some little point, and never know what little point we're going to fight for" (Carney, *Cassavetes on Cassavetes* 415).

The script of *Opening Night* exhibits a defining aspect of naturalism, the primacy of character—characters in a situation, characters in a specific environment. The film is not plotted in the conventional sense. It does not follow a three-act structure with mandatory plot points. There is barely a denouement in the Aristotelian sense. Myrtle arrives just in time to the opening night performance, with the rest of the company thinking they will have to cancel the show. She is drunk and struggles to make her way through the scenes but there is no triumph. Cassavetes explains: "In the end, she doesn't even get anything. She only gets what makes her happy" (Carney, *Cassavetes on Cassavetes* 413).

Cassavetes works purposely against classical Hollywood narrative structure. He says: "Now, all my leanings are *anti*-plot point. I *hate* plot points! I don't like focusing on plot because I think the audiences don't consist of only thirteen-year-old kids and also that each person you see in life has more to them than would meet the eye" (Carney, *Cassavetes on Cassavetes* 419). Indeed, the scenes in *Opening Night* can be seen as a series of "improv exercises." Yet they are not improv scenes that the actors are actually improvising. Instead, they reflect the writing of Cassavetes, who has structured the script into a series of improv situations that create a space for the actors and characters to interact.

In *Opening Night*, Cassavetes's psychologically and socially revealing improv situations ostensibly integrate two important traditions in contemporary acting. These improv situations can be linked to the Method acting techniques developed by Lee Strasberg at the Actors Studio in New York. Such improvisations were designed to help Method performers achieve emotional truth, with the idea being that acting "as if" one had become a specific character in a specific situation or environment would gradually reveal the character's reactions and inner conflicts.

Yet because the situations in Cassavetes's film also serve to reveal recognizable social types, they can be compared to Viola Spolin's theater game exercises that Second City players in Chicago used as a foundation for their improvisational performances. As Virginia Wright Wexman points out, "Spolin's notion of improvisation as a group-oriented game built around a predetermined structure (or story) originated with commedia dell'arte and had little to do with the Method's emphasis on affective memory" (186). Spolin was more interested in social dynamics; her theater games were designed to foster effective "group response in which players see themselves as an organic part of the whole, becoming one body through which all are directly involved in the outcome of the playing" (Spolin xv).[5]

The improv situations in *Opening Night* gradually reveal inner conflicts. They also create circumstances for Cassavetes's players to see themselves as "an organic part of the whole." For example, Ben Gazzara and Zohra Lambert are assigned the parts of an older husband, Manny, with a younger wife, Dorothy. They are told: A husband and wife are having an intimate conversation (plus drinking) at 4:30 in the morning. He is a theater director. She is his younger, totally dependent, stay-at-home wife. The phone rings and it is his leading actress desperately in need of reassurance. He must declare his love and admiration for her while being sensitive to his wife's presence. His wife tries to playfully distract him from the conversation, but she knows that his livelihood, as well as hers, depends on his ability to deal with the actress.

In a second example from *Opening Night* , Meade Roberts and Eleanor Zee are assigned the part of the parents, Eddie and Sylvia Stein, who are grieving over the loss of their seventeen-year-old daughter, Nancy (Laura Johnson). A third character is an actress, Myrtle Gordon (Gena Rowlands), who visits their home. The actors are given the following situation: The actress arrives at the home of a young girl who was hit by a car and killed. The actress is not invited but wants to express her condolences. The family knows that it was she the young girl was trying to see when the car struck her. The parents reject the actress and want her to leave.

These are, of course, examples of "characters in situations" from *Opening Night* but they could just as easily be improvisation exercises in a Method acting class or a Second City performance. The idea in such an improvisational exercise would be to see how the characters would react in those given situations.

In the scripting process, Cassavetes seems to have developed his characters as he placed them in environments that would help explicate his themes, themes that are based on "characters in situations" that reveal psychological and social truths. Cassavetes himself struggled with the complexity of the modern human condition—in fact, he seems to have taken great pleasure in exploring the struggle and finding a way to portray daily life and the concerns that he and his audiences shared. He seems to have worked from the premise that the situations, problems, and issues with which he struggled were of interest to modern viewers because of an undeniable shared experience.

Cassavetes's films are never reducible to one theme, nor are his characters reducible to one goal or desire that moves the action forward. Instead, a film such as *Opening Night* works through a complex problematic of related themes. For example, the film explores the various ways to be loved. Myrtle is loved by the public and (often falsely) by the theatrical company. The film also deals with the nature of physical love and the question of how one can be loved when one no longer possesses sexual appeal. How can an older career woman without children and without a husband be loved? Both Maurice and Manny tell Myrtle that she "doesn't turn them on anymore." This theme is complicated by Maurice (Cassavetes), David Samuels (Stewart), and Manny Victor (Gazzara), who at various times throughout the film all mention that affairs with younger women do not work for them anymore.

Directing

Unique to John Cassavetes's directing style is his rejection of standard Hollywood filmmaking techniques and his commitment to procedures that would free his actors from the constraints that he, as a professional television and film actor, felt worked against the type of performance style that interested him. The combination of his screenwriting and shooting methods leads to a performance style that is not only consistent among his various actors but is the defining characteristic of a Cassavetes film. The performances in *Opening Night* are grounded in a conception of character that shows the influence of both the naturalist and the modernist traditions: the characters are shaped by their specific social environments, yet those environments are the source of fragmented, indeterminate psychological and social identities. The film's modernist view of identity reveals Cassavetes's opposition to the nineteenth-century "romantic" conceptions of character that served as the foundation for "realistic" performances in classical Hollywood cinema. Thus the director's concern with the consequences of social realities confirms that opposition and discloses his attempt to forge a new kind of naturalism, a neonaturalism suited to a modern context.

Opening Night was shot over a five-month period from November 1976 to March 1977, and it was completely financed by Cassavetes himself. (Indeed, he had to take time off in February for an acting job in a TV pilot to make money to complete the film.) He used three main locations: the Lindy Opera House, the Pasadena Civic Auditorium, and the Green Hotel. He believed in shooting on location for artistic reasons, but he also could not afford to build sets in a studio for the films he financed himself.

The three main locations for *Opening Night* were quite extravagant compared to locations used in his earlier self-financed films. He shot the séance scene in *Opening Night* in his own home, which he had used in earlier films such as *A Woman under the Influence* (1974). *Opening Night* was a much larger production with a larger budget (about $1.5 million) than that of his previous self-financed films (Carney, *Cassavetes on Cassavetes* 413–16). Perhaps reflecting that higher budget, the movie has more elaborate production values than his earlier films and more sophisticated camera work in many scenes. Cassavetes does, however, continue to use the handheld camera in various scenes, such as the one between Myrtle and a psychic, in which Myrtle "kills" her vision of the young girl.

Cassavetes developed various methods of working with performers that modified the roles of director and actor. Some of these techniques were designed to free actors from restricted responses and help them "focus on the actual field [in which] the playing (energy exchange) takes place between players." To allow actors to "get beyond the [inhibiting] need for approval and disapproval" (Spolin xv), Cassavetes purposely kept his interpretation of the script from them. He refused to dictate line readings. He felt that if they were given a complete interpretation of the entire narrative in advance it might "simplify" their performance. Joan Blondell, who plays Sarah Goode, said that Cassavetes did not tell her what her character's reaction to the final Maurice-Myrtle "improvisation" on the stage was to be (Carney, *Cassavetes on Cassavetes* 424). The ambiguity at the end of *Opening Night* is so strong that, as Carney points out, even Rowlands and Cassavetes did not agree about whether the final play-within-a-play showed Myrtle's defeat or her victory (424).

Cassavetes shot a tremendous amount of footage for *Opening Night* to capture his players' unorthodox and complex performances—such as those small, subtle expressions that sweep for a split second over Rowlands's face as she moves from subtext to subtext. The director shot much more coverage than those working with him thought necessary. The ample footage would, of course, afford him the possibility of rescripting and reworking the film during postproduction, which he did extensively (Carney, *Cassavetes on Cassavetes* 421).

Cassavetes also used directorial methods to elicit fresh, offbeat performances and avoid overrehearsed or "canned" scenes. Cassavetes used shooting techniques that kept the performances edgy and unpredictable. He did not approach directing by working toward the "perfect" picture or the "perfect" line reading. Instead, using an approach closely linked to Method principles, Cassavetes sometimes kept the camera running between takes, shooting several takes one after another, a procedure that puts pressure on the actor, a sort of driving force that keeps him or her insecure and off balance. Like Elia Kazan and others who have used directorial strategies associated with Method acting, Cassavetes would often introduce last-minute changes, either in dialogue or in action, to scenes that had been rehearsed. In a two-person dialogue scene, for instance, he would give instructions or line changes to one of the actors without telling the other (Carney, *Cassavetes Cassavetes* 418–24, 436). All of these disparate methods helped the director capture a spontaneous, unrehearsed quality in the performances that increased the sense of naturalism found in his films.

Performance Style

In the script for *Opening Night* , Cassavetes wrote highly individualized characters who become completely realized people through his directing. They are "modern characters" as August Strindberg defined them in his preface to *Miss Julie* (qtd. in Jacobus 762–63) because they exhibit the "ambiguity of motive" that Strindberg describes. Beginning with his initial work at the Moscow Theater, Stanislavsky explored and developed methods for training actors and creating performances that would convey the complex experiences of "modern characters." The performances in *Opening Night* suggest a committed attempt to embody the principles of acting that Stanislavsky formulated early in his career: to play truthfully, to create the life of a human soul, to live your part internally, and then to give that experience an external embodiment. The film's performances evince many of the objectives articulated in *An Actor Prepares*, the text that introduced American readers to Stanislavsky's early theories on acting, albeit in an abridged and somewhat distorted form. For example, the clearly etched acting styles in *Opening Night* reflect the position: "An actor must learn to recognize quality, to avoid the useless, and to choose essentially right objectives" (112). They are evidence of Cassavetes's view that portrayals of modern characters should "be real, live and human, not dead [or] conventional" (Innes 57).

Examining the performances in *Opening Night* in light of passages from *An Actor Prepares* helps to illuminate Cassavetes's borrowings from naturalist and modernist traditions. The text outlines Stanislavsky's ideas about the "super-objective" (the "through line" of action), explaining that "all the minor lines are headed toward the same goal and fuse into one main current" (261). It describes what happens when an actor has not established his or her ultimate purpose and illustrates what the line looks like if the smaller lines lead in various directions. "If all the minor objectives in a part are aimed in different directions it is, of course, impossible to form a solid, unbroken line. Consequently the action is fragmentary, uncoordinated, unrelated to any whole" (261). This observation is an uncannily accurate description of an actor playing a Cassavetes character, especially in *Opening Night*.

Cassavetes gets his unique style of performance from his actors by creating double, and sometimes triple, subtexts played out simultaneously. In theatrical practice, the term *subtext* is used for what is not being said, what lies under the dialogue. As Robert Benedetti explains: "When there is an obstacle to direct action, the character may choose an *indirect* action; we call these hidden intentions *subtext*" (152). For example, there are many variations on a line reading, depending on which subtext the actor is working. One of the goals in rehearsal is to find the subtext that best works for a given scene. The character may hide the subtext beneath the dialogue either for external or internal reasons, and the character may be either conscious or unconscious of the subtext. The actor is not supposed to play the subtext (that is, the audience should not be aware of it), but rather be able to deduce it (Benedetti 149). Describing the way "realistic" productions require acting that makes the characters' intentions easily intelligible, *An Actor Prepares* explains: "The whole stream of individual, minor objectives, all the imaginative thoughts, feelings, and actions of an actor, should converge to carry out the super-objective of the plot" (256).

Hollywood "realism" often requires actors to play one specific subtext at a time in order to achieve the clarity of intention that Stanislavsky describes. In contrast, Cassavetes's neonaturalistic approach does not seek this clarity of intention—either through his dialogue or through the performances he elicits from his actors. The basic actions and reactions of his characters come from multiple and often divergent subtexts that play out simultaneously.

For example, early on in *Opening Night*, Myrtle (Rowlands) leaves the theater and is mobbed by fans. One young woman in particular pursues her and runs alongside the limousine as it takes the theater group to a restaurant. The young woman, Nancy Stein, is hit by another car. Myrtle is upset and has the limousine stop at her hotel. Maurice escorts her up to her apartment as the others wait in the limo. Myrtle is rattled and fixes herself a drink.

> **Myrtle**: Don't be distant, Maurice. Come on and have a drink.
> **Maurice**: I'm hungry. There are people waiting downstairs in the car.
> **Myrtle**: What's the matter with us? We lose sight of everything. There's a girl killed tonight. All we can think about is dinner.
> **Maurice**: I gotta go.
> *Myrtle walks over to him and—in a way that suggests past intimacies and present passion—kisses him. Maurice pulls back.*
> **Maurice**: (*shaking his head no*) You're not a woman to me anymore. You're a professional. You don't care about anything. You don't care about personal relationships, love, sex, affection.
> **Myrtle**: Okay.
> **Maurice**: I have a small part. It's unsympathetic. The audience doesn't like me. I can't afford to be in love with you.
> **Myrtle**: Good night.
> **Maurice**: Yeah, good night.
> *He leaves. Myrtle pours herself a drink and with a cigarette jutting out of her mouth walks with what is presumably her script into the bedroom. She almost breaks into tears for a moment.*[6]

Myrtle's character spine for this scene is to get away from the others, to sort out her feelings about the girl hit by the car, and to test her ability, as presumably she has in the past, to seduce Maurice.

Her double subtext is to get Maurice to want her so as to ease the pain of the death of the young girl and to test her sexual powers to see if she can still seduce Maurice—two very complex subtexts to be performed at the same time. When he does not respond, she gives up with a meek "okay," but with a double subtext: I want to save face and I just wanted to try, but I really do not care much anyway. A superficial reading of the scene would see Myrtle as an eccentric (or crazy) woman "under the influence," based on her erratic and strange behavior. If her intentions were diagrammed, as per Stanislavsky's through line, the small lines making up the super-objective would lead in varying directions. Rowlands's creation of Myrtle comes out of the difficult, complex, and varying subtexts that she must play at the same time. As with the character, Rowlands may not be aware of them all, but the performance approved by Cassavetes as director contains them.

All of the main players in *Opening Night* have to portray characters that deal with a multiplicity of subtexts. The performances in the following scene reveal the highly complex subtextual work going on. This scene follows closely after the preceding scene between Myrtle and Maurice and is, in a way, even more complex and enigmatic. Manny and Dorothy Victor are together in their hotel room. It is 4:30 in the morning.

> **Manny**: I need your help. . . . [*unintelligible*] But I'm going to go crazy if you don't tell me what it's like to be alone as a woman. What do you do? Okay, that's it. Will you make me another drink, please?
> **Dorothy**: Sure.
> **Manny**: I'm going to get drunk.
> **Dorothy**: Ah . . .
> **Manny**: Eh, if you want to get hostile, you go ahead. My goddamn life depends on this play. And you should go to all the rehearsals. You should watch everything. You should sit with Myrtle. Fill her in on yourself and be part of it.
> **Dorothy**: Do I get paid for this?
> **Manny**: If you understudy, I'll pay you.

The irony of the word "understudy" sinks in. Dorothy fools around as if she is considering the offer. They laugh.

> **Manny**: That's right. 'Cause, I tell you, my life is getting boring. I'm getting somber. My own tricks bore me.
> **Dorothy**: Do you want ice?
> **Manny**: Yeah. There's no humor anymore and all the glamour's dead.

> You notice that? I can't even stand how they come to rehearsal. They come to rehearsal dressed in terrible clothes.
> **Dorothy**: Manny, I'm dying. I'm dying. I know I'm dying because I'm getting tired. It's always the same. You talk. I sleep. If I'd known what a boring man you were when I married you, I wouldn't have gone through all those emotional crises.

She means it, but she doesn't mean it, but she really does mean it. He pours her a drink. They awkwardly try to embrace. Just as they get it right, the phone rings. He leaves to answer it.

If given this text to direct, one could come up with several plausible intentions for the actors. Manny wants to get drunk, wants to share his pain with his wife, or wants to communicate with her. Dorothy wants to get along with her husband or wants to connect with him to ease her loneliness. The point is there are very workable intentions in the text for these two characters. These or similar intentions may have been used by Lambert and Gazzara in the development of this part of the scene.

One can, of course, never know what process Cassavetes and his actors used to develop the performances in this scene, but the result is totally unexpected from what the text indicates. The result violates all conventional wisdom on performance. The actors do not give the characters a clear intention. We do not know what they want. They seem needy, but we do not know what they need. There is no clear goal that moves the action forward. One cannot deduce the subtext of these two characters. Whatever subtext the actors are playing, it does not seem to match the text. As the actors play what appear to be multiple subtexts at all times, although we do not know exactly what these subtexts are, we get two highly original, deeply complex performances that show two human beings in some kind of state of pain, boredom, and passivity who are unable to communicate.

Much of the multiplicity or ambiguity of motivation is conveyed through the actors' gestures and physicality. For example, Lambert's strangely graceful body goes "in all directions at once," materially expressing the idea that Dorothy means it, but she doesn't mean it, but she really does mean it, but she doesn't care anyway. Some of the "ambiguity of motive" featured in the film's performances may come from Cassavetes's choice to have the actors play a subtext or, more likely, several subtexts that do not correspond in the expected way to his written text. What is clear is that this is exactly the style of performance Cassavetes was trying to achieve because he thought it closer to how modern people "really" behave.

The scene continues. Manny picks up the phone in the bedroom.

> **Manny**: Hello. Oh, Myrtle. No, sweetheart, I'm still up. I'm sorry you're not feeling well. You have a fever? What? What girl? The young girl got killed in front of the theater tonight. Alright, sweetheart.
> **Dorothy**: It's 4:30 in the morning.
> **Manny**: Yes, I know it's lonely. I hate out of town, too. Of course, I love you. Hold it, will you please. It's nothing. It's just my wife. Right. Of course, I'll leave the phone on. Yeah. She doesn't mind at all.
> **Dorothy**: Tell her you'll talk to her in the morning.
> **Manny**: I don't sleep anyway.
> **Dorothy**: You'll see her in the morning.
> **Manny**: (*to Myrtle*) Right.
> **Dorothy**: Right.
> **Manny**: (*to Myrtle*) Right. There's no one I love more than you this moment. You know I love you. What? Yes, sweetheart. Okay. Well, what's wrong with being slapped. (*to Dorothy, who distracts him*) Cut it out. (*to Myrtle*) Just a second. (*to Dorothy*) Cut it out, will you please? (*to Myrtle*) There is nothing humiliating about it. You're on the stage for crissake. He's not slapping you for real. Myrtle. Ah, Myrtle. Myrtle. It has nothing to do with being a woman. Now, you're not a woman, anyway. No, no, you're a beautiful woman. I was kidding. And you see, you have no sense of humor. I told you that. I don't want to argue with it, darling. We'll rehearse it. Well, how . . . If we don't rehearse it, we won't get it. But it's not humiliating. It's a tradition. Actresses get slapped. It's a tradition. You want to be a star. You want to be unsympathetic? It's mandatory you get hit. That's it. Now go to sleep.
> *He hangs up the phone.*
> **Manny**: A young girl got killed by the theater tonight.

We cut to the rehearsal scene where Myrtle gets slapped. During Manny's phone conversation, Dorothy dances into the room, daintily holding her robe out as if it were a ball gown. She does a classical ballet step, moving to him as he sits at the top of the bed. She jumps on the bed and pretends to swim on her back. She goes into a pretend boxing match, catches one of her blows on her chin and falls back, rolling off the bed onto the floor. She leaves the room.

In this part of the scene, Manny has three goals: (1) he wants to soothe and comfort Myrtle so she will behave at the rehearsal the next day; (2) he wants to assure his wife that he loves her; and (3) he wants to test his ability to control Myrtle. Along with these three subtexts, which Manny/Gazzara plays simultaneously, he is also testing his sexual powers and past attraction to Myrtle, with whom he presumably has had an affair. He wants to really assure her so she will continue in the role, but at the same time that he reassures her of his "undying devotion," he is playing with her and even making fun of himself to himself. In addition to all this, Gazzara's performance adds to the main theme of boredom and ennui. This theme is carried mainly by the dialogue, but we also see it in Manny's posture, unvoiced sighs, and facial expressions. Manny has done it all before.

During this scene, Zohra Lambert, as Dorothy, plays various objectives: (1) to get Manny's attention; (2) to show she has a place in the world (she matters); and (3) to do this without really demanding his attention since his livelihood (and hers) depend on his ability to handle Myrtle. Dorothy/Lambert also contributes to a larger theme in the film, boredom, at the same time that she shows that her character is someone who stands outside the emotional machinations of life. Dorothy lives on the perimeter. When Lambert dances, pantomimes, and horses around by falling off the bed, she not only reveals Dorothy's character as a meek nonparticipant—as an observer outside the main action of her husband's life—but she also reveals her need to hold Manny's attention as he soothes the extravagant Myrtle. She cares, but she really doesn't care. Even though she has little dialogue, Dorothy's "ambiguity of motive" is vividly expressed by Lambert's gestures and movements.

In a later scene, when Myrtle storms out of the theater with Sarah (Joan Blondell) chasing her, Dorothy stands in the background, against the wall, out of the situation, unobserved, unnoticed, withdrawn from the Sturm und Drang of Myrtle's emotional roller-coaster ride. Dorothy carries the traits of the nonparticipant, a recurring minor character found in many Cassavetes films. She is one of several characters throughout his films who insulate themselves from "the perils of emotional exploration" (Carney, *Films of John Cassavetes* 240).[7]

Many of Cassavetes's characters are inarticulate, only able to express themselves in fits and starts. Cassavetes finds ways and opportunities for these characters, such as Dorothy, to be revealed through physicality because the very nature of their characters makes words less appropriate. However, just as the dialogue of the characters has various subtexts at work under it, so do their movements and gestures. The facial expressions, gestures, and movements of Cassavetes's actors can be as expressive and complex as the intonations and rhythms of the lines of dialogue they speak. For example, when Myrtle sits at the table at the séance, her body movement and gestures, especially the way she smokes her cigarette in defiance, tell us that she will not participate. She is cornered, trapped, and ready "to jump out of her skin." Here, Cassavetes's strategy of using multiple subtexts simultaneously works with and without words.

Playing with Performance

At the end of the film, Myrtle arrives at the theater falling-down drunk and proceeds to work her way through the opening night performance. Gradually sobering up, she gains control of herself by the final scene of the play. As Maurice passes by her backstage to make his entrance, she says, "I'll bury him," and when she goes on stage, Myrtle forces the scene into an improvisation that Maurice must pick up on. Rowlands and Cassavetes thus portray two actors in a play performing an improv in a "theatrical" acting style—rather hammy and playing to the audience. We are very aware of the skill Rowlands and Cassavetes have to move from a naturalistic performance style to a more theatrical one. The improv answers one of the film's major dramatic questions—what gives meaning to life? The answer is: all there is, is love—or, said another way, love may be all there is. By showing us the various reactions Sarah, David, and Manny have to the improv, the scene also makes the point that "the lines" characters/people say are not all that important. Even more important, the scene implies that the best (and perhaps the only) way to get through modern life is to improvise as we make the best of what we can.

As if to underscore that idea, the final scene in the film is shot in documentary style with people coming backstage for the opening night reception. Here the distinction between the "real" and the "filmic real" breaks down entirely, especially with the appearance of Seymour Cassel and Peter Falk, longtime associates of Cassavetes. The last line of the film has Manny introducing Peter Bogdanovich, as himself, to Dorothy: "Do you know Peter Bogdanovich?"

Cassavetes is again playing here, as he has throughout the film. As Carney points out, Cassavetes sought to move beyond the working methods of Lee Strasberg's Actors Studio, calling their process "organized introversion" (*Cassavetes on Cassavetes* 52). Like Viola Spolin and Bertolt Brecht, who at the end of his career moved away from his didactic "epic" theater to a freer, more playful approach, Cassavetes came to believe that acting should be fun and playful, not the serious, laborious work he attributed to the Actors Studio. As Carney says, "In Strasberg's vision, the theater was a church; in Cassavetes's it was a playground" (53).

Conclusion

Modernist tendencies bear on the whole of Cassavetes's directorial enterprise. Though highly idiosyncratic, his films nevertheless present characters that can be understood as belonging to a naturalistic trend in modern American cinema. Cassavetes's uniquely defined characters struggle with challenges emblematic of certain contemporary social realities. The performance style he develops with his actors is a reaction to and a departure from performance styles that belong to classic Hollywood cinema. By breaking with the conventions of Hollywood "realism," Cassavetes's actors create performances that are infused with an off-balance spontaneity that cannot be expressed in "perfect" frame compositions and "Hollywood movie dialogue."[8]

His directorial choices in terms of the technical aspects of his films are marked by a self-consciousness and by a simplicity and functionalism designed to disrupt the "realist" conventions of classical Hollywood cinema. It was not only that Cassavetes could not afford the Hollywood methods of filmmaking (and he could not), but that he saw the studio process as an obstacle to the kind of performances he wanted. He describes the Hollywood set from the point of view of the actor and then adds: "And a different kind of acting is born of that, and that is a professionalism, a professional . . . kind of acting, which all actors have done" (Carney, *Cassavetes on Cassavetes* 44). Cassavetes wanted to find another way of making films and to do that he had to eliminate the "pictorially perfected" shot, the "auditorally perfected" sound track, and the shooting techniques used to create them.[9] Thus the self-reflexive aspects of his filmmaking techniques arise from issues of functionality, not from a political agenda.

Christopher Innes argues that naturalism, as a historical style in theater, introduced "a quintessentially modern approach, and defined the qualities of modern drama" (1). Since the terms *naturalism* and *realism* are particularly ambiguous, Innes suggests that both need to be understood as applying to the historical movement as a whole.[10] However, he locates a "subtle distinction" that he believes adds to a "greater critical precision" (6). Innes explains that "it would be logical to use 'Naturalism' to refer to the theoretical basis shared by all the dramatists who formed the movement, and their approach to representing the world. 'Realism' could then apply to the intended effect, and the stage techniques associated with it." This distinction allows both terms to be used for the same text, "with each term describing a different aspect of the work" (6).

Applying this distinction to film, we see that Cassavetes's movies are "realistic" in terms of their intended effect, but that they do not follow the techniques and conventions that comprise classical Hollywood realism. Cassavetes shares the theoretical basis of theatrical naturalism because he is committed to exploring characters in situations. He is not interested merely in the psychological conflicts of a character. Instead, he frames character reactions to given situations in ways that reveal the dynamic interaction between individual psychology and social circumstance. What is uniquely original about the performance style in a Cassavetes film and what makes watching a Cassavetes film a consistently demanding but exhilarating experience is the sense that we are in the presence of an artist who is completely uncompromising as he reworks naturalism in a modern context.

NOTES

1. I use "Cassavetes films" to refer only to the eight films over which he had complete control: *Shadows* (1959), *Faces* (16mm in 1965, 35mm in 1968), *Husbands* (1970), *Minnie and Moskowitz* (1971), *A Woman under the Influence* (1974), *The Killing of a Chinese Bookie* (1976 and 1978), *Opening Night* (1977), and *Love Streams* (1984).

2. Brecht's first detailed treatment of epic theater appears in a 1930 essay, "Notes to the Opera," which attacked "the old 'culinary' form of grand opera" (Wilbern 67). It was published shortly after the Leipzig premiere of *The Rise and Fall of the City of Mahagony*, an opera Brecht created with Kurt Weill that adopted the basic attitude of traditional opera but began to challenge "the society that need[ed] operas of that sort" (Willett 157).

3. This is a major theme in Ray Carney's extensive work on Cassavetes and appears in various places, such as Carney's *American Dreaming: The Films of John Cassavetes and the American Experience*.

4. In *Cassavetes on Cassavetes*, Ray Carney reiterates numerous examples of material in *Opening Night* that come directly from Cassavetes's and Rowlands's professional experiences. Ray Carney spent

eleven years compiling all possible material from interviews with Cassavetes. He then edited, structured, and wrote invaluable explanations making sense of this extensive amount of research. This effort culminated in *Cassavetes on Cassavetes*, a book Carney calls the autobiography Cassavetes would have written. Carney once and for all clears up innumerable questions and ambiguities about Cassavetes that the filmmaker-actor himself had propagated. The book provides deeply rich insights into Cassavetes as a person and as an artist. A valuable source is Carney's Web site: www.Cassavetes.com.

5. John Cassavetes was acquainted with Strasberg's and Spolin's use of improvisation. In the late 1950s, Cassavetes and Burt Lane formed an acting workshop that explored methods similar to Viola Spolin's theater games, which had their first professional application in 1956 at the Compass Theater. Differentiating their approach from the Method Strasberg developed at the Actors Studio, Burns explains: "In focusing on core emotions, [the Method] removed the masks of the characters and deprived them of personalities. In real life, we rarely act directly from our emotions. Feeling is simply the first link in a chain. It is followed by an adjustment of the individual to the situation and to the other people involved in it, and this in turn leads to the projection of an attitude which initiates the involvement with other persons" (qtd. in Carney, *Cassavetes on Cassavetes* 53).

In addition, the year before Cassavetes produced *Opening Night*, he worked with Second City alumnae Elaine May. Virginia Wright Wexman discusses the difficulty of bringing Second City's audience-interactive performance style into a film production context. She notes that May's *Mikey and Nicky* (1976), "starring Peter Falk and Method-influenced John Cassavetes, made extensive use of improvisation but that the effect was closer to" the psychological studies favored by Strasberg than to the satirical social observation found in Second City's skits (189).

6. Quotations from *Opening Night* are my transcriptions.

7. Carney cites examples of this recurring character type in other Cassavetes films in his discussion of *Love Streams* in *The Films of John Cassavetes*, 235–70.

8. See Berliner for a useful analysis of Cassavetes's dialogue.

9. It would have been interesting to see John Cassavetes's reaction to Mike Leigh's work as well as to the films of Dogma 95. One also wonders what Cassavetes might have done with the digital video systems now available.

10. Raymond Williams, among many others, has tackled the ambiguity between naturalism and realism.

Works Cited

Benedetti, Robert. *The Actor at Work*. 8th ed. Boston: Allyn and Bacon, 2001.

Berliner, Todd. "Hollywood Movie Dialogue and the 'Real Realism' of John Cassavetes." *Film Quarterly* 52.3 (1999): 2–16.

Carney, Ray. *American Dreaming: The Films of John Cassavetes and the American Experience*. Berkeley: U of California P, 1985.

———. *Cassavetes on Cassavetes* . London: Faber and Faber, 2001.

———. *The Films of John Cassavetes: Pragmatism, Modernism, and the Movies*. Cambridge: Cambridge UP, 1994.

Ewen, Fredric. *Bertolt Brecht*. New York: Citadel, 1967.

Gritten, David. "Names Upstairs and Down." *Los Angeles Times Calendar* 4 Nov. 2001: 73.

Innes, Christopher. *A Sourcebook on Naturalist Theater*. London: Routledge, 2000.

Jacobus, Lee A. *The Bedford Introduction to Drama*. 4th ed. Boston: Bedford/St. Martin's, 2001.

Spolin, Viola. *Improvisation for the Theater*. Evanston: Northwestern UP, 1983.

Stanislavsky, Konstantin. *An Actor Prepares*. Trans. Elizabeth Hapgood. New York: Theater Arts, 1936.

Wexman, Virginia Wright. *Creating the Couple: Love, Marriage, and Hollywood Performance*. Princeton: Princeton UP, 1993.

Wilbern, Julian H. *Brecht and Ionesco: Commitment in Context*. Chicago: U of Illinois P, 1971.

Willett, John. *Brecht in Context*. New York: Methuen, 1984.

Williams, Raymond. *English Drama: Forms and Development*. Cambridge: Cambridge UP, 1977.

———. *Keywords: A Vocabulary of Culture and Society*. London: Fontana, 1976.

7

Plain and Simple
Masculinity through John Sayles's Lens

Diane Carson

••

Known internationally for his principled, long-standing commitment to independent filmmaking, John Sayles commands respect for his provocative and diverse narratives.[1] With its impressive variety of films over a sustained career, Sayles's output stretches from *The Return of the Secaucus Seven* (1980) to *Silver City* (2004). Geographically democratic, he has situated narratives from Alaska to Florida, from New Jersey to South America, and from Ireland to Louisiana. He has employed the vehicle of science fiction in *The Brother from Another Planet* (1984) and myth in *The Secret of Roan Inish* (1994) to elaborate his ideas. Whatever the location or the narrative device, Sayles selects a neonaturalistic style of performance to convey his atypical and confrontational themes, eschewing mindless, escapist entertainment.

In so doing, Sayles reinterprets what is conventionally considered Hollywood "realism" in order to arrive at a remarkably honest, straightforward, and complex representation, particularly of his male characters.[2] Sayles's preferred performance style certainly embraces many naturalistic acting characteristics, specifically the attempt "to conceal or modify all the rhetorical devices," "to rid acting of arty, stylized gentility" (Naremore 44, 49). Sayles also promotes the impression of "the actor's speech, posture, or gesture as relatively 'organic' phenomenon" (49). Or, as the audience would respond, "Viewing a naturalistic performance, it's easy to assume that the gestures, actions, and expressions are the only appropriate ones . . . the decisions the actor has made are invisible." Each character is consistent and coherent, behaving as expected: "The actor disappears into the character" (Lovell and Krämer 5).

Sayles's directorial technique necessitates a distinction between Hollywood realism and naturalism, a difference succinctly defined by David Mayer. Whereas realism requires no action from the spectator beyond appreciation, naturalism offers "a comprehensive scientific, philosophical, and sociopolitical system in which human behavior and environment are inextricably linked" (Lovell and Krämer 26). Furthermore, just as neorealism embodies a "hunger for reality" that goes beyond Americans' "sweetened version of truth produced through transpositions" (Zavattini 69), Sayles's neonaturalism propels the spectator, in a similar vein, toward a less idyllic, more multifaceted perspective. Conventional cinema ascribes stereotypical, usually gender-bound, qualities to characters in narratives driving toward satisfying resolutions. In contrast, Sayles presents provocative subjects in distinctive ways: through accessible performances that redefine the male protagonist.

Although not as well known as many directors with marquee names, with action-adventure pedigrees, or who exploit more titillating content to command mainstream exposure, Sayles has established a respected and respectable cinematic position on his own terms. From his earliest to his latest works, Sayles challenges the viewer to reevaluate mainstream themes and their reassuring presentational style. Sayles's concerns include: friends' reunion and reassessment of their political resistance and disenchantment in *Return of the Secaucus Seven* (1980); a middle-class married woman discovering her lesbian identity and suffering the prejudice of its revelation in *Lianna* (1983); the racism and social injustice experienced by a mute black alien who arrives in Harlem in *The Brother from Another Planet* (1984); striking 1920s Appalachian coal miners and the company violence used to combat unionization in *Matewan* (1987); and the political corruption and tribalism that rule urban life in *City of Hope* (1991). *Lone Star* (1996) explores the reactionary power and restrictive pressures of cultural icons and the dangers of crossing literal and metaphoric borders. *Baby, It's You* (1983) indicts class and ethnic prejudice as it exposes paralyzing personal and social barriers. *Men with Guns* (1997) admonishes those who avoid tough moral choices, those who remain comfortably ignorant of and oblivious to governmental abuse, and implicitly urges constructive reform to destructive civil strife.

Throughout these films, Sayles's casting choices and visual presentations resist simplistic categorization. Characters do not win against all odds, nor do their attitudes and values always prevail. To encourage spectatorial engagement in his radical (by Hollywood standards) undertaking, Sayles chooses carefully, trying not to alienate his audience. Sayles says, "I look for actors who can inhabit the character so if I change lines, they can do those lines exactly as the character would" (*Limbo* press conference). Examination of the dominant acting style that defines masculine performances in Sayles's films leads to the compelling conclusion that Sayles's atypical male characters listen carefully, consider their situations conscientiously, and then act decisively but quietly. Verbal and nonverbal acting choices sustain the believability of such behavior while defying plot predictability and disrupting formulaic poses. In creating the central male characters, actors eschew the postmodern affectations of ironic distanciation, self-conscious cynicism, or allusions to contemporary cultural artifacts and media images. In other words, Sayles navigates a course away from Hollywood's faux realism as exemplified in the action-adventure fantasy *Indiana Jones and the Temple of Doom* (1984) while also steering clear of the modernism of an Altman or an Antonioni and the postmodern style of a Kubrick or Woo, directors studied elsewhere in this volume.

Matewan and Chris Cooper's Performance

Matewan presents an exemplary case study. Joe Kenehan (Chris Cooper) first appears on screen in a medium close-up, roughly six minutes into *Matewan*. He sits alone on a train nearing Matewan, West Virginia, facing toward the camera. The bottom half of his face is obscured by the *Fayette Tribune*, the newspaper he is reading. Directional daylight (motivated lighting) floods through the railroad car window, illuminating the left side of his face. As the train slows to a stop, the conductor moves through the car, edge of screen left, his back to the camera, and announces matter of factly, "Just gotta stop for a few repairs. Sorry for the inconvenience." In both the seats behind Joe, two men abreast in each row continue to speak to each other, their exchanges barely audible. Joe does not say a word as he quietly folds the newspaper and moves calmly toward the door at the back of the car.

Sayles cuts to a long shot outside the passenger car a beat before Joe leans out of the platform (figure 7.1) to watch Few Clothes (James Earl Jones) and other African American coal miner scabs step down from the boxcar located just behind the passenger

7.1. From a safe distance, Joe Kenehan (Chris Cooper) watches the scuffle.

7.2. The imposing Few Clothes (James Earl Jones) runs to catch the train.

car. As Few Clothes exits the boxcar, he pauses before moving powerfully toward the camera. Two quick cuts establish an eyeline match between Joe and Few Clothes. With a shout, striking Matewan coal miners immediately swarm from the woods to attack with fists, sticks, and baseball bats. As the train begins to roll, scabs scramble to jump back into the boxcar. Few Clothes throws off two attackers, muscles past those who gang up on him, and hustles to catch the caboose as it pulls away (figure 7.2). Joe leans back into the car, having remained motionless during the scuffle, having uttered no sounds and having made no attempt to abet or stop either group.[3]

Though a mute observer throughout the altercation, Chris Cooper conveys masterfully and nonverbally Joe's curiosity mixed with apprehension. As the railroad car slows, Joe reacts unhurriedly but promptly, Cooper communicating unease and tension through pinched lips and shifts of his eyes. As the visual composition and editing establish Joe's centrality to the narrative, he anchors, but never dominates, the action. Joe's cautious manner and his abstention from the brawl communicate his, and implicitly ask our, thoughtful perspective.

Driven by his commitment to unionizing these 1920s Appalachian miners, Joe is the vested witness who asks pertinent questions while expressing adamant opposition to violence as the solution to the company's exploitation of labor. As a participant with contested opinions, Joe poses no threat to the miners' proceedings despite his firm conviction. Throughout the debate, he maintains a characteristically attentive—albeit passive—presence, hovering in the background, watching and weighing what he sees and hears.

Cooper's neonaturalistic, accessible performance aligns our empathetic identification with Joe, and we thereby participate in the narrative. In contrast to the often distancing emotional and behavioral choices of both the modernist and postmodern styles, neonaturalistic acting invites audience receptivity to and involvement in the story and with the characters.[4] The low-key, cool introduction to Joe Kenehan, presented with calm, convincing restraint through Chris Cooper's subdued acting, exemplifies writer/director John Sayles's preferred performance style, one with significant consequences for his message. And the casting choice of Cooper, his amenable, nonthreatening presence as Joe, further fortifies the appeal of a decidedly untraditional "hero." The atypical male at the center of this and most of Sayles's narratives becomes the ingenious, likable vehicle for redefinition of courage through accessible, neonaturalistic acting. As a tool, it is a clever strategy to so slyly and agreeably undermine our cultural stereotypes and make us rethink our perspective.

Since Joe remains the pivotal character throughout *Matewan*, his opening and subsequent scenes shatter any expectations for an authoritative, dynamic, and aggressive male presence. In contrast to Joe's relative physical fragility, Sayles visually emphasizes Few Clothes's stature, girth, and self-confidence. The script accurately describes Few Clothes as "a huge man" and Joe as "nervous" (Sayles, *Thinking in Pictures* 7–8). In his supporting role, James Earl

Jones, a bear of a man, dominates the frame verbally and nonverbally in the opening and in the subsequent scenes in which he figures. In this skirmish scene, Few Clothes steps into view and fills the boxcar door in a low-angle one-shot that contrasts dramatically with the diagonal angle looking down the tracks/train of Joe as he leans halfway out of the passenger car in medium long shot.

Emphasizing his stature literally and figuratively, Few Clothes looms and pauses, a suspended power, before he steps down from the boxcar. In the first shot of Joe, he was just there, as if accidentally discovered by the camera half hiding behind his newspaper. Several other details reinforce Few Clothes's, not Joe's, impressive appearance: Jones's considerable physical size and his recognizable, resonant voice, and Few Clothes's movement toward screen right, combined with his halting and facing forward in medium shot. As Paul McDonald explains in chapter 1, minute details in actors' choices communicate content powerfully and convey strong emotional registers. Impressive—but very different—actors, both Cooper and Jones illustrate this principle with their consistent, multifaceted verbal and nonverbal presentations of their personas.

These actors embody the contrast between their respective characters. James Earl Jones maintains an upright posture and challenging gaze; Chris Cooper averts his eyes, hunches his shoulders forward, and meekly withdraws into the passenger car, diminishing any power he might be expected to wield as the central character. Shot at an angle, Cooper's slim body appears almost delicate, and his lack of rugged features makes him seem vulnerable, ineffectual. In Joe's initial introduction, he walks quietly away from the camera, while in sharp contrast, Few Clothes powers his bulk toward the camera, which retreats from him, yielding command of the composition to him. It is axiomatic in film that the character from whom the camera retreats possesses the power, for good or ill, to author the narrative. Since Joe does not say a word, participate in the scuffle, or command the camera, he must redefine authority and authoring.

Throughout the introductory and subsequent scenes, Joe appears shy, halting, and unsure of himself. He never exhibits the predictable attributes of the typical Hollywood male—a man who acts more than he reacts and who claims dominant positions in the compositions while taking controlling, forceful stands on issues central to the plot. Further, Sayles chooses not to inflect this passive character with a Brechtian alienation or a postmodern disaffec-

7.3. Joe Kenehan's (Chris Cooper) clothes and expression define him as an atypical male protagonist.

tion. Instead, he insists on a reconfigured male—without an attitude, without power, and without defensive posturing.

At the conclusion of this same scene, Joe hunches over on screen right and asks the conductor, "When we gonna get to Matewan?" "You don't want to go there, Mister. There ain't nothing there but crazy people," the conductor replies. Sayles cuts to an extreme long shot of the Matewan railroad platform with Joe at the edge of the frame, screen left, quiet until Bridey Mae (Nancy Mette) initiates conversation. Squeezed screen left, Joe looks around as if lost and walks screen right, still in extreme long shot. During their dialogue, Bridey Mae faces the camera while Joe stands sideways, slightly tucking his chin when he reacts and speaks, still a tentative, reticent man. His appearance complements his verbal inadequacy, dressed in decidedly unglamorous rumpled clothes. The dark jacket secured midway across his chest with one button makes it look too small for him (figure 7.3), and he completely lacks the sartorial appeal of a conventional hero. Contrast

Joe's appearance, for example, with Indiana Jones's beautifully cut trademark rich brown leather jacket that moves sensuously when Harrison Ford springs into action.

Joe's self-deprecating appearance and presence persist throughout the film, qualified only, albeit vitally, by Joe's firm commitment to nonviolence. Cooper's acting choices reveal a proficiency and consistency in conveying this character. Sayles's equally unambiguous visual choices effect a coherent and impressive synchronicity of actor and director working to redefine the concept of male integrity. Joe often stammers slightly, interjecting "uhs" in his comments and questions. He frequently occupies a lower position or background space in the frame. Even in the miners' meeting, when the white men accept the "colored" workers, Joe leans to balance himself, arms crossed or fiddling with his cap. When he does speak forcefully, his body is turned away from the camera for part of his speech. Coming immediately after the scene in which the preacher (played by Sayles) vigorously throws his arms about, loudly proclaiming the Lord, Joe appears adamant but immensely reserved by comparison. Later, when Joe asserts himself by reiterating the labor union gospel at the river, voice-over narration takes control within ten seconds, supplanting Joe's single authority with "we" and interpreting the progress of unionization for the audience.

Joe's relative passivity, communicated by Cooper's deferential manner and softly spoken lines, culminates in the film's dramatic, violent conclusion, which includes Joe's death, one of many. Curiously, unlike in a conventional film, the death is not seen on camera and not emphasized. The killing occurs one breathless moment before the final shootout begins. Sheriff Sid Hatfield (David Strathairn) and the company's hired guns stand apprehensively facing each other on the railroad tracks, a showdown imminent. Joe sprints around the corner of a building yelling, "No!" Violence immediately erupts as Sayles cuts to the men drawing their guns. At the conclusion of the shooting, a cut to a medium long shot finds Joe, dead, slumped on the railroad tracks.

Seldom has an American leading man been so easily eclipsed by compositions favoring other actors, and seldom has an actor used his verbal delivery and nonverbal gestures to convey so reserved a pivotal male character. In contrast to Hollywood theme-park realism, even a reluctant hero like Bruce Willis in *Die Hard* (1988, the year after *Matewan*) possesses a ferocity and bravado completely absent from Cooper's acting choices and Sayles's visual compositions. Cooper's atypical male performance and the Joe Kenehan persona espouse Sayles's principles and promote his attempt to reconfigure incidental as well as the deeply embedded features.

Sayles's Working Methods and Their Impact

Understanding Sayles's working methods gives glimpses into his strategies for countering Hollywood "realism" and may also elicit some appreciation of his accomplishments. Actors, of course, come to film and stage work with varied techniques and espouse diverse theories, from interpretations and misinterpretations of the Stanislavsky System (see Carnicke for important clarifications regarding Stanislavsky's teachings), the Method School, and Brechtian distanciation, to cite just three.[5] Similarly, in analyzing performance, some critics foreground the cinematic apparatus while others champion actors' verbal and nonverbal elements or the narrative function of the character per se (Heath 113–29). Productive analytical constructs also employ what James Naremore calls the "performance frame" (9). Star studies, semiotic concepts, historical stylistic indexing, cultural indexing, and many other tools of analysis can offer insights into actors' contributions to the film under scrutiny. But most directors establish a working method that fuses their personalities with a comfortable level of control over the production. Their direction or nondirection of the actors results, at best, in stylistically coherent work that advances the work's theoretical underpinnings.

This is the case with John Sayles, who approaches continuous negotiations between director and actor with diverse strategies, melding actors' techniques in the interest of thematic unity. Moreover, Sayles's character and plot complexities place unique demands on every performance. As Emanuel Levy observes, "Unlike Cassavetes, Sayles uses large ensembles, and his characters are more intelligent and complex" (84).[6] An independent filmmaker working on a tight production budget, Sayles involves a range of experienced and inexperienced actors from whom he must extract and guide performances. Since individuals bring a multiplicity of skills and approaches to the set, methodologies can conflict as well as complement each other. And Sayles directs uniquely individualistic, as well as unified, works. "Each of his films has utilized a different stylistic idiom" (Levy 85)—for example, the rhythm of a

7.4. John Sayles on the set of *Matewan*; Chris Cooper in background.

mountain ballad for *Matewan*'s 1920 coal miners (appropriate to Cooper's performance as well) and the beat and riffs of jazz for *Eight Men Out*'s 1919 Chicago baseball scandal.

Sayles manages to adapt each actor to the genre and historical particulars of his distinctive narratives. At the 1999 Cannes International Film Festival, where he premiered *Limbo* in competition for the Palme d'Or, Sayles talked about his strategies for dealing with dissimilar actors and demanding narratives. During every film production, he holds to one constant: that the actors listen carefully to each other. For example, Sayles said that while shooting *Limbo*, to intensify the interaction and attentiveness between Donna (Mary Elizabeth Mastrantonio) and Joe (David Strathairn), he directed Mastrantonio to respond with unscripted answers to questions posed by Strathairn. In *Passion Fish*, while attempting to blend the contrasting acting methods of Alfre Woodard and Mary McDonnell, Sayles said he worked with each in very different ways: McDonnell wanted little direction, preferring to find Mary-Alice (her character) through her own methods; in contrast, Woodard told

Sayles to tell her in precise detail exactly how he wanted Chantelle (her character) to appear and sound. Woodard told Sayles that she would absorb this information and those expectations to make Chantelle "hers."

Such tales of contrasting acting processes are part of the Sayles legend and not surprising. Nevertheless, Sayles has said that he "rarely asks actors how they do things. I just trust them to do it. Each has his own technique" (Cannes interview). Sayles quotes David Strathairn as knowing that "there are a hundred different ways to say, 'Hello.'" The directorial talent required to integrate disparate approaches and to channel multiple possibilities into a coherent cinematic presentation is exceptional.

The difficulty of Sayles's task multiplies for ensemble pieces such as *The Return of the Secaucus Seven, Eight Men Out* (about the "Black Sox" baseball scandal), and *City of Hope* (an urban drama). Nevertheless, from the 1919 baseball scandal to a politically charged city in 1991, from the Irish mythopoetic tale *The Secret of Roan Inish* to the Mexican troubles of *Hombres armados* (*Men with Guns*), a recognizable acting ambience defines Sayles's films. Whatever the plot, the country, or the time period, as Sayles told *American Cinematographer*, "My first priority is always with the acting and the believability of the characters" (Carson 53).

Naturalistic and Neonaturalistic Characteristics

Clearly, Sayles's emphasis on "the believability of the characters" and on "authenticity" anchors his films firmly within a traditionally naturalistic acting style, whatever the actors' theoretical approaches. Sayles's concern for acting verisimilitude, location shooting, and the "rendering of human action in clearly delineated social environments" (Baron 182) each contributes to this naturalistic effect, his adaptation of "Stanislavskian aesthetics" (Naremore 2). As Cole and Chinoy explain its expression in the early twentieth century, audiences perceive naturalism as "the simple gestures and natural movements of a modern man living in our everyday world" (214). Moving from Ireland to Mexico, from the inner city to the Appalachian coal mines, Sayles elicits the immediacy of a specific moment as it is lived by characters who exhibit "no mood of detachment" (Connor 135). Each actor fully occupies a specific, recognizable time period and place, one consistent with Sayles's "singular and iconoclastic" vision (Levy 84). In other words, Sayles captures a world right here, right now, via a visceral and corporeal potency. At the same time, he reinvents the essence of his central male characters through comprehensive visual and thespian presentations: a new naturalism presides.

Several factors contribute to the accessibility and immediacy of this conception. Shooting on location as much as physically and financially possible, Sayles crafts his actors' interactions with their immediate environment, as well as with each other, through a unified and consistent set of traits, mannerisms, and actions. To establish a complement between person and place, before shooting begins Sayles insists on traveling to the film's location to make final script revisions (Sayles, *Limbo* press conference). His intent, one consistent with his films' neonaturalistic acting style, is clear. He approaches the location "like a reporter, asking, 'How do you do this? What does this feel like?'" Sayles then revises the script to sound and feel authentic and directs his actors accordingly.

Working his way throughout the narrative with this approach, Sayles produces a satisfying unity of verbal and nonverbal elements with a full complement of human qualities, as opposed to a modernist or postmodernist minimalist offering. Rather than moving toward the theatrical in using broad, emphatic gestures and amplified, inflated language, Sayles's actors convey the immediacy of recognizable emotions and understandable reactions. They are inextricably linked to their moment with the impact the director choreographs through atypical immersion in genuine complexity. For example, even the final shootout in *Matewan* lacks the hyperbolic, sensationalistic features of violent encounters in faux realism films since the early 1970s. Sayles notes that in the last ten years "there have been so many shootouts with automatic weapons, great squibs of blood, and people flying through the air, John Woo style. I can't top that and astonish people, so what I'll do is what we haven't seen—three-dimensional characters whom you meet and start to feel something for the way you would a real person in a violent situation. [This is] humanistic violence, which is much more upsetting" (*Limbo* press conference).

Determined to present realistic dramas, Sayles is partial to those creative and technical individuals whom he admires and with whom he has built a track record. Several actors appear in more than one Sayles film, among them David Strathairn, Chris Cooper, Mary McDonnell, Joe Morton, Kris Kristofferson, and Gordon Clapp. But Sayles notes that he never uses them "in iconic ways, for the same qualities over and over again. These are versatile, real actors" (*Limbo* press conference). In fact, he admires them precisely because they disappear into their roles.

In many ways, Strathairn and Cooper define the Sayles male. They command more screen time than any of his other actors and represent, to a greater or lesser degree, the atypical masculine personas dominant in Sayles's films. These personas exhibit remarkable differences from conventional Hollywood male characters. They include: David Strathairn as the sensitive, tentative Rennie in *Passion Fish*; Joe Gastineau as the conflicted man groping for redemption in *Limbo*; the older, fatherly Federico Luppi as Dr. Fuentes in *Men with Guns/Hombres armados*; Mick Lally as the sweet Grandfather Hugh in *The Secret of Roan Inish*; and conflicted, struggling Vincent Spano as Nick Rinaldi and Joe Morton as the idealistic, frustrated Wynn in *City of Hope*, neither far from earlier roles, with Spano portraying "Sheik" in *Baby, It's You* and Morton as the hunted, haunted Brother in *The Brother from Another Planet*. Similarly, Jon deVries plays fragile husband Dick in *Lianna*, and the majority of the baseball players in *Eight Men Out* resist the usual braggart-athlete stereotypes: John Cusack as Buck Weaver, Charlie Sheen as Hap Felsch, D. B. Sweeney as "Shoeless" Joe, and Jace Alexander as Dickie Kerr—not a conventionally impressive athletic presence in the lot.

At one time or another, each man's acting conveys a measure of the alienation that experience has conferred on him. Each is an existentialist struggling to gain perspective on, and to find meaning in, life. But each engages in his effort without the detachment exhibited by characters in modernist works by, for example, Antonioni or Godard. On the whole, Sayles's protagonists are soft-spoken, physically and verbally nonassertive, sensitive, intelligent, and thoughtful. They tend to be loners, detached but caring, sometimes almost bewildered. As representative of Sayles's men, Cooper's acting presents the most illuminating example of Sayles's neonaturalistic style. On screen in *Matewan* and *Lone Star*, Cooper projects the reserved, understated, and sometimes even tentative presence of a Sayles "hero." Analysis of almost any representative scene in either film demonstrates the atypical presentation of this and other male characters.

Another illuminating comparison made possible through this collection is a consideration of John Sayles and John Cassavetes (see Maria Viera's essay). In part because their working practices differ, Sayles and Cassavetes reflect the variation within the neonaturalistic continuum. Cassavetes's ensemble actors (especially Gena Rowlands, Ben Gazarra, and Peter Falk) differ dramatically from Sayles's actors and the emotional register he effects. Levy compares and contrasts the two directors: "Like Cassavetes, Sayles loves performers—even in small roles, his actors shine—though acting in his films is less self-indulgent than it is in Cassavetes's work" (84). At least in part, this derives from Sayles's firm direction and control as writer, director, and—usually—editor. For despite the feeling of spontaneity and improvisation in his films, Sayles asserts, "I change about two lines of dialogue per movie. That's usually because the actors are having a hard time saying them" (Cannes interview).

Working often with Cooper, Sayles completely trusts the performer's acting choices, trusts him, like Strathairn, to play both the text and the subtext, and to use every acting nuance to communicate a purposeful performance. He underplays to provide tension. To summarize the opening description, as Cooper embodies Kenehan, the actor seldom raises his voice even when he disagrees with someone or opposes his or her action. As Kenehan, Cooper often turns his body away from the camera, slightly hunched over, gaze cast down, to avoid a challenging or aggressive stare. Nonverbally a subordinate male, he does not cower so much as graciously defer to others. Sayles often intensifies this effect by placing Joe on the weaker screen left side of the frame and/or in the middle or background planes rather than in the dominant position of foreground screen right. In *Matewan*, Cooper keeps Joe's gestures and incidental mannerisms to a minimum, projecting a still, thoughtful presence.

In addition, Cooper uses his average-sized body in nonthreatening ways, often positioning himself slightly slumped or crouched over. For an exaggerated, revealing contrast, consider Cooper's ramrod and aggressive posture as the inflexible, tough Marine, Colonel Frank Fitts, the Burnhams's next-door neighbor in *American Beauty* (Sam Mendes 1999). On more than one occasion, a harsh Colonel Fitts confronts his son. Cooper adopts a physically threatening posture as Fitts and uses his rigidity in this postmodern film to suggest that he might explode at any moment.[7] But time after time in Sayles's films, Cooper emphasizes his character's reticence. In *Matewan*, as a newcomer interrogated by the coal miners about labor heroes and their deaths, Joe must earn his way into the miners' meeting. As knowledgeable as he is, Joe visibly thinks before giving each correct answer. With the camera angled down from C. E. Lively's (Bob Gunton) point of view and partially obscured by shadow, Joe's accuracy comes across as less than authoritative, an impression enhanced by Cooper's low-key performance. Positioned at an angle with his back against the wall, Joe again speaks quietly, while shifting his eyes, repeatedly looking down, and opening and closing his lips. Paradoxically, seldom has a character been so determined, as the plot unfolds, while seeming so tentative. Others repeatedly command attention more compellingly than does Joe.

From *Matewan* to *Lone Star*

Nine years after *Matewan*, Sayles made *Lone Star*, also starring Chris Cooper. Its narrative design is analogous to the former film in presentational style and acting choices. Throughout *Lone Star*, Cooper's character, Sheriff Sam Deeds, investigates the "lone star" badge found in the desert, an inquiry that uncovers corruption and murder. As unusual in its own way as *Limbo*'s unexpected ending, the conclusion to *Lone Star* romantically unites Sam and his newly discovered half sister, Pilar Cruz (Elizabeth Peña). In one pivotal scene involving the dedication of a statue to his deceased father, Sheriff Buddy Deeds, Sam is called on to speak. Immediately thereafter, he and Pilar walk to the river and begin to heal their relationship. Sam admits his disillusionment with his job as sheriff: "I gotta admit it's not what I thought it would be. . . . Hell, I'm just a jailer."

During this scene, which is shot primarily in medium shot and medium long shot, Sam nervously looks down, turns and taps his hat, and speaks tentatively—most of the time in profile. The encounter feels honest, natural. We identify, perhaps even empathize, with Sam's awkwardness. Pilar ends the conversation with only a nod good-bye from him. As in several scenes throughout the film, Sam stands thinking as the camera pans away from him and into a flashback. Sam spends the next few scenes looking at evidence while saying nothing, in a montage of information—reports, letters, and maps—superimposed over Sam. The narrative elision shifts attention away from the character's presence to the objects of "evidence." All the data and analysis ultimately lead Sam to his investigative conclusion—and he's wrong despite his certainty. Seldom has an anchoring male character been so physically and intellectually undermined.

Throughout these critical scenes, Cooper looks up, head tilted down, while shot from a slightly high angle, even when he talks to the cleaning man in the office. Here he is more assertive than as Joe Kenehan in *Matewan* but pales by contrast with the unprincipled Kris Kristofferson character. In *Lone Star*, Sam crosses to "the other side," that is, Mexico, to learn what he can about the case. But Montoya, the man who knows the truth, defies Sam and his questions. Sam stands in the background, with his hands in his back pockets, answering Montoya but never assertively. Similarly, during his drive to watch Pilar, Sam looks straight ahead. Instead of bravura acting, the music expresses his emotions and his impassive face reveals repressed longing, an echo of his subdued acting in *Matewan*. But the minute inflections in his acting choices in *Matewan* and *Lone Star* capture and express the significant differences between the two contrasting characters. Whereas Joe remains tentative and on guard, Sam does get to relax with Pilar, smiling and even half laughing.

In both cases, Cooper seems thoroughly immersed in the character and the scene. But Sayles's refusal to cut to close-ups endorses empathy without identification. Or, to apply what Tomlinson (see his chapter 3 in this collection) explains with reference to Robert Bresson, Sayles invites "projection" through Cooper's neonaturalistic acting. But, like Jean Renoir, Sayles avoids a cinematic style that demands identification.

As a result, "His pictures are less emotionally draining than those of Cassavetes, and they benefit from sharp dialogue and clear dramatic structure" (Levy 84). While Hollywood realism relies on both projection *and* identification, thus fulfilling audience expectations in traditional ways (for example, the central male character discovers the truth and solves the mystery, punishes the bad, and rewards the good in competent, decisive, and impressive fashion), Sayles consistently uses characters who watch and listen. They elicit the same response from us precisely because we watch from a comfortable position, but one at a distance from the characters. The director counts on our own intelligence, on our desire and willingness to listen. Ultimately, Sayles presents central male actors who elect nuanced verbal and nonverbal interpretations. When we recognize the unconventional narrative content and the authenticity of the actors' choices to deliver their performances in a compelling but atypical way, we will have acceded to Sayles's desire—that his audience, like his actors, listen and think.

Notes

1. See, for example, Carson; Levy; Merritt; Molyneaux; Pierson; and Holmlund and Wyatt.

2. Sayles's female characters also depart in some significant ways from Hollywood's dominant depictions. Elma Radnor (Mary McDonnell) in *Matewan* and Pilar Cruz (Elizabeth Peña) in *Lone Star*, the films most thoroughly discussed in this essay, are integral to the action, functioning as much more than figures of romantic interest. Further, the sexual abuse of Bridey Mae (Nancy Mette) in *Matewan* differs radically from the often titillating, sensationalistic exploitation found in so many mainstream films.

3. In a conventional film, Joe would probably jump in on the strikers' side, land several good punches, prove his mettle, and thus establish his credentials. So Joe's first scene announces his unusual persona. *Matewan* tells the story of the 1920 Matewan, West Virginia, coal miners' strike and Joe's attempt to unionize white and black miners while avoiding violent clashes with the company enforcers.

4. See the essays in the modernist and postmodern sections of this collection for more in-depth exploration of these acting styles and their effects in contemporary films. I use the term neonaturalistic acting to refer to performance in the second half of the twentieth century from the vantage point of the modernist break with earlier tradition. For the most part, *neonaturalistic acting* adopts and reflects the characteristics of naturalistic acting, described later in the essay. A director like John Sayles who chooses this style does so to circumvent the distancing and self-consciousness of the postmodern style and its attendant characteristics. Again, see the essays in the postmodern section and the introduction for a fuller discussion of this issue.

5. See, for example, Comey and Weston for various approaches and suggestions for directing performers.

6. For more illuminating comparisons and contrasts, see Maria Viera's chapter 6 on Cassavetes.

7. *American Beauty* employs a sarcastic tone of smugness characteristic of some contemporary films. Moreover, the digital video recording by Colonel Fitts's son and the use of that medium express a self-conscious awareness of the mediated world in which we live, a prevalent postmodern motif.

WORKS CONSULTED

Andrew, G. *Stranger Than Paradise: Maverick Film-Makers in Recent American Cinema*. New York: Limelight, 1999.

Baron, Cynthia. "The Cybernetic Logic of the Lumière Actualities, 1895–1897." *Quarterly Review of Film and Video* 18.2 (2001): 169–90.

Barr, Tony. *Acting for the Camera*. Boston: Allyn and Bacon, 1982.

Butler, Jeremy G. *Star Texts: Image and Performance in Film and Television*. Detroit: Wayne State UP, 1991.

Cardullo, Bert, Harry Geduld, Ronald Gottesman, and Leigh Woods, eds.

Playing to the Camera: Film Actors Discuss Their Craft. New Haven: Yale UP, 1998.

Carnicke, Sharon Marie. *Stanislavsky in Focus.* Amsterdam: Harwood, 1998.

Carson, Diane, ed. *John Sayles: Interviews.* Jackson: UP of Mississippi, 1999.

Cole, Toby, and Helen Krich Chinoy. "France." *Actors on Acting: The Theories, Techniques, and Practices of the World's Great Actors, Told in Their Own Words.* Ed. Toby Cole and Helen Krich Chinoy. New York: Crown, 1970.

Comey, Jeremiah. *The Art of Film Acting.* New York: Focal, 2002.

Connor, Steven. *Postmodernist Culture: An Introduction to Theories of the Contemporary.* Oxford: Blackwell, 1992.

Heath, Stephen. *Questions of Cinema.* Bloomington: Indiana UP, 1981.

Holmlund, Christine, and Justin Wyatt, eds. *American Independent Cinema.* London: Routledge, 2004.

Levy, Emanuel. *Cinema of Outsiders: The Rise of American Independent Film.* New York: New York UP, 1999.

Lovell, Alan, and Peter Krämer, eds. *Screen Acting.* New York: Routledge, 1999.

Mayer, David. "Acting in Silent Film: Which Legacy of the Theatre." *Screen Acting.* Ed. Alan Lovell and Peter Krämer. New York: Routledge, 1999. 10–30.

McDonald, Paul. "Film Acting." *The Oxford Guide to Film Studies.* Ed. John Hill and Pamela Church Gibson. New York: Oxford UP, 1998.

Merritt, Greg. *Celluloid Mavericks: The History of American Independent Film.* Berkeley: Thunder's Mouth, 2000.

Molyneaux, Gerard. *John Sayles: An Unauthorized Biography of the Pioneering Indie Filmmaker.* Los Angeles: Renaissance, 2000.

Montoya, M. E. "Lines of Demarcation in a Town Called *Frontera*: A Review of John Sayles's Movie *Lone Star.*" *New Mexico Law Review* 27 (1997): 223–40.

Naremore, James. *Acting in the Cinema.* Berkeley: U of California P, 1988.

Pierson, John. *Spike, Mike, Slackers, and Dykes: A Guided Tour across a Decade of American Independent Cinema.* New York: Hyperion, 1995.

Ryan, Jack. *John Sayles, Filmmaker.* Jefferson: McFarland, 1998.

Sayles, John. *Limbo* press conference. Cannes International Film Festival 22 May 1999.

———. Personal interview. Cannes International Film Festival. 22 May 1999.

———. Personal interview. Toronto Film Festival. 8 Sept. 1997.

———. *Thinking in Pictures: The Making of the Movie "Matewan."* Boston: Houghton Mifflin, 1987.

———. *Variety* panel discussion on independent filmmaking. Cannes International Film Festival. 18 May 1999.

Sayles, John, and Gavin Smith. *Sayles on Sayles*. Boston: Faber and Faber, 1998.

Weston, Judith. *Directing Actors: Creating Memorable Performances for Film and Television*. Studio City: M. Wiese, 1996.

Zavattini, Cesare. "A Thesis on Neo-Realism." *Springtime in Italy: A Reader on Neo-Realism*. Ed. and trans. David Overbey. Hamden: Archon, 1978. 67–78.

8

Passionate Engagement
Performance in the Films of Neil Jordan

Carole Zucker

Surely all art is the result of having been in danger, of having gone
through an experience all the way to the end, to where no one can go
any further.
  Rainer Maria Rilke

Acting is not an imitation of life but a greater truth.
  Sanford Meisner

· ·

With each successive outing, the Irish filmmaker Neil Jordan aston-
ishes the viewer with the eclectic, catholic range of his interests.
This is especially evident when one examines *The Butcher Boy*
(1997), a black tragicomic tale of "rural Irish dementia" (Lacey 50);
In Dreams (1998), a psychological horror/thriller; *The End of the
Affair* (1999), an understated melodrama; *Not I* (2000), a film based
on one of Samuel Beckett's most eccentric plays; and *The Good
Thief* (2003), a remake of Jean-Pierre Melville's gangster classic,
Bob le Flambeur (1955). Jordan's peregrinations through and transformations of classical genre often loosen or immolate the conventional boundaries between existing categories. Jordan's oeuvre is
truly idiosyncratic, filled as it is with formal experimentation and
stylistic changes from film to film. He often creates moods and
situations that can be sensed but that are too complex to be grasped
immediately. Jordan is one of the rare filmmakers who uses both
the image and language to express and transform meaning. He has
no trepidations about making bold, outré gestures in his work.

Jordan is thus one of the most audacious, poetic, and intelligent of contemporary filmmakers.

As much as Jordan experiments with form and generic convention, his work tends to circulate around repeated themes. Among them are: a fascination with storytelling; impossible love and erotic tension; the quest for identity; contemporary permutations of the family unit; violence and its attendant psychic and physical damage; the dark and irrational aspects of the human impulse; and characters who are, in some way, haunted by loss. His films continually ask a question that is at once simple and magnificently complicated: What does it mean to be human?

Jordan's attachment to the plurality and permeability of the boundaries of human behavior leads him to investigate diverse styles of acting. After all, how can one style possibly serve to depict the complex and heterogeneous worlds he explores? Given his penchant for pluralism, the performances in his films have no discernible signature; one cannot perceive a "Neil Jordan" style of acting. As with form and genre, he is committed to experimentation and diversity in performance, always in response to the particular story he is telling. One constant in Jordan's films—apart from his skill with casting—is that there is rarely an elemental or univocal meaning that can be taken from witnessing a given performance (Falsetto 251).[1] His films are replete with moments that work on multifarious levels. As writer/director, Jordan portrays the mystery and complexity of human feeling, where subtextual meanings abound.

This essay will investigate three of Jordan's films that serve as examples of his formidable work with actors and best represent the range of performance styles in his films. *The Crying Game* (1992) tackles several performance issues: work with a nonactor and professional actors, a mix of radically different performance styles within the same film, and the way in which film style engages with and is a determining factor in performance. *Interview with the Vampire* (1994) is a study in the uses of ritual, hyperbole, and theatricality in performance. Finally, *The End of the Affair* (1999), in complete opposition to *Vampire*, is a meditation on minimalism.

The Crying Game: "Who knows the secrets of the human heart?"

In the aftermath of *The Crying Game*'s surprising success—the film enjoyed large-scale public support and garnered mostly excellent reviews in the popular press—critics of a certain persuasion targeted the filmmaker's perceived lack of correctness in the handling of gender, race, and postcolonial politics.[2] Because the film is occupied, at least on a certain level, with a veritable hornet's nest of loaded issues such as homosociality, homosexuality, transvestitism, interracial romance, and sectarian violence in Ireland, it would have been odd for critics to overlook the representation of these matters. However, the denunciations of Jordan's films stem from a fundamental misapprehension of the director's artistic project. Jordan, even while using identity politics as an arena in which the narrative is played out, is much more intrigued by the fundamental humanity of his characters. As Jack Boozer writes, "Jordan can hardly be accused of unawareness of the crises and conditions that exist. His focus simply emphasizes the microcosm of individual character development, of any possibility of finding a path through the circulating signifiers that pass for contemporary meaning and truth" (179). Jordan is much more in sympathy with the ideas expressed by the poet/writer Tom Paulin when he said in an interview, "I just wanted to displace the concept of national identity, the concept of belonging to your tribe, the idea of tradition and so on. I wanted to wreck that and replace it with something that's plural and infinite, something that's moving all the time" (Hughes 125). Jordan's concern with the multiplicity of meanings inherent in human interactions is very much at the core of his filmmaking practice, and a signal aspect of his responsive working relationship with actors.

The first segment of *The Crying Game* presents the taking as hostage of a black British soldier, Jody (Forest Whitaker), by an IRA unit. The paramilitary cell is led by Peter (Adrian Dunbar) and it includes Fergus (Stephen Rea) and Jude (Miranda Richardson), who, as the only woman in the unit, is given the task of seducing Jody to facilitate his capture. Fergus, alone among his comrades, almost instantly bonds with Jody. Most of the scenes that take place in this section are between Jody and Fergus—a flirtatious interplay immediately surfaces between the two men. It begins when Fergus suggests that Jody eat something and lifts his hood to delicately place bits of food in his mouth. There is something touching, with intimations of the erotic about this gesture, which, as the hostage sequence evolves, maneuvers toward more profound feelings between the two men.

In these scenes, Stephen Rea is fairly relaxed as Fergus, and not given to a great deal of movement; he does very little "emoting." As the segments of the first part of the film progress toward Jody's eventual death, the emotional range, particularly on Rea's part, remains subtle and completely lacking in ostentation. For example, when Jody asserts that Fergus will have to kill him, Rea's response is to look up and away; his anxiety is betrayed primarily by little more than the noticeable shallowness of his breathing. One of the few times Rea displays more externalized emotion is when Jody remarks on the innate lack of compassion of Fergus's "people." Fergus's anger is manifestly straightforward; he says, "What the *fuck* do you know about my people?" In one beat, through the use of vocal intonation, a collision transpires between Fergus's IRA sympathies and his verboten connection with the British soldier's humanity, thus compromising his allegiance to the terrorist agenda. Furthermore, Fergus resents Jody's dehumanizing circumscription of his identity; he fights throughout the film to retain his individuality, to resist categorization by others. In terms of acting, as Neil Jordan has said:

> This guy Fergus is a Catholic and a nationalist, and he identifies himself with certain parameters. He thinks this is what he is, a political animal. He's wedded to violence. He feels that he's a soldier, and is justified in killing people he doesn't know for this cause. I was interested in setting this person up with his polar opposite, someone who is so far away from his experience: a black soldier who is gay, although Fergus didn't know it. If you throw this character on this journey, will he survive and will he change. (Falsetto 237)

Most of the hostage scenes are shot in a fairly conventional way; the cutting follows the semantic flow with shot/reverse shot editing patterns dominating. A greater sense of urgency develops as Jody comes to the realization that he is unlikely to survive. Jordan begins to cut to closer shots of each actor. Jody asks Fergus to look up Dil, his "wife," and "tell her I was thinking of her." Fergus, now attached to the hostage, is visibly moved by Jody's request; tears are barely suppressed as he contorts his face in the effort not to cry.

Fergus is told that he must kill Jody and finds the prisoner sobbing. The expression on Rea's face reveals many different emotions at the same time—feelings of impotence, guilt, confusion, pain, and empathy. He wants to help, but he cannot. Rea's face is truly a study, because one can sense this complex of feelings without a great deal of motion or effort on the actor's part. As Rea has said, "The camera likes to watch actors thinking" (qtd. in Zucker, *In the Company of Actors* 116). Jody is desperately frightened, and Rea's face is charged with desperation and loss, a privation that will resonate in the film's second half. There are cuts to closer and closer shots of each actor's face, with the camera moving in on each actor as he speaks. This penultimate scene between Fergus and Jody is brimming with constrained but very full emotion. It plays very much like a passionate love scene.

In every way, the first section of the film is very much a chamber piece. The shooting style is integral to defining the spatial parameters of Jody's imprisonment. But perhaps more importantly, in terms of the emotional and psychological universe Jordan sets up in the film, the tightly constructed and constricted style reflects the affective oppression of the IRA. This is a milieu that allows for little expressivity, other than the muted affection shared by the prisoner and his "keeper." In fact, Peter, the group leader, says later in the film (after stubbing a cigarette out on Fergus's hand and whacking him in the face), "I'm getting fuckin' emotional, and I don't want to get fuckin' emotional." In the opening section, Jordan might easily have moved the camera more, or had less conventional setups. I will argue that the film's style changes utterly—as does the latitude for expression—once Fergus "crosses the water" to London (an idiomatic Irish expression that means going to England) and is released, fleetingly, from the suffocating world of IRA politics.

Each Fergus/Jody scene has a very clear dramatic arc; as each scene is played out chronologically, the intensity builds. A great deal of this has to do with Jordan's talent as a writer, and the fact that two excellent, professional actors perform the scenes.

And if I have shortchanged Forest Whitaker in this section, it is not because he is any less skilled, committed, and truthful in these scenes than Stephen Rea. But Rea is so heavily inscribed in Neil Jordan's work—he has worked thus far on nine of the director's twelve films—that he deserves pride of place when discussing Jordan's work. As the director himself has said of Rea, "Stephen's a remarkable actor. . . . He's one of the best, genuinely one of the most intelligent actors in the world" (qtd. in Falsetto 251). And what I believe Jordan means in this statement is Rea's capacity for *emotional intelligence*—the ability to assess and embody the needs of a part—rather than (but not excluding) the actor's intellectual faculties. The profundity of an actor's emotional intelligence marks the difference between an actor who is simplistic and banal, and one who is inspired. Rea has very definite ideas about film acting— what belongs on film and what does not. He has said: "I've always had a great love of Robert Mitchum. . . . What it is I admire about his acting is that he's one of the great narrative actors. Nowadays everybody wants to 'show emotion'; everyone since the post-

8.1. Forest Whitaker and Stephen Rea in *The Crying Game*. (Courtesy of the British Film Institute)

Brando Italian actors wants to scream the house down and show their innards, and Mitchum simply thinks.[3] He must have been wonderful for a director" (qtd. in Zucker, *In the Company of Actors* 110–11).

And one can readily see that frugality in Rea's performance in *The Crying Game*. The ability to *let oneself alone* in front of the camera, to allow oneself, and have the ability, to *be, in character*, is one of the most demanding and difficult styles of acting to achieve. One must have the focus, the relaxation, the technique, and the naturalness to allow the camera to record the unimpeded beauty, the simplicity, and complexity of *being*—to, as Sanford Meisner put it, "live truthfully in imaginary circumstances" (15).[4] One may call this "naturalism" or simply good acting. Lindsay Crouse has said of acting for film: "You're a symbol. . . . You're very translucent when you're on film. You are a figure of light; your soul comes through. You can tell, easily, when someone is really doing it or not" (qtd. in Zucker, *Figures of Light* 28). It is this type of "dangerous" acting, letting the camera reveal your "visible soul" that Stephen Rea displays in *The Crying Game.*[5] It serves Neil Jordan's desire to construct multiple layers of meaning through the complex medium of his characters (figure 8.1).

Once Fergus "crosses the water," and meets Jody's "wife," Dil, the shooting style changes markedly. Most of the time the actors are seen together in two-shots; the shot/reverse shot pattern is used sparingly. The takes are longer and more expansive; there is greater depth of field. More of the environment is revealed, whether in the Metro—the gay bar where Dil and Fergus meet—or in Dil's flat; the camera follows the actors around and through space. There is a sense of liberation in Fergus's relocation to new surroundings; he has a new job as a construction worker and a new name, Jimmy. This section of the film is altogether less formal and restrictive.

Fergus's range of expression is given more latitude; although still subdued, Rea's performance in the London locale has more color and variation than in the Jody sequence. After the "discovery scene," when Fergus realizes that Dil is a cross-dressing male,[6] they meet at her workplace, Millie's hairdressing salon.[7] A long dialogue scene ensues as the camera continually tracks with both characters. Fergus expresses incredulity at his own naïveté, while Dil—at least on the surface—stages a show of nonchalance. (Fergus: "Thing is, you're not a girl, Dil." Dil: "Details, baby, details.") When they arrive at Dil's flat, she attempts to touch Fergus's face. Fergus refuses Dil's offer of intimacy; he instinctively moves away from Dil's outstretched hand. She says, "Don't be cruel." Fergus, in a very delicate move, cocks his head and submits; he says, "O.K." in a whisper that is an aural caress. It is a particularly telling, highly nuanced, and unexpected response on the actor's part, coming directly out of the "given circumstances" of the situation rather than the result of a premeditated, manipulated reality. Rea is showing us rather than telling us how his character feels with the most subtle and understated gestures and barely articulated dialogue.

He then reaches out to pat Dil in a big-brotherly, patronizing way, almost as if trying to reinstate their relationship on a "normal" footing. He says, "Be a good girl, go inside." Dil stands her ground and looks directly at Fergus: "Only if you kiss me." Fergus stops for a moment, taken aback by the bluntness of the request. His body literally rocks backward, then forward on his heels as he moves closer to kiss Dil lightly on the lips; his eyes are closed. Fergus then moves slightly backward. The expression on his face is at once amorous, aroused, surprised, and perplexed—a confused range of emotions his character might experience kissing another man. He lets out a short snort; he can't believe what he has done. It's also a self-protective pulling back, as if to deny that he kissed Dil for any reason other than to satisfy a petulant request. Or perhaps it is partly an apology for his physical aggression on learning Dil's "secret." His eyes remain in contact with hers, as Fergus tries to deny the significance of the kiss by asking, "Are ya happy now?" Dil maintains her cool, but suppressed anger shades her deadpan reply, "Delirious." Fergus lets out a big breath. Again, there is a play of emotions—pleasure, fear, disbelief, and perturbation—that transfuses his expression.

This long scene is notable for several things. First, it is often through the feelings rather than the words that contact is made. The tension between Dil and Fergus and the attraction/repulsion of their erotic interplay is largely declared in their movements toward and away from one another; their hesitant touching or refusal to make contact; the awkward, defeated, or defiant postures each of them adopts. Language is secondary to this interchange; they are in response to one another in a way that transcends language. Each is emotionally available to the other, and the audience, like the characters, doesn't know what is going to happen next. There is an exquisite feeling of aliveness, of living in the unknown, of "the first time" in this scene. As Meisner said, "The quality of your acting depends on how fully you are doing what you are doing" (qtd. in Silverberg 61). Each actor responds to the minute changes in his partner; they work off of one another and give up control for the sake of the truth of each moment. Neither partner directs the scene toward a goal. There is never a moment in which you feel either actor withdraw from the scene to determine the next move or the next response; they remain in sensitive contact with the gradations of each other's behavior. In terms of the script, the sequence moves from point A to point B but the unique way it moves, working with the moment-to-moment emotional fullness of the actors' responses to one another, is always exciting and unexpected.

Jaye Davidson gives a remarkable first performance, and while we must give him credit for allowing himself to engage so fully in the proceedings, other factors are at play. When working with non-actors, because they have no technique, the director usually has to film quite fast.[8] This precisely suits Jordan's shooting style; he rehearses very little, and then only for the purpose of rewriting dialogue that does not work. The director rarely does more than one or two takes. So we are getting the raw moments of film acting. A nonactor like Davidson will not have the technique, the skill, or the experience to know how to build a scene. A professional actor like Rea, while working partly on an instinctual level, will have the working experience to know when he has achieved the goals of a scene. He will know how to tap into his emotions with facility rather than producing facile emotions; it is Rea's job, particularly as a film actor, to be able to express himself with immediacy. Rea comments on working with a nonactor:

> Working with a non-actor is tricky. . . . It's not that they're not talented, it's not that they're not conscientuous. . . . What non-actors sometimes do is pick up your tone. Like that scene at the end of *The Crying Game* where I'm tied to the bed and my character says he's sorry. We started doing that, take one, and I started to fill up with tears, right? So take two Jaye [Davidson] starts to fill up with tears as well. Take three, he's crying more than me, so that's the un-discipline that happens, because you don't just start a scene and go wherever it goes . . . and you don't let it knock you about all over the place. . . . What happens with a non-actor is that a scene more quickly loses its shape. That doesn't mean they're not brilliant—and Jaye was absolutely brilliant in it—but when they're being brilliant, you have to get it right then. The professional actor will get it, be able to do it again, and develop it. If I was doing a scene with Miranda, the scene would automatically develop, because she's a fine professional actor. (qtd. in Zucker, *In the Company of Actors* 115)

It is interesting to contemplate a remark Rea made about Lauren Bacall in *To Have and Have Not* (1944): "They all said she was so cool, but she says she was terrified, and if you look at it knowing that, all you can see is her fear. She's a young girl of nineteen" (qtd. in Zucker, *In the Company of Actors* 116). I think this is true to a certain extent of Davidson. While he seems at ease with his gender "performance," there are moments of fear and uncertainty, often masked by cool. But whatever underlying panic there might have been—as a nonactor playing a leading role in a feature—it is integrated into the performance and serves to make it more real. And happily, there is none of the flamboyance that one might associate with transgender role-playing.

Ultimately, *The Crying Game* is a film resolutely entwined with the notion of identity as a sort of performance. If one fully engages with a role, one becomes something other, and new amplitude and fluidity is given to one's notion of self. Jordan says, "Could people's narrow identifications of themselves change? . . . It was an exploration of self. That's what I wanted to do with it. If you strip away all these masks human beings wear, is anything left underneath? Is anything left of Fergus when all this stuff is stripped away from him? In fact, there is, and he turns out to be a human being" (qtd. in Falsetto 238). Those that are capable of acting on feeling and instinct and act in response to the possibilities offered to them—Fergus and Dil—are the survivors in the film. Whether these characters are or will become connected in a sexual relationship is irrelevant. What is important is that both have broken through boundaries that had previously constricted their notions of selfhood; each can embrace unsettled positions regarding his identity.[9]

Stephen Rea says:

> The emotional journey is that Fergus realizes that you can love anyone. He goes from being a man who's got a very rigid code about who you can offer love to, and it doesn't include British soldiers, it doesn't include the British, it doesn't include loving other men, and it probably doesn't include black men, or black people. So by the end of the movie, he knows, and we all know and feel it, you can love anyone—race, gender, nationality are all meaningless. That wasn't a challenge for me, because I believe that with all my heart. It's wonderful to be in a movie where it really happens. I think that's what everyone responded to. (qtd. in Zucker, *In the Company of Actors* 115)

Interview with the Vampire: "I was waiting for you. Watching you watching me."

If *The Crying Game* can be seen to turn on a patently outrageous premise—"A tranny meets an IRA terrorist," as Stephen Rea put it (qtd. in Zucker, *In the Company of Actors* 116)—the initial transgressive plot is made both sympathetic and believable through the small moments of truth that lie at the heart of the film. It is a paean to Neil Jordan's eclecticism that, several years later, he would be drawn to a project so different in dimension, scope, and generic origin as to signal a significant movement in the director's oeuvre, *Interview with the Vampire*. Yet if one examines the attraction more closely, one sees that Neil Jordan was drawn to Anne Rice's best-selling novel because of the book's sense of "loss, inner anguish, and pain" (Jordan, *Interview with the Vampire*), an aggregate of sentiments that might also describe *The Crying Game*.

Again, the filmmaker is attracted to a dramatic situation that is played out in extremis. The fact that the main characters are vampires does not change Jordan's essential priorities, as he asks in *Vampire*: What is love? What place does feeling have in the world? What makes people (or vampires) behave as they do? The question is, at base: What does it mean to be human? And what makes this eternal mystery all the more complicated is that in this case, the director is not dealing with ordinary mortals. As Armand (Antonio Banderas), the oldest vampire on earth, says of Louis (Brad Pitt): "A vampire with a human soul. An immortal with a mortal's passion. You are beautiful, my friend." Louis's dilemma—caught between his humanity and his inhuman appetite for blood—becomes the film's central dramatic conflict. (Lestat can be seen as Louis's antagonist, but it is essentially Louis's internal discord that provides the film's most powerful dramatic material.)

The differences between *The Crying Game* and *Vampire* that interest us in this context are the ways in which the two films present performance. While in the former film (and in the last film to be discussed, *The End of the Affair*), the multifarious meanings of the narrative reside almost wholly in the intimate realm of the actors' expressions, gestures, postures, and so on, in *Vampire* we must negotiate our way through the varied tones of the scenes. The import is not so much in the release of little feelings that may be witnessed in a naturalistic film but in the unstable thrust of the material presented to us. Often it is difficult to determine whether to gape in horror or to respond with laughter to a particular scene in *Vampire*, if not both at once. So the movement in terms of acting is from the representational to the presentational. The more naturalistic films might be called "microresponsive," while *Vampire* works on a canvas that is painted in an altogether bolder and more astonishingly flamboyant palette of colors (figure 8.2).

The Crying Game tenders provocative and naturalistic performances within the framework of Jordan's imaginative universe. In *Vampire*, the performances defy the prototypical traits of naturalistic performance (the valorization of truthfulness and consistency, recognizable conventions of behavior, the representation of "authenticated life" [Burns 144], and the like) and position the acting style firmly within the compass of excess. I have written at length on this subject elsewhere and thus will comment only briefly on the most salient aspects of "excess" as a performative mode. First, there is an emphasis on irony, commentary, and self-consciousness. While I will argue later that *Vampire* uses the spatial configuration of the theater in its mise-en-scène, it wreaks utter havoc with the Stanislavskian notion of being "private in

8.2. Antonio Banderas and company in *Interview with the Vampire*. (Courtesy of the British Film Institute)

public." If anything, the performances are meant to invoke the presence of the spectator; we are meant to know the actors are performing. Further, to explicate the notion of "excess":

> Our absorption in the performance largely depends on the actor's abilities, and further, on his or her capacity to choose creatively and well. The criteria by which these choices are more or less apt hinges on the style and demands of the narrative, i.e., in a narrative that is closer on the spectrum to realism, the criteria of "truthfulness" and "naturalness" would obtain. But [in cases where] the diegetic world presents a very heightened or otherwise distorted version of reality . . . the style of acting—governed by this weakened resemblance to the world we know—is not bound by the laws of naturalistic behavior. And where the stricture to play naturalistically is relaxed, the style of performance may be inclined, in more interesting cases, to "excess," to a de-familiarized notion of human behavior. (Zucker, "Concept of 'Excess'" 56)

Vampire, situated in a particular subgenre of horror, lays prior claim to a "weakened resemblance" to the world of normality. But not all vampire films engage in the degree of ritual, stylization, and exaggeration so abundantly displayed in Jordan's film.

In great measure, *Vampire* is about performance as spectacle, funded, as it is for much of the film, by copious amounts of theatrical rhetoric. And the other necessary component of spectacle is the audience—the watcher. Jordan repeatedly sets up a relay between that which is presented to us and the trope of the watching figure, through the use of camera placement or movement and/or an actual embodied onlooker, thus acknowledging our spectatorial position. I believe Jordan is interested not only in the watcher/ watched motif. Equally—as a director heavily invested in horror and the gothic—he is deeply intrigued by the human hunger for destruction and violence, a fascination going back to traditions of oral storytelling in preliterate cultures.

A scene from *Vampire* that is heavily inscribed with the patterns of spectacle and spectatorship takes place in a New Orleans brothel. The set is arranged very like a stage, with deep red brocade wallpaper and vivid color throughout.[10] Candles light the corners of the room. The characters—a young prostitute, Lestat, and Louis— are all positioned frontally with respect to the camera; one has a strong sense of peering at the scene through the "fourth wall." Lestat playfully (at first) bites the breast of the woman. Only slightly later do we—and she—perceive that her ivory dress is drenched in blood. She begins to scream.

Lestat slits the prostitute's wrist and fills a wineglass with her blood. In a long shot emphasizing the proscenium arch–like nature of the set, Lestat offers Louis the beverage; Lestat is rectitude and courtliness personified. Louis reacts with revulsion to the liquid benefaction. Both actors are positioned in the foreground on opposing sides of the frame, the moaning woman is seated dead center in the background; it is a strong, highly stylized composition.

Lestat moves to the frightened woman and, with a great flourish, kicks open a coffin lid and drops her body in with a thud. Lestat hops onto the lid of the closed coffin with the panache and elegance of Errol Flynn. Louis watches the proceedings, horrified by Lestat's cruelty. The latter continues to toy with the shuddering prostitute; he is humorous and light-hearted. She states the obvious: "It's a coffin," to which Lestat responds, "So it is. You must be dead." He strikes a pose, hand on cheek, as if contemplating the situation. It is a campy gesture, and he stares at Louis as he performs it. The scene ends with a high-angle shot of the decimation; another prostitute lies dead in the foreground; Lestat has finished off the pitiful victim in the coffin. The audience is watching from a height, as if from the balcony of a theater.

One can see the way in which sexuality, cruelty, and theatricality are imbricated in this scene. There is a tension created between the icy barbarity of Lestat's actions and the highly mannered and decorous behavior with which he performs them. And this theatricalized cruelty is again in opposition to the more humane and human demeanor of Louis as he witnesses Lestat's remorseless conduct. The scene is paradigmatic of *Vampire's* complex fusion of tones. We are amused by Tom Cruise's stylized dandy but at the same time horrified by his cool infliction of suffering. Again, one sees Neil Jordan's penchant for working close to the edge and for placing viewers in a position of discomfort where they must traverse a network of conflicting moods and emotions.[11]

The theatricality of the first part of the film is displaced in its second half by scenes that take place in a real theater, Le Théâtre des Vampires. The audience within the film is unaware that this is a company of genuine vampires, who actually kill people on stage. Before viewing the main spectacle of the vampires' show, we see bits of a Grand Guignol performance, which was popular in Paris at the time. (A reference to a different style of theater, commedia dell'arte, is found earlier in the film, intercut with another theatrical and painterly rendering of Louis and Lestat feasting on a prostitute.) Armand, the leader of these "decadent" vampires, is played with great authority and elegance by Banderas.[12]

A young girl is brought onstage, obviously terrified, calling out for help. Her outer garments are stripped off and her breasts sensuously bared. Just as a vampire is about to sink his fangs into her neck, a sound resonates like a cannon shot. We see Armand, upstage, dressed entirely in crimson, toss his long mane of black hair as flames shoot out of either side of the foreground. He is extraordinarily regal and moves with the assurance of privilege. Armand holds his arms out to the victim. (The stage set looks very much like many of the New Orleans sets, with rich, deep colors lit by evocative candlelight.) The girl runs to Armand's open arms and buries her face in his chest, as though he had come to rescue her. He, in turn, puts on a show of solicitude, caressing her and stroking her hair. Suddenly he pushes her downstage and raises both her arms to shoulder height. He whispers in one of her ears and then the other, saying, "No pain. No pain"; it is a rhythmic ritual. She seems either resigned, hypnotized, or fully paralyzed with fear; she does not move. Armand removes her petticoat so that she is completely nude. The girl faints or collapses in his arms as he bites her neck. The moment he sinks his teeth into her flesh, he looks directly at Louis in the balcony, who whispers, "Monstrous." Armand then raises the supine body of the girl over his head as the others in the troupe carry her off. An overhead shot shows the black-cloaked figures converging like famished rats on the girl's body. The curtain closes.

Thus desire and death coalesce in ritualized spectacle. Eroticism is presented as a threat, lethally entangled with mortality. Louis—watching and passive—is a surrogate for the film audience, as the viewers of this gruesome spectacle. What makes this highly reflexive scene so disquieting is that it is performed in public. At one point, a woman in the audience, just as Armand is about to bite the young girl, stands up and cries out, "Take me, M. Vampire." It is like watching a rock show in which the entrance of the star (Armand) is charged with electric anticipation and a frisson of eroticism. The public's fascination with this ritual of submission to a diabolical figure is all the more haunting because it cannot differentiate between dramatized death (Grand Guignol) and a real murder that is played out for its delectation: that is a truly appalling idea. Yet surely Jordan is reminding us of our own thralldom to the profane. The spectacle demands to be watched; it merges the monstrous and the beautiful. We cannot fail to look, and that enraptured passivity, that magnetism provoked by ritual and spectacle, however evil or macabre, has a universal, timeless dimension. It is not limited to the world of vampires; it is endemic to humanity.[13]

Apart from the scenes of spectacular theatricality, Jordan varies the temperature of the performances with more naturalistic moments. A sequence striking in its poignancy is the one in which Claudia (Kirsten Dunst) comes to understand that while her emotions and mentality change as she continues her existence, she will retain the physiognomy of a dolllike little girl. She anguishes, "It means that I shall never, ever grow up. . . . Tell me how I came to be this . . . thing." There are no histrionics; the scene is very quiet and low-keyed—just a sad admission of who she is and what she can never become. As Claudia expresses her anguish, Louis silently weeps, averting his eyes from the girl and finally admits that it was he who made her. It is important to be reminded that even among the undead, there are redemptive moments of genuine sorrow and pain. The more naturalistic moments, though limited, provide a conduit between the imagined cosmos of the grotesque and the excessive and a world without severity and violence, a place of identifiable feeling.

Jordan knows that he cannot sustain a long film with a nonstop show of pyrotechnics. He weaves scenes of ritual power and energy with moments of mournful tenderness, distancing us with potent images of heightened intensity, and then moving us toward a position of sympathy for the devil.

The End of the Affair:
"For a moment I was free of feeling . . . and it felt like happiness."

The End of the Affair is a departure from Neil Jordan's previous films in many significant ways. Formally, it is his most sophisticated and complex work to date. The director/writer has fabricated a narrative structure that traverses the events of a six-year period, gracefully spanning and interweaving disparate temporal periods. It takes a number of viewings, in fact, to piece together what Jordan has called both a "metaphysical detective story" and "a visual, semantic, emotional puzzle (*End of the Affair*). The same event is seen several times from different characters' perspectives. Jordan, who began his career as an award-winning fiction writer, was heavily influenced by *le nouvel roman* and by Alain Robbe-Grillet and Marguerite Duras in particular (McIllroy 112). Throughout his career, both as a writer and a filmmaker, he has shown a highly developed sensitivity to the phenomenal existents of the world.

The invocation of *le nouvel roman* is highly relevant to the director's work with actors in *The End of the Affair*. One of the hallmarks of the literary movement is the writer's interest in the provisional, the contingent, and fleeting sensations of the moment. In addition, there is no attempt to enter into the psychology of the characters in works of *le nouvel roman*; one observes from a perspective *with* the characters, having access to their external sensorial world, rather than as seen from an interior point of view. Much the same can be said of Jordan's treatment of the performances in *Affair*, as we shall see.

The Irish director said he watched two films repeatedly to prepare for the film: Robert Bresson's *Les dames du Bois de Boulogne* (1945) and Max Ophuls's *Letter from an Unknown Woman* (1948). The impact of Bresson's style can be readily detected in Jordan's use of synecdoche at various points in the film,[14] as well as in the highly rhythmical sound and image montage (for example, the movement of figures ascending stairs, opening and closing doors, a typewriter clacking on the sound track). Perhaps the most powerful relationship Jordan bears to Bresson is what critic Hugh Linehan has called "the intertwining of eroticism, death and an equivocal sense of the sacred." And *The End of the Affair* is deeply connected with questions of belief and faith, issues that have never achieved such naked articulation in Jordan's previous work. Religion has a special resonance for Jordan, who says he is a nonbeliever but was a believer as a child, and that his fall from Catholicism "left a hole in my life" (*End of the Affair*).

To represent this freighted material, Jordan worked only with professional leads of the highest caliber for the first time in his career: children, nonactors, and novices were not employed. The result is an exquisitely modulated chamber piece. The actors are Ralph Fiennes as Maurice Bendrix, the semisuccessful writer, Julianne Moore as his lover, Sarah, and Stephen Rea as her husband, Henry, a high-ranking government bureaucrat. The film takes place just before and during the Blitz in London, when, as the director says, people lived every day as though it could be their last (*End of the Affair*).

Jordan talks of resisting the temptation to "broaden the film out" and wanting to "make everything as small as it could possibly be" (*End of the Affair*). The most succinct way to deal with Jordan's treatment of actors is to examine several pivotal scenes in depth, as many of the strategies that are employed throughout the film can be found in these sequences. It is important to set up the prior circumstances of one of the scenes to be scrutinized: Henry has told Bendrix that he believes Sarah may be having an affair. He has the business card of a detective agency, but thinks it beneath his dignity or does not want to know the truth, and so declines to pursue the matter. Bendrix, whose passionate affair with Sarah terminated abruptly several years before, suggests that he will go to the detective in Henry's place: "Jealous lovers are far less ridiculous than jealous husbands."[15] Henry drops the matter but Bendrix, who measures his love by the degree of his jealousy, visits the detective and instigates an investigation. Henry and Bendrix meet later in the rain that drenches most of the film, and Bendrix suggests a drink (figure 8.3).

The crucial scene commences in a pub, as Bendrix inquires with seeming nonchalance about Sarah. Henry responds offhandedly but one can sense his discomfiture as he twists a tumbler of whiskey in his hands, gripping it far more tightly than necessary. Bendrix announces that he has taken matters into his own hands and consulted the private detective; he now has all the documentation—photos, love letters—that prove Sarah's infidelity. During this conversation, Henry is appalled by Bendrix's "infernal cheek." Henry's expression of consternation is largely made manifest through the extraordinary tightness of his facial muscles and the rigidity of his posture. Rea's voice is reduced to a whisper, an effective tool for the stage-trained actor to communicate Henry's strangled emotion.

8.3. Stephen Rea and Ralph Fiennes in *The End of the Affair.* (Courtesy of the British Film Institute)

Bendrix's assault becomes physical when he places his leg across a stool, obstructing Henry's departure. He is provoked by Henry's passivity and charged with an anger that emerges as belligerent sarcasm. Henry, ever the meek gentleman, looks astonished but paralyzed; his distress and indignation is held in check by dint of habitual and capacious reserves of repression. His one action is to seize the incriminating evidence and ram it into a fireplace with a poker; it is a sudden and kinetic display of heretofore suppressed fury. As Henry rushes out of the pub, Bendrix lowers his head and shouts after the object of his derision, "I can always get you a carbon copy." Now Bendrix's face becomes a study of conflicting feelings. Neil Jordan has remarked that he likes actors who are able to communicate two entirely different things at the same time (*End of the Affair*). But here Fiennes registers arrogance, malice, pity, and gravitas all at once. The activity is internal, only a slight smirk is legible on his face.

Bendrix notices that Henry has left his hat on the table, thus providing an excuse for him to follow his victim. He finds Henry outside in the pouring rain, seated very stiffly on a bench. Bendrix apologizes to Henry, who looks bewildered, lost, on the verge of tears, and terribly wounded. He physically recoils as Bendrix sits next to him. The rain streaks down his face, making him all the more pitiable. Henry asks if Bendrix and his wife were lovers. He swallows hard in an effort to contain his rage, pain, and confusion. He is near tears; a tremendous sadness and sense of betrayal suffuse his face. Rea again uses his voice to great advantage, employing the most minimal inflection and affecting a near monotone. His face is such a mask of mastered inexpressivity that each tiny movement and delicate change reveal the deep feelings he is stifling with great difficulty. His breathing is crucial during this interchange; he often stops breathing, overcome by emotion, and must gasp for air.

The tone of the confrontation changes, as Bendrix's cruelty and anger rise in pitch. He calls Henry Sarah's "pimp." As Bendrix says the word, Henry reacts as though he has been punctured by a sharp instrument. He closes his eyes in unbearable misery and defeat. During this dialogue, the camera moves in close on Bendrix's face; he is thinking very deeply. But the key to Bendrix's thinking is that while remaining Ralph Fiennes, he is thinking as his character. Simon Callow puts this notion quite beautifully:

> I do believe there's a shamanistic aspect to acting. . . . I profoundly disagree that acting should only ever be a reflection of life, a kind of mirror. . . . I think that acting performance is life itself, it's a manifestation of life, it's an organic thing. It's a living, hugely complicated thing with its own ecology, its own biology. . . . If it's working . . . it's a point of success when you cease to play the character and the character starts to play you. Then, something's really happening; within the framework the author has created, the character must have its dangerous life. (qtd. in Zucker, *In the Company of Actors* 45)

Jordan says of *The End of the Affair* that it was like casting Mitchum and Bogart in the same film (*End of the Affair*). What he means is that Fiennes and Rea are merely thinking and reacting in barely perceptible ways; they are not overtly expressing emotion. One can view this scene repeatedly and find new emotions, always very subtly etched in both actors' faces. The degree of understatement and the ability of both actors to convey the depth and pitch of their emotions is extraordinary. Rea uses the smallest movements of his face and body and the constriction of his voice to articulate the wounds to his selfhood. And it is interesting that the little Rea does in this scene is quite different from the "little" he does as Fergus in *The Crying Game*. Both are subdued, highly internalized performances; nonetheless, each performance is informed by the given circumstances of the narrative. The physical expression, however limited, and the modulation of a quintessential spirit—call it soul or psyche—animates the presence of two distinctive characters, Fergus and Henry. Fiennes works primarily through the matchless intensity of his gaze and the translucence of his eyes that allow one to see into him, to the very core of his feelings. Fiennes displays vulnerability and transparency, even while he appears to be doing nothing; his focus and concentration are fierce and total. He has an almost uncanny ability to inhabit and embody the soul of a character; that is what—at least in part—we mean when we speak of charisma; certainly, it is great film acting. In describing what one sees in the performances in *The End of the Affair*, one is addressing a very essential conundrum as well as acknowledging one of the preeminent skills of film acting: How does one communicate highly interiorized states? How does an actor make emotion visible?

There is one other scene to describe, briefly, because it provides some of the most extraordinarily powerful moments I can remember seeing in any film. Sarah is dying and Henry has asked Bendrix to live in their house, to be there "when the time comes." Henry is watching over Sarah as Bendrix types in another room. We hear Henry scream Bendrix's name. Henry embraces Bendrix, crying openly, and says, "You have to help me, Bendrix. I can't live in a world where she's gone." The camera then captures Bendrix's face as he says, "I'll help you." The moment reveals the depth of Henry's love for Sarah, his fragility, and his capacity for profound feeling. It has an explosive impact because of the degree to which Henry has suppressed his feelings throughout the film and because of the way his emotions now detonate with full expression in the face of his loss. Bendrix's eyes stare intently, and the look on his face is somewhere between devastation and resignation. There is also, if only for a fleeting moment, a look of contentment. He is finally able to give of himself without ego or the expectation of reciprocity. The stigma of selfish interest has been removed (just as the boy may have been miraculously cleansed of his birthmark at the film's end). The actors, of course, don't say any of these things. But we can *feel* what lies beneath the simple gesture of the two men embracing. That is subtext, and that is what great actors know how to communicate so brilliantly. The scene is intensely moving and unforgettable in its dimensionality. As in the whole film, the key is in the simplicity and the utter conviction of the performances. *Affair* resonates with Helen Mirren's wonderfully economical advice to actors: "Don't think. Be" (qtd. in Zucker, *Conversations with Actors* 256).

Conclusion

I have considered three films in which Neil Jordan's work with actors is played out in very different registers. However disparate his projects, Jordan consistently manifests a passionate engagement with the material; there is no sense in which he is a "director for hire." There are other commonalities among the films under discussion. A signal aspect of Jordan's work is his approach, as writer/director, to character. He does not have a strong investment in probing the characters' psychology in the traditional sense; he is more interested in their immediate feelings. One knows very little about these characters; their backstories are minimal because, at best, we enter their lives in medias res. And yet one cannot call these films apsychological (in the way one might consider the work of Michelangelo Antonioni), because there is access to the emotional sensibilities and temperature of the characters: characters have definition and amplitude; feelings are experienced and enacted; and emotional journeys take place that result in major alterations of a character's life. Jordan is more interested in what I would call "sensual meaning," that which is provisional and made up of the melding of image, sound, performance, narrative, and dialogue. One intuits not only from characterological traits but from sensory materials. Although Jordan's films may be read through the filter of theoretical, historical, and cultural perspectives, it is really the experiential component that most interests the filmmaker.

I think of Neil Jordan as a postmodern romantic: postmodern in that he destabilizes boundaries, appropriates a variety of artistic referents, and transfuses genres, romantic in his embrace of perception, intuition, and sensation. Perhaps Jordan offered an important gesture toward understanding the complexity of his work when he said: "When you begin to work artistically, you throw yourself to a certain extent into chaos, into the area of your mind and experiences which is very volatile, even in some cases dangerous. The attraction of art, and perhaps the beauty of it, is that it can encapsulate all the beauty of sensual experience and at the same time allow you to meet this chaos and the darker side of your personality in, perhaps, the most meaningful way" (qtd. in Comiskey).

Thus the director does not want to diminish the irreducible mystery that subtends human behavior and being-in-the-world; rather, Jordan wishes to set forth the kaleidoscopic array of feel-

ing—whether through bold theatricality or fragile minimalism—
that makes the human condition so sublimely enigmatic.

NOTES

1. Since *Interview with the Vampire*, Jordan has enjoyed a privileged
relationship with Hollywood, largely due to the support of producer/mogul
David Geffen (now of DreamWorks). As Geffen said, "I'll enable you to
make . . . an independent film, so you can do exactly what you want."
Jordan is essentially an independent filmmaker with creative control over
his films, whether making a $70 million film like *Vampire* or smaller pro-
jects like *The Butcher Boy* (1998).

2. See, for example, Edge; Handler; Hennessy; Kotsopoulos and Mill;
Lurie; Russell; and Zilliax.

3. Rea is referring primarily to Robert De Niro and Al Pacino when
he speaks about "post-Brando Italian actors."

4. Elsewhere Meisner writes, "You don't have to play at being the
character; it's right there in your doing it" (24).

5. See Zucker, *In the Company of Actors*. Antony Sher speaks of
these elements as the most prized in acting: "The good ones keep danger
in the air" (172) and "That's what I want when I go to the theater: to see
the actor's visible soul. I always find that very moving" (174).

6. Even in this scene, which was the "twist" that distributor
Miramax used quite brilliantly in their press releases and advertising to
tantalize audiences, it is interesting to watch the way Rea underplays his
reaction to Dil's revelation. As they prepare to make love, Dil opens his
kimono to reveal a hairless male chest and his penis. Fergus (whose point
of view the camera has duplicated in the pan down Dil's body) looks up at
Dil's face, then turns frontally toward the camera, looking downward. We
can hear him breathing heavily. There is no need for a substantial reaction
from the actor because in the next shot, as Dil reaches out to touch him,
he hits Dil and then runs to the washroom to throw up. We see and hear
Fergus retching in the background while Dil occupies the foreground space,
saying, with almost preternatural calm, "It's all right, Jimmy. I can take it.
Just not on the face." The situation largely supplants the need for a great
deal of dialogue or reaction from Rea.

7. I will refer to Jaye Davidson as "she" because that is the way he
names himself in the film.

8. See Zucker, *Figures of Light*. Henry Jaglom is quite good on working with nonactors. He says:

> An actor knows the language, and you can work with them to collaborate, cre-
> ate something. A non-actor . . . I trick them into not being self-conscious, into
> trying to be as available and natural and spontaneous as they are in life.

People are very interesting in life, but they start censoring it when they're in front of a camera, when there are lights, makeup, a script, when there are specific things they must say or accomplish. So I try to take away all of those things that inhibit their acting. . . . But it's much more exciting to work with a well-trained actor. . . . When actors are really not prepared for the moment, but they've actually been prepared by their years of training to allow that moment to fully happen, those are the most exciting film moments. (250)

9. The importance of selfhood and its relationship to performance cannot be emphasized enough. No one can be anything but her- or himself, although the performer may filter the character through that self. Lindsay Crouse speaks with eloquence on the subject:

The most difficult part of the art is the struggle to bring out the truth of your being, the fullest dimension of yourself. . . . It's amazing how people will avoid using themselves in art, because we instinctively know that everything we do is a self-portrait. Acting is the art of self-revelation. We want to avoid that knowledge like the plague because of all the ambivalence we have about ourselves. We are not good enough . . . and if what we are doing is a self-portrait, everybody is going to see us. Oh my god, what will happen then? Technique is there to enable us to step forward and shine and remove all that fear, remove the tension, the self-consciousness, the defenses, all the reasons we say we can't step out. But what a great example we set when we do. (qtd. in Zucker, *Conversations with Actors* 14)

10. Jordan has called these "venereal kinds of colors," a strange but apt designation (qtd. in Whooley 10).

11. Jordan remarks that this scene is a pivotal one because Lestat forces Louis to realize what he is. The director also discusses how difficult the scene was to film because of the level of cruelty involved (*Interview with the Vampire*).

12. Armand says of his entourage of vampires, "They reflect nothing. Decadent, useless. They can't reflect anything." He says to Louis, "But you do. You reflect [this age's] broken heart." As a four-hundred-year-old vampire, he looks longingly to Louis to make contact with the present day.

13. Here one is forcefully reminded of Edmund Burke (59–61). Burke discusses how the "sublime power" completely transcends the boundaries of the individual and the mortal, and that one has the sense of being threatened with obliteration upon encountering it. The sublime is the "terrifying thrill," one filled with "pain and terror" rather than pleasure and love, terms that would most appropriately describe the spectacles of *Vampire*.

14. At the beginning of the film, when two of the main characters meet, we see them enter a house. As they climb a staircase there are intercut shots of hands caressing stockinged legs and then another insert of two pairs of hands clasped near a woman's genital area. We do not yet know to whom these body parts belong until they are repeated in a different context later in the film.

15. Surprisingly, for a director so devoted to the erotic on a variety of levels, *The End of the Affair* contains the first lovemaking scenes Jordan has filmed.

Works Cited

Boozer, Jack. "Bending Phallic Patriarchy in *The Crying Game.*" *Journal of Popular Film and Television* 22.4 (1995): 174–79.

Burke, Edmund. *A Philosophical Enquiry into the Origins of Our Ideas of the Sublime and Beautiful.* New York: Oxford UP, 1990.

Burns, Elizabeth. *Theatricality.* London: Longman, 1972.

Comiskey, Ray. "Interview with Neil Jordan." *Irish Times* 11 May 1982: 8.

Edge, Sarah. "'Women Are Trouble, Did You Know That Fergus?'" *Feminist Review* 50 (summer 1995): 173–85.

Falsetto, Mario. *Personal Visions: Conversations with Contemporary Film Directors.* Los Angeles: Silman-James, 2000.

Handler, Kristen. "Sexing *The Crying Game*: Difference, Identity, Ethics," *Film Quarterly* 47.3 (1994): 31–42.

Hennessy, Rosemary. "Ambivalence as Alibi: On the Historical Materiality of Late Capitalist Myth in *The Crying Game* and Cultural Theory." *Genders 24: On Your Left, Historical Materialism in the 1990s.* Ed. Ann Kibbey, Thomas Foster, Carol Siegel, and Ellen Berry. New York: New York UP, 1996. 1–34.

Hughes, Eamonn. "Tom Paulin." *Writing Irish: Selected Interviews with Irish Writers from the Irish Literary Supplement.* Ed. James P. Myers, Jr. Syracuse: Syracuse UP, 1998. 115–27.

Jordan, Neil. Commentary. *The End of the Affair.* DVD. Columbia Pictures, 1999.

———. Commentary. *Interview with the Vampire.* DVD. Warner Home Video, 2000.

Kotsopoulos, Aspasia, and Josephine Mill. "Gender, Genre, and Post-Feminism: *The Crying Game.*" *Jump Cut* 39 (1994): 15–24.

Lacey, Colin. "Patrick McCabe: A Comedy of Horrors." *Publishers Weekly* 16 Nov. 1998: 50–51.

Linehan, Hugh. "Greene Giant." *Irish Times* 27 Jan. 2000: 15.

Lurie, Susan. "Performativity in Disguise: Ideology and the Denaturalization of Identity in Theory in *The Crying Game.*" *Velvet Light Trap* 43 (spring 1999): 51–62.

McIllroy, Brian. *World Cinema 4: Ireland.* London: Flicks, 1986.

Meisner, Sanford. *On Acting.* New York: Vintage, 1987.

Russell, Hawley. "Crossing Games: Reading Black Transvestism at the Movies." *Critical Matrix* 8.1 (1994): 109–25.

Silverberg, Larry. *The Sanford Meisner Approach.* Lyme: Smith and Kraus, 1994.

Whooley, Sharon, ed. "Neil Jordan: In Conversation with Michael Dwyer."

The Fleadh Papers, Vol. II, 13 July 1997, 1–20.

Zilliax, Amy. "The Scorpion and the Frog: Agency and Identity in Neil Jordan's *The Crying Game.*" *Camera Obscura* 35 (May 1994): 25–52.

Zucker, Carole. "The Concept of 'Excess' in Film Acting: Notes toward an Understanding of Non-naturalistic Performance." *Postscript* 12.2 (1993): 54–62.

———. *Conversations with Actors on Film, Television, and Stage Performance.* Portsmouth: Heinemann, 2002.

———. *Figures of Light: Actors and Directors Illuminate the Art of Film Acting.* New York: Plenum, 1995.

———. *In the Company of Actors.* London: A & C Black, 1999.

4

....

POSTMODERN

FILM

PERFORMANCE

9

Acting Prima Donna Politics in Tomás Gutiérrez Alea's *Strawberry and Chocolate*

Ronald E. Shields

The Cuban film *Strawberry and Chocolate*, with screenplay by Senel Paz and direction by Tomás Gutiérrez Alea and Juan Carlos Tabio, created a sensation when released in Havana and throughout the world in 1994. According to film historian and critic Emilio Bejel, the film exposes what it meant to be a homosexual artist in Castro's Cuba in 1979 (69). Bejel argues that the film provides an exploration of "how personal identity must connect to some accepted cultural identity if a sense of collective identity is to develop" (66). Within the context of the film's date of release in Cuba, the film offered "a radical proposition" by calling for the "acceptance and integration of homosexuality in the concept of Cuban nationality," along with other disenfranchised social groups, as imperatives to save a dying Cuba (66). The film arrived in the United States in September 1994 as part of the Latin American Film Festival in New York. Soon after, it was distributed throughout the United States and became the first Cuban film (with English subtitles) ever to reach major American markets (65–66).

Strawberry and Chocolate, a product of Cuban national cinema and American marketing, serves up telling social drama as an operatic and ironic comedy, a compassionate treatment of homosexual life within an intolerant culture. The film stands in stark contrast to Nestor Almendros's bleak documentary, *Improper Conduct* (1983), which revealed Castro's evil plots to purge homosexuality from Cuban soil (forced labor camps, electroshock therapy, and worse). Based on a story by Senel Paz, *Strawberry and Chocolate* explores the layered terrain between an attractive young Marxist, David (Vladimir Cruz), who learns tolerance, and a bourgeois homosexual artist, Diego (Jorge Perugorria), who defects from Cuba to seek acceptance elsewhere. Film critic Edward Guthmann called the film "a gentle, sometimes long-winded plea for tolerance" that positions the homosexual character "as a mirror—not only for David's homosexual biases and Communist Party cant, but also for Cuba's resistance to anyone who falls outside the established norm."

Film scholar Bert Cardullo notes that the film's cinematographer, Mario Garcia Joya, felt that the film was a "slyly propagandistic film about homosexuality from the Cuban government's point of view" (480). Indeed, Joya argues, the film presents a "safe" treatment of the subject of homosexual repression in Cuba. The events of the film are placed "in the past, *after* the shutting down of Cuba's concentration camps for gays and *before* the Mariel boatlift as well as the AIDS epidemic (and AIDS-quarantining)." The film presents a heterosexual Marxist "overcoming his aversion to homosexuals, if not embracing homosexuality itself" (481). The film captures and exploits the Cuban political dynamic through an ironic cinematic style, an aesthetic approach framing the space in which oppositional discourses interpret social configurations of power and desire, repression and revolt.

According to Linda Hutcheon, the postmodernist use of irony as an aesthetic and rhetorical strategy includes "an increased ability to subvert *from within*, to speak the language of the dominant order and, at the same time, suggest another meaning and another evaluation" (16). In postmodern aesthetic terms, particularly comic juxtapositions and the use of assimilated gesture, *Strawberry and Chocolate* evokes the grim realities of Cuban oppression within the facade of a normalized social discourse about homosexuality. Cuban politics during the closing decades of the twentieth century can be read as prima donna politics—a rousing national opera complete with onstage and offstage voices, a diverting cast of supporting characters, sustained and heightened emotions, ridiculous plots, flights of virtuoso display, and compelling prima donnas center stage and off. Alea's lifelong visionary politics play out in this film in surprising ways. The film connects the political and the personal through assimilated acting techniques (gesture collected from life and presented as quotation), ironic operatic frames, musical quotations, and references to gay culture and the diva Maria Callas.

The film opens with a brief comic prologue. David, a university student at Havana University and a good communist, brings his girlfriend to a cheap hotel to make love. While she undresses in the bathroom, David finds a hole in the wall and briefly glimpses a couple in the next room noisily copulating. To underscore the comic moment and to suggest David's imagined desire, this pornographic glimpse is presented in black-and-white footage juxtaposed to the realistic color film used in the framing scene. Embarrassed by what he sees and responding to his girlfriend's obviously false protestations of virtue, he nobly announces that he won't make love to her until they are married. Her startled response, presented in a tightly framed close-up, is "What?" As spectators, we are as surprised as the young woman—a comic shift that establishes the narrative perspective of the film away from sex and toward issues of idealism, desire, and personal choice.

The scene cuts to her wedding day with another man, and we see David moving away to find solace in ice cream. Attracted to David, Diego also orders ice cream (strawberry rather than chocolate) and invites the young man to his apartment with promises of novels by Vargas Llosa. In the apartment, the gay artist Diego tries to seduce the young David. He plays a tape of Maria Callas before going into the kitchen to make coffee and tea. Diego pauses, listens to the voice, and says: "God, what a voice! Why can't the island produce a voice like that? We need another voice so badly." When questioned about this passage, the director Tomás Gutiérrez Alea laughed and confirmed it as a reference to Fidel Castro's vast political power and the need to open the Cuban political system: "Well, it seems obvious, doesn't it? Of course, that line is said as a joke, but a joke that contains a great measure of truth" (qtd. in West 16).

With this second scene of failed seduction, Alea once again plays against expectations. Using the voice of Maria Callas to foreground issues of gay identity and underscore particular operatic aspects of character and plot in the film, the filmmaker comically renders homosexual desire through an adroit use of assimilated gesture. Diego embodies his sexuality through an assimilated acting style that shifts from lyrical realism to flights of excess—aesthetic and emotive qualities mirrored in the operatic arias he loves. As argued by Cynthia Baron, postmodern cinema fixates on "commerce with popular culture, the eschewing of psychological realism, an opposition to realism in general, an alleged inability to be politically progressive, and a marked tendency of excess" (19). This describes the postmodern force of *Strawberry and Chocolate*: the nexus of acting choices, gay politics, and opera, presented as comedy.

My explication of the postmodern acting used to express gay desire in *Strawberry and Chocolate* focuses on the use of Callas as a signifier, the surprising "politically progressive" use of a comedy, and the "marked tendency" toward excess and camp, specifically in the use of an assimilated acting style. My analysis of Diego's seduction scene begins with a discussion of assimilated acting and Alea's use of comedy as political critique. In doing so, I address Alea's debt to neorealism and "imperfect cinema"—cinematic and ideological preoccupations central to Cuban national cinema. My argument explicitly links Callas to the politics present in *Strawberry and Chocolate* through an explication of specific acting choices used to reference gay desire in the film. Finally, I contrast the operatic excess in *Strawberry and Chocolate* with the physical restraint used to express gay desire in a similar scene in Jonathan Demme's film *Philadelphia* (1993). My reading of these operatic moments traces the power of Callas's circulating image within and beyond the borders of the gay community. Both films expose the cultural forces that shape the embodiment of homosexual desire and police the boundaries of gesture, political and aesthetic.

Neorealism, Imperfect Cinema, and Assimilated Acting

Within the traditions of the Western drama, the dramatic genre known as the "comedy of manners" refers to works originally presented on the English stage during the closing decades of the seventeenth century and throughout the eighteenth. These plays featured a highly ordered society and stock characters governed by decorum. Urbane and often cynical in tone, these plays used stock characters, wit, and elaborate plots to expose the excesses and shallowness of English social life and the foibles of personality. As popular taste shifted to embrace sentimentality onstage, stage comedy changed to embrace wit as well as satire on contemporary subjects, a dramatic form using laughter as well as tears as a lens for social critique (Brockett 327–28, 335). In this regard, Alea's use of comedy as part of his ideological project within Cuban national cinema can be defined as an extension of this traditional comic impulse. For example, in his film *Death of a Bureaucrat* (1966), a worker dies in a work-related accident and is buried with his worker's card. When his widow finds that she cannot claim her husband's pension, she goes to elaborate steps to reclaim this literal symbol of his proletarian standing. As a black comedy, the film exposes the foibles of individuals acting their roles within a highly bureaucratic society. In *Strawberry and Chocolate*, Alea again uses comedy to expose the limitations of life under Castro. He also uses excess to embody gay desire and, in doing so, connects gesture to his larger ideological project.

Speaking to the Association of Third World Studies in October 1993, Alea discussed his career in film, Cuban cinema, and the role of the artist in the Third World. Arguing that cinema should function as an ideological weapon, the filmmaker placed his cinematic practice within the tenets of neorealism and Garcia Espinosa's "imperfect cinema." According to Alea, "because of its forms of production, its dramaturgy and its aesthetics" neorealism created an "authenticity" of expression in Cuban national cinema, qualities lacking in Hollywood cinema at the time. Dismissing the claims of those critics who rejected imperfect cinema as "praise for clumsiness, for ugliness, or for a lack of professionalism," Alea stressed the "ironic tone" underlying the theory of an imperfect cinema, an approach directed "against the hollow perfection" of Hollywood's "ostentatious display of technique." According to Alea, Espinosa influenced him by inviting him "to place technique at the service of imagination and not vice-versa" (102–3). Stressing the power of colonialism to shape economic structures as well as spectatorship, Alea argued that Cuban films should be able to compete profitably with other cinemas: "We ought to be able to compete in equal circumstances with our colleagues anywhere in the world; we should be able to compete for both spectators and screens—that is the heart of the matter" (103). He concluded by blaming "the transnationals" for controlling access to distribution and calling for the "diversification" in audience taste through exposure to multiple cinematic traditions (106–7).

Given that Alea's speech was delivered shortly before the release of *Strawberry and Chocolate*, it is instructive to consider how the various aesthetic and political ideas outlined in the address manifest themselves in this particular film. Certainly the popularity of *Strawberry and Chocolate* in Cuba and around the world testifies to his desire to diversify audience taste by bringing his mature imperfect cinema to an international audience. But how is this film an example of Alea's grounding in neorealism? At first glance, *Strawberry and Chocolate* does not appear to contain any elements of neorealism. Seamlessly edited and filmed in color, the film does not feature nonactors in leading roles; in fact, Alea chose not to cast a homosexual actor to portray the gay artist, Diego. Nevertheless, in a nod toward neorealism's quest for authenticity, he did instruct Jorge Perugorria to gather physical behaviors and attitudes from Cuban homosexuals as part of the acting style central to his characterization of Diego. In doing so, he opened the door to the postmodern.

According to Perugorria, although Alea could have cast several gay actors as Diego, he selected a heterosexual because of the actor's ability to "find the truth he wanted." In an interview with Johannes Birringer, Perugorria describes his preparation for the role as a process of assimilation. He notes that Alea introduced him to "several of his friends who are intellectuals and homosexuals," individuals who "he thought had something of Diego's character in them" (21). He also gathered impressions from his own circle of gay friends "to discover how they relate to each other, as well as their way of seeing things." From these experiences, he "began to select from each one some detail, some story, some quotation" and ultimately began to "formulate Diego's role" (22).

Critical responses to Perugorria's performance underscore his use of stereotypical gesture to convey character. Film critic Rita Kempley acknowledges Perugorria's performance, specifically his success in revealing how "Diego the unique human being 'emerges' from Diego the stereotypical Queen" (B7). But to dismiss the acting as predictable camp would be reductive. An example of postmodern acting, the performance of gay desire in *Strawberry and Chocolate* exploits the perspectives of spectator and actor in a single body. As described by theorist Philip Auslander, the formulation of the "spectactor" provides "a way of reconceptualizing postmodern subjectivity without denying its fracturing, so as to recover a space for critical distance and, hence, politics in postmodern performance" (8). This self-aware gestural collage grounded in neorealism's quest for authenticity assumes aesthetic form in *Strawberry and Chocolate*, a film that exposes the critical force of assimilated acting through the presentation of character as cultural sign. Whereas neorealism's quest for psychological or material realities serves as the base essence of expression through most of the film, the occasional comic use of assimilated acting to present gay desire pushes the film into the postmodern. Assimilated acting purposely manipulates surfaces and mirrors how individuals navigate and view the individual and cultural landscape. Consequently, through gestural excess, gay desire in *Strawberry and Chocolate* plays out a telling satire of Cuban society's attitudes about homosexuality (figure 9.1).

9.1. Contrived
gestural excess as
assimilated acting
(Jorge Perugorria
as Diego).

Elinor Fuchs explicates the social and economic forces framing postmodern politics and art by arguing that "the stunning collapse of communism and the retreat of democratic socialism
destroyed the compass by which most nations in the twentieth century organized themselves ideologically, whether for or against,
willingly or under compulsion." Change, she continues, is neither
uniform nor universal. Nevertheless, "all are forced to acknowledge and respond to the irresistible advance of transnational economic and electronic forces" (16). Perhaps Alea's surprisingly accessible depiction of homosexuality in the comedy *Strawberry and
Chocolate* can be attributed to his continuous growth as an ideologically committed artist, a filmmaker seeking new audiences and
modes of expression through an appropriation of the transnational
imperative. Ultimately, the film was constructed to succeed in a
variety of markets—a subversive postmodern act of reverse colonialism (the telling irony of Miramax distributing Cuban national
cinema as popular entertainment).

Callas Sings in Castro's Cuba: Prima Donna Voice and Gay Identity

Strawberry and Chocolate is set in 1979, right before the Mariel
boatlift in 1980, an event that brought about great changes in
Cuba—a nation ready for a new voice, well aware that change will

225

come only when new worlds are welcomed and embraced. This is the world dreamed and preached by Diego: a world literally played out in his apartment, filled with emblems of his imagined yet forbidden place. His apartment contains American whiskey, a poster of Marilyn Monroe from *Some Like It Hot*, forbidden magazines and novels, music by Cuban expatriates, political art filled with disturbing religious imagery, and the voice of Maria Callas singing Leonara from Giuseppe Verdi's *Il trovatore*. Alea's use of Callas's voice resonates with details of the diva's legend and her progress as a prima donna. The opera is based on an older sword-and-honor play replete with Latino cultural representations of masculinity, cultural norms still prevalent in Castro's Cuba and problematized in comic and more serious ways in the film (see Murray; Smith 248–60). Ultimately, the aria itself provides ironic and comic commentary on the action of the scene.

Callas's performance of "D'amor sull'a li rosee" (an aria that leads directly into the choral "Miserere") was originally prepared for performances during her Latin America tour in 1950. She sang in *Il trovatore* for the first time in Mexico City on 20 June, along with the great American baritone Leonard Warren. Although Callas had earlier made her mark in Venice and Florence, she had not yet conquered La Scala. Her exuberant singing came out of a strong and youthful, though unglamorous, body. These performances (in Mexico, Brazil, and Argentina) were marked by flamboyant vocal excess and dramatic overstatement. During those years, she began to acquire wealth, popularity, and critical success as a prima donna (Galatopoulos 93–111). Listening to recordings of these performances today and viewing photographs of Callas taken in the early 1950s, one can hardly imagine the radical changes in her voice and body yet to come. By the summer of 1954, she was a slender, beautiful woman. In becoming so, she distanced herself from images from her past. Callas biographies document glimpses of the unattractive young Callas as she moved through the war-torn streets of Athens on her way to the conservatory. Production photographs show the heavy young singer singing out for freedom as Leonora in Beethoven's *Fidelio*. Family photographs show the young woman with bad skin who was forced to leave Greece to seek a career elsewhere because she feared both the fascists and the communists.

Unlike the characters in *Strawberry and Chocolate*, Callas rarely expressed political opinions in her letters. However, like David in the film, when politics obstructed her work as an artist, Callas did speak out. In a letter written while in Argentina, Callas expressed her frustration working in the country under Eva Peron: "Buenos Aires is quite hateful to me. The climate is awful. Too much smog everywhere. And then it is very fascist. All the fascists of the universe are here. Even the theater is under the control of Evita" (qtd. in Allegri 72). Reading her letters to her husband, Meneghini, from this period reveal a Callas who is a terribly ambitious performer desperate for opportunities, personal love, and public adoration, as well as an artist intolerant of political oppression.

The Maria Callas referenced in the film *Strawberry and Chocolate* reflects specific moments in her progress as a prima donna, a time of personal and professional transitions. Adapting Ferdinand de Saussure's structuralist approach to linguistics as a critical lens by which to read cultural texts, it could be argued that Callas serves as a cultural icon. Given her celebrity status, she emerges as a "culturally agreed link" connecting the signifier with the sign so that "the signifier immediately invokes the idea associated with it" (Counsell 11–12). Leonora was a major Callas role during the early stages of her career and this particular aria was occasionally programmed during the later years of her career as well. Indeed, *Il trovatore* was associated with significant turning points in Callas's life and career: both the soaring voice of the emerging diva in Latin America and the faltering voice of the slim haute couture diva in Paris.

Contemporary theorists interested in the intersection of opera and homosexuality often focus on the anguish and triumphant anger of the prima donna, particularly Maria Callas, as an archetype for gay opera culture. Voice has emerged as a useful trope by which to investigate the cultural and performative dimensions of opera within the convergent economies of race, gender, and sexuality. For instance, Catherine Clément, in her book *Opera, or the Undoing of Women*, argues that traditional operatic plots mute the female voice in subordinate cultural roles, a necessary dramatic construction to control and defuse female energy that often leaves the dying soprano rendered voiceless. According to critic Paul Robinson, Clément's focus on operatic plots as literary and cultural constructs misses a source of female triumph, the actual sound of the diva's singing voice. Robinson argues that operatic character can best be understood as sonorous voice, an embodied critical perspective that rises above competing characters, orchestras, and predictable misogynistic plots. To do so shifts the focus from one aspect of textuality (the scripted) to another (the embodied). A critical preoccupation with voice (embodied expression as well as social code) can also serve as an important part of promoting and defining the "voice" of a public persona, including operatic divas such as Maria Callas. As Wayne Koestenbaum reminds us, although "opera is an elite form, and though Callas's fans were usually at least middle-class, and usually white, her image circulated beyond opera culture's borders" (135). Leonardi and Pope go so far as to suggest that the diva, "even if we give her a recognizable name—Maria Callas, Joan Sutherland, Marilyn Horne, Leontyne Price, Marian Anderson—is not so much a person as a position, a condition, a situation" (9). Whereas in general terms, a psychoanalytic tradition of identification emphasizes a preoccupation with self and consciousness, postmodern identification focuses on reflections and shifting surfaces. As such, the sensual voice of the diva serves as a site of inquiry for the projections and desires of others, a shifting surface and postmodern signifier.

Callas's operatic career coincided with advances in recording technology (the long-playing [LP] record) and the paparazzi. These powerful venues of cultural circulation (and the dramatic events of her life and talent that prompted this circulation) soon became part of the story. Perhaps her eventual circulation as a cultural icon originates, in part, from the unique "grain" of her sound and technique. As articulated by Roland Barthes, the grain of a voice is what a listener hears and experiences, a combination of "pheno-song" and "geno-song" that constitutes performance. Combining technique and taste, musical understanding and style, talent and personality, Barthes's "grain of the voice" is "the body in the voice as it sings, the hand as it writes, the limb as it performs." He goes on to confess his highly personal response to the embodied voice: "I am determined to listen to my relation with the body of the man or woman singing or playing and that relation is erotic" (188). The emphases on body, as well as voice and issues of identification, circulate around the power of the prima donna as cultural signifier. Photographs, recordings, and videos of Callas in performance document that her technique was extremely physical; reviews of her performances also verify that her audiences were rarely passive in response to her embodied voice. The recorded voice of Callas is as flexible and telling as her constructed myth; each found sonorous expression in a variety of dramatic bodies and plots (real and operatic).

In *Strawberry and Chocolate*, Diego's response to Callas's voice is articulated through his quick gasp, his audible response to her singing, and it serves as a catalyst for all that follows. Indeed, his response to the grain of her voice quickly turns to identification, a postmodern preoccupation with surfaces and significations. As argued by Leonardi and Pope, the diva's voice within gay culture ultimately emerges as "a political force." Bold and assertive, "the diva's voice moves and transforms women (and a few men), gives them (or helps them to discover in themselves) new vision, strength, desire" (19). As cultural sign, the diva's voice enters the consciousness only in a culturally shaped and mediated form, a constructed meaning.

As theatrical onstage as off, Callas dramatically reshaped her body in mid-career; soon afterward, she reshaped her personal life (moving from a conventional marriage with Meneghini to accepting her role as the mistress kept on Aristotle Onassis's yacht). Her diverse operatic repertoire also shifted as she moved through her career (changes connected to the state of voice, her opportunities, and her personal choices). Biographies and coffee-table books document Callas "in both her personal and professional capacities (the boundaries sometimes proving hard to distinguish)" (Lindenberger 2). The circulating visual and recorded Callas legacy documents that she often looked and sounded quite differently. This ability to exploit the wide dramatic and musical range of her voice characterizes the diva's career and recorded oeuvre. Ultimately, these connections between her personal life and her art shape the critical controversy surrounding her rapid vocal decline and combine to construct Callas as an icon within parts of the gay community. As Roland Barthes reminds us, cultural myths (a socially determined "reflection") are a type of collective representation, the constructed product of images and values circulating within the popular press and marketplace (165–67).

Acknowledging the idiosyncratic and transitory nature of cultural mythmaking, the failed seduction scene in *Strawberry and Chocolate* exploits the voice of Callas and the Callas myth to construct political critique and character development through an operatic acting style. To do so opens the door to the postmodern. In an interview with Dennis West, Alea rejected any critical reading of Jorge Perugorria's acting in the film as a parade of gay stereotypes: "No, no. He's definitely not a stereotype. Diego is not really even a *loca*. The equivalent in English of *loca* is 'queen'—a gay who expresses himself in a very extroverted, very spectacular manner, who flaunts his homosexuality" (16). Alea's rejection of the limitations of stereotype underscores the constructed nature of Diego's character in the film. Building character through contrasting

9.2. Acting gay desire as prima donna politics (Jorge Perugorria as Diego).

physical responses, Perugorria's specific acting choices at times appear as contrived excess, operatic moments in the extreme. As film theorist Paul Burston notes in describing vestiges of gay culture and identity, "a diva creates herself" through display of voice and gesture: "Her gestures are rehearsed, her appearances staged" (107). Much the same could be said about Perugorria's preparation and portrayal of Diego in *Strawberry and Chocolate* (figure 9.2).

Assimilated Acting and Gay Desire in *Strawberry and Chocolate*

In his theory of postmodern acting, Philip Auslander notes the difficulty of reading the body as a sign. He argues that "to posit the body as an absolute, originary presence beyond signification is neither accurate nor theoretically defensible." Ultimately, "the problematic of the performing body lies in the tension between the body's inevitably serving as a signifier while simultaneously exceeding, without transcending, that function" (8). A close reading of Jorge Perugorria's acting choices as Diego in the seduction scene illustrates postmodernism's preoccupation with signification and embodiment, specifically the actor's use of assimilated gesture and his identification with and referencing of Maria Callas as a gay icon (a mirrored act that exceeds but does not transcend).

The Verdi aria used in this scene is a construction of extended lyrical phrases punctuated with moments of coloratura display. Perugorria's performance as Diego mirrors this operatic construction and ranges from moments of subtle understatement to expansive, clichéd gestures. When Diego turns on the tape to play the aria, he presses his middle finger to his forehead when he hears her voice. Slowly, he moves his fingers down over his face to his lips and briefly caresses his throat before crossing his arms over his chest: "God, what a voice!" With that lyrical operatic gesture of devotion, he places gay desire and his identification with the diva's voice within the mind, the throat, and the heart of his character. Moments later, as he turns to leave the room, he theatrically throws his arm over his head as he grandly exits to make coffee.

Other moments in this scene repeat this pattern of controlled lyrical embodiment set against expansive flights of emotion and physical display. For example, when Diego enters with the coffee and prepares to spill the drink onto David's shirt, he carefully bends over and slowly closes the door by backing into it. Suddenly, like a scene out of a comic opera, he spills the coffee onto David's shirt and then urges him to take it off so that he can remove the stain. This action, played quickly and with full comic effect as farce, is underscored with Diego's furtive glances at David's naked chest and a flurry of worried gestures as he takes the shirt and brings a towel to provide a modest covering for David.

As the aria draws to an end and the seduction is obviously over, Diego brings the operatic reference full circle by declaring, "Isn't it wonderful. People out there pushing on buses, everyone shouting, and you and I here, listening to Maria Callas." As he speaks these words, he carefully holds his cup and rubs his finger along the edge, signaling frustrated desire. The aria is over, literally and figuratively. As the conversation turns to Cuban politics and literature, Diego's use of gesture is restrained and devoid of excess. The obvious shift in acting style can only be understood as a deliberate juxtaposition in performance choices designed for rhetorical effect. The choice is made to exploit details of assimilated behavior for comic effect (the film as a comedy of manners) in contrast to the more acceptable group of behaviors appropriate for a social drama (the film as a polemic).

It could be argued that Alea knew that for Diego to be accepted as a sympathetic character by the general public, his homosexual desire would have to be embodied as operatic excess and framed as comic farce. In contrast, Diego's politics and discourse on art and artistic freedom evokes a subdued and restrained embodiment, controlled and free from affectation. These aesthetic contrasts in acting choices clearly underscore the ironic tone of the film as postmodern parody (sex farce as social critique) and illustrate Alea's self-articulated artistic agenda to use film as "an ideological weapon," merging "entertainment, artistic expression, and cultural product" as "a bearer of ideas" (112).

The scene ends with Callas singing Leonora's words, "But, oh, if our ways should forever part, he will not know the torment, the breaking of my heart, he will not know the torment, the woe, the woe in my heart." As argued by Wayne Koestenbaum in his personal gay reading of *Il trovatore*, the power of the opera plays out in the theoretical and erotic space surrounding and connecting the characters, a dynamic personal space embodied through gesture and voice: "Only Leonora is visible. The voices of the unseen monks provide miasma; to make an impression, Leonora needs their somber chant as backdrop. If you're deprived of erotic freedom, imitate Leonora. Banish comedy from your body. Dive below the staff to summon chest notes, and quickly re-ascend to your head" (223).

Diego, accepting of David's heterosexuality, turns his seduction toward David's intellect, his sense of nationalism, and his cultural consciousness. Hence the lines, "Isn't it wonderful. People out there pushing on buses, everyone shouting, and you and I here, listening to Maria Callas." In the opera, Leonora has left the convent to seek out her beloved Manrico, who has been thrown into a tower prison by the evil political ruler, Count di Luna (who also happens to be—unknown to all but the gypsy Azucena—Manrico's long-lost brother). As Koestenbaum notes, "Manrico lacks an onstage body: he is just a tower, a tower that warns, in its stiff salute, that a man will soon be missing" (224).

In *Strawberry and Chocolate*, Diego's flirtatious ways in the obviously contrived situation call out to David through Leonora's replies to Manrico's voice in words as ironic (and hilarious) ruptures of high art; the film's plot is, in many ways, as contrived as opera itself. The juxtaposition establishes several comic and ironic parallels: Leonora's leaving the convent as opposed to Diego's leaving the closet; David's ideological prison as opposed to Manrico's tower; and Leonora's call for "gentle breezes" as a parallel to Diego's inner monologue "sighing" while he tries to seduce David. Thus in postmodern aesthetic terms, Alea creates a contrived comedy of manners through ironic juxtaposition.

Concurrently—and pointedly—for the thematic richness of *Strawberry and Chocolate*, Callas's voice and the dramatic action of *Il trovatore* work together to critique the cultural and political oppression in Cuba. As noted by Auslander, "the postmodern political artist has no choice but to operate within the culture whose representation he or she must both recycle and critique" (89). In this film, Alea circulates operatic references, a postmodern juxtaposition linking high and low cultural forms.

According to Alea, the year 1979 marked one of the darkest periods of artistic and homophobic persecution in Cuba (qtd. in West 16). In the opera, Count di Luna discovers the true identity of his brother, Manrico, moments after ordering his execution. Reading the Cuban political scene through the opera, the film asks the question: Will change bring Cuba's brothers together before it is too late? Expressed another way: Will silence create death as well as desire? Koestenbaum points out that in the opera desire *and* politics prompt character and plot: "From his tower, which looms on the stage like an abstract, harmless phallus, Manrico delivers a real melody, more lyrical and arching than Leonora's separate spasms of distress. Hysterical Manrico spills outward, displays his symptoms, forbids containment" (223). Manrico, like Diego, longs to escape his prison. Established as a Leonora surrogate early in the scene through his identification with Callas, Diego also plays Manrico while in the kitchen singing a Cuban folk song against the voice of Callas. As Diego leaves David to look around the apartment while he makes coffee, Diego's relationship to the singing Callas is altered. His absence shares and shifts Leonora's longing onto David. The pursuer and the pursued become one in the chase. Both seek fulfillment. Both reach out against the voices of political oppression.

Callas Sings in the City of Brotherly Love: A Hollywood Leading Man Acts Gay Desire

More than background music, Maria Callas's voice in *Philadelphia* appears at a crucial moment in the film and allows the central gay character to emotionally connect with his heterosexual attorney. In this way, Callas's voice serves as a bridge of understanding parallel to the use of her voice in *Strawberry and Chocolate*. In both films, her singing resonates within and beyond the personal and social isolation experienced by the gay men, individuals separated by sexuality and politics, ignorance and desire, ethnicity and class. In

Philadelphia, we see Andrew Beckett, a white gay man dying from AIDS in the city of brotherly love. *Strawberry and Chocolate*, a film about contrasting tastes, details a gay Latino's story about surviving a life of sexual and artistic censorship in Castro's Cuba. Both films present a story of transformation and change. Both films present a gay central character through carefully controlled acting styles. However, whereas Diego's homosexuality is indicated through an assimilated acting style, Tom Hanks's portrayal of Andrew Beckett is devoid of any deliberate assimilations of gay desire.

In an interview with the critic Michael Fleming, gay comedian Scott Thompson expressed dismay with Demme's casting of Hanks in the lead role—an example of our culture's homophobia. According to Thompson, casting Hanks as a gay character was Hollywood's way of coping. In the interview, Thompson was quoted as saying that the film did not go far enough to reveal the physicality of gay expressiveness: "If you're an opera queen listening to your favorite aria, aren't you lip-synching? Lip-synching is the most popular gay sport, after figure skating" (2). Despite this reductive comic turn toward cliché, Thompson's observation speaks to his awareness of the specific acting choices used to embody homosexuality and the diva's voice in *Philadelphia*, acting choices selected to foreground the AIDS crisis in acceptable dramatic terms.

According to Quentin Curtis, "Great scenes usually grace great films or redeem mediocre ones," and the confession scene featuring the voice of Callas makes this film important. During this scene, the melodrama "comes out of the closet. Before, it has been all things to all multiplexes: a love story that dares not speak its name, a legal thriller that's fixed, a message movie that pulls its punches. Now it's about living with AIDS—and dying with it." Demme's cinematic approach, an aesthetic of indirection in both the acting and the visual narrative, illustrates the cautious commercialism of the entire project (the first "AIDS film" from a major studio) and serves as an example of cinematic realism, Hollywood style (figure 9.3).

As noted by Ronald Mark Kraft, commercialism shapes the film: "Gays and lesbians may very well feel cheated by *Philadelphia*—it's AIDS 101 and Gay 101 all neatly tied up with a red ribbon—but this movie wasn't necessarily made with them in mind" ("Philadelphia Freedom" 72). Doug Tomlinson avers that in its quest for realism, "traditional narrative cinema . . . encourages both projection and identification" through the use of close-up and reac-

9.3. A high-angle establishing shot frames an operatic entrance (Tom Hanks as Andrew Beckett and Denzel Washington as Joe Miller).

tion shots to trace emotion and reaction (372). This is the editing style favored in this film. Consequently, what we think and feel about Andrew Beckett (Tom Hanks) is shaped by how others respond to him and his situation, particularly Joe Miller (Denzel Washington), his lawyer. Tom Hanks avoids the operatic gestures of the diva and speaks through the verbal and physical rhythms of a Hollywood leading man—an acting style based on bodily and vocal restraint. Acting style *and* editing practice within the Callas scene illustrate these elements of traditional narrative cinema.

The Callas referenced in *Philadelphia* links directly to Callas's performance of Maddalena's aria, "La mama morte," from *Andrea Chenier*, composed by Umberto Giordano. Andrew Beckett introduces Callas's voice as an example of his "favorite aria" during a late-night session working with his attorney in preparation for the upcoming trial. Beckett is suing his former employers, accusing them of discrimination because he is homosexual and dying from AIDS. From earlier scenes in the film, it is clear that he has a case; he was dismissed from his position after his employers learned of his illness. It now is necessary for Beckett to prove discrimination in court, despite painful revelations and personal intrusions. While Callas sings, Maddalena's words blend with Beckett's explanation of the operatic text, a performance revealing the depths and intensity of the dying man's despair and human ability to love. What is important in this scene is Hanks's refusal to embody the voice of Callas. What we see is his translation of what she is saying. During the scene Beckett's emotional identification with the voice echoes his friend's ability to understand. Only once does his voice suggest the flirting tones of gay desire—on the phrase "Heaven is in your

9.4. A tight close-up breaks the silence about AIDS (Tom Hanks as Andrew Beckett).

eyes." However, immediately after saying these words, Beckett's face contorts in pain in response to the tender memory. In framing this moment with this strong physical response, a connection is made between gay desire and AIDS and the assumed universal emotion of memory and regret (figure 9.4).

When Tom Hanks as Andrew Beckett begins this scene, he references the stereotype of the opera queen, the homosexual who finds absolution and inspiration in diva worship. However, his embodiment of the scene avoids physical cliché. His movements are slow and deliberate, and his vocal inflections are introspective and haunting. The context of the scene, the fact that he wants to share his love of Callas's performance, might well have been portrayed in the operatic excess of lip-synching or drag performance. However, Hanks's acting avoids excess and his verbal text explains rather than duplicates the aria, a deliberate rhetorical approach to character. He speaks *alongside* the text of the aria, making connections among his life, his world, and the world of the aria. As he works to explain, his voice and body bear witness. His performance avoids direct physical and vocal identification with the diva. What we see and hear is his explanation of how Callas's performance makes sense of what he is living through. Identification is established, but indirectly.

An operatic confession witnessed by his belligerently heterosexual counsel, this scene serves as a turning point within the film. Joe Miller's realization of his homophobia is revealed through a series of reaction shots used to track his reluctant but inevitable reversal. When viewed in isolation, these reaction shots (with the soft romantic lighting, tight framing, and fashion-plate attire) appear

9.5. Hollywood-
style reaction shot
(Denzel Washington
as Joe Miller).

as bizarre commercials for romance novels. (Is he listening to Maria
Callas or a torch singer?) Juxtaposed against the intense and jarring
images of Beckett's explanation of the aria, these mainstream
images blend to sustain a cinematic style appropriate to traditional
narrative cinema: Joe watches, listens, and responds, and slowly,
vicariously, enters into the hell of Beckett's reality (figure 9.5). Joe's
reversal, prompted by Beckett's performance, mirrors Maddalena's
change in the first act of the opera. After hearing Chenier's inspira-
tional poetry, Maddalena's aristocratic indifference to human suffering crumbles. In this Hollywood drama, as in the opera, love triumphs, and understanding follows. And, of course, the suffering
lover ultimately dies in each.

The contrast between Joe's slow progress toward empathy and
Andrew's emotional confession during the aria scene can be traced
in the careful use of lighting, blocking, and camera angle. As Amy
Taubin notes, "Despite the close-ups that put the actors in the viewers' laps and the percussive use of camera movement, *Philadelphia*
is extremely theatrical: it seems like opera" (25). Earlier in the
scene, Andrew enters the room pushing his medical-drip stand,
much like the character of Tosca during her first entrance—a diva
standing alone onstage. The scene ends with him standing alone in
the center of the room, leaning heavily on the stand for support—a
diva spent, standing alone onstage. Both images are established
through a high-angle shot circling above the wooden floor of the
apartment. At key moments, Andrew pushes his medical-drip into
and out of frame—a lonely solo dance. These moments carry visible
reminders of his disease, his struggle, and his mortality. In addition,
the use of a moving camera, the pulsating red light alternating with

darkness on Andrew's face, and the layered line readings by Tom Hanks, all work together to bring the audience directly into Andrew Beckett's world, his hope, and his hell. This is what Joe sees as well and, in watching, he is changed.

Callas sang *Andrea Chenier* only once during her career, a series of stormy performances in January and February 1955, with the tenor Mario Del Monaco. They were supposed to have opened the new year's season in a production of *Il trovatore*, but the tenor claimed illness and requested that Giordano's opera be substituted for the Verdi. That this substitution was allowed speaks to more backstage intrigues at La Scala. Indeed, Del Monoco's requested substitution was a clumsy attempt to upstage Callas. Leonora in *Trovatore* was considered a Callas specialty—something a jealous tenor colleague would rather avoid. In addition, the character of Maddalena was a favorite role of Callas's rival, Renata Tebaldi. Perhaps the tenor, who frequently was paired with Tebaldi on London Records, preferred a different leading lady. Be that as it may, Callas surprised them all: she learned the role in less than five days and gave an electric performance (Galatopoulos 110, 177–80). Could it be that Andrew Beckett identifies with Callas and this aria because he knows what it means to work against the clock and strive against impossible odds, knows what it takes to speak out against intrigues?

Callas's close friend Stelios Galatopoulos later reported that Callas "found Maddalena interesting in the way she develops from a frivolous girl to a serious and dignified woman," a woman capable of the "ultimate sacrifice" (178). In the film, Beckett reaches into and surrenders to Callas's performance of the aria as index to his own struggles and trials, both literal and figurative: a response made physically visible during his visceral responses to details in the musical score (such as the solo cello lines). The words of the aria describe Maddalena's circumstances and emotions as she anticipates the trial in which the life of Chenier hangs in the balance. Recalling her despair on seeing her mother murdered and her home burned, she characterizes Chenier as the embodiment of divine love, oblivion brought to earth to comfort her. On the opening night of *Andrea Chenier* in 1955 at La Scala, Maria Callas lost control of the climactic B-flat in the aria, and the audience responded with competing catcalls and cheers. At this climactic note in *Philadelphia*, Andrew Beckett's silent cry, clenched fist, and contorted face reflect his deepest emotions as he exposes his own mortality: a personal state and private moment, a public scream against our society's indifference to AIDS and those who live it.[1]

In a bitterly pessimistic interpretation of this moment, Moshe Sluhovsky concludes that this scene's ultimate failure is that the world's silence and indifference will in the end collapse back onto those who suffer. Hope is an illusion. Although both men seem transformed by the music, Miller goes home and crawls into bed with his wife while Beckett is left alone in his empty apartment attached to his IV stand. "Apparently, the aria's comforting words 'You are not alone' do not apply to gay life" (1266). Koestenbaum directly connects Callas, death, and gay desire in equally pessimistic terms:

> In the era of Silence = Death, the opera queen's silence is freighted with fatality. The silent opera queen, drowned out by Callas, is an image of gay helplessness, the persistence of the closet, and a tragic inability to awaken the body politic. But the opera queen and Callas share a biography: opera was ultimately as deadly to Callas as to the opera queen. According to the Callas myth, opera disqualified her for love, and when she lost opera, she lost her life. In the brutal, intoxicating dream of opera which framed the life of Maria Callas and the lives of countless opera queens, the gate to opera is guarded by twin thugs, Death and Silence. If you want admission to the realm of bliss and expressivity that opera promises, you must leave your throat at the door. (45)

What both critics ignore is that Callas's voice serves as a sound bridge and carries over as sound track into the next scene. Whereas her voice serves as an acoustical frame for the earlier scene, when the aria is repeated as the sound bridge, the volume is increased as it underscores all that follows. As Joe Miller goes home, he cannot get the diva's sound out of his head. Following the traditional practice in narrative cinema of allowing musical repetition to serve as an acoustical bridge framing time and place with significance, Callas serves as the narrative frame singing the film's idealism. Her voice brings understanding in *Philadelphia*. Certainly, a wobbly high note is nothing compared to AIDS, but within the context of this scene, Callas's artistic and personal struggle and ultimate triumph give voice to that which Andrew Beckett has been unable to share with those around him. In this scene, the voice of Callas as signifier compels and allows him to speak.[2]

Intended for a mainstream Hollywood audience, Jonathan Demme's *Philadelphia* uses the expressive language of traditional narrative cinema to provide arresting visual images, edited in skillful ways, and to work with the musical structures of Giordano's score to guide audience response toward Andrew Beckett's homo-sexuality. In doing so, Demme reveals multiple perspectives within and around the silence about AIDS in America at that time. In *Philadelphia*, the commanding Callas of La Scala is referenced. Her performance of Maddalena from *Andrea Chenier*, as explained by Beckett, creates the turning point in the action, a moment when the killing silence about AIDS and personal desire is broken by love and understanding. Ultimately, because Beckett and Miller were able to find a way to break the silence, both men speak out against homophobic intrigue and injustice. Following the expectations of commercial cinema, the climatic courtroom scene keeps Demme's film "hetero-friendly" while at the same time delivering a timely social message and critique (Davies and Smith 139).

Conclusion

But how does the Callas in *Philadelphia* (as quoted and translated by the gay, white, upper-middle-class lawyer dying from AIDS) dif-fer from the Callas in *Strawberry and Chocolate* (as evoked and praised by the Latino gay artist and political activist)? In *Strawberry and Chocolate*, the filmmakers reference the Latin American Callas (the Callas of Transition) as metaphor for the struggles within Castro's Cuba. Indexing particular moments in Callas's career and life, as well as specific associations with character, plot, and theme in *Il trovatore*, the Cuban film uses an assimilated acting style to foreground issues of identity, artistic expression, sexuality, and per-sonal freedom in Castro's Cuba.

Both films use specific acting strategies to avoid cultural resis-tance to gay bodies. Whereas Demme plays to Hollywood's expec-tations of a leading man through an acting style that avoids identi-fication with homosexual cliché, Alea exploits the power of quota-tion to create a postmodern acting style to present gay desire and thus enables the film's ironic surface to open to cultural critique. By exploiting the immediate cultural depth of Callas's evoked image and voice and the potent theatricality of her memory and performances within and outside the gay community, these films quote Callas to reach across the borders of high and low culture as well as homosexual and heterosexual life. The power of her voice to be heard and understood in these films testifies to the malleable richness of Callas's circulating image as a cultural icon.

A final biographical note about Callas and her recording of Leonora underscores her circulation as a cultural sign in *Strawberry and Chocolate.* The specific recording of the aria used in the film came from a television broadcast of a Callas concert presented in Paris, 19 September 1958 (Scott 216). This was a crucial year of transition for Callas in both her professional and personal life. Her appearances at La Scala continued to be artistic triumphs during the mid-1950s but by 1958 it was clear that the voice was changing from the fearsome instrument of the earlier years into something more fragile and unsteady, darker and more introspective. It was soon after this concert that Callas began her love affair with Onassis. Once she left her husband and assumed her life with the tycoon, her La Scala career soon ended; what continued was a career as the Diva in Exile and, eventually, the Silent Diva (the Callas who haunts Terrance McNally's play *Masterclass*) (see Galatopoulos 320–80). However, in the Cuban film, what we hear is a different Callas, the Latin American Callas, Callas in Transition.

Indeed, all of the major characters in the film connect with this theme of transition. One exception is Miguel, the stereotypical foil, the unchanging homophobic revolutionary whose machismo interaction with his friend David, ironically, reads as gay as Diego's operatic manners. In sharp contrast, the friendship that develops between David and Diego can be traced through the story's development of David's expanding sensibilities and transitions as a sexual being, as an intellectual, and as a Cuban. In the words of Emilio Bejel, "David's role in this film is quite clear—the idealistic revolutionary of a generation born precisely at the triumph of the Revolution, who, while supporting the nationalist/Socialist system, insists on a new vision of the nation and the Revolution. Within the semantics of *Strawberry and Chocolate*, David represents the complex term: the utopian horizon of the film's explicit ideology" (72).

Following Bejel's thematic and symbolic explication of the film, perhaps the most interesting character in transition is the suicidal Nancy, the Marxist "lumpen," (an unemployed, promiscuous individual who lives by selling American dollars). Bejels states that "Nancy is that part of the Cuban nation that desperately needs to be saved from suicide." Diego saves her life and cares for her; in addition, David literally gives her his blood and eventually his love. Together the two men "represent an alliance needed to bring about Cuba's 'utopian salvation.'"(71). This melodramatic formulation of character and theme mirrors Callas's performance in *Il trovatore* as well as character and theme in the opera itself, specifically the absolute and binding versions of accepted masculine honor that underscore character and action in the opera. These cultural norms in the opera (and alive and well in Castro's Cuba) explicitly create the final tragic moments when fratricide brings down the curtain.

In *Strawberry and Chocolate*, Diego and David struggle to speak beyond the walls of Cuban cultural and political oppression to avoid such a fate for themselves and their nation. Against Callas's pirated voice on the tape (music played so that the neighbors will not hear them talking alone), Diego indirectly references Leonora's fate through his dialogue with David. While doing so, he reveals his understanding of what it means to be at a turning point, a point of transition and no return. Diego's desire for David and his desperation to change the way David thinks and feels about sexuality, human rights, and Cuba can all be heard in Callas's understanding of the plight of Leonora. All find expression in contrived, idealistic, and erotically desperate terms. By using Callas as postmodern sign and referencing Diego's transitional state as a gay artist through assimilated gesture, Alea's film (in a subversive act of simulation and shifting reference) acts gay desire as prima donna politics.

As Emilio Bejel argues, *Strawberry and Chocolate* marked the "coming out" of homosexuality in Cuba from private to public space, a cultural and social phenomenon and an important marker of cultural, political, and social transition (68). The film presents a story of transformation and change through a postmodern process of image making, specifically, the blending of high- and low-cultural appeals and the postmodern concern with excess and the play of signifiers. The Callas icon referenced in the dialogue and sound track is, paradoxically, the image of the opera star as the emerging diva in Latin America juxtaposed against her later image as the slim haute-couture diva in Paris (a diva in transition, a signifier of shifting form, shifting bodies, and shifting contexts).

In closing, it is useful to reflect on the various meanings of the word *assimilate*. In biological terms, the word refers to the process of bringing nourishment into the body to build living tissue. In linguistics, the word refers to the manipulation of sound to blend with adjacent sounds. A sociologist would use *assimilation* to describe the process of cultural blending or merging of various minority voices into the dominant cultural landscape. In *Strawberry and Chocolate*, the camp acting style used to indicate gay desire when read as assimilated acting literally and theoretically embodies a postmodern critical perspective as cultural critique. Played as a gay opera queen who knows and enjoys the effectiveness of expansive operatic gesture, a glance, and a grand entrance and exit, Diego's body—when identified with Callas—becomes the literal and figurative site of personal and ideological conflict, a prima donna moving center stage to be heard.

NOTES

1. The Callas in this scene is the Callas of La Scala, the reigning queen of the operatic stage during the mid-1950s. Callas was a controversial singer and personality with an unconventional voice; her appearances at La Scala were always considered events, not solely for their musical merits but also for what they revealed about less artistic matters. Frequently, disruptive claques competed with each other in the gallery with raucous convictions. Indeed, Callas's conflicts with other singers and the La Scala management were publicized events, conflicts that played out onstage and off.

One of the most famous examples occurred when Callas performed in a revival of Donizetti's *Anna Bolena* in 1958. Illness had forced Callas to walk out of a performance of *Norma* at the Rome Opera a few weeks earlier on 2 January 1958, a gala occasion broadcast live across Italy to honor important political figures, including the president. The Rome Opera had not arranged for an understudy, so the performance concluded after the first act. No explanation was given when the announcement was made. Immediately, the audience in Rome and the national press branded her cancellation as caprice, an affront to national pride (when in fact, as was proven later in court, she was truly ill). But scandal spoke louder than truth. One newspaper even went so far as to suggest that such irresponsible behavior was to be expected from Callas, given her "dangerous association" with Elsa Maxwell, a thinly veiled sneer at Maxwell's sexual orientation (Galatopoulos 270–74).

The La Scala audience was ready to punish their queen. When Callas entered as Anna Bolena, certain members of the audience created a disruption. At the moment when Anna confronts her judges, Callas quickly moved toward the front of the stage and threw out Anna's words as her own: "Judges? For me!?" The combination of her brilliant vocal execution and audacious challenge to the La Scala audience won the day. The audience, stunned into silence, later cheered (Galatopoulos 278–83). Indeed, audiences at La Scala during these years were sensitive to these rivalries, dramas, and personalities and looked for them; they relished the opportunity for histrionic showmanship and partisan response.

Record producers also played to these operatic intrigues. For example, the specific Callas recording used in *Philadelphia* was originally recorded in 1954 and released in September 1955. The arias performed on this recital album were carefully selected to demonstrate the stupendous range and flexibility of Callas's voice. Several selections were from operas rarely or never performed by Callas onstage (including the aria from

Andrea Chenier); however, some of these Callas rarities were closely associated with her rival at La Scala, Renata Tebaldi. Perhaps this repertoire was chosen to conquer rival territory as well.

2. In *Philadelphia*, Andrew Beckett's last name summons associations with the writings of Samuel Beckett, existential playwright for the theater of the absurd, a theater in quest of meaningful silence. The subject matter and cultural moment shaping the story of Andrew Beckett's trial and death (homophobia and AIDS) evoke themes in Samuel Beckett's theater, which are dramas of isolation, games, and waiting. Andrew Beckett's operatic moment (playing himself playing Callas playing Maddalena and finding his voice between these spaces) recalls striking images in Samuel Beckett's dramas. Examples would include images such as the circular waiting for death in *Endgame* or the woman buried alive and waiting in *Happy Days* (up to her waist in the first act, up to her neck in the second). Samuel Beckett's characters display great courage in the face of this silence and approaching darkness. These characters evoke the power of voice, an emotional aesthetic and rhetorical conduit to the soul, as a means to break the silence. Andrew Beckett, quoting Callas, does too.

Works Cited

Abbate, Carolyn. *Unsung Voices: Opera and Musical Narrative in the Nineteenth Century*. Princeton: Princeton UP, 1991.

Alea, Tomás Gutiérrez. "Another Cinema, Another World, Another Society." *Journal of Third World Studies* 11.1 (1994): 90–113.

Allegri, Renzo, and Roberto Allegri. *Callas by Callas: The Secret Writings of "La Maria."* New York: Universe, 1998.

Auslander, Philip. *From Acting to Performance: Essays in Modernism and Postmodernism*. London: Routledge, 1997.

Baron, Cynthia. "Nicolas Roeg's *Track 29*: Acting Out a Critique of Theory in a Postmodern Melodrama." *Spectator* 14.1 (1993): 16–25.

Barthes, Roland. *Image, Music, Text*. Trans. Stephen Heath. New York: Hill and Wang, 1977.

Bejel, Emilio. "*Strawberry and Chocolate*: Coming out of the Cuban Closet?" *South Atlantic Quarterly* 96.1 (1997): 65–82.

Birringer, Johannes. "Homosexuality and the Revolution: An Interview with Jorge Perugorria." *Cineaste* 21 (1995): 21–24.

Brockett, Oscar. *History of the Theater*. Boston: Allyn and Bacon, 1987.

Burston, Paul. *What Are You Looking At?: Queer Sex, Style, and Cinema*. New York: Cassell, 1995.

Cardullo, Bert. "*Strawberry and Chocolate*: A Review." *Hudson Review* 48 (autumn 1995): 476–84.

Chanan, Michael. "Bittersweet Offerings." *Guardian* [London] 24 Nov. 1994: T9.

Clément, Catherine. *Opera, or the Undoing of Women*. Trans. Betsy Wing. Minneapolis: U of Minnesota P, 1988.

Counsell, Colin. *Signs of Performance*. London: Routledge, 1996.

Curtis, Quentin. "Hesitation and Deviation." *Independent* [London] 27 Feb. 1994: 126.

Davies, Jude, and Carol R. Smith. *Gender, Ethnicity, and Sexuality in Contemporary American Film*. Edinburgh: Keele UP, 1997.

Ehmke, Ronald. "Notorious Stereotypes Bedevil *Strawberry and Chocolate*." *Buffalo News* 31 Mar. 1995: 1.

Esslin, Martin. *The Theater of the Absurd*. Garden City: Doubleday, 1969.

Fleming, Michael. "*Philadelphia* Draws Fire from Gay Kid in the Hall." *Variety* 24 Jan. 1994: 2.

Fuchs, Elinor. *The Death of Character: Perspectives on Theater after Modernism*. Bloomington: Indiana UP, 1996.

Galatopoulos, Stelios. *Maria Callas: Sacred Monster*. New York: Simon and Schuster, 1998.

Giordano, Umberto. *Andrea Chenier*. Vocal score. New York: International Music, 1955.

Grossberg, Michael. "McNally Puts Gay Stereotype to Sound Dramatic Use." *Columbus Dispatch* 10 Jan. 1995: 10C.

Guthmann, Edward. "*Strawberry* Explores the Flavors of Cuban Life." *San Francisco Chronicle* 10 Feb. 1995: C3.

Hutcheon, Linda. "Introduction." *Double Talking: Essays on Verbal and Visual Ironies in Contemporary Canadian Art and Literature*. Ed. Linda Hutcheon. Toronto: ECW Press, 1992. 11–38.

Kaufman, Frederick. "Polemical Pillow Talk." *Aperture* 141 (autumn 1995): 70–71.

Kempley, Rita. "Bittersweet Chocolate." *Washington Post* 10 Feb. 1995: B7.

Koestenbaum, Wayne. *The Queen's Throat: Opera, Homosexuality, and the Mystery of Desire*. New York: Random House, 1993.

Kraft, Ronald Mark. "Philadelphia Freedom—*Philadelphia* Directed by Jonathan Demme." *Advocate* 28 Dec. 1993: 71–72.

———. "Ron Nyswaner: Writing the Gay *Philadelphia* Story." *Advocate* 21 Sept. 1993: 4–49.

Leonardi, Susan J., and Rebecca A. Pope. *The Diva's Mouth: Body, Voice, Prima Donna Politics*. New Brunswick: Rutgers UP, 1996.

Lindenberger, Herbert. *Opera in History: From Monteverdi to Cage*. Stanford: Stanford UP, 1998.

McNally, Terrance. *The Lisbon Traviata*. New York: Dramatists Play Service, 1990.

Miller, Mark. "The Selling of *Philadelphia*." *Newsweek* 20 Dec. 1993: 99.

Murray, Stephen. *Latin American Male Homosexualities*. Albuquerque: U of New Mexico P, 1995.

Robinson, Paul. "Review of Catherine Clément, *Opera, or the Undoing of Women*." *New York Times Book Review* 1 Jan. 1989: 3.

Scott, Michael. *Maria Meneghini Callas*. Boston: Northeastern UP, 1991.

Sluhovsky, Moshe. "*Philadelphia* (motion picture review)." *American Historical Review* 99 (Oct. 1994): 1266–70.

Smith, Paul Julien. "Cuban Homosexualities: On the Beach with Nestor Almendros and Reinaldo Arenas." *Hispanisms and Homosexualities*. Ed. Sylvia Molloy and Robert McKee. Durham: Duke UP, 1998. 248–67.

Taubin, Amy. "The Odd Couple." *Sight and Sound* 4.3 (Mar. 1994): 24–25, 45–46.

Tomlinson, Doug. "Performance in the Films of Robert Bresson: The Aesthetics of Denial." *Making Visible the Invisible: An Anthology of Original Essays on Film Acting*. Ed. Carole Zucker. Metuchen: Scarecrow, 1990. 365–90.

Verdi, Giuseppe. *Il trovatore*. Reduced orchestra score. New York: Edwin Kalmus, n.d.

West, Dennis. "*Strawberry and Chocolate*, Ice Cream and Tolerance: Interviews with Tomás Gutiérrez Alea and Juan Carlos Tabio." *Cineaste* 21.1–2 (1995): 16–24.

10

Kidman, Cruise, and Kubrick
A Brechtian Pastiche

Dennis Bingham

....

Although acting in Anglo-American films of the post–silent era has
been dominated by Delsartean, Stanislavskian, and Strasbergian
traditions, these realist/illusionist styles have been countered by
the subversive influences of Brechtian "epic" acting. The Marxist
aesthetics of the playwright-theorist Bertolt Brecht, like those of
his cinematic counterpart Sergei Eisenstein, were in rebellion
against the genteel theater that nurtured late-nineteenth and early-
twentieth-century representational drama. They were steeped in
such low- and middlebrow forms as the circus, popular melodrama,
the operetta, vaudeville, music hall, and cabaret, as well as the
"primitive" cinema of attractions. Violating realism by crossing
representation with such frankly presentational modes, Brecht dis-
abled the easy belief of audiences in any created reality. Urging
actors to play episodes rather than continuous, cause-and-effect
action, he wanted from them "the most objective possible exposition of a contradictory internal process." The audience watching an
actor's performance should not think "'How true!' but 'How surprising!'; not 'Just as I thought,' but 'I hadn't thought of that!'"
(Callow 168).

When Brechtian performance involves well-known actors,
attempts to separate acting from stardom should be fruitless;
Brecht greatly admired Charlie Chaplin and the Marx Brothers. He
valued "the performer's self-presentation as the possessor of a special skill, . . . the elegance and aplomb with which the actor should
deliver a finished product, showing clearly that it has been thoroughly rehearsed, thought-out, and mastered, rather than on the

'method's' ideal of a performance, which seems to be forming itself at the moment of its being shown" (Esslin 138–39).

His favorite exemplar of "epic" acting was the outsize Hollywood star Charles Laughton, who originated the title role in *Galileo* in Los Angeles in 1947. When Laughton himself turned to movie directing for the first and only time, in *Night of the Hunter* (1955), he encouraged Robert Mitchum and Lillian Gish to enact, in a Brechtian manner, deeply archetypal renderings of their star personas. Mitchum's performance, which superimposed mythical monsters and melodramatic scoundrels onto his own "bad boy" persona, was a forebear of Jack Nicholson's multilayered horror-film madman in Stanley Kubrick's *The Shining* (1980).

Most film actors will say that their job is to serve the script or contribute to the director's vision. However, in films where postmodernism meets Brecht, the director's purpose and the performer's intelligent contribution intersect. *Eyes Wide Shut* (1999) feels like a return to author-centered modernism for its director, Stanley Kubrick, after a run of films, beginning with *2001: A Space Odyssey* (1968), which play like postmodern pastiches (see Bingham). The final Kubrick film's links to postmodernism are found largely in the performances of Tom Cruise and Nicole Kidman. They represent in the Brechtian manner Hollywood ideals of gendered behavior, then turn to an exploration of the class and gender typology of these ideals. The publicity for and media coverage of this film before it opened in July 1999 encouraged the spectator to watch the film for hints of the couple's "real-life" relationship. Subsequent viewers might scrutinize it for signs of their breakup, announced a year and a half after the film's release. Either reading attests to Kubrick's tendency to emphasize the star as a larger-than-life presentation of cultural conventions and types.

The anomalous quality of Stanley Kubrick's success may not yet be fully understood. He was an independent filmmaker tied to a single studio (Warner Bros.) for the final three decades of his career, a maker of Hollywood blockbusters who lived and worked like a European artisan, and a conjurer of popular genres and stars whose work remains for many their introduction to nonclassical forms of cinematic image-interpretation. Moreover, he was a big-budget capitalist director whose films often have at their center virulent critiques of capitalism, notably in *Barry Lyndon* (1975), a late-eighteenth-century picaresque romance whose dominant motivation and most recurrent motif is money, and *The Shining*, in which an angry white male in paid servitude amid the splendor of a luxury hotel built atop an Indian burial ground ventures into homicidal insanity for his crack at the American Dream. Clearly the author at the center of works that explored the power of machines, the disintegration of the individual, and the prominence of the materials of cinema in the experience and meaning systems of his films, Kubrick may have been the filmmaker most responsible for establishing modernism in Hollywood cinema.

Later, Kubrick's authorial presence seemed to recede from films in which an anomic postmodern playing space is marked by allusive performances and free-floating, increasingly hollow cultural artifacts. If *A Clockwork Orange* (1971) and *Full Metal Jacket* (1987) present the lethal junkyards of Western civilization, *Barry Lyndon* and *The Shining* lay out its no less dangerous playgrounds. Postmodernism concerns itself with the dominance of the sign and the loss of all reality behind it. The problems posed for Brechtian theory in both modernist and postmodernist practice have been widely discussed. Brecht's political activism stood opposed to the sometimes closed formalism of high aesthetic modernism. However, what Thomas Elsaesser calls Brecht's "appeal to a reality outside representation, outside the world of signs" makes the dramatist a quaint, naively idealistic figure in a bombed-out world like that depicted in *A Clockwork Orange* (183). It follows that Kubrick's most postmodernist film would be also his least Brechtian.

Kubrick often used the materials of cinema disjunctively and against each other. The acting styles and characterizations in his films are often stylized, flat, and exaggerated, much more in the manner of Brechtian "epic" acting than of naturalistic, interactive styles. Indeed, when Steven Spielberg took over Kubrick's project *A.I.: Artificial Intelligence* (2001) after the latter's death, he apparently tried to hew closely to Kubrick's episodic, elliptical, and nonempathetic style. The one Kubrickian element he evidently decided not to utilize was the variously but consistently stylized acting. Instead, the performances in Spielberg's film stay within the interactive, embodied norms of most Western film and theater.

In contrast to traditional performance norms, epic acting demands a decentered subjectivity along with a strong hint of cultural references and influence. This made it a key influence on postmodern performance. In the epic mode, a character is a set of ideological and social roles and traditions, not a discrete personality, just as character is a compilation of performance codes and conventions, not a differentiated person. Acting is a showing of the character, not an embodiment of it. Such a performance aesthetic is at the center of Kubrickian narrative technique. Cause-and-effect logic is turned on its head: we see the effect, but the cause is buried and unclear. In Kubrick's films, acting consists of surfaces, not depths, making them appear superficial and obvious at first viewing, but mysterious and even unlimited on further reflection.

P. L. Titterington, in a much-noted 1981 *Sight and Sound* article, said that Kubrick's style "seeks to combine the theater of Brecht, with its emphasis on intellectual scrutiny and alienation techniques designed to prevent indiscriminate emotional identification, with the theater of total, overwhelming subjective emotional involvement conceived by Artaud." In common with Brecht's theater of thought and social criticism, Kubrick's cinema is "the search . . . for a language of film that will convey complex ideas directly . . . very much a cinema of ideas" (120–21). Aside from profoundly deconstructive and didactic political films made far outside commercial filmmaking systems, such as the works of Jean-Luc Godard or Rainer Werner Fassbinder, Brecht's influence on oeuvres like Kubrick's, made within mainstream cinema, has rarely been acknowledged. This is because even when Brechtian style, particularly Brechtian acting style, has been used, as in *Night of the Hunter*, the social mission of Brecht's theater often is lost. There is usually a subtle but fundamental divergence from the Brechtian conviction that "We must find means of 'shedding light on' the human being at that point where he seems capable of being changed by society's intervention" (Callow 169). For instance, "Laughton might have felt," writes Simon Callow, "with Kierkegaard, that 'an artist cannot change society; all that he can do is to express that it is sick'" (170).

The most critical of artists working within the American commercial cinema—in his time, he was matched only by Robert Altman as a diagnostician of social sickness—Kubrick made complexly layered films that intimated in detail the deep structure of social illness and violence. Nevertheless, *Eyes Wide Shut* represents new departures for Kubrick. For once, the director is not dealing with structures of war and genocide, tribal hierarchies, the destructiveness of patriarchal systems, and the small space between pre-evolutionary and civilized people. Or is he? Perhaps it is more accurate to say that the topic here is heterosexuality rather than global war. Or perhaps it is the war that men keep from breaking out within themselves between their various repressed sexual identities and possibilities.

The self-contained sexuality of *Eyes Wide Shut*'s female protagonist, Alice (Nicole Kidman), is managed by fantasy, dreams, self-knowledge, and an attenuated flirtation at a party that she totally savors but makes sure that it stops well short of infidelity. Her husband, Bill (Tom Cruise), lacks full understanding of the couple's sexual dynamics, of his wife's simultaneous indulgence in sexual fantasy and in monogamy, and indeed of female desire. "Millions of years of evolution," a sarcastic and stoned Alice/Kidman declares in a remarkable monologue, "men have been sticking it in wherever they can, while women just want commitment and security." When Bill swallows the bait and agrees with this Neanderthal scenario, Alice tells him of her willingness, in fantasy, to end her marriage and family life for one night of passion with a "young naval officer" she saw once in a hotel restaurant and never even spoke to.

Kubrick, reading this passage in the novella *Traumnovelle* by Arthur Schnitzler, may have recognized that the movies have always permitted men such lingering fantasies of pleasure, but that women have never been allowed such transgressions, at least not without being punished for them. He may have remembered the wistful moment in *Citizen Kane* (Orson Welles, 1941) when Mr. Bernstein (Everett Sloane) remembers a girl he saw boarding a ship fifty years before and declares, "I'll bet a day hasn't gone by, when I haven't thought of that girl." Alice is not punished for her fantasy; rather, it causes Bill inadvertently to punish himself. Where Schnitzler's novella describes the husband as jealous, retaliatory, and contemptuous, Kubrick's film shows the man turning the signifier of the woman's fantasy into a mental image, the signified of a literal betrayal—a monochrome image of a military man invading his wife. Unlike Alice, who evidently channels her fantasies and flirtations into her sex life with her husband, Bill cannot merge himself into Alice's fantasy, as Tom Cruise, who played Navy men in two of his best-known films, *Top Gun* (Tony Scott, 1986) and *A Few Good Men* (Rob Reiner, 1992), might be expected to do.

Instead, when Alice tells Bill about her fantasy and, much later, about a dream in which she fornicates with numerous men while Bill is left a humiliated outcast, she crosses a heretofore invisible line between an organic reality that unites actuality, spirit, and fantasy and Bill's concept of a reality characterized by experience. In essence, this is how Kubrick sees gender difference, a gap between femininity and masculinity that for the man extends like the intolerable "no man's land" that stretches between the

French and German battle lines in the director's *Paths of Glory* (1957). The man sees his wife's stories as challenges to his sexuality, and he responds in the forum traditionally open to men in our culture, the external world. Bill's eyes are certainly wide, but they're not open. The fantasy Alice tells of sex with the naval officer takes on a life of its own, or rather, a life of *his* own. It serves a similar function to that of the monolith in *2001: A Space Odyssey*, an ambiguous, recurring motivation, an obscure mindscreen that, by its very inscrutability, seems to promise understanding and satisfaction. As opposed to the female sexuality that Alice owns, Bill's adventures in reality attract him by their danger, a danger that reveals male power structures, that dehumanizes sex, and that infects, addicts, exploits, and kills women.

Tom Cruise's Dr. Bill Harford is a paragon of caring professionalism and family values in the Big City (Kubrick's own father was a physician in the Bronx). He, like many men in middle-class America, has been trained to be the "hero," the benevolent patriarch, the symbolic good man who can be counted on. "You're awfully sure of yourself, aren't you," his wife Alice taunts him. "No, Alice," he replies, "I'm sure of you." It's the kind of line that a man says, expecting to hear "My hero!" in return. Instead, he gets Alice's bust-a-gut laughter. This is the standard Kubrick man, also the absurdist theater man, and the Brechtian man—a collection of roles with no thought, just conditioning, the man who plays doctor, father, lover—whatever you want. But he is hollow.

This concept of the everyday man as hero dovetails nicely with the Hollywood star system. Although no one knows exactly what makes some performers stars and others mere actors, certainly stars are cast and sold as "contemporary ideas of what it is to be an individual in the culture" (Dyer 8). At the same time, stars conform unconsciously to national, gender-bound, and even universal, archetypes. The most common star type is the magnetic, average guy, a plausible, likable, and subtly strong figure whose "I want" may match the strivings and aspirations of the time, but who can play virtuous characters whose heroism is intrinsic, but not overwhelming, and at times may even be in doubt. In terms of acting, the heroic male lead usually appears to be "playing himself." His is a strong, still presence almost to be taken for granted. As a rule, the male star "acts less," in the sense of emoting, than any of the performers around him, male or female. The more interesting the star, the more the persona is in tension with the star's acting and the varied roles he may take on.

Tom Cruise was the most successful of the men who became stars at unprecedentedly young ages during the youth film mania of the mid-1980s. He developed the persona of a callow but cocky young man whose excess of confidence, expressed with a 100-watt smile, makes him attractive but also suggests that he needs tempering and maturing. Most of Cruise's films knock him off his pedestal and make him earn back his confidence in a maturer framework. The narratives of *Top Gun*, *The Color of Money* (Martin Scorsese, 1986), *Rain Man* (Barry Levinson, 1988), *A Few Good Men*, *The Firm* (Sydney Pollack, 1993), *Jerry Maguire* (Cameron Crowe, 1996) and, since *Eyes Wide Shut*, *Magnolia* (Paul Thomas Anderson, 1999), *Vanilla Sky* (Cameron Crowe, 2001), and *Minority Report* (Steven Spielberg, 2002) all work variations on this remarkably various and durable formula. Oliver Stone's political biopic *Born on the Fourth of July* (1989) starts the Cruise character off as a young Marine recruit who must undergo a harsh political education.

Essentially, Tom Cruise is a highly efficient mime, good at projecting honesty, strength, and sincerity. Through his hairstyle, costuming, and stance, he represents ambition, complacency, materialism, success, and superficiality. Cruise gives the kinds of performances conventionally expected of a male lead, emoting much less than the other actors around him. He tends to react, to be the still center around whom things happen, the initiator of action, about whom the audience does not give much thought because none is necessary. This kind of film actor traditionally performs "naturally"; that is, his acting is disciplined and minimal in its movement. Thus it does not call attention to itself.

When Stanley Kubrick works with a star in the heroic Everyman tradition, he boils the archetype down to its barest outline. With star actors like Kirk Douglas, Ryan O'Neal, and Cruise, Kubrick reduces the archetype to a sincere, earnest, forthright, and heroic nub and has the actor play the skeletal outline with a Brechtian awareness of the type as a type. Thus the actor is not called on to embody a character or to enact emotions. He is there to show the type, or, maybe better yet, why that type is at the heart of American male stardom, and more important, why it is a desirable model for American masculinity. This, Kubrick suggests, is all one needs to know about the male protagonist as a type, while what the type stands for is middle-class, white, Western masculinity. He is oriented toward goals and action, directed toward the outer world of experience, authority, and exploitation. The type is lacking in self-knowledge, compelled to repeat his patterns all the way back to the primordial scene, which, in Kubrick's evolutionary scheme, is not so far away, as in the graphic match from bone to satellite in *2001: A Space Odyssey*, the "master scene" of Kubrick's oeuvre.

In his yuppie doctor's nightmarish walk with love, money, and death, Cruise acts out several sign systems at once: the cocky, competent, hail-fellow-well-met *as role*, the flirtatious, deferential young urban male professional *as role*, the passionate, trustworthy, breadwinner male *as role*, the overconfident up-and-comer who eventually discovers he has walked into a trap—and all of these roles *as Tom Cruise*, and *Tom Cruise as the signifier of all these roles*. The spectator is invited to think about what the heroic Everyman archetype means and what Tom Cruise in particular means as a star. Kubrick uses the heroic male star type and the performer who signifies that type less like an actor and more like a model, in the sense in which Robert Bresson used his nonprofessional performers. When the hero confronts stimuli outside his programming, however, his response takes the form of ambiguous, enigmatic reactions that suggest why Kubrick required a legendarily high number of takes to get the desired effects from his actors.

This is why Alice's laugh is subversive at Bill's moment of bottom-line earnestness, a Tom Cruise movie's equivalent of "the money shot," the romantic commitment that audiences of both genders come to the theater to see Cruise make. That the audience knows that this is Tom Cruise's real-life spouse (and now his ex-wife) howling at his "Here I come to save the day" stance gives her laughter more authority than it would have coming from another actress. (Compare the aggressiveness of Cameron Diaz's character toward Cruise in *Vanilla Sky*, which plays as threatening and crazy, if necessary for Cruise's comeuppance.) In line with Kubrick's tendency not to define a character, not to impose a point of view, and not to allow the spectator a catharsis, actors in his films play either a set of gests or they exaggerate in ways that set them off from the character. Jack Nicholson's performance in *The Shining* and George C. Scott's in *Dr. Strangelove* are right in line with Brecht's dictum for actors that the audience ought to "laugh when they weep and weep when they laugh" (71).

Whereas Hollywood leads act in a style of invisible craft, naturalism, and interaction with other actors, Kubrick defamiliarizes these conventions. In the moment after Alice/Kidman recounts her long soliloquy about her fantasized desire to leave behind "everything" for one night of love with a naval officer, Bill/Cruise's facial reaction is held for the audience to think about. He leans forward,

10.1. As Bill Harford, Tom Cruise enacts an essentially unreadable reaction to his wife's fantasy.

naked above the waist, lips apart, as the Steadicam slowly inches in. Cruise reacts, but we have no idea how (figure 10.1). Ambiguous response is not an easy code for an actor to perform, a difficulty that may explain why Kubrick was known to elicit upwards of fifty takes of a single line or reaction, and a major reason why his shoots took so epically long to complete. Kubrick tries to ensure that his actors' responses will not lose the audience in definitive, explanatory emotion (LoBrutto 441). "Empathy," Brecht's nemesis, is difficult because it is hard to know what one would be empathizing with. Is it jealousy, envy, fascination, astonishment, horror, disbelief, or dumbstruck momentary incapacitation? This reverses Steve Neale's now axiomatic assertion that woman is a mystery whereas man is implicitly known (16). It is the man's motives that are enigmatic here; his response, which is to take action in the external world of which he is presumably master, is completely predictable, but so much so that it eventually becomes revealed as instinctive and thoughtless.

After Bill's interrupted decorum is itself interrupted by a phone call from a patient, Kubrick cuts to the sight and sound of a speeding cab on a nocturnal street, as if expressing cinematically the sentence, "Bill could not wait to get away from there." What follows is a darkly lit shot of Cruise, wearing black, sitting in the right side of a cab, looking left, a strand of hair falling over the right edge of his forehead. His face, though grim, is expressionless. The camera begins an almost imperceptibly slow zoom-in as Kubrick cuts to a monochromatic shot: Alice seduced by her imaginary sailor. The film cuts back to the shot of Cruise's face, closer now and moving in. The editing pattern produces a new rendition of the Kuleshov effect, in which the audience is moved to provide an emotional response for the image of a blank-faced actor. Kubrick invites the spectator to put a figurative mask on the face of Bill/Cruise, in advance of the literal party mask Bill will be required to rent, put on, remove, and then find again.

The figurative donning of masks is what Brechtian acting by means of "gests" is about. For Brecht, an action "split up according to gests," or gestures, fragments the continuity of action and the cause-and-effect sequentiality that permits an audience to follow a character emotionally but without thought. The sequence from Kidman's monologue, to Cruise's stricken reaction, to Cruise's taxi-cab getaway, to the image of Kidman and the seaman, and back to Cruise (the return shot that would conventionally suggest that a decision or plan of action has formed in his mind) leads us to assume a cause-and-effect chain. But the assumption is groundless. In his explanation of Peter Lorre's performance in the play *Mann Ist Mann* in 1931, Brecht describes a courtroom scene in which the character reads a case for the defense as if it were "prepared at some quite different period, without understanding what it meant as he did so" (54).

In *Eyes Wide Shut*, Cruise's "action split up into gests" is what produces the effect of a man flying off into action without knowing why he does so. Moreover, as Brecht explains in regard to the same play, "the character's development has been carefully divided into four phases, for which masks are employed—the packer's face, up to the trial; the 'natural' face, up to his awakening after being shot; the 'blank page' up to his reassembly after the funeral speech; finally the soldier's face" (55). Likewise, the character of Bill can be seen as split up according to the masks that he wears when he plays his various roles: the face of the hail-fellow (at the party), the face of the ardent lover and the trusting husband, the face of the caring doctor, the face of the husband after he has heard of his wife's desire to be unfaithful, the face of the thrill-seeker, the face of the man who has been exposed and humiliated, the desperate face of a man who believes he has caused a woman to be killed, and, finally, the face of a guilty husband.

This exchange of masks, which Brecht also referred to as "acting in episodes" (54–55), is made more resonant in its seeming exchange of roles in other Cruise films, from the hail-fellows of *Top Gun* and *Rain Man*, the righteous seeker of truth in *A Few Good*

Men (the courtroom exchange between Cruise and Jack Nicholson's Guantanamo Bay Marine commander—"I want the truth!" "You can't handle the truth!" is echoed here), and especially to the humiliated hotshot lawyer who finds himself in the center of a conspiracy in *The Firm*.

As the film plays out, Bill's impotence and final lack of consciousness of what he has done or what has happened to him are proved by his inability to react in any way but to exchange one mask for another. So in the scene in which the rapacious robber baron Ziegler (Sydney Pollack) explains the sex rituals of the rich and powerful that Bill stumbled into, Bill/Cruise moves from deferential and dutiful doctor to desperate pursuer of the truth to humiliated, chastened unmasked man. First, he is called to Ziegler's palatial home and led by a manservant through labyrinthine, Kubrickian corridors to a side door. Then Bill/Cruise stands rigidly, his arms folded, his lips pursed into a polite smile. With quiet interest, he queries his powerful patient. While holding a drink, he waves an arm and tries to be casual. "What kind of problem are you having?" he asks.

As Ziegler/Pollack, who carries the bulk of the dialogue, tells Bill about the staged ritual for masters of the universe that the thrill-seeking doctor had gotten himself into, Cruise is seen mostly in close-up reaction shots that show in gests his decorum being broken down. First reaction shot: his smile begins to look pained and forced; the second: his eyes fixed on the speaker, as his brows begin to furrow, slight shadow over his eyes, lips apart, mouth still drawn in the mildest vestige of a grin. Third reaction: similar to the second one, except that the mouth is now beginning to draw downward. The impression made by this small change is profound: Bill begins to look worried, as if the facade might crumble into hysteria. Indeed, in the same shot, his mouth falls open, he draws in a gasp of air, faces downward, takes two deep breaths, tightens his face until creases appear under his chin. He then raises his head, fixes his mouth into a "brave" grin, and says, "I'm sorry, Victor, I uh . . ." He tightens his mouth yet again—"collecting" himself—then closes his eyes on the word "What . . ." then, addressing Ziegler, "in the hell [pause] are you talking about?" As he says this, he attempts a laugh that sounds more like a sob, then fixes his mouth again into a smile.

Just describing Cruise's performance this way demonstrates that his acting is more complicated than it at first seems. Under Kubrick's direction, Cruise merely overemphasizes his usual "heroic-naturalistic" style, and not even that very much. The

10.2. The seeker after truth: in prosecutorial mode, Bill/Cruise leans forward, chopping the air as he pleads his case.

effect, however, is for the character to act in excess of the dramatic situation as it is thus far revealed, and to behave in contradiction to his line. This is standard acting in contemporary American film, whereby behavior betrays subtext, character is fully revealed, and, when it happens late in a film, catharsis is achieved.

Furthermore, as the Ziegler scene progresses, Cruise deliberately confronts his host with a newspaper clipping about a woman at the orgy who died later of an overdose, thereby going into his "seeker-after-truth" mode. In a shot on Cruise (from the hips up), the actor leans forward, pressing his point, cutting the air with his "upstage" arm as he builds, quietly but intensely, to the line, "Do you mind telling me what kind of fucking char*ade ends* with *somebody* turning up *dead*?" Before he speaks these lines, the camera backtracks, and Cruise moves, so that he is now in profile, directing his attack out of the shot to the left. As he comes down for emphasis on the words and syllables indicated above, Cruise brings his arm to the "nine o'clock" point on a clock, as it were, cutting the air in the manner of a prosecutor (figure 10.2).

These are familiar acting codes, of which Cruise has been a highly successful contemporary exemplar; here, however, Kubrick manages to move the spectator to recognize their familiarity. The spectator can either conclude, as many critics did, that Cruise is a limited actor and Kubrick is "using" him for his power to attract and connect with an audience while mocking his range. Or the spectator can think about what those codes represent, why they are such powerful signifiers in the first place, and how the "episodes" can be seen to play as "the stages of man," the roles that define manhood in our culture.

If "acting in episodes" translates in Cruise's character to the playing of roles and the exchange of masks, in the more thoughtful character played by Nicole Kidman the concept is seen in a more subtle presentation of the character's thoughts as a not quite connected set of faces, postures, and gestures. Alice is Kubrick's most fully realized female character. If anything, he has overidealized her, while still appearing uncertain about women's place in the world. A more physical and more animated actor than Cruise, Kidman telegraphs her character through actions and reactions that, by means of slight exaggeration, appear as disconnected gests. By thus acting outside the role, Kidman suggests Alice's inner life, though in a way that does not proceed from internal processes but is conveyed in surfaces. Kidman often exaggerates the time it takes Alice to have a thought, speak a line, or complete a sentence—all without the interjection by other actors that one would find both in life and in more naturalistic, interactive kinds of performance. Furthermore, in her ability to convey through Brechtian gestic performance attitudes and positions from myriad depictions of women through the ages, Kidman demonstrates, perhaps better than any actress of her time besides Jennifer Jason Leigh (*The Hudsucker Proxy*, Joel Coen, 1994; *Kansas City*, Robert Altman, 1996), female character as postmodern pastiche.

There is a moment early in *Moulin Rouge* (Baz Luhrmann, 2001), a film for which Nicole Kidman's experiences working with Kubrick clearly prepared her, when Kidman offers a succinct selection of dramatic masks. She plays Satine, the courtesan who is set up for a night of lust with a wealthy backer who will stake the company of the dance theater-cum-brothel, the Moulin Rouge, to a show in a legitimate theater. Amid the dizzying exposition of Luhrmann's pastiche of archetypal musical plots and themes, Satine and Zidler (Jim Broadbent), her employer, change costume behind an impromptu but showy screen made up of showgirls' long skirts. In a series of quick head-and-shoulders shot/reverse shots (1) Satine/Kidman, eyes to the camera, asks in a way both candid and businesslike, "Will he invest?" (2) motioning to wardrobe assistants and busily undressing, she asks, more insistently, "What's his type?" as the timbre of her voice goes up on each line; (3) hat off, hair down, chin lowered, she begins, "Wilting flower?" (4)

"Frightened bunny?" her face level and her voice in a childish chirp
(as Ziglar/Broadbent emphatically shakes his head no); (5) "or smol-
dering temptress?"

The latter obviously will carry the day, obviousness being the
pastiche's operating assumption. As Kidman speaks the line, her
voice slightly mocks it, her eyes look directly at the camera, and
her thick red hair shakes a bit more like a lion's mane than a
temptress's unlocked locks. In the following shot, with Satine's bit
of performance over for the moment, the courtesan goes back to
dressing before erupting back out into the center ring. The expressions look like items on an epicurean Delsartean menu after 150
years of sampling. In this way, postmodernism claims both fakery
and authenticity, nostalgia and timelessness, technological change
and universal human patterns that do not change. "Men grow cold
as girls grow old," sings Kidman in the cruel *Gentlemen Prefer
Blondes* (Howard Hawks, 1953) song, "and we all lose our charms
in the end." Will this happen to the thirty-three-year-old actress we
watch here, whose uniqueness comes in an ability to objectify and
fragment herself before the cinematic apparatus does it to her? Or
is Kidman's coconspirator the motion picture, which preserves
youth for all time (cameras, not diamonds, are a girl's best friend)?
Are we left to think about the throwaway quality of cinema's treatment of actresses? Does Nicole Kidman make us think of every
actress cast aside at forty to play villains or mothers?

At the time of the release of *Eyes Wide Shut*, Nicole Kidman
was known to the general public mainly as Tom Cruise's wife.
Within the industry, however, she was considered, though not
nearly so big a star, much more of an actor than Cruise. And she,
much more than he, is in "performance mode" in *Eyes Wide Shut*,
in which she affects an American accent and plays a part rather
than a familiar star archetype. Furthermore, Kidman and Kubrick
are free to explore a new topic for Kubrick: female subjectivity. In
1996, Dana Polan called Kubrick "simultaneously a sexist director
and one of the most interesting depicters of a fundamental sexism
in men's treatment of women" (90). Cindy Fuchs, in her review of
Eyes Wide Shut, agreed: "Kubrick has never been prone to insight
concerning his women characters, but he has in the past offered
notoriously astute dissections of masculinity" (2).

Although Kubrick's evolved response to his earlier ignorance
of women might be to overidealize his heroine, Kidman acts always
a step or two outside the character, telegraphing her reactions, elon-
gating the time she takes to articulate her decisions and conclu-

sions. Even her emotional responses are presented as signs, not as experiences for the audience to "share" unproblematically. While Bill/Cruise goes through his paces in the quietly disastrous external male world of exploitation and death, Kidman's Alice inhabits an essentialist "feminine" realm of self-knowledge, controlled extra-marital flirtation, self-contained fantasy, and subtly conscious discontent. Consider, for example, Kidman's line readings in the expository scene in which she dances with the seductive Szavost (Sky Dumont) at a lavish party. The dialogue goes as follows:

> **Szavost**: What do you do, Alice?
> **Alice**: Well, at the moment I'm looking for a job. I used to manage a gallery in SoHo, but it went broke.
> **Szavosi**: Oh, what a shame! I have some friends in the art game. Perhaps they can be of some help.
> **Alice**: Oh, thank you. (Kubrick and Raphael 20)

While the older Lothario asks the question as no more than dance-floor small talk, Alice/Kidman makes her reply slowly, taking a beat between "Well" and "at the moment." She goes up on "the moment," turning it into a question in way that feminist linguists have found female speakers frequently do as an unconscious expression of a lack of confidence. However, after taking another beat, she says more decisively, "I'm looking for a job," speaking the words deliberately, but without emphasis, except for a slight "hmmmmming" laugh that takes some of the seriousness out of it. The sentence "I used to manage a gallery" she speaks breathily but almost monotonically, simply rattling off the information it imparts. She exaggerates the next line, "but it went broke," singing it, as it were, operatically, rising to one note, and recalling the pig-tailed damsel at the top window of the tower. She laughs while she says this, not wishing to break the light tone of a social event.

Nonetheless, the line conveys significant exposition; it establishes that Alice is frustrated in her career, no longer making her own money, while her successful husband gets to play the bread-winner by default. The effect within the scene is to trivialize her experience before the man can; moreover, the effect on the audience is to make it difficult to know how seriously she is taking herself or, more to the point, how seriously she takes her encounter with the Hungarian. At the same time, the information is being put out there for the spectator to keep for later reference. When Alice confronts Bill for thinking of her only as a sexual object of men, without sexuality of her own, her discontent at being strictly a doctor's wife is clearly what is in back of the lines, not to provide conventional "character motivation" but to elucidate the general political condition whereby women are subordinated to their husbands.

While the Hungarian's reply that he knows people "in the art game" makes Alice's profession sound slightly crass, as he pounces on any opportunity to ingratiate himself, her reply again is unexpected. Keeping her head back, locking onto his eyes, she murmurs "Ohhh . . . thank you," as if this casual and insincere offer of help were the most wonderful thing anyone ever did for her. Kidman takes eight seconds to pronounce those three monosyllables, even inserting a two-second pause between "oh" and "thank you." These may seem to be trivial points, but it is exactly such moments, or rather seconds, that have made Kubrick's films odd and baffling for many. To an audience expecting naturalistic performances in a film billed as a drama of love and sex, performance codes like Kidman's seem inappropriate to the narrative situation and are off-putting besides. Just what they put off is the revelation of meaning behind the lines, which is not immediately apparent and can emerge only later. This requires the spectator, in a Brechtian spirit, to remain alert and thoughtful.

Furthermore, Kidman's performance style is attuned to Kubrick's new concern with female subjectivity, which is stated at the beginning in a subtle proclamation of how the film will proceed. *Eyes Wide Shut* begins with a waltz and a quick view, as if through a keyhole, of a woman (clearly Nicole Kidman) with her back to us, removing her clothing. What does this signify? A male gaze objectifying the female body? Male desire? Or perhaps these plus something else. We soon learn that this opening is out of time sequence. When we move to the diegetic present, we see Tom Cruise and Nicole Kidman getting dressed, whereas we had just seen Kidman get undressed. Next we see her on the toilet, nothing unusual for a married couple accustomed to seeing each other every which way. However, the shot is at least a mild demystification of the first shot.

Kidman enacts Alice's behavior at the Christmas party, where she flirts long and languorously with a cliché of a Continental seducer, "showing the role," rather than embodying the character (Brecht 137). The actress plays Alice in the midst of playing a performance but feeling it as well, letting herself go out of control but knowing exactly when to reel herself back in and when to firmly say no. Kidman's performance in this scene is very precise in showing Alice's flirtation with the Hungarian as a series of plainly defined episodes. First, Kidman makes it very clear from her first appearance that Alice is a kind of facial blank slate until she enters a social interaction; then she turns on the requisite expression. In the long sequence of tracking shots in which Cruise and Kidman finish getting themselves ready for the Ziegler party, Kidman, wearing a stunning barebacked, split-leg evening gown, walks, a bit robotic and expressionless, into the living room where the babysitter waits with the couple's little girl. When Bill asks the babysitter's name, Alice says blankly, "Roz," then lights her face up as they approach the sitter, whom Kidman greets brightly.

While Cruise's "acting in episodes" seems the stuff of Kuleshovian montage, with Kidman, the masks are more in the mise-en-scène as we see the woman's life as a series of public and familial roles. When she is not playing a role—when she is not "on"—she is blank, not in the way that the man seems hollow and empty but like a performer offstage or a singer between sets. While Kidman projects Alice as "turned on" or "turned off" in the sexual sense, she also shows a third dimension in Alice—the person who channels dreams, of the day- and nighttime varieties, into her conscious personality. Thus Alice is shown in three broad juxtaposing "episodes": offstage or off-duty; onstage playing the roles expected of a woman in family and society; and in her inner life as dreamer but also, crucially, as an artist. Alice, we learn, is an unemployed art dealer who had managed a small shop. Her closeness to the art world is reflected in the paintings that adorn the Harfords' apartment, and which are actually the works of Kubrick's wife, Christiane, and daughter Katherina.

In his essentialist approach to gender, Kubrick appears to see "feminine nature" as an inner beauty and creativity that bloom in opposition to the exploitative scheming of men, who rarely look down from their power centers to notice. Ordinary men, the ones at the service of the powerful, must be brought down from their illusions of importance and capitalist-inspired self-identity to see that they have more in common with the women who get "played" by patriarchy than with the architects of phallocracy, the powers that be, who reign unseen in nearly every Kubrick film. (Here they dwell behind masks at the ritualistic orgy that Bill worms his way into.) One of the most poignant things about *Eyes Wide Shut* is that Kubrick finally steps out from his accustomed authorial vantage point in what turned out to be his final film. He struggles to make a film that expresses the quiet, productive, and secluded life that he lived in England with Christiane and their daughters for most of the couple's forty-year marriage. If we see the paintings as metonymic for the director, then the paintings, like Alice's dreams and the sexuality that emerges from them, give disembodied expression to that which they cannot express in the world. Therefore, in Kidman's performance not only are "episodes" separate from each other, but so are vocal, mental, spiritual, and physical registers. Kidman and Kubrick emerge as co-orchestrators of all of these. On one hand, Tom Cruise's star persona seems not only larger than the character he plays but also, in a somewhat demeaning sense, bigger than Cruise himself as an actor. Nicole Kidman, on the other hand, stands over Alice, controlling the character she plays while that character also controls herself and the reactions of other characters and the audience to her.

We see this earliest and most tellingly in the lengthy sequence at Ziegler's party. The sequence begins as Bill and Alice dance. Kidman's face is blank and her eyes wander, projecting boredom and uncertainty at this party, where she knows no one and where she is present only because it is the home of one of Bill's wealthier patients. As the band takes a break and Bill takes her arm to lead her somewhere else, Alice's body goes stiff: "I desperately need to go to the bathroom." After Alice arranges to meet Bill at the bar, the Steadicam follows Kidman past a waiter bearing champagne flutes; she takes one, drains it, and turns her head as if to show: "I'm getting drunk. I need to get a grip on myself."

When next we see her, amid a parallel-edited sequence that contrasts her activities at the party to Bill's, she is standing at the bar, drinking and looking around. The camera circles, until it shows the bar from behind, as a man turns from the conversation he's been having. This is the Hungarian; we watch him watching. Here is where Kubrick's style matches the acting styles in which the characters act, as Brecht recommended, as if everything they do had been prearranged and rehearsed. In allowing us several beats to size up the setup whereby a man's gaze takes in a woman and he prepares to approach her, symbolically drinking her in as he downs the champagne from her glass, the action takes place not by chance, but as if it were preordained, dull in its predictability. Thus we write the scene before it takes place. Kubrick, whose work was once disdained by a reviewer as "film theory at work" (Harvey 64), restages the scene in a "dead style" (to use Fredric Jameson's phrase), puts the audience at a distance, creates a tableau (the composition *as* composition), draws the action out just a bit longer in a naturalistic rendition, and allows the gest (and Alice's jest) to be made obvious.

At the bar with the Hungarian, Alice switches from "blank waiting-for-husband" episode to flirtation, as Kubrick cuts to the reverse angle from her side of the bar, an abrupt change in episode and register that recalls the moment in *The Shining* when the film-maker cuts suddenly from Jack Torrance (Jack Nicholson), alone at a secluded bar, to Lloyd the bartender standing before rows of liquor bottles on shelves that had been bare in the previous shot. The cut in *Eyes Wide Shut* is made after the man introduces himself as "Sandor Szavost. I'm Hungarian" and just before she responds, "My name is Alice Harford. I'm . . . American," presenting herself with a physical flourish that nearly turns into a curtsy. Her line, in Kidman's reading, is multilayered. As written, it is the sort of mean-ingless, awkward banality that Kubrick characters constantly say to each other as if it were awfully clever banter that was being uttered for the first time. Alice/Kidman speaks it with winning panache that seems charmingly naive. Moreover, most viewers would know that Nicole Kidman is an Australian playing an American and affecting a more than passable American accent. Therefore, the scene presents Alice/Kidman as an actress playing a character who is playing roles, without reverting to sexist "woman as actress, woman as duplicitous" traditions.

A passage toward the end of the long sequence with Alice and the Hungarian demonstrates the time that Kidman and Kubrick take to lead the spectator to *think* along with Alice, rather than to empathize with her. The Hungarian, a friend of Ziegler's, invites Alice to see the wealthy host's "collection of Renaissance bronzes"; he wants, Alice will later tell Bill, "Sex. Then and there. Upstairs." When Szavost makes his veiled yet blatant proposition, Alice looks into his eyes and smiles languorously. She deeply enjoys the idea of being ravished by a seducer so obvious he could have slid out of a romance paperback. He could also be out of *The Earrings of Madame De* (1953), directed by Max Ophuls, who filmed several adaptations of works by Arthur Schnitzler and was one of Kubrick's favorite directors (see LoBrutto 138). Her enjoyment becomes increasingly private, within herself; Kidman leans her head back and Szavost leans his in so far their noses and mouths nearly touch. Alice's answer comes very slowly: "Maybe . . . not . . . just . . . now," a line which is very cryptic in Kidman's reading of it and from which Kubrick, characteristically, cuts away.

10.3. After awakening from her reverie, Alice/Kidman makes clear to the Hungarian seducer that her "no" means "no."

When next we see her, she is still dancing with Szavost, her eyes "wide shut," her head swaying dreamily to the music. As the song ends, she comes to, as if from a dream. She looks at him, and says, laughingly, almost to herself, "I think . . . I've had a little too much champagne," a socially acceptable explanation for the reverie she has just allowed herself. Her head moves, her eyes stray; toward the camera, her face begins to turn back into its offstage blankness (figure 10.3). Pulling away, Alice has mentally already left the Hungarian, who twice tries to convince her that she does not have to go. Finally, she turns, looks up at him, and this time she is the one who does the convincing: "Yes, I do," she says firmly.

In short, Alice's "no" means "no . . . I'd like to, if I were somehow somebody else under different circumstances; it's been fun playing the 'bad girl' for a few minutes, but *hell*, no." Kidman has shown Alice facing the fact that she has to pull herself away from this exquisite moment. In gests, Kidman displays a private *jouissance*, an ecstasy. This character owns her sexuality and she is having this experience for herself. The guy is so slimy and so unreal that he could be out of one of her dreams. The spectator is not invited to blame her as a tease, in familiar misogynistic ways. The actress has established Alice as a heroine as earnest and forthright as Cruise's hero archetype—who indeed is upstairs, promising the powerful libertine Ziegler that he *will not* be forthright about the prostitute he has just medically attended to after she nearly overdosed while screwing Ziegler in a cathedral-like bathroom, with the magnate's wife downstairs.

Moreover, the opening shot of Kidman undressing is revealed to be a flash-forward after Alice and Bill come home from the party. Put in sequential order, it would go after Alice's farewell to Szavost and before the mirror shot, used in ads and poster art, of Cruise and Kidman naked, Cruise ravishing her as she looks off. Together, this active female sexuality complicates the male gaze and makes it anxious, which is certainly the effect Alice's talk has later on Bill. Moreover, the mirror has often been used, as in film noir, to signify a woman's private space. Female directors, from Gillian Armstrong (*My Brilliant Career*, 1979) and Jane Campion (*The Piano*, 1993) to Kasi Lemmons (*Eve's Bayou*, 1997) and Sally Potter (*Orlando*, 1993), have co-opted it as a way to establish a woman's ownership of her body and to head off the aura of a male gaze when a female body is shown. With the sequence book-ended in this way, Alice/Kidman emerges, established in the subject position, in the driver's seat, with Bill/Cruise in control but unconscious, like men in general, as they are depicted in all Kubrick films from *Dr. Strangelove* onward.

Brecht wanted epic theater to combine "instruction" with "pleasure," although the latter concept has been forgotten in most latter-day interpretations of both Brecht the theorist and Brecht the playwright (see Wright 113). Kubrick's tendency has been to alter cause-and-effect narrative by showing the effect only, moving the spectator either to try to figure out the cause or simply to tune out. This is not to say that there is not an emotional effect with Kubrick but simply that it does not arise from empathizing with a character who can be experienced as if he or she were a real person. This approach calls for a reversal of the way the narrative unfolds. After Ziegler tells Bill the full story of the masked orgy for the rich and powerful, Bill returns home. Before he gets there, however, Kubrick cuts to a close-up of the mask Bill wore at the party, the mask that was missing when he returned the costume to the rental shop. The camera pans, revealing the mask next to Alice sleeping in bed. Her decision to leave it there, or any motivation for doing so, has been elided.

Moreover, once the mask is revealed, Kubrick shows Bill walking into the apartment and turning out the lights on the Christmas tree—the first time anyone has shut off one of the Christmas trees that adorn every scene, enforcing a sense of carnival that Bill's snuffing of the tree lights finally dispels. Bill then casually walks into the kitchen, opens a beer, all in one shot and in real time, creating a kind of suspense that distances us from the situation as well. Kubrick cuts to inside the bedroom as Bill

10.4. The face as mask: Cruise's earnest pathos is mocked by the impassivity of the gaudy mask that has triggered it.

enters it; in full shot, Bill looks and the camera, from the same position, sweeps the distance from him to the mask. Kubrick "ruins" the effect of a point-of-view shot that would reveal the mask to us at the same time it is revealed to Bill and puts us in his position as he responds emotionally to the revelation that his wife knows that he has been up to something.

Cruise's emotional breakdown is viewed from outside, which recalls a similar outburst by Ryan O'Neal in *Barry Lyndon* when Barry's beloved son Brian dies. In an important sense, it does not matter how Cruise performs it, and he happens to perform it all out. Nonetheless, we see it as a tableau, a "scene" in a narrative. This story will not simply show that a man is destroyed, without recognizing it, by a system that exploits and dehumanizes. Rather, it will teach him a lesson, however ambiguous that lesson is. Therefore, Kubrick "presents" the action, rather than "represents" it, in order to instruct his audience (figure 10.4). Pleasure derives from the way that the film, by means of art, presents an experience, rather than makes a statement. But that experience is one that we see from a thoughtful distance—one of space as well as of the time that Kubrick takes to play out situations that other directors would move more "efficiently" through. It is not an experience that the audience feels it "shares."

After Bill tells Alice about all of his maladroit sexual misadventures, Kubrick cuts from Cruise's ever earnest vow, spoken through sobs, to "tell you everything," to a close-up of Kidman, red-faced, covered in tears. The emotion happens offscreen. Kidman

10.5. The face as mask: in the very next shot, Kidman's face encapsulates the effect of her husband's confession.

later told an interviewer that she looks as if she'd been crying for hours because "I'd been crying for hours." That realism produces a physical and visual effect, rather than one that is visceral and emotional. The shot is similar to that of a placard in Brecht's theater, or in the silent cinema, that might read "She cried" (figure 10.5).

In the film's final scene, Kubrick uses a motif of rebirth that he has used in all his films from *Dr. Strangelove* on. The endings of *A Clockwork Orange*, *The Shining*, and *Full Metal Jacket*, for example, return their protagonists to that original violent primal scene, the start of civilization, the beginning of patriarchy. *Eyes Wide Shut* ends somewhat more gently but not much less disturbingly, as the couple find that they have each pursued a sexual fantasy that has brought their marriage to a precipice. In a toy store with their daughter, they watch as she looks at a baby carriage, then discuss how to give new birth to their marriage.

During this scene, Kubrick never shows Alice and Bill in the same shot, except in full body. Even in their reconciliation, they seem isolated. In the toy store, which is apparently FAO Schwarz, this couple being upscale to the end, the actors walk past a large display for "K'Nex," a construction toy marketed mostly to boys, as we wait to see what still "k'nex" (connects) this husband and wife. The display's two whirling windmills, on either side of the shot, suggest once again that the world is supposed to be engineered and built by boys (who tilt at windmills?).

The last cutaway from Bill and Alice is to the daughter holding up a Princess Barbie toy. Bill's quest has been in pursuit of nothing but live Barbies, including perhaps the one he married. While the nocturnal Barbies in the outside world have all been toys in the hands of patriarchy, his wife is an unpredictable, independent force—who will not be toyed with. In the shot/reverse shots, Bill/Cruise appears "guilty": his black coat matches his dark brown hair, which in turn matches the disheveled brown stubble on his face. With light glinting off the side of Alice's one visible wire-framed eyeglass lens, he stands as if before a judge, awaiting sentencing. His play at prosecutor in the final scene with Ziegler having failed, he now appears as one convicted. His coat is open, revealing an open white shirt and a red v-neck that stands out over his chest like a scarlet "A." The lighting is gentle Hollywood three-point illumination, but with an extra side light that makes him look like he is on the spot. He stands to the sinister left of his wife, his head reared back slightly, but also hanging a bit toward her, as if in defeat, with his eyes fixed on her but also a little downcast (which is some trick, considering that Cruise is, famously, shorter than Kidman).

In the reverse shot, Bill recedes into the left side of the shot; and Alice is more animated than he is. Her head bobs as she thinks. He appears to be an automaton, unconscious to the end. She appears to be a consciously thinking agent; her position is a bit like that of HAL in *2001*. Indeed, in Kubrick's later films, the objects that come to vex the presumptuous male are usually females who had been considered, as a species, to be objects incapable of their own thoughts or responses. These are, in *The Shining*, Wendy, who is able to arrange Jack's demise, despite her fright; the female sniper in *Full Metal Jacket*, who embodies a fierceness and determination that has to be programmed in the American fighting men; and Alice in *Eyes Wide Shut*, who is continually a couple of steps ahead of Bill. The actors' delivery remains deliberate. Alice's every gesture and word appears to have been produced after some thought.

In addition, Bill looks to Alice for her reaction; his demeanor is of one who is being carefully prompted, looking to the coach for every cue. Cruise's head cocks to the right in a classic gesture that with a male romantic lead always signifies sincerity. Here the character, like Cruise himself, appears trained to use this gesture to produce that sincerity effect. When Alice says, "The important thing is we're awake now, and hopefully, for a long time to come," Bill/Cruise straightens his head, looks at her earnestly, and promises, "Forever."

10.6. A remorseful Bill offers his wife the insipid resolve of a Hollywood ending.

10.7. While also acting in episodes, Kidman invests her character with a realism that comes from having fewer illusions about the world than the man does.

Of course, if Bill/Cruise gets his way, this story will get a mindless Hollywood ending. Kubrick and Cruise show that the character has learned nothing, that he is still playing "hero," feeding his wife the stock lines that he thinks the plot calls for (figure 10.6). Kidman continues to act in episodes, putting her hands to her eyes at one instant, to control her emotions, then launching into a rational utterance, her emotions well in check. The realist, in a seemingly non-Kubrickian world that exists outside signification, Alice answers, "Let's not use that word. It frightens me." Again, while Cruise's gestures quote familiar codes, Kidman's gestures do not. She even moistens her lips with her tongue between the two

271

sentences, again making her much less programmed, more real, than he is, and certainly more lifelike than the Barbie doll scenarios Bill seeks out (figure 10.7). Thus each actor proceeds, very differently, to act along a line of distinct gests.

The marriage of Bill and Alice is still going to be a balance, and perhaps it won't last very much longer after the film's ending than the union of Cruise and Kidman did. Bill wears the black overcoat and scarf of a professional; she wears what could almost pass for a housecoat. This suggests that his career is still the important one; she remains at loose ends. Nonetheless, he defers to her: "Tell me, what should we do?" "Fuck." She still dictates the terms, or term, of the relationship, and these expressions—in their crudity and directness—are no less threatening to the male than before. It is here that we might wonder if Kubrick's own newly awake sense of sexual politics is a bit musty. While the female orgasm might have been news to men in 1968, when Kubrick first thought of adapting Schnitzler's novella, would a man in 1999 be threatened by a woman's utterance of the "f-word"?

One Kubrick Web site went so far as to suggest that Kidman, in shots in which she peers over the top of her glasses, comes to resemble the director, who is shown in a nearly identical pose in a portrait released by Warner Bros. This, along with the explanation of a *The Firm*-like conspiracy from a character played by Sydney Pollack, Cruise's director on *The Firm*, reinforces an impression that Bill/Cruise is being "directed," his course authored by others, and that this, and not the archetype of the strong self-determining male, is the essence of masculinity in Western culture. Furthermore, Gaylyn Studlar argues that in *Eyes Wide Shut*, "Nicole Kidman's body rather than Cruise's becomes the focus of the camera's attention" (182). Studlar maintains that while earlier Tom Cruise vehicles, specifically *Risky Business* (Paul Brickman, 1983), *Cocktail* (Roger Donaldson, 1988), *Days of Thunder* (Tony Scott, 1990), and *Interview with the Vampire* (Neil Jordan, 1994), appeared to posit Cruise's body as the object of a homosexual look in films in which relationships between men were far more important in the narrative than heterosexual romances, which were treated in a perfunctory, obligatory manner, most of his more recent films have presented him as a conventional male subject. However, the attention given, in Cruise's self-examining performance for Kubrick, to the faltering and illusory elements of the male subject position disrupts the smoothness one expects of a simple male-subject, female-object pattern. So does the unpredictable discontinuousness of Kidman's behavior as Alice.

Cruise had preceded *Eyes Wide Shut* with Jerry Maguire, a role that demanded some emotional exposure of him. Notwithstanding his supporting turn as a misogynist demagogue in *Magnolia*, Cruise's films since working with Kubrick, *Mission Impossible 2* (John Woo, 2000), *Vanilla Sky*, and, to a certain extent, *Minority Report*, have been about masks. It is as if Cruise were dramatizing a desire to obscure his famous face, to cover it, and to acknowledge it as a meaningless facade, a hindrance to expression.

Jonathan Rosenbaum wrote that Kubrick concluded his career "with the closest thing in his work to a happy ending" (2). The ending of *Eyes Wide Shut* suggests that the world is beyond change and that the only way to deal with the way things are is to create your own world, a solution Brecht would have loathed. In short, Kubrick, who believed that what he wanted of the world could be brought to him in Boreham Wood, England, and everything else could be avoided, finally made his solution the world's. Kubrick's most conservative film is also his most honest and his most personal. What is more, this conclusion is arrived at by means of a Brechtian model of instruction. Kubrick finally could do no better than to instruct from his own experience. The performances of his stars, who turn behavior into gesture, action into process, and character into type, move audiences to think in idiosyncratic ways about what men and women want within a structure put in place to serve the interests of men in power.

WORKS CITED

Bingham, Dennis. "The Displaced Auteur: A Reception History of Kubrick's *The Shining*." *Perspectives on Stanley Kubrick*. Ed. Mario Falsetto. New York: G. K. Hall, 1996. 284–307.

Brecht, Bertolt. *Brecht on Theatre: The Development of an Aesthetic*. Ed. and trans. John Willett. New York: Hill and Wang, 1964.

Callow, Simon. *Charles Laughton: A Difficult Actor*. New York: Grove, 1987.

Dyer, Richard. *Heavenly Bodies: Film Stars and Society*. New York: St. Martin's, 1986.

Elsaesser, Thomas. "From Anti-illusionism to Hyper-realism: Bertolt Brecht and Contemporary Film." *Re-interpreting Brecht: His Influence on Contemporary Drama and Film*. Ed. Pia Kleber and Colin Visser.

Cambridge: Cambridge UP, 1990. 170–85.

Esslin, Martin. "Some Reflections on Brecht and Acting." *Re-interpreting Brecht: His Influence on Contemporary Drama and Film.* Ed. Pia Kleber and Colin Visser. Cambridge: Cambridge UP, 1990. 135–47.

Fuchs, Cindy. Rev. of *Eyes Wide Shut. Philadelphia City Paper* 22–29 July 1999 <http://www.citypaper.net>

Harvey, Stephen. "Shining It Isn't." *Saturday Review* (July 1980):64.

Kidman, Nicole. Interview with Paul Joyce. 12 July 1999. *Eyes Wide Shut.* DVD. Warner Home Video, 2000.

Kubrick, Stanley, and Frederic Raphael. *"Eyes Wide Shut": A Screenplay.* New York: Warner, 1999.

LoBrutto, Vincent. *Stanley Kubrick: A Biography.* New York: Donald I. Fine, 1997.

Neale, Steve. "Masculinity as Spectacle: Reflections on Men and Mainstream Cinema." *Screen* 24.4 (1983): 2–16.

Polan, Dana. "Materiality and Sociality in *Killer's Kiss.*" *Perspectives on Stanley Kubrick.* Ed. Mario Falsetto. New York: G. K. Hall, 1996. 87–99.

Rosenbaum, Jonathan. "In Dreams Begin Responsibilities." *Chicago Reader* 23 July 1999. <http://www.chireader.com/movies/archives>

Studlar, Gaylyn. "Cruise-ing into the Millennium: Performative Masculinity, Stardom, and the All-American Boy's Body." *Ladies and Gentlemen, Boys and Girls: Gender in Film at the End of the Twentieth Century.* Ed. Murray Pomerance. Albany: SUNY Press, 2001. 171–184.

Titterington, P. L. "Kubrick and *The Shining.*" *Sight and Sound* 50.2 (1981): 117–21.

Wright, Elizabeth. *Postmodern Brecht: A Representation.* London: Routledge, 1989.

11

Thinking through Jim Carrey

Vivian Sobchack

> The object . . . [is] to describe the animation of the human body, not in terms of the descent into it of pure consciousness or reflection, but as a metamorphosis of life.
>
> *Maurice Merleau-Ponty*

> Whoever invented the mirror destroyed us.
>
> *Jim Carrey*

••

Consider the following scene in comedian Jim Carrey's first hit movie, *Ace Ventura: Pet Detective* (Tom Shadyac, 1994): Ace—a totally self-reflexive eccentric who has an emotional and behavioral affinity with animals and is incredibly responsive to the physical environment and dogged and doggylike in his commitment to his job—is on the trail of the stolen mascot of the Miami Dolphins. He is "playing insane" so as to get committed to a mental institution, where he needs to follow up on one of the case's major clues. Brought in by his supposed "sister," he is twice over a bizarre figure: first as Ace, with his cockatoo hairdo, an overabundance of self-confidence, and a bouncing walk informed by a "sick, cocky vigor" (Sherrill 104); then as his chosen "character," a mentally disturbed ex-football player whose disguise of plaid shorts, pajama top, and unlaced combat boots is enhanced most noticeably by a pink tulle ballerina's tutu. With intense, monomaniacal glee figured through both his bright and unblinking stare and a voracious grin, he rises to meet the psychiatrist as if the latter were a football coach. He then proceeds to deliver a self-referential bodily monologue of a clichéd, televisual "big game" moment—not only verbally describing but also physically enacting "a button hook pass in super slo-mo," first in forward and then in reverse sound and motion.

This is an extraordinary performance. Slowed down, hyperbolically exaggerated, and enacted in real time (that is, the time of human physical action), the strenuous stretching and contraction of facial and neck muscles—particularly the jaw and mouth—convey microunits of bodily effort. Arms and legs flail and pump up and down in a rhythm we can inspect, and the hands claw for the air ball in grotesque contortions of strain and desire. Language is also temporally distended both forward and backward. Transformed into both chirpy and guttural unintelligibility, its meaning is lost in a vocal microanalysis of words and sound made completely arbitrary no matter their direction. In this particular and comic narrative context, Carrey's controlled deployment of his body and voice to exaggerate and deconstruct what is already a highly mediated and exaggerated moment of "spontaneous" masculine bodily action is not just grotesque and very funny. It is also quite astonishing in its critical attention to the reflexive and incredibly self-conscious manipulation of both physical behavior and mass-mediated discourse in what has come to be called "postmodern culture" (however one defines it, a culture particularly marked by its constant use of quotation, sampling, and recycling of both identities and texts).[1]

Given its self-awareness and its virtuosity, how might we meaningfully think through and talk about such an in-your-face physical performance—both as it is accomplished and as it is physically and socially comprehended by an audience? Popular reviewers, of course, tend to rely heavily on metaphor and hyperbole to evoke the physical "look" and "feel" of the performer qua performance. Thus Chris Willman writes exuberantly of Carrey as Ace: "When . . . Carrey goes on a crying jag, his enormous mouth turns into such a gaping canyon that your mind might wander to wondering just how many whole grapefruits could be stuffed into it. When he deigns to close those choppers, he doesn't so much smile as he clinches every muscle within a six-inch radius of his overbite into a maniacal grin that makes him look like a handsomely-dimpled gerbil" (6). Nonetheless, however evocative, these descriptions do not tell us *enough* about Carrey's art—about what he does or how he does it. Nor would the usual "star study," which often focuses on the construction of a star "persona"—looking more at biography, production histories, and fan culture than at the present "presence" of a corporeal figure on screen.

Here, then, I am particularly interested in quite literally "thinking through" Jim Carrey's body—that is, trying to match this extraordinary performer's complex and critical "corporeal intelligence" with some form of analysis and description adequate not only to it but also to our own "corporeal comprehension" of it as his audience. As Jodi Brooks aptly puts it, what seems needed is "both *a resensitization of the spectator's body* and *a refiguring of the imaged body* which is not only available to new forms of visibility but [also] renders visible new spatial and temporal configurations" (17). Thus linked together in the cinematic experience, the performer's body and the spectator's body could be said to constitute and literally *incorporate* what Lesley Stern calls a "'loopy system' of energy transference" that circulates in an "erratic manner among actor, the film itself and the viewer" (Stern and Kouvaros 25). This "loopy system" is enabled and influenced not only by narrative structure and such cinematic operations as cinematography, camera movement, and editing but also by the *bodies* of the actor and the viewer.[2] Expansive and dynamic, this notion of energy transference—"its operations, end-points and forms of engagement"—allows us "an understanding of performance in which the focus is on *the way energy is deployed and transmitted by and through the body* rather than privileging psychological or mimetic principles" (Stern and Kouvaros 26; emphasis added). Thus it is to the "loopy system" of the transference of bodily energy and corporeal intelligence that constitutes Jim Carrey's performances that I now want to turn—looking not only to these performances' connected operations but also to the ways in which they refigure the imaged body spatially and temporally and resensitize the spectator's body in a dialogue or circuit of coconstituted attention and corporeal expressivity. In this regard, as Stern and Kouvaros suggest: "Much more is at stake here than a reading of a particular bravura comic performance" (25). Indeed, in what follows, although I certainly hope to illuminate the nature of Carrey's particular bravura performances, I am much more interested in attempting to understand and adequately describe forms of "being on the screen." Thus I have chosen Carrey not so much because he is a "star," but because his body is so "in our face" that his flamboyant corporeal presence on-screen intensifies and foregrounds what other performers do, but which may be much harder to see with them.

It seems appropriate to begin at the "end point" that is also its beginning: Carrey before the mirror, analyzing and practicing—through his own reflection—what will eventually appear on-screen.

Here, "everything that appears spontaneous is the result of hours and hours of preparation"—although, I would argue, *nothing* Carrey does on-screen *ever* appears completely "spontaneous" (Sherrill 100). Indeed, part of what we marvel at (or loathe) is the performer's constant self-reflexivity that points to all those hours of bodily scrutiny, practice, and preparation—recognition of which (both by him and by us) calls into question even his most seemingly "natural" actorly behavior. Calling himself "a bit of a control freak," Carrey tells us, for example, that "when I made *The Mask* [Chuck Russell, 1994], I knew every move I was going to make" (qtd. in Franklin 51). Bringing his prior acts of attention and reflection to the screen, he layers the characters he plays with the corporeal exaggerations of the very attentive and intense reflective processes that produced them. As Richard Corliss notes, Carrey "can turn the simple act of listening into power aerobics": his "laser stare becomes maniacally penetrating," and "turning to hear a question, he nearly gives himself whiplash" ("World's Only Living Cartoon" 56).

Carrey, of course, began his career as a comic impressionist who could do caricatures of more than 150 mass-media celebrities ranging from Elvis Presley and Sammy Davis Jr. to Leonid Brezhnev. Many of these show up in such films as *The Mask* or, with a dizzying verticality, in *Man on the Moon* (Milos Forman, 1999), in which he impersonates Andy Kaufman impersonating Elvis. Carrey was also an amateur cartoonist. Both these talents for caricature call for the microscrutiny, isolation, and exaggeration of the human body's meaningful behavior. Indeed, Carrey has said that he creates both his impersonations and his fictional characters "by first discovering the appropriate gestures, twitches, body shapes" (qtd. in Knelman 33). Voice, too, plays a crucial part. In his microanalyses of the body, vocal and facial muscles are in exaggerated concert, slowing down and stretching out or flattening sound and behavior into the musicality of a particular person's speech (such as Andy Kaufman's or Elvis's), or into irony (Ace's "Alllll-rrrighty, then" or the Cable Guy's too quickly delivered monotone: "God bless you. You're too good to me. You really are"), or into a loss of intelligibility (Ace's "slo-mo" football commentary or his frequent self-congratulatory deconstruction of the epithet, "Lo—ooo—uh—ser"). As Corliss says of his vocal virtuosity, "He can torture the most innocent banalities . . . into delirious comedy" (Rev.).

Carrey's detailed microanalysis of the way in which the body inflects gesture and voice to constitute not only "personality" but also incredibly nuanced social and cultural meaning is fore-grounded both offscreen and on through the rhetorical exaggera-tions of *hyperbole*. That is, through a physical exaggeration of ges-ture and voice that visibly inscribes a *more extensive space* than is the norm, Carrey shows us how complex desires, emotions, and thought processes are literally incorporated and performed—both as oneself and for others. Think here, perhaps, not merely of the facial difference but also of the spatial difference between our own slightly raised eyebrow inscribing skepticism and ironic distancia-tion and one of Carrey's superarched and arch ones. Correlatively, by virtue of their expansion in space, Carrey's exaggerations also (to varying degree) *slow down and extend time and action*, allowing him (before the mirror) and us (before the screen) to inspect more carefully how our bodies shape and "perform" our intentions in the world, both for the eyes of others and ourselves. In this sense, the hyperbolic "super slo-mo" sequence in *Ace Ventura*, while singu-lar, is not only exemplary of the microanalysis Carrey performs before the mirror but also exemplary of the microanalysis he per-forms on-screen—even at whirling dervish speed as in *The Mask* or as he appears to conform more closely to the temporality and rhythms of "normal" human action in parts of *Liar, Liar* (Tom Shadyac, 1997) and *The Truman Show* (Peter Weir, 1998). In sum, it is through the rhetorical figure of hyperbole as it is physically enacted and corporeally understood that Carrey foregrounds the lived body's behavior as always—and often histrionically—both self-reflexive and performative in its grasp on being.

In an admirable essay focused on Charlie Chaplin, Laleen Jayamanne writes that to understand comic performance in what she calls "slapstick time," we must learn "how to perceive mimet-ically the slapstick bodies that move too fast or, as the case might be, too slow" and also map out "the temporalities invented by them" (110). In regard to such spatial mapping, she suggests that "mimetic gestural performance has the power to create *any-space-whatever*, which is a way of disorganizing spatialized arrangements of power" (131). Carrey's gestural power in this regard is quite extraordinary. He does more than appropriate and *extend space* through the elastic and hyperbolic distensions of his body: the attentive turn of a head spatially exaggerated into whiplash; the self-confident cockiness and "come on" of a slightly tilted hip hyperbolized into celebratory priapic pumping; the eager friendly grin expanded to a size that not only overtakes the face but also threatens to engorge its human object.

Carrey also *transforms space* with his body and voice, throughout his films physically performing and thus constituting the world as infinitely capacious and able to entertain and combine an infinite number of actual and virtual scenarios. Here, we might think of Ace transforming what seems a mundane space into a virtual generic "action thriller" or into the bridge of the *Starship Enterprise*: the already half-virtual Mask not only invoking a virtual but suddenly presenced Sally Field, Clark Gable, and Desi Arnaz in dizzying succession but also transforming a generic police chase action sequence into a big "Latin" samba number straight out of a Carmen Miranda musical. We might also recall sociopath "Chip Douglas" in *The Cable Guy* (Ben Stiller, 1996) turning the search for the location of interior wiring into a highly charged (and disturbingly funny) sexual encounter with a suddenly (and startlingly) eroticized apartment wall.

What Carrey performs and provokes, then, are a multitude of spatial "double takes" that emphasize the infinite extensibility not only of the space of the body but also the space of the world. This is rather different from the kind of "double take" that emphasizes and extends (or "doubles") time through a heightened, if slight, repetition of action. This latter double take is best illustrated by Cary Grant who, in his comedies, was physically adept at following his "natural" response with a suddenly startled turn of the head, a horrified look, and a small but noticeable backward and horizontal motion of his upper body, these indicating (and sharing with the audience) his delayed recognition of and self-critical commentary on an initial incomprehension. Carrey, instead, constitutes the double take in space less through temporal repetition than through what we might call a *vertical* physical layering of chimerical changes of behavior, reflexive self-commentary, and fragmented temporality. That is, he fluidly (if schizophrenically) inhabits, dramatizes, and transforms characters, scenarios, and virtual worlds through and on his body—moving in elasticized and exaggerated metamorphic response to the multiple forms and fragmented rhythms of postmodernity.

Adding further complexity and richness to the layered aspects of Carrey's physical performance are the films' narratives—almost all of which complement Carrey's vertical double takes by sequentially "horizontalizing" and deconstructing his near simultaneous layering of human self-contradiction. The narratives of the films in which he performs all temporally split and contrast contradictory behavioral components into "doubled" characters—for example, sweet and meek Stanley Ipkiss and aggressive and in-your-face Mask in *The Mask*; nerdy inventor Ed Nygma and Nijinsky-like archvillain the Riddler in *Batman Forever* (Joel Schumacher, 1995); Fletcher Reede as liar and truth-teller in *Liar, Liar*; abject comic Andy Kaufman and hostile lounge singer Tony Clifton in *Man on the Moon*; the "schizophrenic" mild-mannered state trooper Charlie Baileygates and his pathologically nasty and aggressive alter ego, Hank Evans in *Me, Myself & Irene* (Bob and Peter Farrelly, 2000); and, most recently, the complacent and self-serving screenwriter Peter Applegate become amnesiac war hero Luke Trimble in *The Majestic* (Frank Darabont, 2001). Nonetheless, even when playing characters who are split and thus "doubly taken" in the narrative, Carrey himself is not. That is, his physical performance displays such control and virtuosity that the dialectic of character he enacts is synthesized into a higher-order—and exhilaratingly smooth—temporal and spatial tension. The fragmentations and contradictions in postmodern culture between "authenticity" and social convention, intense engagement and distanced irony, between heartfelt sentiment and its deprecation are all "composited"—become simultaneous—on his incredibly nuanced and responsive body.

Carrey, then, not only performs "in" but also "refigures" space through his hyperbolic but layered and nuanced physicality. How might this physicality also perform and refigure *time*? Discussing temporality and slapstick performance, Jayamanne contends that it is "the differential rhythms and speeds" at which tactical violations and transformations of conventionally circumscribed or "ritual time" and objects are performed that "make us convulse with laughter or shudder in terror" (118). In this regard, along with the power of his gestural performance to create "any-space-whatever," Carrey's body also seems able to "seize the 'tiny' or brief instant chance proffers . . . to transform ritually structured time into mimetic play and to tactically deploy ritualized objects as toys" (Jayamanne 134). Jayamanne also emphasizes the slapstick comic's general "mimetic capacity to *endlessly divide time*" (127). For example, she describes the rhythms of Charlie Chaplin's gags and his interactions with objects as an "evasion and side-stepping of the present" that divides and extends its temporality into what, after Deleuze, she sees as a "present of pure operation, not of incorporation" (129).

Carrey, I would argue, divides and extends time quite differently. His performances do not evade and sidestep the present;

instead, they are completely immersed in the present and in the exploration of its transcendent (not transcendental or "pure") possibilities. Indeed, Carrey's physical inventiveness does not aim at some "pure operation" but rather seeks to realize the "incorporation" of his imagination. Thus Carrey inhabits the present fully, taking advantage of both his own embodiment and the world's materiality to test, play out, thicken, and extend the present's alternative scenarios and its polysemic possibilities. Here, we might recall Ace Ventura at an upscale party, loping along the buffet table, putting hard-boiled egg halves on his eyes and hanging a row of asparagus spears from his mouth to materially embody first a movie monster and then becoming a socially self-conscious party guest asking another sotto voce, "Do I have something in my teeth?" Or, in an extended sequence of *Liar, Liar*, horrified "truthteller-for-a-day" lawyer Fletcher Reede struggling to make his blue pen write on a piece of paper the lie that its color is red.

Although she does not deal directly with hyperbole, Jayamanne's discussion of how, through mimetic gestural performance, the slapstick clown is able to both create "*any-space-whatever*" and "*endlessly divide time*" allows us not only a more specific description of Carrey's hyperbolic physical idiolect, it also sheds light on the *rhetorical argument* that is constructed through his exaggerated physical performance. In this regard, it seems more than a comic accident that in the utterly sober *The New Rhetoric: A Treatise on Argumentation*, a chapter entitled "Arguments Based on the Structure of Reality" addresses what is called the "argument of unlimited development." Such an argument insists "on the possibility of always going further in a certain direction without being able to foresee a limit to this direction, and this progress is accompanied by a continuous increase in value" (Perelman and Olbrechts-Tyteca 287). This increase in rhetorical value, however, has less to do with the *content* of the argument than with its *progress*—and the increasing fascination this progress exerts as it escalates. Thus, the authors write:

> What is important is not the achievement of a certain objective, the arrival at a certain stage, but continuing, going further, passing beyond, in the direction indicated by two or three stepping stones. The important thing is not a well-defined end: Each situation, on the contrary, serves as a stepping stone or springboard permitting indefinite advance in a certain direction. . . . This kind of reasoning is used not only to promote certain behavior but also . . . to define certain

"purified" notions, stemming from common-sense conceptions which are presented as a starting point. (288)

The reasoning behind the argument of unlimited development informs not only Carrey's characterization of his own personality and avowed appetite for self-improvement books but also his investments in performing. In interviews, for example, he has said: "My mother used to say to me, 'You're never satisfied.' And it's true" (qtd. in Handy 80) and "It all comes down to: Am I going to be able to do something I haven't done before? . . . Is it something that hasn't been seen?" (82). Even more telling is his self-description as a compulsive and "circular thinker": "I get on the carousel of thought and break things down about a thousand times. It's exhausting. I guess they call it obsessive-compulsion" (qtd. in Franklin 59).

Carrey's offscreen purchase on the argument of unlimited development is, of course, a great deal less funny (or, if you prefer, less horrifying) than those arguments of unlimited development he plays out in most of his films. *The Cable Guy* never gives up on— and, indeed, escalates—both "Chip Douglas's" voraciously needy search for friendship and his later sociopathic attempts at revenge. In *Liar, Liar*, attempting to avoid arguing a court case because he is supernaturally bound to tell the truth for a day, lawyer Fletcher Reede mugs himself in the men's room, subjecting his body to every conceivable torture the space and appliances make available. Forced to argue his case nonetheless, as one reviewer notes, "Carrey's courtroom self-destruction takes the expressive portrayal of comic suffering *as far as it can go*" (Atkinson, rev. of *Liar, Liar*; emphasis added). The argument is there, too, in permutations of Carrey's dialogue and delivery. In *Dumb and Dumber* (Peter Farrelly, 1994), when told by the woman he loves that his romantic chances with her are more like one in a million than the one in a hundred he has suggested, love-struck Lloyd glows with hopeful optimism as he slowly breaks a smile, "You're telling me . . . there *is* a chance." In *Batman Forever*, after a major performative outburst of rage, the Riddler coyly asks, "Was that over the top? I can never tell." And, indeed, a great part of the pleasure (or dismay) we feel watching Carrey perform is his own immense and unfailing energy—a not-to-be-stopped life force or "vitalism" (both impulsive and compulsive) that makes manifest his performative joy or drivenness in precisely going "over the top." The very opening of *Ace Ventura: Pet Detective* exemplifies Carrey enacting not only a version of the argument of unlimited development but also this capacious joy of performance as, still unknown to us and disguised as a parcel delivery man, the pet detective consciously, gracefully, and with precise timing from truck to door commits every conceivable—and then some—damage to a package he is delivering to a pet-napper. Thus—and it has much to do with the promise (and folly) of unlimited development—as Nancy Franklin notes, in Carrey's comedy "there is a potent rage to live" (51).

Given that the argument of unlimited development seems well suited to both comic performance and comic narrative, it should be no surprise that one of the main rhetorical figures put to its service is hyperbole—which, "when it has an argumentative purpose, as it almost always does"—encompasses not only *enlargement* but also *diminution* (Perelman and Olbrechts-Tyteca 291, emphasis added). Here, in relation to enlargement, we might think, for example, of Mack Sennett's Keystone Kops in chases that involve more and more people, of Laurel and Hardy's *Big Business* (James W. Horne and Leo McCarey, 1929), in which a house and automobile are totally demolished, and of *It's a Mad Mad Mad Mad World* (Stanley Kramer, 1963), which in scope, activity, and comic cast extends "madness" to epic proportions. And in relation to diminution, we might recall *Dumb and Dumber*, which keeps asking and answering the question: "How dumb can you get?" Furthermore, as *The New Rhetoric* points out, the use of hyperbole in such an argument need not only build gradually but may also arise suddenly and be "fired with brutality" (Perelman and Olbrechts-Tyteca 290). This sense of brutality is certainly apposite to the hostile exaggerations of Ace, the Cable Guy, and pathological alter ego Hank in *Me, Myself & Irene*—as well as to Carrey's comments to an interviewer that he uses comedy "as a lethal weapon" and that "there are times in my shower where I'll think of a person and I'll be mad at them and I'll arm myself with twenty good things if they ever say anything to me. That's what comedians do: prepare themselves for war" (qtd. in Daly 294).

While most often gradual (if sometimes brutal), the major function of hyperbole in an argument of unlimited development (whether its goal is enlargement or diminution) is "to provide a reference which draws the mind in a certain direction only to force it later to retreat a little to the extreme limit of what seems compatible with its idea of the human, the possible, the probable, with all the other things it admits" (Perelman and Olbrechts-Tyteca 291). The audience to such an argumentative performance becomes rhetorically complicit with it—on the one hand caught up in and appreciative of the spectacular exaggerations of its rhetorical moves and, on the other, also aware of the argument's developmental limits beyond which one confronts the impossible, the inhuman, the ridiculous. Thus as the audience engages and enjoys the exuberance of the argument, it also grasps the commonsensical terms of its refutation. This rhetorical rebuttal emerges from the recognition "that it is impossible to go indefinitely in the direction indicated, either because one encounters an *absolute* or because one ends up with an *incompatibility*" or is in "danger of *appearing ridiculous* as a result of incompatibility with values one is loath to give up" (Perelman and Olbrechts-Tyteca 289; emphasis added).

In comedy, of course, these limits to and rebuttal of the argument of unlimited development are—through their physical incorporation and narrative dramatization—precisely what provide the "ridiculous" grounds for humor. Posing these limits, often it is the narrative that rebuts the argument. In *Dumb and Dumber*, for example, the absolute limit is figured as the film's arbitrary ending—at a point that absolutely cuts off what might otherwise be an unlimited series of variations on a single gag of diminution. In *The Cable Guy*, the absolute limit is reached as complete exhaustion— "Chip Douglas" taken off to the hospital on a stretcher. *The Mask*'s narrative reconciles the "incompatible values" of grandiose desire and acceptable social behavior in the final refiguring of Stanley Ipkiss as less "over the top" as the Mask but also more bold than his earlier milquetoast character—and *Liar, Liar* ends similarly with the "reformation" of Fletcher Reede, who is now able to reconcile being a "liar/lawyer" and a good and "truthful" father/husband.

Ultimately, however, these incompatibilities of value and the ridiculous extremes of the argument as it strives for its furthest extension are precisely what are foregrounded on-screen in both Carrey's performances and the comedies that frame them. These are what provoke in the audience not only the complicity of rhetorical appreciation but also the critical distance of rational judgment—the latter emerging, however, not in reflective thought but in the corporeal rebuttal of laughter.

In this regard, *Man on the Moon* resonates as a complex and ambiguous counterexample. Structured as an argument of unlimited development focused around the escalating exaggerations and extremes of ambiguously comic performer Andy Kaufman, the film does not allow its audiences (both within the text and within the theater) clear grounds for the argument's rebuttal—and thus for rational judgment enacted as critical laughter. This is not only because *Man on the Moon* marks itself generically as a "bio-pic" of Andy Kaufman, an ambiguous comic genius, but also because the only limit placed on the argument is its subject's very real death, itself made ambiguous as, at once, both the absolute and furthest extension of Kaufman's unsettling performance of the argument in his life and career—and its ultimate rebuttal. Here the argument of unlimited development (and Carrey's performance of it as Kaufman) is ambivalently comic and tragic—and too ambiguous to judge in the form of critical laughter.

Man on the Moon aside, however, the argument of unlimited development is an organizing structure of any number of hyperbolic comic routines and narratives. Thus what is particular to Jim Carrey's use of that structure is that unlimited development is not only *narratively* argued in his gags and films, but also *corporeally* argued in his physical performance. His skill in hyperbolically creating and transforming enlargements and diminutions of his bodily comportment, gesture, voice, and character literally embodies the argument. Furthermore, through his vertically layered physical gestures, vocal inflections, and explicit self-reflexive dialogic commentaries, Carrey's body is a palimpsest—not only able to perform the argument but also (and amazingly) to perform its rebuttal. That is, part of Carrey's embodied persona is, to varying degrees, always making manifest a critical judgment—both about the hyperbolic nature of the argument of unlimited development he is performing and about the specificity of his own rhetorical performance in arguing it. Indeed, as Carrey tells one interviewer, "I . . . could sit here and dissect what I think comedy is and make it really boring for everybody, but I know what it is. . . . Freud talks about jokes being judgments, and that's what they are; *the job of a comic is to judge*" (qtd. in Daly 294).

In this regard, Carrey has larger interests than the mere physical and verbal self-reflexivity, self-referentiality, and self-judgment *of* his performance *in* his performance—what might be taken as an extreme form of narcissism. In both his comic dramatizations and his physical and verbal metacommentaries and judgments upon them, he uses the argument of unlimited development to focus on and heighten our attention to the thoroughly acculturated and performative nature of human behavior in mass-mediated culture. While his work constantly draws attention to the always social visibility of our corporeal behavior, it also emphasizes both the mediating cultural templates (or conventions) that make of us all actors and performers in our own and other people's scenarios—and our heightened self-consciousness of this fact about our mass-mediated lives. Indeed, in nearly all his films, Carrey's iterations of unlimited development are played out, both corporeally and narratively, within a social and cultural context in which "spontaneous" or "authentic" behavior is always—and from the first—generated by and filtered through mass-mediated imagery and desire. What we learn from Carrey's hyper- and metacritical performances is that in contemporary postmodern culture we are all "actors": "spontaneously" living our lives as conventional performances of characters and scenes from movies and television shows and comic books and advertisements and self-consciously, ironically, and judgmentally adjusting our comportment in relation to the characters, desires, dialogues, and scenarios we see on the screens that surround us.

Yet Carrey adds something more to the discourses on postmodernity that foreground the culture's heightened intertextuality, self-reflexivity, and the contemporary insight (always uncanny) that even in our most seemingly "authentic" behavior, we are always performing the performances of others. What is unique about his complex corporeal literalizations is their emphasis on how popular mass media have not only coconstituted our culture's resources, behavioral repertoire, and tastes, but have also coconstituted our bodies and our visible comportment. Thus as Michael Atkinson summarizes:

> Jim Carrey is more than a rubber-faced comic . . . he is the human animal shaped, corrupted, and fueled by the irrational, behavioral hyperbole of television. As such, he is funny while still being self-referential; every gesticulation and grimace is a dense text of pop-culture history and, often, a flagellating self-critique. . . . Carrey's persona is beyond humor; the most interesting aspects of his films are not the ones that make us laugh . . . [but those that] can be read as a scathing interrogation of media culture. (rev. of *Liar, Liar*)

As both star persona in his interviews and character in his films—and sometimes with a sadness quickly undercut by his self-consciousness about its possible appearance as an "act"—Carrey consistently points to and understands himself as *nothing less yet also something more* than a completely exteriorized and textual being born of mass-mediated culture. (If he gets serious or sentimental or slightly tearful in interviews, for example, he will catch himself, physically exaggerate his behavior, and say something explicit that indicates awareness that as an "actor" and "performer" on the big or small screen, the "authenticity" of his feelings and behavior are always questionable and may, indeed, be deemed "insincere.") Indeed, albeit in a much more deeply self-conscious and certainly less sociopathic and malevolent form, Jim Carrey *is* the Cable Guy. Atkinson is right on the money when he writes:

> The movie is nothing less than the self-interrogation of a postmodern superstar. Who is the Cable Guy, whose lonesome adult person is a raving juggernaut of broadcast reflexes and received media myth, but Carrey himself? . . . On the surface a familiarly absurd study of misplaced obsession, *The Cable Guy* is really Carrey's lacerating self-portrait-under-pressure, a there-but-for-the-grace-of-God vision of what the man could have very well become with just a little less wit, luck and satire smarts. (rev. of *The Cable Guy*)

Unlike the metacritical Carrey, however, the Cable Guy is the ultimate production of mass-mediated culture. His "real" name— "Chip Douglas"—is only televisually authentic (he also calls himself "Larry Tate" and "Ricky Ricardo"); indeed, he has nothing but TV to ground his identity, and both the character and the film overtly and darkly criticize (to disturbing degree for most audiences) the virtuality of mass-mediated being and its real consequences. The virtual—and yet real—nature of mass-mediated being informs all of Carrey's films, characters, and performances. Many of his characters have "every genre tic imaginable" (Skinner). Ace, for example, is always creating movie, TV, and radio serial scenarios and always talking in his own self-referential and mangled idiolect of imagined media dialogue that presumes a mass-media audience. For example, he describes aloud to himself and his imagined audience a room whose walls are covered with hunting trophies: "This is a lovely room of death"; or coming into an African village, he announces: "I will slip among them as a transparent thing"; or after accomplishing a task, he speaks of himself in third person: "'Wunderbar,' he exclaimed with great relish." And, in mimetic sympathy with Ace, the films' narratives also have "every genre tic imaginable." For example, *Ace Ventura: When Nature Calls* (Steve Oedekerk, 1995) begins as a parody of the Sylvester Stallone action picture *Cliffhanger* (Renny Harlin, 1993) wackily inflected by the opening sequence of Alfred Hitchcock's *Vertigo* (1958) (figure 11.1).

11.1. Jim Carrey as Ace Ventura in *Ace Ventura: When Nature Calls*.

Along with their generic movie references, Carrey's films also give us "a razor-sharp vision of televisual sensibility invading reality" (Atkinson, rev. of *Liar, Liar*). The Mask, as performer/character, not only becomes an array of Chuck Jones–like cartoon caricatures of media celebrities but is also media-savvy in other ways: he functions, for example, as a crazed television game show host—or, accused of a bank robbery, he mock moans: "It was the one-armed man" (referring not only to the villain in the television series *The Fugitive* [1963–67] but also to the extremely popular film version released in 1993, the year before *The Mask*). Here, too, the narrative is aware of and plays with the media: it does a riff on itself through the person of a television psychologist who has written a pop self-help book called *The Masks We Wear* but says these masks are only "metaphorical"—when, through the magic of cinema, computer-graphic imaging techniques, and Carrey's body, we and Stanley know for a fact that such masks can be quite real.

In a similar vein, in *The Truman Show*, our first introduction to "normal" Truman Burbank (the unknowing "star" and only "authentic non-actor" in a wildly popular "reality" TV program

11.2. Jim Carrey as Truman Burbank in *The Truman Show*.

that runs twenty-four hours a day) shows him performing a generic movie scenario of manly heroic sacrifice in front of his bathroom mirror (and a hidden TV camera). Later, we return to this ritual spot to watch him horrify the production staff of the Ur–television show by drawing in soap on his mirror what seems at first a knowing acknowledgment of the television screen on which he lives, but then turns out (to their relief) to be a space helmet in yet another of Truman's imaginary generic scenarios. Again—in a loopy transfer of energy and interest—the narrative itself enlarges on Truman's small performances before the bathroom mirror. That is, we not only watch Truman's performances but we also watch Truman's watchers performing: both the director/god Cristof and his television crew and the mass audience watching Truman on the ubiquitous television screens that are a "natural" part of public and private space. Indeed, *The Truman Show* is an explicit and critical interrogation of "authentic being" as always already mass-mediated—and thus its argument of unlimited development (television that has hyperbolically escalated to encompass an entire life and an entire nation) can stop only at the "absolute limit" of a painted backdrop and a door that opens into a black hole and, presumably, a still televised—and televisual—world. Thus just what Truman escapes from—and to— is not at all clear to his generically satisfied but also troubled audience (both in the film and in the theater) (figure 11.2).

In *Man on the Moon*, the transfer of energy from performer to film to audience has become even more complex and troubling, the relation between being and acting brought, as David Denby notes, "to the edge of metaphysical uncertainty" (130). Indeed, Owen Glieberman writes that Carrey ambiguously turns—as Andy Kaufman himself did—"existence into performance and vice versa" (55). Documented by the press, behaving "in" character off- as well as on-screen while shooting the film, Carrey as comedian qua performance artist Kaufman thus becomes similarly "undecidable." (In this sense, Kaufman was ahead of his time: a postmodernist performer relatively underappreciated in a modernist age.) Here, too, the film's narrative mimetically enlarges on the undecidable contours of both the "real" actor and his "real" character to present "Kaufman's life as a series of madly intricate reality-and-illusion stunts that escalated in orchestration and intensity until they burst the fourth wall of the media age" (Glieberman 55). Indeed (and true to the argument of unlimited development), watching *Man on the Moon*, the viewer may feel as if he or she is "watching not just comedy but the psychotic breakdown of comedy" (55).

In the "'loopy system' of energy transference" that Stern sees circulating in an "erratic manner among actor, the film itself, and the viewers," Carrey's on-screen persona, the narrative's structure, and we in the contemporary audience, who "get" all the allusions and references and express our self-congratulation in appreciative laughter, are all implicated in both the postmodern mediascape and its critique. Breaking that "fourth wall of the media age," Carrey's performances and the films in which they appear transfer—in erratically varying ratio—to those of us in the audience not only his comic energy but also his corporeal exploration and critique of what "authentic" being might be in a mass-mediated culture. We, along with Carrey, become aware of how we are caught up in a network of self-conscious appearances, self-reflexive performances, and self-constructed identities constituted through "sampling" the identities of others (figure 11.3).

Here, we should not just see Carrey's exploration and critique of "nonauthentic" being as playful and positive but should also remember *The Cable Guy*, in which "nonauthentic" and truly "mediated" being is sociopathic. Conversely, however, "mediated"

11.3. Jim Carrey as Andy Kaufman in *Man on the Moon*.

and "inauthentic" being is not all bad; when Fletcher Reede in *Liar, Liar* is forced to "tell the truth" as he sees it, the comically painful—and very, very funny—dramatization of "authenticity" foregrounds "the agony our culture would go through if truth suddenly became an unstoppable reflex" (Atkinson, rev. of *Liar, Liar*). As social beings, Carrey points out, we are—even at our most sincere—*condemned* to performance from the beginning; the mass media only highlight and hyperbolize our being as, from the first, culturally mediated. In postmodern culture, this is something we all know intimately both consciously and corporeally—if only tacitly—on a daily basis. Carrey's performances and films make this knowledge deliriously (and sometimes painfully) explicit and they trouble (to both comic and disturbing effect) our comforting (if now superficial) notions of some private and fixed core that grounds our identity or being as somehow—underneath it all—"really authentic." What Carrey shows us through his performance and his films is that "really authentic" being is "really performative" and immersed in the social conventions and textual productions wrought by history and culture.

And this is why there is a certain amusing and ironic poignancy in Carrey's expressed and continuing desire to be taken seriously as a "real actor." He *is* taken seriously as a real actor—only not quite in the way he might wish. Indeed, perhaps more than any other contemporary screen performer, he is the one who has taught us about the complexity of "real acting." The very nature and precision of his deeply thoughtful corporeal performances have solicited from us, as embodied spectators, a mode of deep and thoughtful corporeal attention. That is, his bodily double takes, his corporeal transformation and expansion of space and time, his argumentative exaggerations and escalations, and his constant self-commentary will not allow us—or allow Carrey himself, in his off-screen persona—to see him as transparently "being," as spontaneously "natural." Thus even in his most serious and "straight" moments, we do not watch him as we watch other actors who perform in the conventionally "transparent" or "natural" mode of verisimilar acting style.

Indeed, in terms of our general viewing habits (even as film scholars), have we ever so consistently or deeply scrutinized the discrete and minute bodily and facial movements of the verisimilar performances of, say, Robert Redford or Robert De Niro? Or, in the comic mode, of Jerry Lewis or Steve Martin (with whom Carrey has been compared)? In the first instance, "real" (read "verisimilar") actors like Redford and De Niro create homogenous (if complex) performances that are conventionally taken up as a whole within the compass of the narrative (and sometimes, as with Redford, also within the compass of stardom). In the second instance, film comedians like Lewis and Martin (a neat reversal!) may be as precise in the achievement of their corporeal art as is Carrey, but they solicit our attention differently. Lewis and Martin perform with such broadly hyperbolic but generally undifferentiated exaggerations of their bodies that, on-screen, they seem less self-reflexive and microanalytic than Carrey—this reflected in their lack of explicit self-commentary and self-judgment. This is not to say, however, that both these extremely physically aware performers are not part of Carrey's "cultural iconography" of comic performance. (Indeed, as Frank P. Tomasulo has indicated in a note to the author, one might argue that Lewis—dumb and, on-screen, physically "out of control" and in constant pratfall—"plus" Martin—physically broad and always in braggadocio mode—"equals" Carrey: the "pratfall" now in total control and the braggadocio mode aware and metacritical of its own exaggerations.)

Unlike Lewis and Martin, however (or, for that matter, De Niro and Redford), Jim Carrey has taught us not merely to watch but also to *scrutinize* and read bodily action as highly complex, extraordinarily differentiated, and incredibly nuanced in social meaning—and, watching him, we cannot do otherwise. Here, we might think of Carrey's "straight" performance as Truman Burbank (supposedly the only "nonactor" in Seahaven) and his even "straighter" (more dramatic) one as Andy Kaufman. With Truman, how aware we are of Carrey's slightest self-reflexive gesture or bodily exaggeration: a smile just a bit too wide, a tilt of the head at an angle just a bit too sharp, an overly bright but genial jocularity that self-references its own polite social rhetoric as he tells his neighbors, "Good morning—and in case I don't see you—good afternoon, good evening, and good night." With Andy, how conscious we are of Carrey's pursed and tightened mouth, the stiffness of his shoulders and neck and head, the overly widened and unblinking eyes that often seem glazed by a lack of expression. (The experience of watching these differentiated and precise transformations of comportment is especially uncanny if one is familiar with Kaufman's persona.)

In sum, Jim Carrey is always self-reflexively "thinking through" his body—and he teaches us to watch him with the commensurate attention of our own. That is, he brings to the fore and refines our general attention to the incredibly nuanced expression of our own incorporation and behavior to seriously point out and explore how we are all "real actors." What he accomplishes is precisely what Brooks speaks of as "a refiguring of the imaged body" and "a resensitization of the spectator's body" (17). Thus, even though he may never get an Academy Award for his refusal of actorly transparence, and even though it is not quite what he had in mind, Jim Carrey demonstrates through his body that he is, indeed, not only a "real actor" but also a serious one.

NOTES

1. In what follows, reference to the postmodern draws from both Fredric Jameson's characterization of postmodernity as a totalizing "cultural logic" born of late capitalism that manifests the structure of late capital in works marked by a variety of aesthetic breaks with modernism and from Linda Hutcheon's characterization of the postmodern as a historical and political mode of reflexive and critical consciousness rather than a totalizing cultural logic. While Jameson's and Hutcheon's characterizations are essentially contradictory—even as they meet in description of many of the aesthetic features of postmodernism, I will argue that Carrey embodies both versions as both fragmented and euphoric "postmodern subject" and its historical and political critic.

2. While this "'loopy system' of energy transference" includes the work of the director, what I am particularly interested in here is corporeal performance and how it means. It is telling that Carrey has worked with a wide variety of directors: on the one hand, those like Peter Weir and Milos Forman, who are acknowledged "auteurs" (insofar as that attribution is used anymore), and on the other, those like Tom Shadyac, Joel Schumacher, and Ron Howard, who may not have a "style" or a particular "thematic" but who helm successful Hollywood films. Perhaps the most interesting directorial association with Carrey—because the most suited to both his outrageous and critical sensibilities—are the Farrelly brothers. Nonetheless, it would be exceedingly difficult to make any significant observations about Carrey in relation to his work with specific directors since, in relation to his career in major features, he has only worked with the same directors twice: Tom Shadyac and the Farrellys.

WORKS CITED

Atkinson, Michael. Rev. of *The Cable Guy*. *Village Voice* 9 July 1996: 48.
———. Rev. of *Liar, Liar*. Mr. Showbiz Web site <http://www.mrshowbiz.go.com>
Brooks, Jodi. "Rituals of the Filmic Body." *Writings on Dance* [Melbourne] 17 (1998): 16–25.
Corliss, Richard. Rev. of *Batman Forever*. *Time* 16 June 1995: 79.
———. "World's Only Living Cartoon." *Time* 8 Aug. 1994: 56–58.
Daly, Steven. "Jim Carrey: The Naked Truth." *Vanity Fair* Nov. 1999: 240+.
Denby, David. "Under the Lights." *New Yorker* 27 Dec. 1999–3 Jan. 2000: 130–31.
Franklin, Nancy. "The Best Pretender." *New Yorker* 17 Dec. 2001: 48–61.
Glieberman, Owen. "Andy Hardy." Rev. of *Man in the Moon*. *Entertainment Weekly* 17 Dec. 1999: 55–56.
Handy, Bruce. "Don't Laugh." *Time* 1 June 1998: 80–82.

Jayamanne, Laleen. "A Slapstick Time: Mimetic Convulsion, Convulsive Knowing." *Falling for You: Essays on Cinema and Performance.* Ed. Lesley Stern and George Kouvaros. Sydney: Power, 1999. 105–45.

Knelman, Martin. *Jim Carrey: The Joker Is Wild.* Buffalo: Firefly, 2000.

Perelman, Chaim, and Lucie Olbrechts-Tyteca. *The New Rhetoric: A Treatise on Argumentation.* Trans. John Wilkinson and Purcell Weaver. Notre Dame: U of Notre Dame P, 1969.

Sherrill, Martha. "Renaissance Man." *Esquire* Dec. 1995: 99–106.

Skinner, Richard. Rev. of *Ace Ventura: Pet Detective. Sight and Sound* 4.5 (1994): 38.

Stern, Lesley, and George Kouvaros. "Introduction: Descriptive Acts." *Falling for You: Essays on Cinema and Performance.* Ed. Lesley Stern and George Kouvaros. Sydney: Power, 1999. 1–35.

Willman, Chris. Rev. of *Ace Ventura: Pet Detective. Los Angeles Times Calendar* 4 Feb. 1994: 6.

12

Suiting Up for Postmodern Performance in John Woo's *The Killer*

Cynthia Baron

....

John Woo's film known internationally as *The Killer* (*Die xue shuang xiong*, 1989) was the first Hong Kong film to be a crossover success in the North American market since *Fists of Fury* (*Tang shan da xiong*, 1971), directed by Wei Lo and starring Bruce Lee, made kung fu movies an important part of international cinema. Perhaps taking their cue from the fact that Woo dedicated *The Killer* to proto–New Wave director Jean-Pierre Melville and New American Cinema auteur Martin Scorsese (Woo), reviewers in the United States categorized the film in rather disparate ways. To describe the retro-epic character of Woo's postmodern knight-errant film, Maitland McDonagh referred to *The Killer* as a "mythopoetic fantasy" (46). Taking a somewhat different tack, James Wolcott called attention to the "cool" surface of Woo's postmodern blood opera when he proposed that with the release of *The Killer* John Woo became "the most exciting cult-icon director from overseas since Sergio Leone put Clint Eastwood in a poncho" (63). J. Hoberman selected yet another focus and emphasized the "hot" emotionality of Woo's postmodern male melodrama, arguing that *The Killer* suggested "nothing so much as *Magnificent Obsession* remade by Sam Peckinpah" (33). Echoing that point, Stephen Holden described the film as "an unlikely fusion of *The Wild Bunch* and *Dark Victory*" (qtd. in McDonagh 47).

Observations such as these offer a glimpse of how Western audiences accessed and interpreted *The Killer* when it was first released internationally. The reviewers' comments also provide a useful starting point for analyzing the performances in this film, portrayals that exemplify one trajectory in postmodern cinema. McDonagh's remarks are especially pertinent, for she points out that Woo's pastiche-like approach incorporates not only divergent narrative formulas but disparate styles of performance as well. Writing about what she describes as "bizarrely stressed acting," McDonagh argues that in Woo's films "individual performers slip back and forth between low-key naturalism and exaggerated theatricalism" (48). Given Westerners' sense that "good acting" is "realistic acting" and that authentic works of art are distinguished by their wholeness, harmony, and radiance, McDonagh's observation could be seen as a mark against the film. Yet her observation about the "bizarrely stressed acting" in Woo's films can also be understood as a neutral description—namely, that the performances do not belong to the realistic, naturalistic, or modernist aesthetic traditions. As a neutral statement, McDonagh's description is directly on target, for performances in *The Killer* slip back and forth between what Westerners would call "low-key naturalism and exaggerated theatricalism" and, as a consequence, are emblematic of certain trends in international postmodern film performance.

Analysis of John Woo's Hong Kong films provides clear evidence that there are rather distinct trends in international postmodernism. The film illustrates the point that "postmodern culture is the culture in which all postmodernisms operate, sometimes in synergy, sometimes in competition" (Appiah 59). For example, *The Killer* is quite different from films like *American Graffiti* (1973), *Chinatown* (1974), *Body Heat* (1981), *Blade Runner* (1982), *Blue Velvet* (1986), *Wall Street* (1987), *sex, lies, and videotape* (1989), and other American films that have been featured in analyses of American postmodern cinema (see Connor; Denzin; Hill; and Jameson). The aesthetic strategies in Woo's film do not represent "an elaborated symptom of the waning of our [American] historicity" (Jameson 576). Moreover, the film's pastiche-like quality is not just mimicry devoid of parodic commentary. Its reworking of familiar images and cinematic conventions is not "simply a kind of surface play (or 'depthlessness')" (Hill 102).

Woo's film does, however, belong squarely within the domain of international postmodern film practice because it features excessive shifts in tone, an eclectic "sampling" of existing cinematic conventions, and a cogent manipulation of commercial imagery. Viewed from a Western perspective, these aesthetic strategies seem to be postmodern adaptations of (Western) modernist collage techniques. When one looks at Woo's Hong Kong film from a Western perspective, *The Killer* also seems to draw on aesthetic strategies associated with (Western) melodrama. It sublimates "dramatic values into decor, color, gesture, and composition of frame" (Elsaesser 7) and deploys structural parallels and dramatic acceleration in ways that produce and sustain contrasting attitudes.[1]

It might be argued that discussing *The Killer* in relation to postmodernism also leads to conclusions that are, at best, provisional. As John Hill and others point out, "The appropriateness of the conceptualization and periodization of postmodernism in relation to non-Western cultures remains controversial" (103). While the focus of this essay does not allow me to address questions of periodization in Hong Kong's (colonial) history, it is possible to directly confront the issue of conceptualization. Put bluntly, postmodern theory will remain incomplete unless it considers, for example, Hong Kong film practice. One reason is that films like *The Killer* provide overwhelming evidence of a cinema on the periphery of Western culture that constructs meaning "through the repositioning of artistic and cultural discourses" (Hill 102).

Like many other Hong Kong films, *The Killer* represents a cultural-aesthetic practice that tacitly questions existing traditions in both the East and the West. It engages those traditions in ways that disclose a self-conscious attempt to make sense of postmodernity in a non-western cultural context. Like other filmmakers who have bypassed "the formal conventions of dramatic realism in favor of [strategies] rooted in non-realist, non-Western, or para-Western cultural traditions," John Woo deploys cinematic conventions in ways that "problematize facile dichotomies such as traditional and modern, realist and modernist, modernist and postmodernist" (Stam 263).[2]

Multiple Avenues of Inquiry

Recognizing the complexity of Hong Kong's multifaceted socioeconomic history, this analysis of film performance will focus on certain artistic practices in *The Killer*. That analysis involves considering Woo's film through conceptual lenses that belong to traditions indigenous to both Western and non-Western cultures. To begin with one of the film's most salient features, it is clear that *The Killer*'s mise-en-scène (sets, lighting design, costuming, props, performance style) addresses international audiences as global consumers. That approach is indicative of the film's immediate cultural origins. As Leo Ou-Fan Lee points out, Hong Kong is "a contemporary culture of multiple styles, combining 'high' and 'low,' East and West" (212). He also proposes that "the talent of Hong Kong's 'postmodern' filmmakers lies perhaps in their seemingly effortless probing and public representation (in the form of commercial product) of the collective 'political unconscious' of the average Hong Kong resident and filmgoer" (213).

In fact, *The Killer* became an effective promotional piece for Hong Kong cinema, for John Woo as a director and for Chow Yun-Fat as an international star, precisely because the "commercial materials" used in its probing of "local" sensibility held significance for "foreign" audiences. Chow Yun-Fat's Armani-suited body served as the film's stable, central norm in a spectacular audiovisual experience that gave expression to the secular (professional, brotherhood-focused) and commercially imperial agendas of the generation that came of age during Hong Kong's meteoric rise in the global marketplace. The city-state's singular advance in the world economy was created by Hong Kong's remarkable demand-responsive *production* of ready-to-wear clothes, toys, electronic appliances, and other household items for the department and dime stores that became a part of American and European post–World War II consumerism.

From the mid-twentieth century forward, Hong Kong has been a site of commercial consumption but, more important, also a center for commercial production. In the 1980s, the city-state ranked second in the world in film exports, third in number of films produced per year. For Hong Kong's black and regulated markets, "land speculation, real estate construction, electronics, apparel and textile manufacture, finance, and tourism" have been central areas of economic activity (Stokes and Hoover 13). Even after becoming the Special Administrative Region of China in 1997, Hong Kong still has the world's second most competitive economy; it is the world's seventh largest trading economy; it has the world's second largest per capita holding of foreign currency; it is the world's fourth largest source of direct foreign investment and the world's ninth leading exporter of services (1). Ranked thirteenth among the 133 countries surveyed by the United Nations, Hong Kong has more millionaires and billionaires per capita than anywhere else in the world (9).[3]

The tiny city-state is not only singularly marked by its intense productivity. It also exemplifies in unparalleled ways what it means to have a media-saturated cultural environment. Hong Kong has the highest per capita consumption of television set ownership and viewership in the world (Palmer 49). For Hong Kong residents, designer-label attire is a preoccupation, and television programs on clothing and fashion are intensely popular. Hong Kong was the first major city in the world to have a fully digitized telephone network. It has the highest rate of telephone concentration and fiber optic cable connections in Asia. It has the world's highest rate of faxes and is the fourth largest printing center in the world.

Thus *The Killer*'s commercially inflected representational approach is indicative of its cultural origins in another more diffuse and global respect as well, for as Hill and other scholars explain, media images have been "increasingly identified as a key, if not *the* key, reality for the modern [global] citizen" (98). Drawing on that key reality, Woo's film mobilizes a familiar mode of address that makes its central characters recognizable and accessible to international consumers. Thus its media-saturated images create a potential bridge for audiences' emotional connection with John (Chow Yun-Fat), Jenny (Sally Yeh), Sidney (Chu Kong), and Inspector Li (Danny Lee).

Yet in contrast to the processes of identification codified in classical Hollywood cinema, *The Killer*'s presentation of character creates a cool identification that allows audiences to become engaged with the film's surface level of cinematic hijinks as much as with the characters themselves. There is suture—the camera work and editing practices that "stitch in" the spectator to the perspective and values of the protagonists—but it is a different kind of suture. *The Killer* generates a type of postmodern pleasure that does not necessarily arise from identification with the characters, the camera, or a reality present elsewhere but that arises instead in the course of making one's way through continually shifting rhythms, moods, and levels of emotional engagement.[4]

The reduced importance of the (formulaic) plot in *The Killer* might be compared to the way "the plot itself is subordinated to the task of coordinating and exposing languages to each other" in (Western) texts that explore the possibilities of parodic stylization (Bakhtin 365). From a Western perspective, Woo's mixing of stylistic levels and his radical shifts in mood, rhythm, and perspective produce an aesthetic experience that seems akin to nineteenth-century melodrama and twentieth-century films in the American melodramatic tradition. For Western audiences, those same elements can even seem reminiscent of French New Wave films like *Shoot the Piano Player* (1960). Confounding the "facile dichotomy" between traditional and modern, the excessive cinematic orchestration of narration and performance in *The Killer* can become more intriguing than the story itself. With cinematic embellishments so dense that they are best appreciated by multiple viewings, *The Killer* generates interest in its diegetic world intermittently and perhaps retrospectively.

Like texts that have been categorized as melodrama, Woo's film brings to mind commerce with popular culture, the eschewing of psychological realism, an opposition to realism in general, an alleged inability to be politically progressive, and a marked tendency toward excess. Situated in an aesthetic domain where melodrama and postmodernism intersect, Woo's film gives expression to "postmodernism's sustained interest in the play of signifiers and melodrama's drive to wring meaning out of surface details" (Baron, "Nicolas Roeg's *Track 29*" 19). The idea that "melodramatic" elements can be found in contemporary Hong Kong film practice is not as preposterous as it might seem. Indeed, *The Killer*'s melodramatic emotionality is so integral to the film that one is required to examine the way it generates intermittent but intense emotional connection with the central characters—even when it is not possible to do justice to the film's complex range of aesthetic antecedents. For example, it is clear that as in other Hong Kong films, *The Killer*'s narrative design owes a great deal to the tradition of Chinese drama as song and play rather than action. *The Killer*'s presentation of performances has been influenced at least in part by Chinese theatrical traditions that emphasize the coordination of codified movements and vocal rhythms. Woo's film also evinces the influence of Chinese theatrical traditions that have made individual characterization and the logical unfolding of the plot secondary to the creation of a production in which visual and aural elements combine to produce emotional effects.

The florid, melodramatic emotionality of *The Killer* points to the influence of traditions within Peking Opera, the *ching-hsi* style of drama that coalesced in China in the mid-nineteenth century. The conventions for performance in Peking Opera seem especially pertinent to understanding the acting styles in *The Killer*. Woo's actors do not create individual characterizations but instead produce the ideal characteristics of the character type they are playing.

The emphasis in Peking Opera that productions consist of play selections "chosen to emphasize the high points" and that staging practices allow for "rapid changes of place" (Brockett 286,

287) are also pertinent antecedents for *The Killer*. Moreover, it is possible to see that Woo's film borrows its presentation of character types through codified forms of costume and movement from Peking Opera. For example, Chow Yun-Fat's gliding walk seems to be a legacy of Peking Opera. The film's Triad boss, Tony Weng (Wing Cho Ip), seems to reprise the Peking Opera role known as painted face or *jing*. Weng exemplifies that role by being a treacherous bandit marked by his "swagger and exaggerated strength" (Brockett 289). His checked and floral patterned shirts recall the spectacular face painting that distinguishes the *jing* characters from the costuming and makeup used to present a *sheng* or male role (John), a *dan* or female role (Jenny), and a *ch'ou* or comic role (Inspector Li).

Still, in some regards, the antecedents for Woo's film are not unique to Hong Kong or Chinese theatrical traditions but instead suggest an orientation found in other non-Western theatrical traditions. For example, Robert Stam points out that popular Indian cinema "inherits a two thousand-year tradition that circles back to the classical Sanskrit drama, whose aesthetic is based less on plausible plot than on subtle modulations of mood and feeling (*rasa*)" (258). Equally important, the aesthetic strategies one finds in Woo's film are not unique to non-Western aesthetic traditions.[5]

Woo's film is marked by eclecticism, erosion of aesthetic boundaries, and a "mixing of different styles, genres, and artistic conventions, including those of [Western] modernism" (Hill 99). Close examination of *The Killer* in the sections that follow will show that the central characters' highly emotional subjective experiences are often conveyed not by material elements of the four lead actors' performances but instead by the film's flamboyant editing strategies and sound-image combinations. The truncated nature of the lead actors' vocal and physical expressivity thus invites comparison with (European) modernist film practice. But *The Killer* breaks with modernist traditions by providing audiences with intermittent moments in which the material elements of the lead actors' performances convey intense emotion.

Yet Woo's film does not use realistic or naturalistic cinematic conventions when the lead actors use their voices, faces, and bodies to project emotional experiences. Instead, it amplifies the actors' well-crafted performances with eye-catching compositions and editing patterns that both support and call attention to strategies that typically increase emotional engagement. The effect these emotion-laden moments might have on different audiences is complicated to assess. That is because Woo's film departs from both the unified, internal logic of (European) modernist films *and* the holistic narrative development of (Euro-American) realist films.

As if following modernist performance traditions, the actors in *The Killer* are primarily, although not exclusively, impassive (Bressonian) models that do not project emotions through their voices, faces, or bodies. But Woo extends strategies linked to modernism by intermittently lifting the restraint placed on the actors' emotional expressivity. At the same time, Woo breaks with the modernist *and* realist traditions by mobilizing performative and cinematic elements in hyperbolic ways to break through the cool, self-parodic tone he establishes and maintains as a baseline.

Thus *The Killer's* presentation of character has the potential to create emotional connection but not through the standard process of accretion that marks the performative and cinematic strategies used by Western realist films to engage audience interest and sympathy. Instead, *The Killer's* audiences can be suddenly caught up in the characters' experiences because the intermittent moments in which actors project emotion are highly expressive. These moments contrast with the minimalist quality that dominates the actors' performances throughout the film; the emotions that Woo's actors project in these moments are also intensified by the director's exaggerated composition, editing, sound, and mise-en-scène selections.

Mobilizing Media-Saturated Rhythms and Imagery

A cool surface that has the potential to engage audiences is, of course, what links *The Killer* to other postmodern aesthetic traditions. Woo's film is an efficiently crafted consumer product designed for international sales. Carefully constructed to engage even (foreign) audiences unable to interpret character interactions in light of the star images of its leading actors, *The Killer* does not depend on international audiences reading the film in relation to *The Occupant* (1984) and *Diary of a Big Man* (1988), the other films that had paired Chow Yun-Fat and Sally Yeh. Nor does it require audiences to be acquainted with the five films that had paired Chow Yun-Fat and Danny Lee.[6] Audiences could become intrigued by Chow's Armani-suited killer even though they were not acquainted with the outsider character Chow had portrayed in Woo's *A Better Tomorrow* (1986) and *A Better Tomorrow II* (1987).

The Killer's international acclaim actually created foreign audiences' interest in the two earlier collaborations between Woo and Chow. *The Killer*'s modest critical and commercial success would also lead foreign audiences to be interested in their subsequent collaborations in *Once a Thief* (1990) and *Hard Boiled* (1992).

The Killer also did not require international audiences to be familiar with the more than fifteen films Woo had directed or the sixty-some films and television programs Chow had appeared in since the mid-1970s. It did not require an intertextual awareness of Woo's collaborations with other actors, such as Kenneth Tsang, Ricky Hui, Fui-on Shing, Leslie Cheung, Waise Lee, Dean Shek, and Lung Ti, all of whom have appeared in three or more Woo films. Woo's film also did not require international audiences to appreciate *The Killer*'s setting: a Hong Kong devoid of British figures and featuring lavish homes and tastefully appointed apartments above the city or on the far side of the island. Instead, Woo's film was accessible to anyone who had flipped through a magazine or surfed their television channels in the 1980s.[7]

The Killer presents its central characters through and in terms of their respective places in a media-saturated society. Important moments in the performances by Chow Yun-Fat, Chu Kong, Sally Yeh, and Danny Lee often feature gestures and poses drawn from the advertising imagery of international consumer culture. The film gives cosmopolitan audiences avenues for emotional contact by framing the characters' significant encounters and experiences in color schemes and compositions one would find in glossy print ads for expensive scotch whiskey, touching TV spots for cellular phones, and programs' cliffhanger scenes that appear just before commercial breaks.

Some of *The Killer*'s most evocative passages employ obvious advertising imagery. A scene that David Bordwell compares to a "melancholic TV commercial," John's cell phone conversation with Jenny, is one of those evocative sequences (109). The scene, which also qualifies as one of Hoberman's "calendar art interludes" (33), takes place rather late in the film. We have seen the bloody shoot-out at John's apartment that takes place when Sidney (Chu Kong) fails to kill John. We have just watched Inspector Li (Danny Lee) sit and smoke a cigarette in John's apartment, listening to the tape of Jenny's ballads and imagining himself to be the man he pursues. Inspector Li's contemplative and transformative moment is broken by Sergeant Chang (Kenneth Tsang), who abruptly enters the apartment to give his report on the bloodbath. Lost in the world of the killer, Inspector Li draws his gun on Sergeant Chang, just as John had when, minutes before, the first of many gunmen sent to kill him burst through the apartment door.

There is a musical bridge that links Inspector Li's scene with the sequence that follows. Taking up the musical motif that has been and will continue to be associated with John's fraught connection to Hong Kong, the plaintive, measured, synthesized music, which recalls the sound of a Chinese *ch'in* or long zither, sets the tone for the pensive phone call between John and Jenny. The sequence opens with blue-gray monochromatic wide-angle shots that show an expensive European car driving into and parking in a private home's stark, concrete-pillared ground-level parking area that looks out over the quiet, far side of Hong Kong harbor. Still in wide shots, we see Chow get out of the car. After pausing to look out over the harbor, he makes a call on his cell phone. During the phone conversation, Chow moves gracefully between the parked car on screen left and one of the structure's concrete pillars at the right side of the frame. As Chow speaks, he pauses occasionally to pose casually, leaning sometimes against the car and at other times against the pillar at the side of the frame.

As if in accord with modernist traditions, throughout the scene Chow's incidental and measured gestures never call attention to themselves. He consistently faces the harbor, his back to the camera. Chow is also shown almost entirely in full shots. Backlighting dominates and so his facial expressions are largely blocked from view. Chow's interactions with the props in the scene (car, cell phone, cigarettes) are not occasions for the actor to project emotion. Instead, when he gets out of the car, places the call, or takes a cigarette out of its pack, his movements are fluid, polished, and functional. In each instance, Chow's gestures exclude realistic details, which might include shuffling or planted feet, trembling or close-fisted hands, and quivering or hard-set lips.

At the same time, Woo's film stretches the conventions of Western modernism by establishing tonal counterpoints to Chow's minimalist performance. One set of contrasts belongs to the changing elements of the background. In contrast to John's circumscribed movements in the confined, concrete parking area, a Chinese junk floats gracefully across the frame in the background. Later, the steady movement of a jet flying from right to left and another junk floating toward the foreground contrast with the static, pensive poses Chow Yun-Fat assumes throughout the scene. Another set of contrasts can be found in the performances of Sally Yeh and Danny

Lee. Marked by conventions often found in traditional narrative cinema, the film's presentation of their performances creates another layer of contrasts with Chow Yun-Fat's performance and the seemingly modernist strategies Woo employs to present it.

During the phone call, the full to medium shots of Chow are intercut with medium close-ups of Yeh in Jenny's apartment. Yeh lies in bed, tucked under a pastel comforter, her head surrounded by and resting on soft, pastel pillows. Diffused high-key lighting enables audiences to see Yeh's more expressive, realistic gestures and facial expressions. For example, underscoring the hushed excitement Yeh projects when she stresses John's name in her response to hearing his voice on the phone, Yeh holds the receiver close to her cheek in a gentle embrace. In another brief shot, we see her nestled in her pillows with her face framed by the phone on one side and her free hand on the other. Yeh, her eyes open wide, looks up as if into the eyes of her love. The diffuse light, the intimate framing, Yeh's expectant facial expression, and the way she gently wraps one hand around the phone and places the other against her face are realistic details that create the impression she is being emotionally embraced by the man she is speaking with.

Yet even on this occasion *The Killer* does not use the eyeline matches and shot/reverse shot sequences that traditional narrative cinema employs to generate audience identification. Instead, as if following soap opera conventions, the intimate connection between John and Jenny in this sequence is created primarily by the sound design. The use of lavalier mikes and/or close-miked post-dubbing allows the actors to speak in hushed voices. That approach affects the evocative features of the actors' line readings, for Chow and Yeh use shifts in breathing and intonation more than changes in volume and rhythm to convey the characters' emotional states. The sound design also signals the film's eclectic postmodernist sampling from disparate traditions, for it combines "hot," emotionally laden aural elements with "cool" images of Chow Yun-Fat overlooking the harbor. The emotion-laden sound design complicates the seemingly unemotional image created by the visual presentation of Chow's character. Presenting Yeh's whispered words over the wide, blue-gray images allows audiences to imagine that John is a man whose tender emotions lie hidden behind a cool exterior.

As if reprising modernist use of the camera as a narrating element, the private, intimate connection established between Jenny and John is disturbed when the camera pulls back and tracks left out of Jenny's bedroom to show Inspector Li poised on the balcony outside her living room, eavesdropping. Shifting immediately to a realistic method of presenting performance, Woo cuts from the tracking shot to a medium close-up of Danny Lee. Bathed in glowing light blue light and with a diaphanous window curtain slightly veiling his face, Lee projects his character's resolved but wistful sadness over planning to come between the lovers. Lee draws his brows, and with his chin held slightly high, he closes his mouth in a thin line.

The moment exemplifies Woo's hybrid style, which combines Hollywood realism with European modernism, for he gives audiences an ideal view of Lee's expressive face but then does not hold the shot long enough for viewers to fully interpret the expression on Lee's face. Feathering one presentational mode into another, Woo then combines short takes with long dissolves until the radiant blue-tinted image of Inspector Li on the balcony dissolves into the blue-gray harbor setting. Returning to John's story, the dramatic significance of the scene is again conveyed by elements of the mise-en-scène. The gliding junk and soaring jet in the background convey John's desire to escape. We know that his desire is doomed, however, because the killer is shown trapped and isolated in the borrowed, concrete space (or cell) where he has parked himself to ponder his fate.

When we return to John's story, the frame composition features Chow Yun-Fat in the foreground in profile. It is the only medium close-up of the actor in the entire sequence. The momentary closer view of Chow's impassive face is still difficult to see, given the backlighting. The shot selection is indicative of a Hong Kong postmodernist who has studied modernist traditions to locate the ruptures that have allowed minimalist work to convey emotion. The tighter framing presents audiences with an evocative, subtle inflection precisely because it represents a shift from the wider shots in which Chow has been shown up to this point in the sequence.

The comparatively closer framing on Chow anchors the scene's next expressive element: the subjective aural flashback in which John hears Sidney ask why John had not left Hong Kong when he had the chance to escape double-crossing Triad boss Tony Weng. Woo amplifies the subtle but significant visual inflection created by the tighter framing on Chow with an evocative (although seemingly mundane) shift in the sound design: the quietly spoken words are, for the first time, completely subjective. Given the close miking used in the dialogue, the change between John and Jenny's conversation and John's memory of Sidney's question appears on the surface to be cool and uninflected. Yet the aural flashback confirms the existence of John's inner life and gives audiences intimate access to the character's most private and emotionally charged thoughts.

To say that *The Killer* gives international audiences access to the central character's most private, most emotional experiences is not to suggest that Woo's film uses conventions central to realistic cinematic traditions. Far from that, the film short-circuits audience expectations that it will abide by the conventions of traditional narrative cinema. Woo makes certain that viewers' increased visual access to Chow's character when the scene shifts back to John overlooking the harbor is marginal and passes in an instant. The medium close-up is framed so that Chow is at the right edge of the frame, occupying only a fraction of the image. In addition, the camera immediately tracks back, making Chow even more distant from the audience and still at the edge of the frame. Here again, the film breaks with conventions of Hollywood realism and at the same time "fails" to conform to modernist conventions. Structured by composition and editing choices that create fleeting moments of emotional engagement, *The Killer* has the potential to activate "very strongly an audience's participation, for there is a desire to make up for the emotional deficiency" (Elsaesser 15). Woo's manipulation of that cognitive-aesthetic process causes his Hong Kong film to share important family resemblances with Douglas Sirk melodramas and other films in the American melodramatic tradition.

The impact of Woo's shot selections becomes amplified by additional elements in the sound design and mise-en-scène. Banking on surefire melodramatic strategies, the film interweaves John's subjective aural flashback of Sidney's questions with John's Hong Kong musical motif. The combined aural elements give the wide shot of Chow in the weighted, lower-right-hand side of the frame a melancholy character. Then, with the music swelling, *The Killer* mobilizes connotations tucked into international fashion imagery to deliver the final expressive punch of the sequence. Given ample time by the long take, audiences are invited to gaze on Chow Yun-Fat dressed in the immaculate Giorgio Armani suit that drapes his body. He sits, looks out over the harbor, and contemplatively smokes his cigarette.

Given the high profile of the fashion industry in the 1980s, this image is far from neutral. The film's production team used connotations bound into internationally recognized clothing designs and fashion labels to convey the moral status and emotional experience of its central character. For 1980s audiences outside Hong Kong, the man in the Armani suit could exist in an entirely different realm from the capricious, convulsive figures that attacked the hero, clothed as they were in ready-to-wear black rayon suits or generic white jogging suits. The exquisitely dressed killer also exists in a world apart from corrupt Triad boss Tony Weng, whose clownish monstrousness is signaled by his gaudy floral scarves and pompous ascots. When international audiences encountered John, the tall, handsome figure elegantly draped in Armani suits with plunging V lines accentuated by subtly patterned ties that connected head to crotch, Chow Yun-Fat could be a safe, commercial fashion model on which to gaze. His attractive but carefully self-censored image anchored the presentation of John as a character who could embody the cross-cultural image of a knight-errant whose Armani suit was a suit of armor.[8]

Equally important in a Hong Kong film tailored for international consumption, Woo punctuates the emotion-laden scene featuring Chow Yun-Fat in his "Armani moment" with an abrupt cut to Sergeant Chang (Kenneth Tsang). In sharp contrast to the killer's pensive cool, Chang fumbles with trash on the back stairs of Jenny's apartment while a tiny gray-haired neighbor woman scolds him for blocking the stairs. The hard break and instant tonal shift at the end of the sequence make the scene between John and Jenny seem like a soap opera episode that has been interrupted by a commercial. Placed at the beginning and end of the "calendar art interlude," Sergeant Chang's entrances break the characters' and the audience's reverie. The design creates a kind of modernist formal elegance or, perhaps more accurately, the kind of repetition postmodern audiences have come to expect in sponsor-driven mass media. Far from being a mark against the film, this sort of pacing and punctuation helped foreign audiences access the characters' inner lives and emotional experiences.

The scene's collage of commercial images also had the potential to emotionally engage international audiences. Borrowing iconography used to advertise luxuries such as tobacco, liquor, expensive cars, international travel, and private real estate, the sequence mobilizes well-established patterns of contemporary consumer desire. The film's sampling from commercial culture does

12.1. Heightened emotionality against a muted blue-gray background: the killer's attempt to change his life is a commercial interlude and/or sequence between commercial breaks.

not render it meaningless. Far from that, the connotations embedded in the iconography contribute to the way the film presents the killer's transformative moment in which John ostensibly chooses a new partner and a new life.[9]

It seems quite possible that the scene's commercial imagery invites audiences acculturated to desire "the better things in life" to understand John's inchoate desire for something better. Moreover, the swirl of luxury lifestyle imagery triggers familiar narratives about unattainable pleasure. With the scene's mood sustained by melancholy music, audiences accustomed to fleeting pleasure and unrealized consumer desire could easily imagine that John's transformative moment is fleeting or impossible to realize. The scene's framing and sound-image relationships support such interpretations. The idea that the lovers are ill fated is confirmed by Inspector Li's position in the background at Jenny's apartment. The blue-gray color scheme underscores John's isolation. The plaintive music allows audiences to interpret Chow's impassive expression and modulated gestures as wistful and pensive. Emblematic of a postmodern approach that openly banks on the evocative connotations of commercial images and the conventions used to punctuate mass-media flow, *The Killer* is marked by a syncretism that fuses disparate trends in modernism and realism in a way that seems beholden to neither Western tradition. The film's performances and its presentation of acting require us to develop new ways of thinking about acting and expressivity, cinematic strategies and audience identification, and meaning and the play of surface details (figure 12.1).

From European Modernism to Hong Kong Postmodernism

The Japanese term in the title of Jean-Pierre Melville's 1967 film, *Le samourai*, can be seen as a synecdoche for the way in which European modernists "invented" new strategies by borrowing from Asian aesthetic traditions, among others. European filmmakers Jean-Luc Godard and Michelangelo Antonioni have perhaps been most closely identified with modernism in the cinema. Yet scholars also see Melville and his contemporaries Robert Bresson, Alain Resnais, and Agnès Varda as quintessential film modernists. Comparing *The Killer* to Melville's *Le samourai* clarifies ways that Woo's postmodern Hong Kong film extends and transforms European modernist traditions.

In *Le samourai* and *The Killer*, the characters are stripped down to their bare essentials. In Melville's film, the central character, hired gunman Jeff Costello (Alain Delon), is defined by his trench coat. In Woo's film, John is defined by his collection of Armani suits. The two films present their central characters' problem in very simple terms: in both instances, the professional killer allows himself to be identified and so must be eliminated.

In Melville's film, this pared-down vision marks the presentation of performance even in the scene in which Costello executes his contract. In a sequence that includes some twenty-five shots, the conventional alternation between Costello's point-of-view shots and other shots that enable us to see the killer move through the nightclub and into its back offices to make the hit never include a close-up of Delon. Delon's purely functional gestures and impassive facial expressions project no emotion. The one line he speaks is in monotone.

The mise-en-scène underscores the cool impression created by the composition and performance choices, for the setting and costumes are dominated by black and chrome with some touches of muted tan, blue, and gray. There are only a few select eye-catching details in the entire sequence. These include the dark skin and lilting voice of Cathy Rosier, the woman featured in the jazz ensemble. The only other accented details are her glittering silver dress, a glimpse of Costello's white gloves, and the moment in the men's room after the room has cleared when Alain Delon flicks a white hand towel to the side.

Like Delon, Chow Yun-Fat projects little if any emotion throughout the film's opening shoot-out. The medium to full shots that show him in action enable audiences to see some facial expressions that at most suggest determined resolve. In Woo's film, the color palette of the mise-en-scène is also essentially limited to black, white, and red. However, when Woo re-creates this scene, he fuses the cool modernist surface of Melville's film with the overheated flow of postmodern audiovisuals. Thus the incidental flip of the towel becomes the slow-motion passage in which John wraps his long white scarf around Jenny's bleeding face as she struggles to break free of his grasp.

There are other significant differences. In Woo's film, our attention is drawn to John's long black evening coat, his billowing white scarf, and the red blood that flows out of the dozens of bodies caught up in the hit. The film breaks completely with modernist methods in the moments just before the scene ends. Rather than cutting quickly between tight, action-filled shots, Woo holds on a wide slow-motion image of Chow Yun-Fat holding Sally Yeh close to him. His long white scarf covers her eyes and face to stop the bleeding his gunshot has inadvertently caused. Facing directly into the camera, Chow twists his face into a horrified grimace. While essentially static, this final tableau is charged with tremendous energy. The visual momentum created by Chow's slow-motion, gliding entrance, the explosive bursts of gunfire, and the bodies flying through the air comes to a screeching halt in this slow-motion image of anguish. Yet the energy is far from dissipated. Woo's cinematic design ensures that the kinetic force of the entire scene is forced into the final melodramatic moment, which actively enlists audience sympathetic engagement in John's anguish.

If we look at the "recognition scenes" in the films by Melville and Woo, it is again possible to see points of contact and distinction. Both filmmakers seem to employ Bresson's modernist approach in which meaning is communicated through the model rather than by an actor. The point of both recognition scenes is to show the central character's fleeting moment of insight or human contact.

In *Le samourai*, the recognition scene takes place in the police station. Witnesses from the nightclub are brought in to identify the man who shot the club's owner. For this scene, Melville again uses about twenty-five shots, and while many of them represent the black jazz singer's point of view, none of the shots are tighter than a medium close-up. The color design of the mise-en-scène is again marked by cool blacks, grays, and blues, and this time it is accented by the leopard skin coat that Rosier wears.

An emblematic modernist sequence, the presentation of performance in this scene is so minimalist, the acting so restrained, and the composition and editing patterns so uninflected that even the slightest shift creates an emotional effect. Tucked inside her leopard skin coat, Rosier remains sitting very still when Delon, wearing a fedora with its brim pulled down and a trench coat with its collar turned up, is brought to stand before her. In answer to the question posed by the police superintendent (François Périer), Rosier states in a hushed monotone that Costello is not the man she saw at the nightclub. A moment passes. Then, lifting his head just enough to reveal his eyes, Delon, speaking for the first time in the scene, thanks her in a hushed monotone. The impassive expression on Rosier's face softens when, for a second, she offers him a half smile in return. Then, blocking any chance that audiences could pause and take in this fleetingly emotional contact between characters, the scene continues, with attention shifting to the police superintendent who must now find another suspect.

Woo also uses the modernist strategy of cutting away from dramatic moments. But he then moves beyond modernist traditions by incorporating the kind of over-the-top imagery often found in Hong Kong cinema. In Woo's film, the recognition scene features rapid-cut images of graphic violence. These images are presented as subjective memories that are triggered when John sees the bloodstains on the white silk scarf that Jenny keeps as a reminder of the accident.

John's flashback takes place after he has beaten up two thugs who have attempted to steal Jenny's purse when she was walking home. Arriving at Jenny's apartment, John gently reassures her that a cat (and not another thug) caused a lamp to crash to the floor. Dressed like an innocent 1950s schoolgirl in a pert white and green plaid dress, Jenny conveys her childlike gratitude to John by asking him to stay for tea. When she leaves the room to prepare it, John turns to gently feel the white silk scarf, which Jenny has hung on the coat stand in her apartment.

The film uses commercial imagery and editing strategies to convey the killer's chivalrous remorse and hard masculinity. In place of dialogue or emotion projected by the actor, John's anguished emotional state and elevated ethical status is expressed by long takes that allow audiences to gaze on Chow in his monochromatic blue-gray Armani suit, complete with matching tailored shirt and gray-accented tie. In concert with those glossy (print) images, Woo bypasses the cinematic convention of shot/reverse shot editing. In place of the brief but significant eye contact between Rosier and Delon featured in Melville's film, Woo presents a single, isolated "picture" of the lovers' momentary touch. In Woo's film, the killer's life-altering moment of human contact is not represented by the cinematic trope of exchanged glances. Instead, Woo presents audiences with a more contemporary and more commercial image by showing Chow's hand softly touch Yeh's as they both reach to feel the scarf.

After this moment of contact, we see John sitting alone, listening to the melancholy music selected by Jenny. Close-ups of Chow's face that show his brows furrowed and his mouth open in shock are then intercut with a few seconds of images from earlier scenes. Excerpts from earlier episodes flash by in rapid succession. First we see a close-up of Jenny's face as she sings in the club the night she was blinded by John's gun firing next to her eyes. Next there is a close-up of John as he enters the club and sees her. Then we see a medium shot of Jenny and John after she gets wounded and the black and white of their clothes is spattered with rivulets of red blood coming from her face. Then there is a medium shot of John's naked back with the same blood spilling down his back as the bullet lodged there is removed. The last image is of a dove perched on a cross in the Catholic church to which John retreated after making the hit.

The Killer rejects the restraint that marks the recognition scene in Melville's modernist film. To give depth to John's character, Woo makes flamboyant use of conventions used in television as he cuts between the tight close-ups of Chow's pained expression and the images from earlier episodes. Thus in Woo's film, the recognition scene is an emblematic postmodern scene designed expressly for cosmopolitan audiences who create their own identities by selecting from an array of menus, products, and program options. Woo gives international audiences the impression they have glimpsed inside the soul of a killer by recapping moments from previous episodes. As if that were not enough, Woo anchors that impression in a product, the long white scarf, which is a visible expression of and synecdoche for the tragic experience that will bind Jenny and John to the end of the film.

In *Le samourai*, evocative close-ups are rare, gestural and vocal expressivity is truncated, and editing patterns communicate ideas and information rather than emotional attributes of characters. By comparison, *The Killer* is marked by moments in which actors project emotion and specific cinematic strategies generate identification with the characters. The distinctions between the two films' presentation of performance depend at least in part on their very different conceptions of identity.

In Melville's modernist film, external identification is necessarily false. Costello is a representative individual because he is passive, quiet, centered, and unified. He is a man in the modern city, an *actant* who makes the final choice about the time and place of his death, a subject defined by his consciousness that he is playing a part in a performance and that there is nothing more than that performance. Isolated by hostile forces on all sides, his true opponent is the state, the police, the voice of authority.

By comparison, Woo's postmodern killer is a representative figure because he is a recognizable type, a character in a conventional narrative, a trope defined by the rules of the formula. The character's subjective experience provides a conceptual space for audience identification insofar as the film establishes points of access. Jostled about in a postapocalyptic world, the killer is threatened on all sides not just by the state but also by the nameless hordes who are the unknowing agents of global capitalism.

Set in a 1980s Hong Kong devoid of Western characters but steeped in Western influences, the film draws on the West's gangster genre. Using a formula in which killers dream big and cops lose sight of the law, Woo's film gives expression to an international sociopolitical identity that is indeterminate and intermittently stable (Teo 233).

Woo's film also seems to express a contemporary Hong Kong sensibility. Scholars like Kwai-Cheung Lo believe that Hong Kong films consistently reveal the performative nature of Hong Kong identity. Looking at developments in the 1980s, Lo finds that the negotiations between the United Kingdom and the People's Republic of China called attention to Hong Kong's status as an extraterritorial site suspended between two empires. Lo argues that Hong Kong films from this period consistently expressed the city-state's indeterminate or even void sociopolitical status.[10]

Surprisingly, rather than disclosing an emptiness at the heart of Hong Kong identity, *The Killer*'s deployment of cinematic strategies and its presentation of performances give voice to a definite, assured mode of address. The film's diegetic world excludes characters that represent British colonial rule. Rather than suggesting that colonial influence has overpowered Hong Kong, Woo's film shows that Western institutions simply provide structures that Hong Kong characters use for their own purposes. John enjoys the quiet of the dilapidated Catholic church and, dressed in her crisp parochial schoolgirl dresses, Jenny offers her visitors (English) tea to smooth over any emotional confrontations.

Woo's film does, however, address the indeterminate identities of global consumers. The Hong Kong film "speaks to" international audiences whose identities have definition only insofar as they are marked by an appetite for "the cutting edge" or "the new and improved." The remarkable social and material realities of Hong Kong in the 1980s made it both a powerless colony and a major player in the global economy that held the power to colonize distant realms of consumer culture. Although Hong Kong had been a colony since 1842, in the 1980s the overwhelming majority of Chinese people living in Hong Kong were related not to conquered people but instead to immigrants who had chosen to become subjects of a foreign power (Wong 170; Stokes 6). Given these considerations, it is possible to see that the indeterminacy embodied by *The Killer* reflects the instability of being both a tiny city-state and a dominant power in the international marketplace of commerce and fashion. That a political entity without diplomatic or military power could influence global commerce and culture should not surprise anyone who recalls that England became the center of pop culture in the 1960s after it had lost its empire.

Hyperbolic Hong Kong Postmodernism versus Hollywood Realism

The Killer has the potential to satisfy similar commercial appetites because it is a syncretic pastiche that fuses elements from disparate cultural-aesthetic traditions and because it deploys familiar conventions in unfamiliar ways. The eclectic strategies Woo uses to present characters sometimes converge to produce the film's most flamboyant displays of emotion. The sequence in which John anguishes over his outcast status is one such moment. Sweating and trembling, John has come to the realization that he is wanted by both the police and the Triads and that his life as a killer has caused nothing but pain to innocents like the little girl who was wounded at the beach. With Chow Yun-Fat's physical features projecting the character's intense emotions, one might imagine that this sequence uses the conventions of Hollywood realism. The distinction, however, between Woo's postmodern approach and that found in traditional narrative cinema is visible in the contrast between this sequence and a scene in *Anna and the King* (Andy

Tennant, 1999) that shows King Mongkut (Chow Yun-Fat) grieving over the death of his favorite daughter.

In Woo's film, the intense emotional experience projected by Chow's appearance, gestures, and facial expressions are amplified by the scene's mise-en-scène and editing design. Dressed in black, his hair wet (with perspiration), and his face covered with sweat, Chow is isolated in tight close-ups and medium close-ups against a bare wall awash in intense colors of light. Behind him on screen left, the light is blue blending into scarlet; on the right, the light is saturated red-orange. Here again, Woo uses the mise-en-scène to express the central character's inner experience, for audiences are invited to imagine that John has worked himself into a sweat because he is torn between feelings of (blue) remorse for endangering innocent young women and (red) hot anger toward his fellow syndicate "brothers."

Throughout the scene, each time we cut to an image of John alone in his room, the camera tracks in slowly, focusing audience attention on the character's emotional crisis. Serving as the foundation for the intense emotional pitch of these cinematic strategies, in a singularly expressive moment, Chow projects John's feeling of guilt and remorse by bringing his hand to his face and covering his eyes. The shots of Chow Yun-Fat are first intercut with slow-motion images of the little girl being wounded in the shoot-out at the beach. As the scene progresses, the images of Chow are intercut with wide shots of Sidney talking (to John) on the phone. With Sidney dressed in black slacks and white business shirt, alone in his austere but luxurious home overlooking Hong Kong harbor, these images are primarily blue and white. The evolving mise-en-scène telegraphs the fact that the sadness John feels about endangering the girl merges into the blue melancholy he feels because he no longer belongs to the "brotherhood." Woo's use of lavalier mikes and/or close-miked postdubbing further inscribes audiences into John's subjective experience. The sound design underscores the effect created by Woo's shot selections and editing choices. It also contrasts with the distancing effect created by the boom miking of Chu Kong's dialogue. The entire passage has fewer than fifteen shots of a few seconds each and thus functions like a television commercial that resonates with power far beyond its apparent insignificance (figure 12.2–figure 12.7).

Brief consideration of a scene from *Anna and the King* clarifies the distinction between Hong Kong postmodernism and Hollywood realism. In the scene in which the king's favorite daughter (Melissa

12.2. The expressive lighting design communicates the killer's intense and conflicted emotional state.

12.3. The images of the wounded child provide intimate access to the killer's subjective experience.

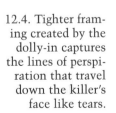

12.4. Tighter framing created by the dolly-in captures the lines of perspiration that travel down the killer's face like tears.

12.5. The framing enlarges the impact of Chow Yun-Fat closing his eyes as if trying to block out the sight of the child.

12.6. Still in close-up, Chow Yun-Fat turns his head slightly to convey a moment of emotional transition.

12.7. Chow Yun-Fat brings his hand to his face and covers his eyes, a gesture that anchors the expression of the killer's anguish and remorse.

Campbell) dies, Chow Yun-Fat is required to portray a character in a moment of anguish that is comparable to the moment we have just considered. Yet in Tennant's film, the scene proceeds according to conventions with which Western audiences are far more familiar. The three-minute scene contains a series of almost forty motivated point-of-view shots that do not allow direct address. Instead, each moment that an actor projects emotion is followed by a glance to another actor. Editing selections thus transform the raw material of the actors' facial expressions into meaningful "responses" and moments that seem to capture authentic expression.

The scene's mise-en-scène helps to convey emotional overtones, yet this Hollywood film is far less flamboyant and far more realistic than Woo's. Anna (Jodie Foster), dressed in a starched blue and white dress that is indicative of her "European" or mental approach to experience, is presented in a harsh yellow-white light that suggests her character is encountering a harsh learning experience. By comparison, King Mongkut and the members of his family, shown in soft, diffused light, are clothed in soft, rich, emotional red and gold colors, as if dying were something non-Westerners eased into with comfort. Dialogue is almost absent from this scene; the emotional force of the sound design is carried by the violins and French horns that fill the aural space with classical European music. Just as the musical score is modulated, measured, and logical, so too are the moments in which Chow Yun-Fat and Jodie Foster project their characters' emotions.

In contrast to Woo's film, which presents us with the protagonist already in a sweat, Tennant's film builds slowly to shots that show emotion, then brings that affecting passage to a close in carefully modulated shots that gradually lower the intensity. It is fifteen shots into the scene before we see Chow embracing little Melissa, his mouth open in dismay. Then, two shots later, we see him hugging and rocking her. Then, another two shots later, we see his body shaking as if he is crying. Dovetailing with these images, we see Foster's lips begin to quiver and then, over the course of the final ten shots of the scene, we are given ideal vantage points from which to see her anguished face.

This poignant scene in *Anna and the King* creates its emotional effects by a process of accretion, for emotion builds and ebbs gradually, imperceptibly, in a seemingly natural way. In the course of the ping-pong shots between the emotional experiences of the central characters (projected by the actors and lovingly lingered on by the composition, music, and editing patterns), audiences are, in the most conventional sense, sutured into the interaction between the characters in the scene.

Hong Kong Postmodernism: "Bizarrely Stressed Acting"

In sharp contrast to films that feature Hollywood realism, *The Killer* and its Hong Kong antecedents deploy unanticipated, intermittent moments of "exaggerated theatricalism." The connection between *The Killer* and other Hong Kong films can be seen if one compares the scene that conveys the killer's remorse to a scene in *Fists of Fury* (Wei Lo, 1971) that concludes with Cheng Chao-an (Bruce Lee) cradling the head of his dead male cousin. In sharp contrast to Tennant's Hollywood film, the three-minute scene in Wei Lo's kung fu film does not build emotional intensity slowly and logically but holds passion back until the final moments of the scene.

Earlier, Cheng has discovered the villain's drug-smuggling operation and beaten or killed dozens of the henchmen who had protected that secret. He returns home late at night, only to find that his housemates have been killed and that his cousin who has cared for him, Chow Mei (Maria Yi), is missing. The scene begins slowly with Cheng first realizing that the home he thought was his refuge had, in his absence, become a graveyard. Until the midpoint of the sequence, which is presented in fourteen shots, Bruce Lee's gestures are even, modulated, and restrained.

At the midpoint of the scene, however, there is a change in his performance and the film's presentation of acting. Once Cheng discovers the corpses, Lee shows that the character literally and figuratively loses his equilibrium, for he runs crazily toward Mei's cottage in back of the main house. For the only time in the film, Lee trips and slips as he zigzags toward the cottage. Discovering that Mei is missing and his youngest male cousin has been stabbed to death, Lee shows audiences that Cheng is horrified. He opens his eyes very wide, claps his hand over his mouth, and spins out of the frame. The camera captures his large gesture and the character's attempt to hide his reaction by pinning himself to the cottage exterior. In a wide shot that emphasizes his slight frame, we then see Lee running back to the house like a fluttering bird searching for a place to land.

The scene concludes with an even more emotionally charged moment. Cheng reenters the room in which his favorite older cousin (Ching-Ying Lam) lies dead on the floor. We hear only the soft sound of Lee's footsteps as he moves toward Lam and lifts his head. The music fades in just as Lee reaches Lam's body. The mournful sound of a Chinese cornet is accompanied by the ethereal sound of reverberating cymbals. Played in languid tempo, the conjoined sound of these instruments conveys Cheng's painful emotional experience. Following a jump cut in the motion that seems almost to mark the transition between action and emotional sequence, a medium close-up shows Lee holding Lam's body in his arms. The shot holds for more than twenty seconds. Lee first cradles Lam's head against his right shoulder, gently stroking Lam's forehead with the fingertips of his left hand. Lee then brings Lam's head close to his chest and, bending even closer, he touches his cheek to Lam's forehead.

This intensely intimate moment has the potential to be evocative because it is so distinct from the largely cool, uninflected approach director Wei Lo uses to present performances throughout the film *and* because the shot is cut short. Having given audiences an overheated moment in which the cinematic strategies almost compel audiences to feel the emotions of the central character, the film instantly returns to its minimalist approach. Creating a hyperbolic shift in tone, the shot of Lee and Lam ends abruptly and the film catapults us to another time and location: a tilt down on sunlit tree branches concludes with an extreme long shot that shows Lee sitting alone at the side of a river.

In contrast to the carefully modulated scene in *Anna and the King*, the scene in *Fists of Fury* does not prepare audiences for the intimate shot that displays Cheng's emotional pain. Instead, like *The Killer*, *Fists of Fury* suddenly changes the strategies it uses to present characters. Viewed through Western eyes, both Hong Kong films feature "bizarrely stressed acting" (McDonagh 48). The eclectic styles of the two films, which both feature a smooth surface intermittently ruptured by moments of intense emotion, lend plausibility to the plight of their central characters, who seem to embody the belief that in spite of or because of men's intense emotionality, coolheaded reason must dominate a man's life.

The emotional turmoil bound into the central characters' failures to achieve a balance between emotive feeling, reason, and personal survival is embedded in the syncretic style that marks the performances in *Fists of Fury* and *The Killer*. The films' intermittent heightened expressivity conveys the complex experiences of the two ill-fated protagonists who, as Hong Kong men, are required to be self-censoring, self-regulating, and self-contained. The two films, which center on characters who engage in strong but fruitless action, convey the unique challenge Hong Kong men face when they seek to honor the code of *yi* (brotherhood) and strive to maintain the proper place of *qing* (emotive feeling) in relation to *li* (reason) and *jing* (cleverness to sustain personal survival).[11]

The two films' disjunctive shifts between "hot" and "cool" sequences and their fragmented glimpses of men's anguish create the impression that for chivalrous men contemporary Hong Kong society is a source of psychic pain. The films' final scenes underscore that idea. Much like Melville's late-1960s film *Le samourai*, Wei Lo's early-1970s film *Fists of Fury* indicates that the hero's true adversary is modern society: Cheng's violent but heroic efforts end with him being taken into police custody. Woo's late-1980s film updates that perception by damning the state and the lethal effects of laissez-faire capitalism: *The Killer* ends with the detective under arrest for putting an end to the Triad boss and with the killer gunned down by the man who had paid him to kill.

Presenting audiences with what some Western critics have seen as a "mythopoetic" vision, Woo's film uses performances and cinematic strategies to reanimate a cross-cultural image of the romantic knight-errant. In contrast to actors in modernist films who truncate the projection of emotion, Chow Yun-Fat and the featured players in Woo's *post*modern film sometimes make expressive use of their voices, facial gestures, poses, and body movements. In contrast to modernist films that employ shot selections that deny identification with characters, the cinematic strategies in Woo's *post*modern film intermittently engage audience identification by displaying his characters' intense emotional experiences.

Designed for international consumers in the postmodern era, *The Killer*'s "calendar-art interludes" (Hoberman 33) are charged with meaning by their integral connection to global advertising imagery. Yet, like other Hong Kong films, Woo's film needs to be considered on its own terms. A syncretic film that integrates actors' work and cinematic strategies in what might seem bizarre ways, *The Killer* invites us to consider postmodern screen performance in an international light.

NOTES

1. Thomas Elsaesser has established a useful framework for analyzing the melodramatic structure of some Hollywood films ("Tales of Sound and Fury"; Baron, "'Tales of Sound and Fury' Reconsidered"). By comparison, the conclusions one can draw from examining the aesthetic strategies

in a Hong Kong film through the lenses of ostensibly Western traditions such as melodrama and modernism are, at best, preliminary. The limitations of this study require that these conceptual frameworks serve as portals for accessing a cinematic practice that has emerged at least in part from non-Western cultural traditions. This first step in cross-cultural analysis is not in any way meant to suggest that a film like *The Killer* can be understood without studying its local and regional aesthetic traditions. Indeed, the next section of this chapter looks at the aesthetic antecedents in Chinese theater, and the chapter concludes with a comparative analysis of scenes in *The Killer* and *Fists of Fury*.

2. It is important to bring analysis of films like *The Killer* into larger studies of postmodernism to circumvent "the strategies of containment that [postmodernist theory itself] can develop" (Connor 181). Analyzing aesthetic practice in "peripheral" regions is especially pertinent to re-visioning postmodern theory. As Linda Hutcheon observes, a great deal of writing on postmodernism and postmodernity has been marked by an "often unconscious ethnocentrism and phallocentrism (not to mention heterocentrism)" that has led to "a devaluing or ignoring of the 'marginalized' challenges (aesthetic and political) of the 'ex-centric'" (17). Bringing a film like *The Killer* into discussions of postmodern film practice makes it possible and even necessary to reconceptualize postmodernism in ways that do not necessarily conform to Fredric Jameson's negative view of American postmodernity.

To effectively study international postmodernism, it is important to recognize that postmodern aesthetics are *not* limited to the stylistic/ideological features that many scholars have linked to the socioeconomic organization of contemporary America. In addition, it is important to understand that while cultural/aesthetic practices and socioeconomic conditions "are no doubt inextricably related," in each instance that relationship must, as Hutcheon points out, "be *argued*, not *assumed* by some verbal sleight of hand" (26). Echoing that point, Hill also finds that although questions about "the scope and grounding of knowledge . . . and the significance of economic and social shifts in contemporary life" are pertinent in studies of "the changing character of artistic practices in the wake of the 'decline' of modernism," it can prove useful to consider questions in each area separately (96).

3. Given these economic statistics, it is not surprising that Hong Kong has the highest per capita consumption of cognac and presence of Rolls-Royces in the world (Palmer 49). It is also not surprising that Hong Kong "is Asia's second largest venture capital center and second largest loan syndication center" (Stokes and Hoover 8).

4. Analyses of suture usually consider "spectator positioning in relation to only two types of film practice: classical-realist texts that lead audiences to identify with fictional characters [and] modernist texts that disrupt conventional modes of narration and identification." Woo's film requires us to "consider different types of suture—for example, instances

in which spectators are alienated from the diegesis but not the text" (Baron, "*The Player*'s Parody of Hollywood" 21).

5. The irregular rhythm that marks *The Killer*'s presentation of characters' intense subjective experience can seem odd, inappropriate, or inadvertently funny to non–Hong Kong audiences. The film's hyperbolic shifts in tone can make audiences attuned to Western traditions of modernism, realism, or naturalism view the performances as instances of bad acting. Yet rather than considering such performances as cases of failed modernism, realism, or naturalism, it seems far more useful to study how *The Killer* might enlarge our understanding of international postmodernism. Descriptive rather than prescriptive analysis of the performances in Woo's film depends on recognizing the "social and cultural specificities of non-Euro-American cinemas" (Hill 103). Lucid analysis of the film's performative and cinematic strategies requires us to articulate distinctions between aesthetic strategies without establishing hierarchies.

6. The five films are *City on Fire* (1987), *Rich and Famous* (1987), *Tragic Hero* (1987), *City War* (1988), and *Code of Honor* (1989).

7. Designed essentially for international consumption, *The Killer* did not generate big box-office receipts when it opened in Hong Kong in July 1989. It may be that the film failed to connect with local audiences because the ostensibly apolitical film premiered just one month after the Tiananmen Square conflict came to a head. An alternative explanation for the film's weak financial performance at home is that Hong Kong audiences found the commercial packaging predictable. To those familiar with Chow's successful career in television and film, *The Killer* was perhaps less stunning than *A Better Tomorrow*, which had made Chow a superstar in 1986. Sally Yeh was a Hong Kong Cantonese pop music star and a movie star since her role in *Peking Opera Blues* (1986). Yet *The Killer* might have failed with local audiences because it paired Yeh and Chow in a film that was less amusing than their previous film, *Diary of a Big Man* (1988). Similarly, while Danny Lee had appeared in dozens of film roles, *The Killer* paired Lee and Chow in a film that was less gripping than Ringo Lam's *City on Fire* (1987). *The Killer* might have lacked the edge required by local audiences attuned to the hard-core social commentary found in the series that opened with Johnny Mak's *Long Arm of the Law* (1984). It may also have lacked the wry social commentary expressed by films like Wong Jing's *God of Gamblers* (1989), which starred Chow Yun-Fat and Andy Lau and sparked a collection of spin-offs and parodies.

8. In *The Killer*, costume designer Shirley Chan contributed to the film's presentation of performance by using symbolic color schemes and contrasting degrees of modernity or elegance in the costuming to convey each character's ethical status and social position. For example, John is the only character to have the fashion sense of a 1980s film star: his suits are made of supple materials that drape and rumple gracefully, that give him "a comfortable, effortless sophistication" (Agins 131). That particular apparel style for cinema heroes and international consumers premiered in

American Gigolo (Paul Schrader, 1980). That film represented a product placement coup that moved Armani sales to the $90 million mark by 1981 (132). It also served as a catalyst for a process that landed Giorgio Armani on the cover of *Time* magazine in 1982 (145). Furthermore, it contributed to developments that by 1991 made it possible for *Women's Wear Daily* to refer to the Oscars as "the Armani Awards" (137).

9. To call attention to the elements drawn from advertising is not meant to suggest that the sequence is somehow unreal. The costumes, props, and settings in this sequence (and throughout the film) create a certain verisimilitude and express a certain lived reality. Given that Hong Kong is a city of mobile phones, pagers, and fiber optic cable connections, John's transformation during a cell-phone conversation actually carries a high degree of plausibility and authenticity.

10. Kwai-Cheung Lo also argues that sublime masculine bodies have been "the unique contribution that Hong Kong has made to cultural production in the world" (106). Lo analyzes the imported images of teddy boys and body builders that were first popular in the 1960s, the 1970s films of Bruce Lee, the 1970s comics of Wong Yuk Long, and the comedic but dangerous stunt work that has been Jackie Chan's signature in films beginning in the 1970s. Lo explains that, from the 1960s to the present, Hong Kong popular culture traditions have presented male bodies in certain dominant, recurring ways: as stylish playboys who lead decadent Western lifestyles, as ascetic muscular heroes, and as heroes marked by their worldliness and their rippling muscles who are stabilized through incessant action and authenticated through displays of pain. Given the many observations on Chow Yun-Fat's stylized clothes and visage, it is possible to locate *The Killer*'s presentation of bodies within the Hong Kong popular culture traditions that Kwai-Cheng Lo outlines (see Cieko 226–27).

11. For a discussion of Hong Kong cinema in relation to these concepts, see Jenny Kwok Wah Lau and Li Cheuk-to.

WORKS CITED

Agins, Teri. *The End of Fashion: The Mass Marketing of the Clothing Business*. New York: William Morrow, 1999.

Appiah, Kwame Anthony. "Is the Post- in Postmodernism the Post- in Postcolonial?" *Contemporary Postcolonial Theory*. Ed. Padmini Mongia. New York: Arnold, 1996. 55–71.

Bakhtin, Mikhail. *The Dialogic Imagination*. Austin: U of Texas P, 1981.

Baron, Cynthia. "Nicolas Roeg's *Track 29*: Acting Out a Critique of Theory in a Postmodern Melodrama." *Spectator* 14.1 (1993): 16–25.

———. "*The Player*'s Parody of Hollywood: A Different Kind of Suture." *Postmodernism in the Cinema*. Ed. Cristina Degli-Esposti. New York: Berghahn, 1998. 21–43.

———. "'Tales of Sound and Fury' Reconsidered: Melodrama as a System of Punctuation." *Spectator* 13.2 (1993): 46–59.

Bordwell, David. *Planet Hong Kong: Popular Cinema and the Art of Entertainment.* Cambridge: Harvard UP, 2000.

Brockett, Oscar G. *History of the Theatre.* 5th ed. Boston: Allyn and Bacon, 1987.

Cieko, Anne. "Transnational Action: John Woo, Hong Kong, Hollywood." *Transnational Chinese Cinemas.* Ed. Sheldon Hsiao-peng Lu. Honolulu: U of Hawaii P, 1997. 221–37.

Connor, Steven. *Postmodernist Culture.* Oxford: Blackwell, 1989.

Denzin, Norman K. *Images of Postmodern Society.* London: Sage, 1991.

Elsaesser, Thomas. "Tales of Sound and Fury." *Monogram* 4 (1972): 2–15.

Hill, John. "Film and Postmodernism." *The Oxford Guide to Film Study.* Ed. John Hill and Pamela Church Gibson. New York: Oxford UP, 1998. 96–105.

Hoberman, J. "Hong Kong Blood and Guts." *Premiere* 3.12 (Aug. 1990): 33, 37.

Hutcheon, Linda. *The Politics of Postmodernism.* New York: Routledge, 1989.

Jameson, Fredric. "Postmodernism, or, The Cultural Logic of Late Capitalism." *American Literature, American Culture.* Ed. Gordon Hunter. New York: Oxford UP, 1999. 573–84.

Lau, Jenny Kwok Wah. "A Cultural Interpretation of the Popular Cinemas of China and Hong Kong." *Perspectives on Chinese Cinema.* Ed. Chris Berry. London: British Film Institute, 1991. 166–74.

Lee, Leo Ou-Fan. "Two Films from Hong Kong: Parody and Allegory." *New Chinese Cinemas: Forms, Identities, Politics.* Ed. Nick Browne, Paul G. Pickowicz, Vivian Sobchack, and Esther Yau. New York: Cambridge UP, 1994. 202–15.

Li, Cheuk-to. "The Return of the Father: Hong Kong New Wave and Its Chinese Context in the 1980s." *New Chinese Cinemas: Forms, Identities, Politics.* Ed. Nick Browne, Paul G. Pickowicz, Vivian Sobchack, and Esther Yau. New York: Cambridge UP, 1994. 160–79.

Lo, Kwai-Cheng. "Muscles and Subjectivity: A Short History of the Masculine Body in Hong Kong Popular Culture." *Camera Obscura* 39 (Sept. 1996): 105–25.

McDonagh, Maitland. "Action Painter John Woo." *Film Comment* 29.5 (Sept. 1993): 46–49.

Palmer, Rhonda. "Media Mix: Wealth and Anxiety: Rules, Regs, Triads, and 1997." *Variety* 24 Aug. 1992: 49, 53.

Stam, Robert. "Introduction: Alternative Aesthetics." *Film and Theory.* Ed. Robert Stam and Toby Miller. Malden: Blackwell, 2000. 257–86.

Stokes, Lisa Odham, and Michael Hoover. *City on Fire: Hong Kong Cinema.* New York: Verso, 1999.

Teo, Stephen. *Hong Kong Cinema: The Extra Dimensions.* London: British Film Institute, 1997.

Wolcott, James. "Blood Test." *New Yorker* 23 Aug. 1993: 62–68.

Wong, Rosanna Yick-Ming. "From Colonial Rule to One Country, Two Systems." *Cosmopolitan Capitalists: Hong Kong and the Chinese Diaspora at the End of the Twentieth Century*. Ed. Gary G. Hamilton. Seattle: U of Washington P. 1999. 167–79.

Woo, John. "Chinese Poetry in Motion." *Sight and Sound* 4.7 (1994): 61.

CONTRIBUTORS

CYNTHIA BARON is an assistant professor in the film studies and American culture studies programs at Bowling Green State University. She is the author of essays in *Postmodernism in the Cinema*, *Screen Acting*, *Headline Hollywood*, *Contemporary Hollywood Stardom*, *The James Bond Phenomenon*, and various academic journals. She is co-authoring a book with Sharon Marie Carnicke titled *Reframing Screen Performance*.

DENNIS BINGHAM is an associate professor in the film studies program at Indiana University - Purdue University, Indianapolis. He is the author of *Acting Male: Masculinity in the Films of James Stewart, Jack Nicholson, and Clint Eastwood* and essays including "*I Want to Live!*: Female Voices, Male Discourse, and Hollywood Biopics," "Unmanning the Self-Made Man: Masculinity and Oliver Stone's *Nixon*," and "The Displaced Auteur: A Reception History of Kubrick's *The Shining*." He is currently writing a book on the post–studio era biopic.

SHARON MARIE CARNICKE, professor and associate dean of the School of Theatre at the University of Southern California, is the author of *Stanislavsky in Focus* and *The Theatrical Instinct: Nikolai Eveinov and the Russian Theatre of the Twentieth Century* and of articles and anthology essays such as "Stanislavsky's System: Pathways for the Actor," "Boleslavsky in America," and "Lee Strasberg's Paradox of the Actor."

DIANE CARSON is a professor of film studies at St. Louis Community College, Meramec. She is the editor of *John Sayles: Interviews* and co-editor of *Shared Differences: Multicultural Media and Practical Pedagogy* and *Multiple Voices in Feminist Film Criticism*. She serves on the editorial boards of *Cinema Journal* and the *Journal of Film and Video*; is the associate producer of *Remembering Bonnie and Clyde*, a documentary shown on PBS;

and has authored articles on Bonnie and Clyde, screwball comedies, John Sayles, and teaching Asian film.

PAUL McDONALD, a reader in film studies at the University of Surrey Roehampton in London, is the author of *The Star System: Hollywood and the Production of Popular Identities*. He is also the author of "Film Acting and Gender: Method Acting and the Male Tantrum"; "Feeling and Fun: Romance, Dance, and the Performing Male Body in the *Take That* Videos"; "Reconceptualising Stardom," the supplementary chapter in the current editions of Richard Dyer's *Stars*; and the contribution on "Film Acting" in *The Oxford Guide to Film Studies*.

ROBERT T. SELF is a professor of English at Northern Illinois University. He is the author of *Robert Altman's Subliminal Reality*, "Troubled Masculinity and Abusive Fathers: Duality and Duplicity in *The Gingerbread Man*," "Redressing the Law in Kathryn Bigelow's *Blue Steel*," "Robert Altman and the Theory of Authorship," "The Sounds of *MASH*," and "Author, Text, and Self in *Buffalo Bill and the Indians*."

RONALD E. SHIELDS is chair of the Department of Theatre and Film at Bowling Green State University. He is on the editorial board of *Text and Performance Quarterly* and is the current editor of *Theatre Annual: A Journal of Performance Studies*. His recent publications have focused on critical readings of postmodern opera stagings and celebrity in postmodern advertising.

VIVIAN SOBCHACK is a professor and associate dean of the Department of Film, Television, and Digital Media at the University of California, Los Angeles. She is the author of *The Address of the Eye: A Phenomenology of Film Experience*, *Screening Space: The American Science Fiction Film*, and *Carnal Thoughts: Embodiment and Moving Image Culture*. She has edited *The Persistence of History: Cinema, Television, and the Modern Event* and *Meta-Morphing: Visual Transformation and the Culture of Quick Change*. Her publications also include many chapters in volumes of collected essays and journal articles.

FRANK P. TOMASULO is a professor and director of the undergraduate studies program at the Florida State University Film School in Tallahassee. The author of over sixty scholarly articles and essays, and over 150 academic papers, Tomasulo has served as editor of both the *Journal of Film and Video* (1991–96) and *Cinema Journal* (1997–2002). He is currently working on a career study of Italian filmmaker Michelangelo Antonioni (SUNY Press).

DOUG TOMLINSON, now deceased, was the editor of the compendium *Actors on Acting for the Screen: Roles and Collaborations* and the author of essays such as "'They Should Be Treated Like Cattle': Hitchcock and the Question of Performance." His work on film acting included his dissertation, "Studies in the Use and Visualization of Film Performance: Alfred Hitchcock, Robert Bresson, Jean Renoir."

MARIA VIERA is a professor and head of critical studies in the Department of Theatre Arts at California State University, Long Beach. She is a filmmaker who has made experimental works, short narratives, and documentaries. A scholar in contemporary film theory who holds a Ph.D. in cinema-television from the University of Southern California, she has published on topics in critical studies and filmmaking practice.

CAROLE ZUCKER, professor of film studies at Concordia University in Montreal, is the author of *The Idea of the Image: Josef von Sternberg's Dietrich Films, Figures of Light: Actors and Directors Illuminate the Art of Film Acting, In the Company of Actors: Reflections on the Craft of Acting,* and *Conversations with Actors on Film, Television, and Stage Performance.* She is currently writing a book, *Beauty and Terror: The Films of Neil Jordan.*

INDEX

Ace Ventura: Pet Detective
(Shadyac), 9, 275–76, 279, 280,
282, 284
Ace Ventura: When Nature Calls
(Oedekerk), 288
Acting: aesthetics of, 3, 7; in Alea,
220, 221, 222, 224, 230, 231, 232,
240; in Altman, 129; in
Antonioni, 98–120; assimilated,
220, 221, 222, 224, 230–31,
242–43; Auslander on, 230; in
Brecht, 247–48, 250; in
Cassavetes, 155, 169, 186; in
Demme, 234, 235; diversity in, 2;
epic, 247–48, 249–50, 255; and
gests, 111, 254, 256, 257, 259,
266; heroic male, 252; historical
context of, 3; and ideology, 3, 7;
in Jordan, 193, 200; in Kubrick, 9,
250, 257–59, 264, 268; in
Luhrmann, 259–60; meaning
from, 39; as mediated performance, 1; minimalist, 6; and modernism, 129, 130; narrative
advancement from, 33; norms for,
2, 3; *vs.* performance style, 45–48,
63; postmodern, 230, 240; in
Sayles, 173, 177, 180, 182–83,
184, 186, 188; scholarly disregard
for, 23–26; in Spielberg, 249; and
Strasberg, 157–58; and time,
30–31; in Woo, 298, 323, 326n5.
See also Actor; Expression;
Method acting
Action: analysis of, 32; in Brecht,
256; and Carrey, 279; dialogue as,
111; meaning through, 23; in
Sayles, 173. *See also* Behavior;
Movement
Active analysis, 47, 52, 53
Actor: in Alea, 229; in Altman, 44,

45, 62, 64n2, 130, 132–44, 146–47;
American training of, 15n1;
antitheatrical prejudice against,
11; in Antonioni, 51, 64n2, 96, 98,
103, 107, 114; as auteur, 98; body
of, 107, 277; and Brecht, 46,
247–48; in Bresson, 71, 73, 74, 75,
77, 78, 79, 313; and camera,
43–45, 46; Carrey as, 293; in
Cassavetes, 153, 157, 158, 159,
160, 161, 169, 186; Cassavetes as,
64n3, 156, 157, 159, 168; character from, 32; as collaborator, 3, 44,
45, 46, 63; contribution of, 44–45,
62; diacritical analysis of, 26–32;
director as former, 64n3; director
chosen by, 43; director's relationship with, 3, 42–64; as Everyman,
253, 254; as expert, 44, 45; in
Jordan, 62, 63, 194–201, 208, 209;
in Kubrick, 45, 52–53, 63, 65n8,
249, 254, 255, 271–72; meaning
from, 24; in Method acting, 98; as
model, 71, 73, 74, 75, 77, 78, 313;
personal life of, 134–35, 137, 138,
142, 143, 248; and postmodernism, 287; as prop, 12, 44, 46,
91n5; Rea on, 196–97; role of,
126; in Sayles, 173–74, 175, 178,
181, 182–83, 184, 185, 186; and
Stanislavsky, 46, 161–63; and
stereotype, 144; as type, 135; *vs.*
mise-en-scène, 12; in Woo, 302,
304. *See also* Acting; Character;
Method acting; Nonactor;
Performance; Star(s)
Actors Studio, 15n1, 168, 169
Adler, Stella, 15n1
Advertisement: and Altman, 145–46;
and Woo, 305, 310–11, 318,
327n9

335